The Divided Nation

The Divided Nation

A History of Germany
1918–1990

MARY FULBROOK

New York   Oxford
OXFORD UNIVERSITY PRESS
1992

Oxford University Press

Oxford   New York   Toronto
Delhi   Bombay   Calcutta   Madras   Karachi
Kuala Lumpur   Singapore   Hong Kong   Tokyo
Nairobi   Dar es Salaam   Cape Town
Melbourne   Auckland

and associated companies in
Berlin   Ibadan

Library of Congress Cataloging-in-Publication Data
Fulbrook, Mary, 1951–
[Fontana history of Germany, 1918–1990]
The divided nation : a history of Germany, 1918–1990 / Mary Fulbrook.
p.   cm.   Originally published in Great Britain
in 1991 by Fontana Press with title:
The Fontana history of Germany, 1918–1990.
Includes bibliographical references and index.
ISBN 0-19-507571-4
ISBN 0-19-507570-6 (pbk)
1. Germany—Politics and government—20th century.
I. Title.
DD240.F85   1992   943.08—dc20   92-7981

3 5 7 9 8 6 4 2
Printed in the United States of America

CONTENTS

Part Three

THE DIVIDED CENTURY

LIST OF ILLUSTRATIONS

LIST OF MAPS

ACKNOWLEDGEMENTS

The story of Germany in the twentieth century is a compelling one, which has profoundly affected European and world history. It has dramatically shaped – and drastically truncated – the lives of millions of people, Germans and non-Germans, and continues to be of central importance in European and world affairs.

At a very personal level, my own interest in German history was stimulated by my mother, a refugee from Nazi Germany. Born during the First World War, growing up in the Berlin of the 1920s and early 1930s, her whole life was radically affected by being the child of a 'mixed marriage', ensuring that as a 'non-Aryan' she would have no future in Hitler's 'national community'. In many ways, this book is for her.

Friends and acquaintances in both Germanies (pre-1990!) provided many insights. It would be invidious to name selected individuals. I am grateful particularly for the willingness of many East Germans to enter into very open and wide-ranging discussions. On a number of visits to the GDR, I spoke with people from a wide variety of backgrounds, including members of the SED, dissenters, committed Protestants of a range of political persuasions, and others. Both arranged interviews and more informal talks turned out, in retrospect, to have taken place in a historic moment before a whole sociopolitical system was about to pass away, and have informed my understanding of the dynamics of pre-revolutionary East Germany. Some of the views and comments made by people to whom I spoke before 1989 could not be captured again except as refracted and distorted with the 'benefit' of hindsight.

While actually engaged in writing this book, the East German revolution unfolded. The wonders of word processing made it relatively easy to change the present to the past tense with respect to discussions of Honecker's Germany; more problematic was the realization that what is of interest to both author and readers changes rather fundamentally when a revolution is known to be on the political agenda. It then becomes apparent which elements of the historical kaleidoscope will prove to be of central importance, and which can be consigned to the sidelines, as, perhaps, of only antiquarian interest. As the focus of current discussion changes, so too do the points of historical interest. The contemporary relevance which lies behind the construction of historical accounts becomes all too clear when the parameters which constitute the 'present' are rapidly changing.

I would like to thank Fontana for bearing with me while I sat on, and periodically altered, the text (sometimes it seemed I would have to update and revise chapter 13 in particular at weekly or even daily intervals). Over a somewhat longer period, I am grateful to colleagues and students at University College London for their stimulation and support. Students of my intercollegiate history seminar on the two Germanies will recognize many of our discussions in the chapters which form Part Two. Participation in conferences organized by, among others, the German History Society, also helped to inform my views and approach. More particularly, I am extremely grateful to Professor William Carr, Dr Jill Stephenson and the reader for Fontana, for their very valuable comments on the manuscript. While I have not been able to act on all their suggestions, they have certainly saved me from a number of errors and helped me to clarify aspects of the account. The responsibility for the inaccuracies and infelicities which remain is, of course, entirely mine.

The maps were produced by the UCL Geography Department, and I would particularly like to thank Louise Saunders for her work. Grants from the British Academy, the University of London Central Research Fund, and the UCL Dean's Fund, have assisted periods of research in Germany. I am very grateful for this support.

Finally, I would like to thank my husband and three children for suffering and sustaining the research for and writing of this book. Without my husband's unfailing support, and more than equal partnership in parenting, the book could not have been written. Without my children, recounting the fates of those who were born into less fortunate historical circumstances might have been much less meaningful.

ONE

The Course of German History

In those extraordinary months after the fall of the Berlin Wall in November 1989, when discussion of the unification of the two Germanies was for the first time in forty years back on the serious political agenda, many voices were raised giving views on 'the German question'. From a variety of quarters, prejudices were aired which had lain dormant – along with the memories, gas masks and other relics of the Second World War – over the years when the Cold War and the balance of terror had seemed to ensure a fragile peace in a divided Europe. Suddenly, the prospect of a united, economically powerful, and politically sovereign Germany, active again in central Europe and in a position to mediate between East and West, aroused powerful emotions among those whose view of Germany had been largely confined to an ill-assorted combination of images of Hitler and sleek West German capitalist competitors. Who were the Germans? What was their national character, if they had one? Who were those people who called themselves Germans, from the other, eastern, side of the rapidly crumbling Iron Curtain, who in many ways seemed not a bit like their western brothers and sisters? Provoked into having to make a rapid response to the collapse of communist rule in Eastern Europe, many people outside Germany found they had a serious deficit of knowledge and understanding. Many Germans, too – both East and West – found that the Iron Curtain, and the proclaimed 'zero hour' of 1945, had raised barriers to informed interpretation. History – although it did not come to an end in 1989, as some pundits, like the American scholar Fukuyama, wished to proclaim – did indeed seem to have stopped, as far as many textbooks were concerned, in 1945. Thereafter, politics and sociology took over

– to provide partial snapshots of an apparently eternal present, unconnected with the radically different past.

But prejudices based on partial perceptions of Hitler's rule, half a century ago, combined with limited impressions of a rapidly changing present, can scarcely provide a secure basis of understanding. The 'land in the centre of Europe', Germany, has always posed something of a problem for the European and world balance of power – as well as being an extraordinary powerhouse of creativity, in cultural and intellectual as well as economic respects. The complexities of German history demand serious and detailed engagement – and many observers have seen it as a most peculiar history, thus provoking heated debates on interpretation.

Over the centuries, there has been a 'German question'. Some analysts see its beginnings – somewhat anachronistically – in the 'failure' to establish a unified state in the Middle Ages. In the days of the politically decentralized 'Holy Roman Empire of the German Nation', the multiplicity of German lands – ranging from the more important secular and ecclesiastical principalities and city states through to the minuscule fiefdoms of 'independent imperial knights' – formed an interdependent system over which the emperors (often pursuing dynastic interests outside the Empire) never quite gained central control. The cultural and political conflicts involved in the Reformation of the sixteenth century helped to institutionalize the decentralization of the German lands. Religious differences coincided and overlapped with political conflicts to confirm this diversity in the course of the seventeenth century, in the series of conflicts which formed the so-called Thirty Years War (1618–48). Yet the Peace of Westphalia in 1648 was effectively able only to seal a stalemate: neither religious uniformity nor political centralization was achieved. The territorial rulers enjoyed sovereignty within their own states, while still remaining formally subordinate to the Emperor. Clashes among states competing for domination in the emerging European state system continued in the 'age of absolutism' of the later seventeenth and eighteenth centuries. While, from the myriad of small states which made up 'Germany',

Prussia emerged as a powerful rival to Austria, the relatively weak German lands were still easily overrun by an expansionist post-revolutionary France under Napoleon.

Under the impact of Napoleonic aggression, a fundamental reorganization of the domestic and external affairs of the German states was begun. In 1806, the Holy Roman Empire was abolished. Legal, social and economic reforms were introduced, either as a direct result of Napoleonic rule or in a form of 'defensive modernization'. After the eventual defeat of Napoleon, the formation of a German Confederation in 1815 included a strengthened and enlarged Prussia as an intended bulwark against France in the west, tsarist Russia in the east. At the same time, with territorial reorganization and a great reduction in the number of German states, other states too had increased in size and importance, many duchies having achieved the status of kingdom for the first time with the demise of the old Empire.

In the course of the nineteenth century, it proved to be the economically more advanced Prussia which was able to gain the edge over Austria in competition for domination over the medium-sized German states. Prussia was in the forefront of moves towards economic integration in the Customs Union, in the century which was to see those dramatic processes of transformation associated with industrialization. Attempts to achieve political unification of the German states under liberal auspices failed in 1848, and it was ultimately the Prussian Chancellor Bismarck's policies of 'blood and iron' that produced the unification, fraught with tensions, of a 'small Germany' (*Kleindeutschland*), excluding Austria, in the second German Empire founded in 1871. First seeking to secure its place in Europe, and then to gain a position among the imperial powers of the world, Imperial Germany proved to be an unstable entity. It came to an end, following defeat in the First World War, in the revolutionary autumn of 1918. After Germany's brief and ill-fated attempt at democracy in the Weimar Republic, the ultimate denouement was to be the genocidal rule of Adolf Hitler and his Third Reich, an empire which was supposed to last a thousand years, but which in the event collapsed in ruins after a mere dozen, characterized by arguably unequalled evil. It was this outcome – this *Götterdämmerung* – which provides the unique twist to the problem of explaining German history.

Many observers have puzzled over this apparently peculiar pattern of German history – this allegedly unique German path, or *Sonderweg*. Diverse attempts have been made to explain its course. Broadly, whether they have wanted to or not, historians of Germany writing after Hitler have had to engage in a long-running battle, characterized by local skirmishes over particular periods and issues, on the questions of 'what went wrong?' and 'when did it go wrong?' A rearguard action has been mounted by those who want to say that not everything did go wrong, or at least, it did not go wrong so early, or it could have been prevented ... However far serious historians have tried to step outside this sort of framework, the shadow of Hitler has stretched a long way backwards, shaping even counter-arguments about the diversity of trends and the non-inevitability of historical outcomes.

Given this sort of context, there has been a widespread (although far from universal) tendency to castigate Germany's past for what it was not: German history has frequently been written in terms of its alleged distortions, failures, 'turning-points where Germany failed to turn' (to use A. J. P. Taylor's phrase). Thus, for example, Germany 'failed' to become a centralized state in the Middle Ages. The 'early bourgeois revolution' of the 1525 Peasants' War 'failed', because Germany lacked a 'mature' bourgeoisie at this very early date (in the view of Marxists following Friedrich Engels). The failure to resolve the religious and political conflicts associated with the Reformation led to the petty backwater, '*Kleinstaaterei*' pattern of the eighteenth century, when a sleepy Germany produced, to be sure, some elevated cultural spirits, but remained at one remove from the real driving forces of history evident in Britain's industrial revolution or the bourgeois revolution which put an end to the '*ancien régime*' in France. The pattern of small states allegedly nurtured the bureaucratic, subject mentality displayed by many Germans. Lutheran doctrines of obedience to worldly authority were compounded by Kantian and Hegelian philosophy in a context of absolutist rule over weak civil societies. In her rude awakening of the nineteenth century, Germany became a 'belated' nation, with the contradictions between an archaic sociopolitical structure and a rapidly modernizing economy ultimately proving too great to bear without unleashing domestic and eventually international conflicts. Germany's by now rather more numerous bourgeoisie proved no less 'immature' in its incapacity for effective politics. And not only were there structural distortions determining Germany's long-term road to catastrophe: the 'land of poets and thinkers' (*Land der Dichter und Denker*) was one allegedly characterized by unique cultural patterns emphasizing docility, apoliticism, an exaggerated faith in bureaucracy, excessive militarism, and so on.

Clearly a brief sketch such as this inevitably bowdlerizes to a certain extent. Nor can justice be done to the full range of attempts to interpret the long sweep of German history. But underlying many such narratives there is a basic, persistent problem which is worth making explicit. To narrate the course of German history in terms of failures and distortions presupposes a 'normal' or 'healthy' pattern of development. Sometimes the (often implicit) model is the development of liberal parliamentary democracy in Britain, or the experience of a 'proper' bourgeois revolution in France; sometimes there is no real country providing a model, but rather a schematic view of 'stages' of historical development. Proponents of 'distorted' versions of German history thus may come from a variety of theoretical traditions, including both liberal and Marxist perspectives. What unites them is the tendency to explain whatever is seen as nasty about recent German history in terms of long-term 'failures' and 'deviations' from some supposedly 'normal' pattern of development.

But there have also been vigorous reactions against this sort of approach, and many historians are trying to ask, with more open minds, about patterns of actual causation – rather than simple depiction of failures – in German history. Determinist views have on the whole been replaced by closer analysis of shorter-term developments in the context of longer-term traditions and trends. While some historians devote major attention to the role of individual personalities in shaping the course of political history in particular, others have concentrated their energies on exploring patterns of social, economic or cultural development in more detail. Greater theoretical awareness has led to rejections of simple empiricism, and of the belief (based on the views of the great German historian Ranke) that one can seek to recount 'how it actually was', while the experience of Hitler has given cause for thought to those who held that historians should seek to empathize with the people about whom they wrote. Lively debates between proponents of different schools of historiography continue with a vengeance, particularly in Germany, where the moral implications of any historical interpretation appear particularly clear. Given the historical outcome in the rule of Hitler, attribution of causality is also in effect allocation of blame. While this is clearly not the place to embark on a comprehensive historiographical survey, the point may be made that there is no single, universally accepted narrative of German history: the field is characterized by vigorous, sometimes quite acerbic, controversy.

Where does this leave current thinking about twentieth-century German history? There are both broad debates about long-term patterns of continuity and discontinuity, as well as more closely focused arguments on specific issues to do with the collapse of Weimar democracy, the rise of the Nazis, and, of course, the explanation of the ultimately inexplicable – the mass murder of over six million people in the death camps. There is also a set of debates about, not only the causation, but also the historical effects or longer-term impact, of the Third Reich. Since the 1960s, there have been discussions about whether the Nazis actually played an important role in putative processes of 'modernization' in twentieth-century Germany.

A further twist to previous debates has been given by develop-ments since 1945. Long-term explanations of the allegedly inherent instability of German history, culminating in the Nazi catastrophe, were faced with the extraordinary success and stability of the Federal Republic. What had become of the supposedly irredeemable German national character? Moreover, there was in a sense a double problem: for, in a very different way, the German Democratic Republic proved to be one of the most stable and productive states in the area of Soviet domination in Eastern Europe. Very often western historians chose largely to ignore the GDR, concentrating most attention on the liberal democracy of western Germany as the new 'culmination' of German history. Even so, attempts to insert developments after 1945 into a longer view were problematic: basic repression in the police state of the East, the allegedly clear superiority of the western system imposed on the West, were to a large extent the underlying premises of Anglo-American interpretations of post-war German history, while Germans themselves (East and West) were caught in the problematic of the morally and politically loaded evaluation of competing systems. In the context of the Cold War, there was a tendency on both sides of the Iron Curtain simply to castigate the other system in terms of one's own values, rather than exploring with sensitivity the actual mode of functioning and inherent problems of each system – a more nuanced approach which could easily be denounced as a form of fifth columnism.

There is now, too, a final twist to the problem. Any new overview of German history must now explain, not only the relative stability – and apparent 'double solution' to the German problem – produced by the division of Germany, but also the dramatic historical transformation which occurred with the East German revolution in the autumn of 1989 and the unification of the two Germanies in October 1990. We have now a certain benefit of hindsight, in that the period from 1945 to 1990 forms a clearly defined historical period; but it is still too early for there to be a systematic body of historiography with well-established lines of argument and debate. To present a coherent account of longer-term trends which culminate in the unification of the two Germanies in October 1990 is to enter into new historiographical terrain.

What then is the argument advanced in this book? Any narrative account is based on certain underlying assumptions about the relative importance of different factors. When dealing with large, complex patterns of historical development, and seeking to tease out the threads of continuity, dynamism and fundamental change, a certain intellectual order must be imposed on the mass of historical material. In the case of twentieth-century Germany, we are dealing with an extraordinary succession of sociopolitical forms and yet also with some basic continuities. In my view, twentieth-century German history cannot be explained in terms primarily of personalities – whatever the undoubted importance of the actions and intentions of certain individuals, most notably of course Adolf Hitler – nor in terms of global, impersonal forces, whether to do with 'national character', 'cultural traditions', or any form of long-term structural determination. The account developed here is premised on the assumption that there is a complex interplay between a number of factors, and that human beings have to act within the constraints of given circumstances: both external structural and cultural conditions and 'internal' limits posed by their own views, knowledge and assumptions.

In seeking to explain patterns of stability and change special attention has to be paid to: Germany's place in the international system; the roles, relationships and activities of different elite groups; the structure and functioning of the economy; the location and aims of dissenting groups; and what may loosely be called the patterns of political culture among different subordinate social groups. Clearly one cannot simply write an abstract formula of this sort, apply it to different historical periods, weigh up the equation, and produce a neat outcome. History is not as straightforward or mechanical a process as that. But when considering the period from 1918 to 1990, the formula just presented does appear to have remarkable explanatory power, as we shall see in more detail in the chapters which follow. Let me preview briefly some of the implications of the elements involved.

The 'land in the centre of Europe' has been intimately affected by, as well as affecting, the international balance of power. Germany played a major role in causing the outbreak of the First World War; but the Treaty of Versailles, particularly in the ammunition it gave to revisionist elements in Germany, also played a role in the causation of the Second World War. However much the latter conflict was Hitler's war, it was also in many respects a continuation of the previous conflict, or of the attempted resolution of that conflict. Defeat in the Second World War was the precondition for the division of Germany – a division that was, however, also predicated on the new Cold War that had arisen between two superpowers who had largely been drawn into European affairs as a result of German aggression. Finally, it was the end of the Cold War, initiated by a crumbling Soviet Union, that was the precondition for the end of the division of Germany. German history cannot be understood without reference to the wider international context.

But nor can it be explained solely in terms of that wider context. Clearly, at every stage the balance of domestic forces played a major role in the pattern of developments. And here we come to the set of domestic factors mentioned above. First, there is the issue of the roles and relations of different elite groups within any particular political system. When elites fail to sustain that system – as in the Weimar Republic – it has little chance of success. When elites condone it, or acquiesce in it – however apparently unjust the system may be – then it has less chance of being brought down by internal unrest. This proved to be the case, in rather different ways, in both the Third Reich (where elite resistance was belated and unsuccessful) and the GDR for a considerable period of time. In the latter case, semi-critical members of the intelligentsia, for example, were in the end accused of having helped to sustain the regime. Interestingly, the speed of the ultimate collapse – effectively a capitulation in the face of mass protest – of the GDR regime had much to do with dissension within the ruling communist party itself as to the best way forward out of a crisis. By contrast, when a variety of elites in the main support a given political system, then it is much easier to maintain stability (provided of course that other factors are favourable). Thus, much of the success of the Federal Republic could be explained in terms of the support for West German democracy (in contrast to that of the Weimar Republic) on the part of the vast majority of political, economic, moral and intellectual elites.

The issue of elite support is a complex one, with cultural and moral elements involved as well as material factors. But the latter certainly play an important, indeed major, role, and need to be singled out for attention in respect of implications for popular as well as elite responses to the regime. Industrial and agrarian elites will clearly prefer a political system that appears to work to their economic advantage – again, contrast the critiques of Weimar democracy on the part of certain hard-pressed sectors of business and owners of impoverished, indebted agrarian estates, with the support for West German democracy among thriving industrialists and the well-represented farming lobby. At the level of mass politics, too, material success is important. Most ordinary working people will for obvious reasons tend to prefer a political system that appears to deliver the material goods. The importance of rapid economic growth for the anchoring of democracy in the early years of the history of West Germany cannot be overstated. Basic material satisfaction need not however be of this standard to ensure a more negative, but no less important, outcome: the *lack* of mass support for political opposition movements. At a rather basic level, people are less likely to rise in protest against an unjust and repressive system if the risks of rising are not counterbalanced by the pressures of acute material distress: consumerism is always a technique for rulers in repressive regimes to seek a modicum of popular quiescence. ('Bread and circuses' policies are as old as Roman civilisation.) This was the case in the peacetime years of the Third Reich: mindful of the need to sustain his personal popularity or 'charisma', on which the political system of the Third Reich was so dependent, Hitler had constantly to balance considerations of consumer satisfaction with the economic imperatives entailed by preparations for war. Similar considerations were pertinent again for much of the 1960s and 1970s in the GDR, when a combination of limited pride in economic achievements, stress on social policies and eventual consumer satisfaction, and hopes that hard work might bring a better future, helped to remove any potential mass support for the more ascetic programmes of dissident intellectuals. In contrast, much of the political turbulence of both the early and the later years of the Weimar Republic had to do with acute material distress for large numbers of people, hit either by catastrophic inflation or by the fear or reality of rising unemployment. This led to the willingness of large numbers to countenance radical political movements – of the Left or Right – claiming to offer some form of future salvation.

Finally, there is the key issue of political dissent and opposition, and of patterns of political culture under given circumstances. It is important for regime stability that political dissent be contained within certain bounds, and that it does not develop into broad, proliferating movements of opposition with mass followings. There are a variety of ways in which this containment may occur: through general satisfaction, for example, squeezing dissenters to a marginal fringe; through massive repression and intimidation, effectively excluding dissent from any articulate body politic; through isolation and limited toleration, allowing controlled ventilation of grievances; and in many other ways. The Weimar Republic was subjected to sustained assaults from a variety of quarters, from left and right; it ultimately fell prey to the latter, and its successor regime dealt exceedingly brutally with opposition from the former. The Third Reich itself was ultimately only felled from without because of lack of effective opposition from within. For much of the GDR's history it proved possible to contain and isolate intellectual dissent. But for a variety of reasons, dissent was able to proliferate in East Germany in the course of the 1980s, providing the foundation for the broad-based pressures on the regime in the situation of crisis which was inaugurated by Hungary's opening of the Iron Curtain and the ensuing flood of refugees in the summer of 1989. Clearly, again, no simple formula will adequately summarize the range of approaches, views and ideals of different groups of dissenters at different times. The character of dissent is affected by inherited cultural traditions as well as institutional and other structural circumstances. But it in turn can closely affect patterns of historical change. Thus, for example, the non-violent dissent shaped under the protection of the East German Protestant churches in the 1980s played a key role in the 'gentle' pattern of the East German revolution, and was a very different phenomenon from earlier 'revolutionary' movements in twentieth-century Germany.

Of course this set of factors cannot in any simple way unlock the course of history: there is a role for chance, for accident, for unforeseen combinations of circumstances, for the impact of personality. It must be the task of a narrative account to bring into play, at each turning, the role of specific elements in the actual pattern of events. But I would contend that the elements briefly introduced here together provide a useful framework for interpreting and seeking to explain the turbulent, often tragic, course of twentieth-century German history. In the chapters which follow, their implications at each stage will be explored in more detail. Let me conclude this chapter by outlining the structure and organization of the book.

The subtitle of this book is '*The Divided Nation*'. Germans in the twentieth century have been 'divided' in at least three different, but interrelated, ways. Most obviously, Germany itself was divided after the war: what remained of Hitler's defeated Reich became two German states, truncated parts of a German nation. This was integrally related to the failure, before 1945, to resolve the problems and tensions of a divided society: tensions which by the end of 1932 had led to near civil war conditions, and which Hitler's enforced creation of a 'national community' merely exacerbated and displaced. Under Hitler, there were divisions between those accepted as 'folk comrades' and those rejected as 'community aliens'; there were also divisions within people themselves, between public and private selves, between conformity and distance, in psychological compromises made in order to survive through a dictatorial regime. Finally, the consciousness of the century itself is divided: by the historical caesura of 1945. For a long time 1945 appeared to be a moment when the 'unmasterable' past seemed to have ended, and the apparently eternal present began. A form of consciousness developed which had serious difficulties in connecting the past with the present, that which had been swept away before and that which had been built up after the 'Zero Hour' (*Stunde Null*) of 1945. Only recently have many Germans sought – in convoluted and problematic ways – to reappropriate and 'normalize' the recent past, to recognize lines of continuity as well as change between the periods before and after 1945. This deep caesura is also only recently being overcome in historical accounts, with historians beginning to cross the divide of 1945 and enter territory previously allotted to political scientists and sociologists.

This book seeks to confront and make connections across these forms of division. It traces the ways in which the problems and conflicts of the Weimar Republic and Third Reich appeared, in very different ways, to have been resolved in the apparently more stable post-war era of divided Germany. It seeks, too, to consider continuities across the abyss of 1945, and to locate the admittedly irreducible evil of the Third Reich in the realities and normalities of the longer sweep of twentieth-century German history.

The book is organized in two main parts. Part One traces the descent of a divided society into the Nazi abyss. Chapters analysing the tensions and strains which led to the collapse of Weimar democracy (chapters 2 and 3), are followed by two chapters (4 and 5) on the Third Reich in the peacetime and wartime years. In contrast to a number of brief overviews of the Third Reich, a relatively large amount of space is allotted to the issue of the 'Final Solution'. It may, with some justice, be asserted that an undue proportion of this text deals with the Holocaust; but given the pivotal role that the Holocaust plays in all popular prejudices about German history, as well as the major difficulties it has caused for the self-understanding, self-representation, and national identities, of post-war Germans – in different ways in East and West – it seems important to give the actual course of events and the difficulties of their explanation a lengthier, more explicit hearing than merely the customary paragraph or two embedded in a wider narrative of the war that is usually found in general histories.

Part Two then explores the extraordinary historical experiment of the divided nation. Three chronological chapters (6, 7, 8) are followed by four thematic chapters (9, 10, 11, 12) exploring certain aspects of the two Germanies in more depth. While the economic development of the two Germanies and the question of inner-German and foreign relations are dealt with in the three narrative chapters, which establish a basic chronological framework, the focus in the thematic chapters is primarily social, political and cultural (in a broad sense, including issues of political culture). There is inevitably a (hopefully minimal) degree of repetition across chapters, but by treating certain themes analytically an interpretation of the dynamics of development of the two Germanies may be developed, exploring the degrees and nature of their divergence, and elucidating the background to the East German revolution of autumn 1989. This revolution, and the radical historical transformation it inaugurated, forms the subject of chapter 13.

In Part Three, a concluding chapter engages directly with the issue of the historical divide, the pivotal date of 1945. It reflects more broadly on the major patterns of development recounted in preceding chapters, and proposes a general framework for interpretation of the course of twentieth-century German history.

The book seeks, ultimately, to treat as a unit what is now a clearly defined historical period, and to present in a readable and intelligible compass an account of some of the major currents of twentieth-century German history in the light of wider debates and controversies.

PART ONE

A DIVIDED SOCIETY

The Weimar Republic and the Third Reich

TWO

The Weimar Republic: Origins and Orientations

The Weimar Republic was Germany's first attempt at parliamentary democracy. Born in 1918 of military defeat and domestic revolution, it was riddled with compromises and burdened with difficulties. After turbulent beginnings, from 1924 to 1928 there was a period of at least apparent stabilization; yet between 1929 and 1933, concerted attacks on democracy in the context of mounting economic difficulties culminated in the collapse of the regime and the appointment of Adolf Hitler, leader of the National Socialist German Workers' Party (NSDAP or Nazi Party), as Germany's Chancellor.

The ultimate demise of the Weimar Republic has inevitably overshadowed interpretations of its course. Some commentators have drawn such a stark and gloomy picture of its early difficulties that the Republic seems foredoomed to failure from the outset; other scholars have placed greater weight on problems arising from the Depression after 1929; and some historians have emphasized the importance of particular decisions and actions made by key political figures in the closing months of the Republic's existence, in 1932–3. It is important to bear in mind, when exploring the complex paths of Weimar history, the constant interplay of structure and action, context and personality; it is important also to bear in mind that under certain circumstances, the scope for human intervention in the course of events may be more limited or constrained than at other times. The conditions in which Weimar democracy was born were certainly not such as to help it flourish; and as it unfolded, it was clearly saddled with a burden of problems, in a range of areas, that would render Weimar democracy peculiarly susceptible to anti-democratic forces in the end.

Germany in the early twentieth century

What was Germany like in the decades prior to 1918? Germany had only been unified – as a result of Prussian chancellor Bismarck's policies of 'blood and iron' – in 1871. Although processes of industrialization had started earlier in the nineteenth century, the pace of change was dramatically quickened by unification. In the period from 1871 to the outbreak of war in 1914, Germany's output of manufactured goods quintupled, while her population grew from 41 million to 67.7 million. Rapid changes in economy and society were associated with a host of strains in the autocratic political system that was Bismarck's legacy for Imperial Germany.

Some areas were experiencing rapid modernization, with expansion in urban areas, such as the great metropolitan capital, Berlin, and in the heavy industry and coal-mining centre of the Ruhr. Workers migrating from the countryside to the towns were lucky if they were housed in the housing estates of paternalistic employers such as Siemens; many more found themselves living in cramped, dark tenement buildings with poor sanitation and limited backyards which were the only areas where their children could play. Meanwhile, the urban upper middle classes led their rather stuffy lives in the somewhat pompous buildings that were characteristic of Imperial Germany. The 'middle classes' were a far from homogenous entity. At the upper levels were the officials, professionals and state servants (the *Beamten*, in Germany a less narrow category than the British 'civil servant'). Then, at a more modest social level, there were the increasing numbers of white-collar employees (*Angestellten*), as well as the older groups of the self-employed, traders and shop-keepers, and small artisans. These latter groups were increasingly challenged by the rise of 'modern', large-scale mechanized industry, run by major entrepreneurs, and by the growth of big department stores as outlets for mass-produced wares. Urban life was clearly changing and expanding at a quickening rate.

Peasants in far-flung rural areas, such as southern Bavaria, might still appear to be living as they had done for centuries, although the notion of a static, unchanging 'traditional' rural society is something of a myth. While the urban bourgeoisie might be enjoying the fruits of modern technology – such as electricity – these peasants would be living in the old, wooden farmhouses, with their religious wall-paintings and flower-bedecked balconies, where they still relied on candlelight, water from the well, and very rudimentary sanitary facilities. Small peasant economies in the south and west had been interpenetrated by artisanal activities for centuries, and had also begun to cater to the newer pursuits of tourism. In the north-east and, particularly, eastern areas of Germany, rural life was characterized by a rather different social pattern: estates owned by the aristocratic land-owning class, the Junkers, were worked by landless agricultural labourers (often Polish), and were increasingly under strain in the competitive atmosphere of a rapidly industrializing nation. While retaining a socially and politically dominant position, the militaristic land-owning caste was suffering a period of economic difficulty, necessitating a series of compromises with, particularly, increasingly important industrial interests.

There were many regional variations: the German Empire had by no means homogenized the differences between its constituent states, and in many ways regional loyalties overrode any 'national' identification. There were traditional antagonisms between, for example, Bavaria and Prussia, based on centuries of political, cultural and social differences. Religious differences, too, were of crucial importance: post-Reformation Germany was divided between Catholicism and a variety of forms of Protestantism (both Lutheran and Reformed). While some states – notably Prussia – were of a mixed religious complexion, divisions between Catholic and Protestant communities in many areas were highly salient. These divisions went right through the community: it was quite possible to live one's life entirely within the framework, for example, of the Catholic church and its political, economic and social institutions: the Catholic Centre party in politics, the Catholic trade unions at the workplace, the reading, cycling, and singing clubs when at leisure. Similarly, Protestants and others had their own penumbra of institutions. Political persuasion might be as important as religious confession: the Social Democrats, for example, had a comparable range of organizations and leisure activities, encompassing many aspects of life and helping to define a particular social and cultural milieu. It is difficult to evaluate the implications of these socio-cultural environments; some have seen them as giving members of those subordinate groups which the architect of Imperial Germany, Bismarck, dubbed 'Enemies of the Empire' (*Reichsfeinde*) an accepted place in society, while others have seen more subversive aspects to their varied activities. Then, too, there were those members of society who constituted different 'underworlds': those who resisted all attempts at organization of whatever kind.[1]

Politically, the old Prussian aristocracy retained pre-eminence nationally, through its domination of the largest constituent state of the federal Empire – Prussia. The inegalitarian three-class voting system obtaining in Prussia entailed the division of the population of each electoral district into three classes according to the payment of wealth taxes. The minority who were the richest then obtained one-third of the votes; the moderately wealthy the next one-third, and the large majority who fell into the poorest category were also allotted only one-third of the votes. The double effect of this system not only greatly disadvantaged the propertyless masses, but also promoted the political position of the landowning Junker class (who were relatively the wealthiest within the sparsely populated rural constituencies) in comparison with the very much wealthier urban bourgeoisie. Dominating Prussian politics, the Junkers were then able to play a major role in the Prussian-dominated Reich. It was a role they were to exercise in the context of the autocratic political structure of the German Empire: real power lay, not so much with the parliament or *Reichstag*, as with the Emperor, his close circle of advisers, his Chancellor, and leaders of the army and the civil service. Influence was exerted on these groups and individuals by the increasingly important pressure groups – many stridently nationalist – which circumvented parliamentary politics in pursuit of their aims. As the German sociologist Max Weber put it, no person with any aspirations to real power would seriously consider becoming a member of parliament in Imperial Germany.

Yet at the same time, Junker domination was not unchallenged. For one thing, with Germany's extraordinarily rapid industrialization, the propertied bourgeoisie (*Besitzbürgertum*) was becoming increasingly important, and compromises had repeatedly to be hammered out between policies reflecting bourgeois economic interests and the often conflicting interests of the land-owning classes. At the same time, the masses were emerging on to the political scene, particularly through the ever-growing Social Democratic Party (SPD). This latter, while professing a certain revolutionary rhetoric deriving from its Marxist heritage, was in practice rather moderate, with a marked focus on parliamentary representation and activity (partly as an ironic result of Bismarck's anti-socialist laws which effectively restricted Social Democratic activity to this sphere). Nevertheless, the growth of an explicitly radical party representing the expanding working classes struck fear in the hearts of the elites, who – on some accounts – resolved certain differences among themselves in order to present a more united front against a perceived threat from below. Whatever the wider merits of this interpretation, certainly one manifestation was the fostering of German nationalism, in the hope that loyalty to the German 'fatherland' would transcend bitter divisions between the classes. Fear of potential civil war at home contributed to willingness to engage in war abroad.

In the event, the First World War did little to resolve the domestic strains of Imperial Germany. Despite a brief moment of apparent and much celebrated (if not exaggerated) national unity in August 1914, social tensions were exacerbated rather than eased by the experience of total war. Industry became more concentrated, with cartels fixing prices and production quantities; but organized labour also became more powerful, since the government and employers had to find ways of avoiding strikes and maximising production in a war economy, and therefore had to treat with the recognized representatives of labour. With the continued expansion of industrial capitalism, the 'old' middle classes – the small producers, shopkeepers and traders – found their already declining position ever more threatened. New sections of the population were increasingly politicized: with many men away at the front, and with the large numbers of war casualties, women and young people were drawn into sectors of the economy in which they had not previously worked, and gained first-hand experience of union organization, confrontation with employers, and notions of 'class war'. Even those women who were not part of the paid labour market may have become somewhat politicized through the sheer struggle for survival, and the realization that the government – rather than the individual – might be held responsible for the difficulties they found in feeding their families. This awareness of the responsibilities of the state continued after the war, heightened by more widespread dependence on state benefits and pensions.

During this protracted war – in which progress was measured from the trenches in terms of yards rather than miles – circumstances on the home front soon deteriorated. Food supplies became a problem as early as 1915. In April 1917 the first major strikes occurred, a consequence of the cutting of bread rations. Civilian government broke down with the resignation of the moderate Chancellor Bethmann-Hollweg in July 1917, and the country was under the effective military rule of Chief-of-Staff Hindenburg and General Ludendorff (in conjunction with two short-lived and ineffective civilian Chancellors, Georg Michaelis until October 1917 and Count von Hertling until October 1918). In 1917, there were two successful revolutions in Tsarist Russia – a far less economically advanced autocracy, and one which, according to a Marxist analysis, should not have been the first to experience communist revolution. Following the Bolsheviks' seizure of power in the autumn, Russia concluded an armistice with Germany and entered into negotiations for peace. After abortive discussions, Germany renewed hostilities in February 1918, and, from a position of strength, was able to impose the annexationist Treaty of Brest-Litovsk on Russia in March 1918. This harsh treaty was greeted with a mixed reception at home, and hardened the attitudes of the western powers against Germany.

Meanwhile, rising domestic unrest in Germany played a role in the Army leaders' decision, in the winter of 1917–18, to ignore the chance of achieving peace with the western powers on relatively moderate terms, since they had begun to believe that only a spectacular military victory could now avert the threat of domestic revolution. In January 1918 there were more strikes, and a widespread war-weariness and desire for peace, even as the Army High Command, supported by the recently founded right-wing *Vaterlandspartei*, propagated ever more extravagant military aims. Yet on the left, the political forces opposing both the military and the right-wing nationalist parties were themselves divided. The Social Democratic Party, since its formation in 1875 out of two pre-existing parties with different traditions, had long experienced tension between its reformist and revolutionary wings. Under the strain of responding to the war effort, the SPD finally split in 1917. The more radical wing formed the so-called Independent Social Democratic Party (USPD), while the majority remained with the more moderate SPD, sometimes known as the Majority Social Democratic Party (MSPD). A loose, more radical grouping further to the left of the Social Democrats was the Spartacus League, whose leading lights were Rosa Luxemburg and Karl Liebknecht. It was in this complex domestic configuration that the new Republic was born.

The 'last revolution from above'

Despite the success of the spring offensive against Russia, by the summer of 1918 it was clear even to the leaders of the Army that the war was lost. The Army High Command now felt that it would be advisable to hand over power to a civilian administration: Army leaders – who were already propagating the myth of a 'stab in the back', the betrayal of an undefeated Germany by Jews and Bolsheviks at home, an enemy within – preferred that a civilian government should have to shoulder the opprobrium of accepting national defeat.

Accordingly, in October 1918 a new civilian government was formed under the chancellorship of Prince Max von Baden. Faced with considerable domestic unrest, this government introduced certain reforms. The reforms were not simply (as they are often described) a 'last revolution from above', a desperate attempt to salvage some credibility for the Imperial system; they also resulted from very strong pressures in parliament, particularly on the part of the moderate Social Democrats. Most notable among the reforms were the introduction of ministerial responsibility to parliament, the control of the armed forces by the civilian government, and the abolition of the iniquitous Prussian three-class voting system. The removal of this system, along with the other reforms, constituted a progressive move in the eyes of democratic forces; but there was one step that Prince Max von Baden's government failed to take. Despite efforts to persuade Emperor Wilhelm II to abdicate in favour of one of his sons, the obdurate Emperor, supported by his sons, refused to assume sole responsibility for Germany's ills. Had he agreed to leave the political scene gracefully in October, the monarchy might have been saved.

The incomplete revolution of November 1918

However, matters developed otherwise. All the cautious moves for reform from above were swept away by a revolutionary tide on the streets which, by early November, it was no longer possible for Max von Baden's government to control. Uprisings all over Germany were sparked off by a sailors' mutiny in Wilhelmshaven and Kiel at the end of October. Ordered out on a last, suicidal mission against the British fleet, the sailors decided they would rather save their own skins than attempt to salvage 'German honour'. News of the mutiny led to the formation, in a large number of places across Germany, of 'sailors', soldiers' and workers' councils', which wrested control of administration from local governments. On 8 November, a Republic was proclaimed in the 'Free State' of Bavaria, under a workers', soldiers' and peasants' council led by Kurt Eisner. The German war effort had clearly collapsed, the authority of the regime was rapidly crumbling, the threat of strikes and civil war on the streets loomed ever larger.

On 9 November Max von Baden made a last-ditch effort to salvage what he could from the situation. He felt that Friedrich Ebert – in his view the most level-headed of the Social Democrats and the one for whom he had most respect – might yet be able to maintain a modicum of control over the situation and avert the threat of radical social revolution headed by the far left. Unable to reach the Emperor (who had fled the unrest of Berlin) by telephone by midday, Max von Baden, in something of a panic, took it upon himself to pronounce the abdication of the Emperor and the intended appointment of Ebert as leader of a new civilian government. The shape of such a government had by no means been decided when, at around two o'clock, Ebert's colleague Philipp Scheidemann went to a balcony of the Reichstag to proclaim a republic, in an attempt to marginalize the almost simultaneous proclamation of a socialist republic by more radical socialists in another part of Berlin. It was clear that Ebert and the moderate Social Democrats would have to move fast to assert control over a situation of strikes, uprisings, mass demonstrations and the breakdown of governmental authority across a Germany which was, formally, still at war.

Rapid negotiations took place between the moderate Social Democrats and the USPD leaders, and a compromise caretaker government was agreed. This consisted of a six-member 'Council of People's Representatives' (*Rat der Volksbeauftragten*), of whom three – Ebert, Scheidemann and Landsberg – were members of the SPD, and three – Haase, Dittmann and Barth – were members of the USPD. Even before this body had been constituted, Ebert had declared his priorities to the people of Germany. The new government was committed to organizing elections for a national constituent assembly, which would be elected by all men and women over twenty years of age. Until this elected body could take power, the temporary government would agree an armistice, lead peace negotiations, seek to ensure an adequate food supply for the people, and oversee an orderly demobilization of troops and the return of former soldiers to civilian life and work. In the mean time, law and order were to be upheld, the people were to desist from plunder and violence, and help to build a better future.

In the context of widespread strikes and demonstrations, the obstacles to a peaceful transition to a new order were formidable. The USPD did agree to co-operate with the SPD, despite their rather different general aims, and the new government – which was to last only a few weeks – was duly given popular legitimization, first by a meeting of council delegates in Berlin in November, and then in December by a wider body of delegates from workers' and soldiers' councils from all over Germany. An armistice was achieved on 11 November, although it was not until the following summer that the terms of the peace treaty would be revealed.

In the first few days after the proclamation of the Republic, two very significant agreements were reached, which embodied compromises which would have a profound effect on the subsequent course of events. The first was between the new government and the Army; the second between leaders of industry and the trade unions.

There were fears among members of the Army High Command, not only of the effects on the troops of the abdication of the Emperor, to whom they had traditionally owed obedience, but also of the possibility of a Soviet-style Bolshevik revolution in Germany. On 10 November, General Groener (who had succeeded Ludendorff as Quarter-Master General) decided that the best approach would be to enter into a pact with Ebert, whom Groener, like Prince Max, considered to be the most sensible and moderate of the Social Democrats. Groener offered Ebert the support of the army in maintaining law and order and suppressing revolutionary uprisings; Ebert accepted. In this pact lay the seeds of many future problems. It illustrated the limited nature of the revolution – not only the Army, but also the other elites of Imperial Germany (including the civil service, the judiciary, and the economic elites), were to remain untouched and unscathed by what remained a purely political, rather than a far-reaching social and economic, revolution. Perhaps more importantly, it also laid the foundations for the repeated repression of radical movements in the following months and years, inaugurating a split between moderate and radical socialists that was ultimately to contribute to their failure to unite in defence of Weimar democracy.

The other early compromise was that negotiated by the trade unionist Carl Legien and the employers' leader Hugo Stinnes. With the 'Stinnes-Legien agreement' of 15 November 1918, the employers made certain crucial concessions to labour. These included: recognition of the legitimacy of trade union representation of the workforce, and agreement no longer to support 'employer-friendly associations'; the smooth reincorporation, so far as possible, of former employees returning from war into their old jobs; the establishment of 'Workers' Committees' (or Works Councils) in enterprises with more than fifty employees, to ensure discussion between employers and employees over conditions of work; the limitation of the working day to eight hours; and the institution of a 'Central Committee' (*Zentralausschuss*) made up of representatives of the unions and the employers to regulate not only the more immediate problems of demobilization and the reconstruction of a war-torn economy, but also the longer-term issues of wages, working conditions, and other contentious matters that might arise in labour affairs. This committee laid the foundations for the *Zentral-Arbeits-Gemeinschaft* (ZAG), which was to give Weimar democracy a corporatist element that later played a role in the economic elites' utter rejection of the 'system' that allowed workers such a considerable voice. Concessions made by employers to workers, when the latter were relatively strong and the former feared a more radical revolution, were to be fundamentally queried and subject to sustained assault – as was the political system that guaranteed those concessions – when the relative circumstances of the parties had changed.

By December 1918, the USPD had fallen out with Ebert's cautious course. The radical socialists had wanted to seize the opportunity for a thorough-going reform of the army, and for the socialization of the means of production; in short, they wanted to effect a genuine revolution, not to administer affairs on a temporary basis pending national elections. The USPD left the government; and at the end of December, the far left formed the German Communist Party (KPD). In January 1919 the split between moderate Social Democrats on the one hand, and radical socialists and communists on the other, became an unbridgeable chasm. A largely spontaneous uprising in Berlin, occasioned by the dismissal of the radical Police Chief Eichhorn, belatedly came under the control of the Spartacist leaders. The SPD overreacted to the demonstrations, requesting the support of the Army and Free Corps (*Freikorps*) units (privately financed paramilitary groups of demobilized soldiers) to suppress the revolt by force. This they did with a vengeance. In the process of being arrested and imprisoned, the Spartacist leaders, Karl Liebknecht and Rosa Luxemburg, were brutally murdered. Radicals never forgave moderate Social Democrats for their use of force – which was to be repeated all over Germany, many times, in response to unrest in the following months and years – and the bitter resentment and hostility aroused at this early date helped to sustain the Communists' later (Moscow-dominated) view of Social Democrats as 'social fascists', a worse enemy even than the Nazis.

Street-fighting, strikes, demonstrations and barricades provided the backdrop for a national campaign for the elections of 19 January 1919. The SPD, which had been relying on this for a solid majority confirming its mandate to govern the new Republic, was disappointed. It gained only thirty-eight per cent of the vote, which under the system of proportional representation entailed forming a coalition government in conjunction with the Catholic Centre Party (*Zentrum*) and the liberal German Democratic Party (DDP). On 6 February 1919 the National Constituent Assembly convened in the town of Weimar (hence the name 'Weimar Republic'), and within a week Ebert had been elected the Republic's first President, while Scheidemann became head of the coalition cabinet.

The Weimar Constitution and the Treaty of Versailles

During December 1918, a group of experts (including Max Weber), under the leadership of Hugo Preuss, a left-liberal

Professor of Law, had been busy developing a draft constitution for the Republic. This constitution was then considered by the National Assembly, and an agreed version took effect on 11 August 1919. It appeared – and indeed was – very progressive, but has subsequently come under much criticism for alleged weaknesses which facilitated the subsequent collapse of democracy.

The electoral system was to be one of proportional representation of parties in the national parliament according to the percentage of votes cast by all men and women over the age of twenty. In the event, the nature of the party system in the Weimar Republic, and what might be called the 'political culture' of a number of Weimar parties, rendered post-election bargaining over possible governmental coalitions much more difficult than it has proved to be in other democracies where proportional representation prevails; thus, as we shall see, it was not so much the rules of the game, as the nature of the parties playing the game, that rendered proportional representation a serious liability for Weimar democracy. The constitution also stressed the participatory, rather than purely representative, aspects of the democratic system. Referenda could be called with direct popular vote on policy issues of considerable importance. The President himself was to be elected by direct popular vote for a seven-year period of office. The elected President, who as a ceremonial head of state replaced the hereditary office of Emperor, was in many ways what has been called an *Ersatz-Kaiser* (substitute Emperor). He had tremendous personal powers, including the right to appoint and dismiss Chancellors, to dissolve the parliament and call new elections, and, in cases where no parliamentary majority could be found in support of governmental policies, to authorize the Chancellor to rule by presidential decree. The notorious Article 48 of the constitution, which gave the President such emergency powers, also permitted military intervention in the affairs of the different local states or *Länder* if it was deemed that a state of emergency obtained. Given the considerable personal power of the President, a lot depended on the particular character who held the office. Friedrich Ebert made use of presidential powers to

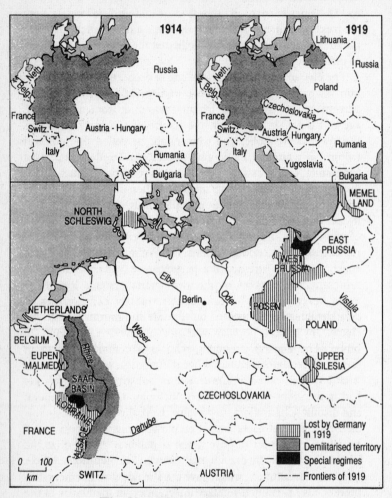

The Versailles settlement, 1919

stabilize democracy; his successor, the ageing military hero Field Marshal Hindenburg, turned out to be much less committed to upholding parliamentary democracy and was to play an important role in its destruction.

One of the first tasks of the new government was to sign a peace treaty with the victorious powers. The provisions of the Versailles Treaty, when they were finally revealed in the early summer of 1919, proved to be harsh. Scheidemann's cabinet resigned, and a delegation from a new cabinet under Bauer went to sign the Treaty on 28 June 1919. Germany lost not only her colonies, but also large areas of German territory in Europe: Alsace-Lorraine was to be returned to France (which was also to enjoy the fruits of coal production in the Saar basin); West Prussia, Upper Silesia and Posen (Poznań) were to be restored to a newly reconstituted Poland, and Danzig was to become a free city under the supervision of the newly established League of Nations. The 'Polish Corridor' thus created separated East Prussia from the rest of Germany. Border areas of Germany were to be demilitarized; the left bank of the Rhine was placed under Allied supervision for a prospective period of fifteen years. There was to be no union of Germany and Austria. The German army was to be reduced to 100,000 men, for domestic and border-guard purposes only, while the German navy was similarly restricted – submarines were forbidden – and an air force was not permitted at all. Article 231 stated that Germany and her allies were responsible for the war and the damage it had caused. In consideration of this responsibility, Germany was to pay an unspecified sum in reparation, to be determined later. When the details of reparations were finally announced at the Paris conference of January 1921, the high sums involved were to arouse great indignation, and to have tremendous political and (politically exacerbated) economic consequences. Altogether, the harsh treatment of Germany after the First World War was to prove a considerable burden for Weimar democracy, and a powerful cause of the persistent, widespread and energetic revisionism on the part of many groups and individuals in the following years. The legend of the 'stab in the back' was to gain considerable currency in the summer of 1919, and for many people 'democracy' became synonymous with national humiliation and, increasingly, economic ruin.

Political unrest and economic chaos

The fledgeling Republic was subjected not only to a hammering from abroad, but also to onslaughts from a variety of quarters at home. Its first four years were characterized by a high level of political violence, with frequent assassinations, coup attempts, strikes and demonstrations, these last generally being put down with considerable force. A second attempt at establishing a Bavarian Republic, following the assassination of Kurt Eisner, was brutally suppressed in May 1919 by Free Corps units, with perhaps a thousand deaths. An attempted national right-wing putsch, with a march on Berlin led by *Generallandschaftsdirektor* Kapp and Infantry General Freiherr von Lüttwitz in March 1920, was only brought down by a general strike, after the army had refused to fire on the putschist troops. Later a successful coup in Bavaria installed a right-wing regime under Kahr, turning Bavaria into a haven in which small nationalist (or *völkisch*) groups could safely organize and foment unrest against democracy. The army, despite its unwillingness to act against the Kapp putsch, was only too happy to fire on the so-called 'Red Army' in the Ruhr, when there were left-wing uprisings against the Republic in the spring of 1920. The army and Free Corps were also keen to intervene to suppress Communist-led uprisings and left-wing regimes in Saxony, Thuringia, and Hamburg in the autumn of 1923. Faced with repeated strikes, demonstrations, and political violence, the SPD sadly misjudged the situation and, instead of responding to the causes of distress, sought to use force to suppress the symptoms of unrest.[2] Moreover, the judiciary throughout the Weimar Republic displayed considerable political bias in treating left-wing offenders very harshly, while meting out lenient sentences to offenders on the right. A deeply polarized society was hardly coming to terms with the new political circumstances of the time.

In the elections of June 1920, there was a swing to the parties of the extreme left and the right, while the more moderate 'Weimar coalition' parties lost ground. The SPD's share of the vote fell from 37.9% to 21.7% while the German Democratic Party's (DDP) vote fell to 8.2%, less than half its former 18.5% and the Centre dropped moderately from 19.7% to 13.6%. The USPD share grew from 7.6% to 17.8% while the KPD (which had not contested the 1919 elections) won 2% of the vote; on the right, the German People's Party (DVP) increased its poll from 4.4% to 13.9%, and the German National People's Party (DNVP) gained 15%, compared to its earlier 10.3% share of the vote. The SPD-led coalition government was replaced by a centre-right coalition.

From 1921 to the summer of 1923, governmental policies served to exacerbate Germany's political and economic difficulties. Wirth's government of 1921–2 pursued a so-called 'policy of fulfilment' which, by attempting to fulfil Germany's reparations obligations, served to demonstrate that the German economy was in fact too weak to pay reparations as envisaged. This coincided with the pursuit by the French of revisionist policies aimed at gaining control of the left bank of the Rhine and setting up a puppet state. Matters came to a head under the government of Cuno, from November 1922 to August 1923, which included the DVP while the SPD remained in opposition. In January 1923, the French and Belgians sent troops to 'supervise' production in the Ruhr, using the shortfall in German wood and coal deliveries to the French as a pretext. This military occupation of the Ruhr entailed the deployment of 100,000 men – equivalent to the total strength of the German army. The Germans responded with a policy of 'passive resistance', ceasing economic production and refusing to co-operate with the occupation. The need to subsidize Germans in the now unproductive Ruhr was exceedingly detrimental to the German economy, and coincided with an extraordinary period of catastrophic inflation.

While the roots of German inflation lay in the earlier financing of war by bonds and loans rather than taxation increases, its explosive growth was fuelled by, among other factors, the printing of paper money for the payment of reparations, and for the financing of heavy social expenditure (on pensions, for example).

This sent the value of money totally out of control. In the course of the spring and summer of 1923, the German Mark progressively became worthless. The American dollar was worth 4.2 Marks in July 1914; it had risen to 8.9 Marks in January 1919, 14 Marks by July 1919, and a peak of 64.8 Marks in January 1920. There was then a brief period of respite, but after January 1921 the snowball started rolling again. By July 1922, the dollar was worth 493.2 Marks; by January 1923 the figure was 17,972; and in an inflationary explosion, the figures rose to 4.62 *million* Marks by August, 98.86 million Marks by September, 25,260 million Marks by October, and an almost unimaginable 4,200,000 million Marks by 15 November 1923.[3] Paper notes were simply stamped with a new increased value; people were paid their wages by the cartload; prices doubled and trebled several times a day, making shopping with money almost impossible; and the savings, hopes, plans, assumptions and aspirations of huge numbers of people were swept away in a chaotic whirlwind.

Those on fixed incomes, and those dependent on money savings, were of course hit the hardest. Even when the worst material impact was over, the psychological shock of the experience was to have longer-lasting effects, confirming a deep-seated dislike of democracy – which was thereafter equated with economic distress – and a heightened fear of the possible consequences of economic instability. A few groups and individuals were by contrast well-placed to benefit, and even to make a profit, from the inflation, such as the industrialist Hugo Stinnes.

In the end, the situation was brought under control by the Stresemann government of August–November 1923. The policy of passive resistance in the Ruhr was terminated, easing the burden on the German economy and defusing international tension, while a currency reform introduced the *Rentenmark* and laid the foundations both of a more stable currency and of a reconsideration of the reparations question in the following year. At the same time, a number of putsch attempts, including communist-inspired uprisings in Saxony, Thuringia and Hamburg, were suppressed. One putsch attempt of this period – which was at the time but one among many – has gained particular historical notoriety. In Bavaria, a number of nationalist groups were laying complex plans for a right-wing 'march on Berlin', copying the successful model of Mussolini's Fascist march on Rome of the previous year. One of the groups associated with these plans was the small party formed out of the earlier German Workers' Party (DAP) led by Anton Drexler, and now known as the National Socialist German Workers' Party (NSDAP, or Nazi) under the leadership of a certain Adolf Hitler. At the time relatively insignificant, the failed 'Beer Hall Putsch' of 8–9 November 1923 – which lost crucial support in high places at the last moment – in the event gave Hitler and his associates considerable national publicity in the trial which ensued. Sentenced to a minimum of five years' detention – of which he served less than a year, in relatively comfortable circumstances in Landsberg prison – Hitler took the opportunity to write the political diatribe entitled *Mein Kampf*, and to ruminate on the future strategy of his party. In the mean time, however, from 1924 the Republic appeared to be recovering from its early turbulence, and entering into a new period of stabilization, on both the domestic and international fronts.

Apparent stabilization, 1924–9

In November 1923, Gustav Stresemann became Foreign Minister. A member of the right-wing liberal DVP, Stresemann only gradually became committed to the Republic, intellectually rather than emotionally (as the German phrase *Vernunftrepublikaner* implied). Despite the frequent changes of governmental coalition during the Weimar Republic, Stresemann retained the position of Foreign Minister until his death in October 1929. During this period he made a major contribution to the stabilization of the Republic as far as foreign affairs were concerned – which, as it sadly turned out, was in the end not quite far enough.

The Versailles Treaty had left a number of outstanding problems. It was clear after the catastrophes of 1923 that the issue of reparations would have to be reconsidered. In

1924 the Dawes Plan was adopted, which aided both German economic recovery and American expansionist economic policies. Essentially postponing a final settlement, this plan allowed Germany a breathing space before full reparations would be payable, with payment staggered over four years before reaching a maximum level in the fifth year. For Germany, it also meant considerable economic dependence on short-term loans from abroad, particularly from America. In the early phases only one-fifth would be paid from Germany's own resources while four-fifths were to come from international 'start-up' loans. Stresemann was quite clear about the difficulties this would entail for the weak German economy, but felt that the potential benefits of normalization of relations with France in particular outweighed the obvious and serious economic problems involved.

In July 1925 the Rhineland began to be cleared and French troops started to leave the Ruhr. After long negotiations, in October 1925, the Locarno Pact was signed by representatives of Germany, Belgium, Britain, France, Italy, together with separate agreements between Germany and Poland, and Germany and Czechoslovakia. Locarno guaranteed the frontiers between Germany and France, and between Germany and Belgium, and its parties mutually renounced the use of force or invasion of each other's territory except in self-defence. Since the militarily emasculated Germany was in no position to use force, and since Locarno entailed further recognition of the validity of the Treaty of Versailles, as well as appearing to favour good relations with Germany's western neighbours at the expense of relations with Russia, the agreement provoked highly hostile responses from both left- and right-wingers at home. On the other hand, Locarno appeared to mark the beginning of the re-entry of Germany into a community of nations seeking a framework for peace and security in Europe, and it paved the way for Germany's entry into the League of Nations in September 1926.

Partly to reassure domestic opinion, and partly to reaffirm Germany's position *vis-à-vis* Russia, Stresemann concluded with Russia the Berlin Treaty of 1926. This confirmed the Rapallo Treaty of 1922, concluded when Rathenau (who was assassinated after the Treaty was signed) was Foreign Minister. Rapallo had re-established diplomatic relations between Germany and Russia, and the two powers had mutually renounced claims to reparations or compensation. This foreign policy initiative, which aroused considerable resentment among the western powers (who were suspicious of a special relationship between Germany and Russia), had also included a secret military agreement allowing German remilitarization inside the territory of the USSR. In the Berlin Treaty of 1926, Russia and Germany reassured each other of their friendly relations, and committed themselves to remaining neutral in the event of the other country being at war with a third power or powers. This meant that if, for example, Poland and Russia were at war, France would not be able to come to Poland's help via German territory. Stresemann was anxious to reassure his opponents at home that Germany was not exclusively western-orientated in her foreign policy, but rather could act as a peace-keeping bridge in the centre of Europe between West and East. It was nevertheless clear that Poland's position was rather weak, and the issue of Germany's eastern frontiers was left sufficiently open to give hope to revisionists in Germany that changes might yet be effected on that front.

In January 1927 the allied military commission overseeing the post-Versailles disarmament of Germany was withdrawn. The reparations question was reopened, as the 'normal' years of full reparations payments, 1928–9, drew closer. In August 1929 the Young Plan revised the reparations schedule yet again, setting a new total figure and a reduced annual average of reparations payments. This was met with an intense campaign of domestic opposition – in which the Nazis gained some respectability and free publicity by associating themselves with conservative nationalists in the DNVP. But the referendum 'against the enslavement of the German people' failed to win the required 21 million votes (receiving the acclamation of 'only' 5.83 million). In the event, under the Young Plan, foreign controls were to be removed and the Rhineland evacuated by the Allied powers in June 1930, five years earlier than envisaged in the Versailles Treaty. To moderate observers, it might appear that under Stresemann's guidance, a considerable amount had been achieved: reparations had been renegotiated to a more manageable level, Germany's relations with her former enemies and neighbours had been regularized, the Ruhr and Rhineland had been evacuated, Germany had been accepted into the League of Nations – and at the same time there still appeared to be the possibility of reconsidering Germany's eastern frontiers, thus pursuing revisionist aims in a peaceful manner.

Yet many observers in the Weimar Republic were far from moderate. Each of the measures negotiated under Stresemann was highly contentious. Moreover, under the facade of apparent stabilization there were many cracks, both political and economic. In the period of renewed crisis after 1929, these cracks were to turn into an earthquake, bringing the shaky edifice of Weimar democracy tumbling down in ruins. We shall consider the intrinsic domestic weaknesses of the Weimar Republic as they affected its eventual collapse in the next chapter. In the mean time, however, on another front 'Weimar culture' was beginning to achieve international renown.

The Golden Twenties? Society and culture in the Weimar Republic

Many people who know little more about the politics of the Weimar Republic than that it ended with the rise of Hitler may know a great deal about 'Weimar culture'. The Weimar years, brief though this political epoch was, saw an explosion of creativity across a wide range of scientific and artistic fields. The German traditions of research in the natural sciences, particularly physics and chemistry, and expertise in psychology and psychoanalysis, continued to develop in the 1920s. In the field of social sciences, great contributions were made by, for example, the 'Frankfurt School' of Critical Theory, members of which included Max Horkheimer, Theodor Adorno and Walter Benjamin. This school of social theory, forced into exile in the Nazi period, was subsequently rediscovered in the 1960s by younger American and European social theorists, influenced particularly by the ageing Marcuse and by a second generation of critical theorists such as Habermas. In the visual arts, tendencies existing before the First World War – particularly the schools known as 'Die Brücke' (based in Dresden) and 'Der blaue Reiter' (based in Munich) – continued to be creative in the early Weimar years. Expressionism – associated with names such as Ernst Ludwig Kirchner and Franz Marc – exploded, and diversified into an array of experimental and avant-garde tendencies: cubism, futurism, Dada, and other styles flourished. In literature, a great range of prose, poetry, and drama was produced which has proved to be of enduring merit and lasting reputation. Names such as Heinrich and Thomas Mann, Hermann Hesse, Rainer Maria Rilke, Bertolt Brecht (and his musical associate Kurt Weill) have achieved international standing. Even in architecture, Weimar Germany produced a phenomenon of enduring interest: the Bauhaus school led by Walter Gropius. In music, too, there was experimentation in the atonal work of Arnold Schönberg.

Given such an extraordinary diversity of talent and creative production, it is difficult to form valid brief generalizations about Weimar culture, or to suggest a periodisation. It is also clear that not all of that which has been termed 'Weimar culture' was actually a direct product of the Weimar period itself: many commentators have pointed to a cultural epoch stretching from the turn of the century to about 1930. Many of the schools, tendencies, and individuals associated with Weimar culture had been creative already in the decade before the outbreak of the First World War. Some elements were, however, new, and corresponded curiously to the political phases of Weimar democracy. Eberhard Kolb has pointed out that the tendency known as 'new objectivity' (*Neue Sachlichkeit*), with which the Bauhaus, for example, was associated, coincided with the period of relative stabilization from 1924 to 1929.[4] After the near-apocalyptic exuberance of the early years – in both the political and artistic realms – a new emphasis was given to a cool, detached combination of utilitarian and aesthetic qualities. The final years of the Weimar Republic witnessed not only a radical political polarization, but also a heightened politicization and polarization in art, particularly in such fields as theatre. And the social conditions and political violence of the closing years of the Republic, with the onset of the depression, were witnessed to in such realist novels as Alexander Döblin's *Berlin Alexanderplatz*.

But there are perhaps more important ways than simple periodisation in which Weimar culture reflected, refracted, and contributed to the complexities of Weimar politics. For Weimar culture, far from being a homogenous entity, was a deeply divided phenomenon: indeed, perhaps it would be more apposite to speak of Weimar cultures in the plural. And, most importantly, the one element that united the most diverse aspects of this culture was the problematic relationship that proponents of both left-wing and right-wing tendencies had to 'modernity' in general and the Weimar Republic in particular. Use was made of modern means of communication, modern machinery and media, to criticize the age of the machine and modern society. On the left, artists such as Georg Grosz, Otto Dix, Käthe Kollwitz, and Heinrich Zille criticized the bourgeois society in which the bourgeois, conservative and nationalist 'pillars of society' (to borrow the title of one of Grosz's most scathing and biting pictures; *see* cover) grew fat at the expense of the masses, who were driven into conditions of abject poverty. This poverty was captured with humour in Zille's drawings of the life of the Berlin working classes in the early twentieth century, and with pathos in Käthe Kollwitz's representations of misery and suffering. While left-wing political cabaret and theatre attacked the pomposity and injustice of bourgeois capitalist society, the right-wing attacked parliamentary democracy, the political form of the Weimar Republic. The influx of new forms, such as American jazz music – held by right-wingers to be the ultimate in decadence – and the perceived 'laxity in morals', particularly in metropolitan centres such as 1920s Berlin, were held to be evidence of cultural decay. The Weimar Republic itself was held responsible for this decadence, and for the penetration of western forms of shallow, superficial 'civilization' into the purer German 'culture', defiling it in the process. So while the left attacked capitalism, the right attacked democracy: neither wing of elite culture – with the exception of a few individuals, most notably (and belatedly) Thomas Mann – spoke out to sustain the Weimar Republic in principle.

Nor was culture in the wider sense to sustain the new Republic. The social institutions which had the most influence on popular attitudes were still the churches and the schools: and both religious and educational institutions by and large tended to undermine Weimar democracy. Both the Catholic and the Protestant churches propagated essentially conservative, monarchist and anti-democratic sympathies; they were moreover highly critical of the moral decadence, as they saw it, of a society in which birth control was for the first time becoming widespread. The education system was also, in general, conservative and anti-democratic in outlook. Many schoolteachers were traditional conservative nationalists. Student fraternities and university teachers were similarly preponderantly right-wing and anti-democratic in sympathy: the Left was only to dominate German student politics for the first time in the West Germany of the late 1960s. However, in the sphere of education, as in virtually every other aspect of Weimar life, quite different tendencies co-existed. Alongside the highly conservative educational establishment ran currents of reform, and progressive schools. After the Second World War, largely unsuccessful attempts were made to resurrect some of the more progressive elements in Weimar education.

The Weimar period saw an explosion in new media of communication. The cinema began to replace the theatre, as films – first silent, then from 1929 with soundtracks – became an increasingly popular form of mass entertainment. Radio ownership spread rapidly among German households, and contributed to the formation of a new national public. There have been suggestions that the commercialization of leisure started to break down the divisions between class-based subcultures, and perhaps also to erode the hold of the SPD over the outlook and organizations of large parts of the working class.[5] Regional isolation was also diminished, in a less than democratic manner, with increased concentration in the newspaper industry: press barons such as Hugenberg not only directly owned and influenced their own newspapers, but also indirectly affected the contents and political bias of 'independent' local papers through their press agency services and the provision of news snippets and commentaries. In film, radio and newsprint, as in other areas of Weimar culture, developments were ambiguous. While certain renowned films, such as Remarque's 'All Quiet on the Western Front' (*Im Westen nichts Neues*), took a firm stand against war, they remained the exception: there were many more, generally ephemeral and of low artistic quality, which glorified nationalism, war, and the fatherland. In the sphere of radio, pro-Republican forces failed to gain political control or make serious use of a medium which was for most of the Weimar period intended to be politically neutral. It was only in 1932 that von Papen (then Chancellor) asserted political control of the radio, leaving a welcome gift for the Nazis to exploit in their propaganda efforts after January 1933.

If one turns from culture, at both elite and mass levels, to society more generally in the Weimar period, then a similar range of complexities, ambiguities and conflicts appear. Women were formally 'emancipated' in what was essentially a highly progressive welfare state. But this was an 'emancipation from above': despite the existence of minority feminist movements, both bourgeois and socialist, the majority of women continued to have rather traditional conceptions of their role. Being a wife and mother was held to be the essential fulfilment of womanhood: paid employment outside the home was preferably to be undertaken only before marriage, or only if economically absolutely essential. Weimar 'emancipation' was more theoretical than real: while women gained the vote (of which they made slowly increasing use), they remained in predominantly low-paid and low-status occupations. While women had always formed a considerable proportion of the agricultural labour force – peasant farms, for example, being family concerns where women brought in the hay, fed the chickens and milked the cows as a matter of course – women in the Weimar Republic were increasingly employed in white-collar occupations in the new middle class, a trend evident since the beginning of the century. A minority of women did achieve a certain status, if not actual power: the first Parliament of the Weimar Republic, for example, had a distinguished group of women Members. But by and large, despite the spread of birth control and the progressive framework of the constitution, attitudes both of and towards women remained highly traditional. In the depression, with rising unemployment after 1929, there was criticism of 'double earners' (*Doppelverdiener*), as people complained of the unfairness of some families having two incomes while others had no income at all. And when women voted they tended to vote disproportionately for parties which did *not* hold progressive attitudes on women's questions, such as the conservative and Christian parties. The two parties with the most progressive views on women's issues, the SPD and the KPD, failed to attract a proportional share of the votes of women.[6] Formal appearances notwithstanding, most women neither were nor seemed to want to be 'emancipated'. The minority who adopted what they held to be an emancipated *style* – smoking cigarettes in long holders, cutting their hair in short fashions, driving cars and indulging in an apparently glittering night life – attracted criticism from many of the more staid and stolid *Hausfrauen* of Weimar Germany.

There was nevertheless widespread experimentation in life styles among some groups, with 'reform' movements in the areas of food and health, for example. There was an emphasis on nature, with members of youth movements indulging in long hiking trips through the German pine forests, swimming in lakes and rivers, camping and youth hostelling at every opportunity. There had been a tradition of such youth movements in Imperial Germany, such as the largely middle-class *Wandervogel* movement, and the comparable SPD youth organizations. Their activities continued to flourish in the Weimar Republic. Perhaps partly in reaction against the constraints and repressions, the restrictions and gloom of life in large cities, emphasis was given to escape into the countryside.

Whatever the ambiguities of Weimar society and culture, perhaps the deepest and most fatal splits were embedded in the Weimar social compromise, and in the institutional framework of relations between the classes. It was these which contributed mightily to the breakdown of the Weimar political system, creating the opportunities which the Nazis were to seize. We must turn now to the complex and contentious task of explaining the ultimate collapse of the short-lived Weimar Republic.

THREE

The Collapse of Democracy
and the Rise of Hitler

Two rather different processes coincided in the late 1920s and early 1930s. One was the collapse of the democratic political system of the Weimar Republic. The other was the rise of Hitler's Nazi Party, immeasurably aided by the economic depression after 1929. The collapse of democracy effectively preceded, and was an essential precondition for, the rise of Hitler; and the appointment of Adolf Hitler to the chancellorship of Germany was by no means the only possible, or inevitable, outcome of the collapse of Weimar democracy. Given the consequences of this appointment, it is scarcely surprising that the causes, the relative contribution and importance of different factors, have been so hotly debated.

The flawed compromise

We have seen that Weimar democracy was born under difficult circumstances. The 1918–19 revolution in effect represented a temporary abdication of responsibility on the part of old elites unwilling to take the opprobrium of defeat or shoulder the burdens of post-war reconstruction. Fearful of more radical revolution, they made crucial concessions to moderate socialist forces; but they did not view these concessions as permanent, and remained in the wings, waiting and watching for chances to revise both the domestic and international settlements of 1918–19. On the part of the urban masses, on the other hand, the participation for the first time in government of the SPD, and the newly recognized and established position of the trade unions, awakened expectations which an impoverished post-war country would find it hard to deliver. Defeated in war, burdened with the harsh provisions of the Versailles Treaty, essentially contested in its very essence and attacked from both left and right, the Weimar Republic certainly bore a considerable weight of problems from the very start.

Yet it survived the difficulties of the early years. A general strike in 1920 served to defeat the Kapp putsch; the hyper-inflation of 1923 was successfully dealt with, reparations were renegotiated, and international affairs apparently brought onto a firmer footing by the mid-1920s. The question thus arises: was Weimar democracy, as some pessimistic accounts tend to suggest, really 'doomed from the start'; or, rather, was its collapse contingent on the immediate effects of the world economic depression after 1929? Were the causes of its collapse essentially structural and long-term or circumstantial and short-term in nature? And, insofar as they were short-term, what roles were played by different groups and individuals, and what, if any, alternative outcomes might have been possible? What options and courses of action might have been available to those key historical actors, who, if they had taken different decisions, might have been in a position to alter the fatal course of Weimar history? Could the economic distress which provided much of the rapidly increasing strength of the Nazi Party after 1928 have been in some way ameliorated? Did Hitler actually 'seize power', or was it rather handed to him? And if so, by whom? Clearly answers to these questions cannot easily be found, and the concomitant debates are by no means resolved.

In February 1925, Friedrich Ebert died, prematurely, from appendicitis. In the ensuing election, the seventy-seven year-old right-wing monarchist Junker Field Marshal Paul von Hindenburg was elected, on a second ballot, President of the Weimar Republic. Unlike the Social Democrat Ebert, Hindenburg was not in principle committed to upholding and strengthening the democratic system: on the contrary, he made little secret of his intention to replace it with a more authoritarian political system as soon as was practicable. The election of Hindenburg was of twofold significance: it illustrated the prevailing political orientations of a little over half of the German electorate in the mid-1920s; and it put into a position of considerable power an individual who would use this power to undermine the democracy which he was empowered to uphold.

Hindenburg's election was symptomatic of wider trends. As far as the actual functioning of parliamentary democracy was concerned, all was far from well even before the onset of the recession. Under an electoral system of proportional representation, in which the relatively numerous parties held radically different opinions on a range of domestic and foreign affairs, it was extremely difficult to form any sort of stable coalition government with majority support in parliament, even in the 'good years'. While some combinations of parties were able to agree on domestic issues, they could not agree on foreign affairs; and other combinations could agree on foreign affairs but not on domestic matters. With no party able to dominate a fragmented political landscape, any coalition was intrinsically unstable, and in the event short-lived. The instability of parliamentary government only helped to discredit a system which was in any event rather lacking in legitimacy among large sectors of the population.

In 1924 Germany saw two governments made up of a bourgeois coalition without a parliamentary majority come and go: the first, headed by Wilhelm Marx, failed to gain support in the May General Election, as did the second Marx cabinet in the General Election of December 1924. In the period up to the next General Election of May 1928, there were four different cabinets. The first, headed by Hans Luther, which lasted from 15 January 1925 to 5 December 1925, was a coalition of the right which collapsed as a result of the opposition of the right-wing German National People's Party (DNVP) to the Locarno Pact. The second, surviving from 20 January 1926 to 12 May 1926, and again headed by Luther, was a bourgeois coalition lacking a parliamentary majority; it was brought down by a combination of forces in the Reichstag. The third flourished only from 16 May to 17 December 1926, headed once more by Marx, and was a renewed bourgeois coalition lacking parliamentary support; it was ultimately brought down by a vote of no confidence in the Reichstag proposed by the SPD and supported by both Communists and Nationalists, as well as by other smaller parties. A new right-wing coalition, headed again by Marx, lasted from 29 January 1927 until after the General Election of 1928. After the short-lived grand coalition of the Stresemann government of 13 August – 23 November 1923, the SPD had chosen to remain on the sidelines of parliamentary politics. In 1928, the SPD returned again to government in a grand coalition under Chancellor Hermann Müller: this was to be the last truly democratic regime of the Weimar Republic. From 1929 onwards, it was faced with mounting economic, social and political problems that finally tore apart the delicate fabric of Weimar democracy and ushered in the period of *de facto* presidential rule. But it is clear that even in the period from 1924 to 1928, the functioning of Weimar parliamentary politics was less than smooth; and the instability of governments only helped to bring the whole 'system' into disrepute.

The problems of Weimar parliamentary democracy cannot be attributed simply to specific constitutional features, such as proportional representation or the ease by which Chancellors could be voted out of office. Party politics reflected the deeper socio-economic and cultural divisions in Weimar Germany, which in turn contributed to the fragmentation and increasing extremism of party politics in the later Weimar years, and the expansion of an effective political vacuum in the centre ground.

For one thing, because of the new and prominent role of the state in economic and social affairs, socio-economic conflicts were inevitably politicised. Particular issues became generalized; criticisms of specific policies widened to become critiques of the 'system' as a whole. Again, these tendencies predated the onset of economic recession, and weakened the internal structure of Weimar democracy even before it was subjected to the sustained battering of the depression years.

As early as 1923, employers had mounted an effective attack on the eight-hour-day agreed in the Stinnes–Legien agreement of 1918; and the failure of the *Zentral-Arbeits-Gemeinschaft* (ZAG) to resolve industrial disputes led to the official resignation of the trade union organization, the *Allgemeiner Deutscher Gewerkschaftsbund* (ADGB), in January 1924. After 1923, trade unions began losing members, funds, and credibility. They had increasingly to rely on the state as the effective guarantor of their position. Yet employers, despite their relatively strong position, remained on the defensive. Although it is difficult to generalize about employers' attitudes, the Ruhr lock-out of 1928 is a significant illustration of one important strand. Unwilling to concede even a modest wage increase (of 2–4 per cent), certain Ruhr industrialists locked out around a quarter of a million workers in protest against the very system of state arbitration. Gradually, significant sectors of industry came to feel that it was the democratic parliamentary system itself, which guaranteed the position of workers and unions, that needed to be revised. As they lost faith in a system for which they had never, in any event, had much love, so also they began to withdraw support – and funds – from the liberal parties of the bourgeois middle. More broadly, the Weimar Republic was identified with the institutionalized power of workers and their political and union organizations – which employers, who had formed their attitudes in what were now seen as the golden days of Imperial Germany, tended to regard as essentially illegitimate, by definition little more than 'enemies of the Empire' (*Reichsfeinde*), in Bismarck's phrase.

Labour relations constituted but one element in undermining support for the Republic among certain economic elites. Far more widespread was the rejection of the Versailles Treaty and all it implied for Germany's geographical boundaries, and for her political and military status. This resentment was extensive – and was to play an important role in the eventual mass popularity of the Nazi Party – but it took on a particular significance in connection with one particular elite: the army. While there are varying analyses of the role of the army in Weimar politics (ranging from older, liberal interpretations of the army as comprising a 'state within a state' to the more recent explorations of the interconnections between army, industry and government), it is clear that in a number of ways the army played a key role in undermining Weimar democracy. The *Reichswehr* was to a degree split within itself; there were differences of attitude towards the Republic and a growth of factions after 1918.[1] Many leading officers claimed that while they supported the German nation, they could not support the democratic state: thus, in the early years, in different ways, Generals Groener, Seeckt and others co-operated with right-wing groups and paramilitary organizations, such as the ex-servicemen's association, the *Stahlhelm*. German military schools were opened in Russia (under the Treaty of Rapallo) to train officers, and secret rearmament programmes were initiated in contravention of the Versailles Treaty. From 1926 onwards, General Kurt von Schleicher played a leading role in supporting and influencing President Hindenburg's plans for a more authoritarian form of government which would reinstate the pre-1918 elites in what they deemed to be their rightful positions of power. Schleicher's role was to become particularly important in the closing stages of the Republic's brief history.

Meanwhile, in the civilian arena, towards the end of the 1920s, increasing disaffection with democracy was reflected in the rightwards shift of a number of 'bourgeois' parties. Most notable among these was the DNVP, which was taken over by the right-wing nationalist press baron Hugenberg in 1928. After the death of Stresemann in 1929, the DVP also moved towards the right. But even as they shifted, so were they being outstripped – and their support sapped away from them – by the emergence and dramatic growth of an infinitely more radical party: the NSDAP. And, unlike the traditional conservative and nationalist parties, the NSDAP was able, in the new era of plebiscitary democracy and economic crisis, to attract a wide popular following. Ultimately, elites disaffected with democracy were to feel they must ally with the Nazis to gain a mass base from which to bring the shaky edifice down.

The rise of the NSDAP

The Nazi Party was, in the early 1920s, but one among many nationalist and *völkisch* radical political groups. It was catapulted to prominence with the onset of economic recession in the late 1920s: having secured only 2.6% of the national vote in the 1928

General Election, the NSDAP became the second largest party in the Reichstag with 18.3% of the vote in September 1930. The Nazis owed their spectacular success to a combination of two discrete sets of factors: first, their distinctive organization and strategy: and secondly, the wider socio-economic conditions which created climates of opinion and sets of grievances on which the Nazis could prey.

Following Hitler's release from imprisonment at the end of 1924, the NSDAP was formally refounded in February 1925. Over the course of the next few years, Hitler rose from his pre-1923 role of 'drummer' to become the undisputed leader or 'Führer', standing to some extent above the organizational fray and exerting his powers of charismatic leadership through his gifts of oratory and control of mass audiences.[2] The eventual semblance of a well-organized, united party – symbolized by the brown-shirt uniforms of the SA, the serried ranks of units marching past the Führer with arms raised in Hitler-salute, the visual and emotional effects of the mass rallies with the leader as the focal point – partially disguised more complex realities.

The paramilitary SA – founded in 1920, one of the many paramilitary groups to spring up in the aftermath of the First World War – was at first organized only at the local level. After the return of the war veteran Ernst Röhm from Bolivia to head the organization in 1930, the SA remained somewhat unruly, and, in conventional political terms, more radical than Hitler's conception of Nazi ideology was to be. Nor were all Nazi leaders united on a clearly definable 'ideology' in any case. An important figure with ideas somewhat different from those of Hitler was Gregor Strasser, whose role in Nazi party organization was strengthened in 1925 when Hitler was banned from making speeches in public. Strasser, who had considerable organizational skills, played a key role in spreading the Nazi party organization across broad areas of Germany, beyond the original Nazi heartland in Bavaria. In some areas, particularly in north-west Germany, the NSDAP had a more 'revolutionary' or radical flavour.

During 1925–6 the NSDAP suffered much infighting. Hitler, on returning to the public rostrum, was able to transcend this factionalism and unite the party under his unique form of leadership. The Berlin party chief Joseph Goebbels was persuaded of Hitler's merits, and made it his task to promote and strengthen the 'Führer myth' through propaganda. At the same time, the 'putschist' strategy of the early years was rejected in favour of following a legal, parliamentary road to the overthrow of parliamentary democracy. New party organizations were founded to begin to penetrate a range of social and professional groups. In 1926, the National Socialist League of German Students and the Hitler Youth were founded. The League of Nazi Lawyers, the League of Nazi Doctors, the League of Nazi Schoolteachers, and the Fighting League for German Culture were all established by 1929. In 1928, the National Socialist Factory Cell Organization (NSBO) was created in an attempt to infiltrate the heartland of left-wing politics, the working class. From 1930 onwards, concerted efforts were made to infiltrate existing agrarian and white-collar worker pressure groups, such as the *Reichslandbund* and the *Deutschnationale Handlungsgehilfenverband*. Attempts were also made to win over – or at least neutralize and allay the suspicions of – important industrialists.

The Nazis propagated, not a coherent doctrine or body of systematically interrelated ideas, but rather a vaguer world-view made up of a number of prejudices with varied appeals to different audiences which could scarcely be dignified with the term 'ideology'. As far as Hitler himself was concerned, two major elements were of decisive importance. One was his radical anti-Semitism; the other was his ambitious set of foreign policy aims – his desire for mastery of Europe, the creation of 'living space' (*Lebensraum*) for the 'Aryan' Germans, and eventually for mastery of the world. Linked to these was Hitler's anti-Communism: 'Jews and Bolsheviks' were often pejoratively associated, even indissolubly equated, as in their alleged responsibility for the debacle of 1918. The fight against the perceived evils of modern capitalism was to be a simultaneous fight against 'international Jewry' and against the threat of Communism. But while anti-Semitism was undoubtedly a major theme for Hitler and for Nazi activists, it was much less important as an element in the Nazi party's appeal to the wider population.[3] At this broader level, Nazi 'ideology' was a somewhat rag-bag collection of largely negative views combined with a utopian vision of a grandiose future coloured by nostalgic appeals to aspects of a mythical past. Thus Nazism opposed certain pernicious, potentially threatening tendencies of 'modern' capitalist society: the evils of big business (large department stores, often owned by Jews), international finance ('Jewish'), and revolutionary Communism. Nazis promoted a vision of a harmonious national community (*Volksgemeinschaft*) which would be racially pure (cleansed of the 'pollution' of Jews, hereditary degenerates, and other supposedly racially or biologically inferior types), and which would overcome the class divisions which beset Imperial and Weimar Germany. Nazism claimed to be able to transcend the divisions and heal the wounds of capitalist society, and to present a new way forwards to a great future, presenting a genuine alternative to both the discredited authoritarianism of the Imperial past and the 'despicable' democracy of the Weimar present. How this transcendence would look in detail and in reality was never fully spelled out: Hitler was able to appeal to a wide range of groups harbouring different resentments – and to allay suspicions on a number of fronts – precisely because he was never very specific on the details of the proposed new order. In addition to particular social grievances and fears, there was very widespread nationalist resentment about the Treaty of Versailles from which Hitler was able to benefit. But most important for the expanding appeal of Nazism were the economic developments in the closing years of the Weimar Republic.

Economic crises and the collapse of democracy

The Weimar Republic had suffered since its inception from major economic problems. The means of financing the First World War – through loans and bonds rather than taxes – had laid the foundations for post-war inflation, which had been fuelled and exacerbated by government policies in connection with reparations in 1922–3. Even after the stabilization of the currency in 1923–4, and the revision of reparations arrangements with the Dawes Plan, the Weimar economy was far from strong.

For one thing, it was heavily reliant on short-term loans from abroad. These could rapidly be withdrawn, with far-reaching consequences – as indeed occurred after the Wall Street Crash of October 1929. For another, as Harold James has put it, 'Weimar's economy suffered from an inherent instability, and like any unstable structure required only a relatively small push to bring down the whole structure.'[4] On both the industrial and agrarian fronts there were difficulties. Workers were heavily reliant on state arbitration to back wage claims that were disputed by employers, and, on some interpretations, relatively high labour costs contributed to the problems of the Weimar economy. Whatever one's view on the question of whether wages were 'too high' in an era characterized by 'Taylorism' and 'Fordism' (the attempted rationalization of labour and enhanced productivity through the introduction of American time-and-motion studies, assembly line methods and the like), distributional struggles certainly contributed to Weimar's political problems. Nor was all well on the agricultural front, and the difficulties in the agrarian sphere were to play a major role in the rise of Hitler. From 1924, when the agricultural protectionism introduced at the beginning of the War came to an end, there was a need for rationalization in agriculture. From the mid-1920s onwards, agricultural indebtedness increased, and every year there were greater numbers of bankrupt estates: a heightened political radicalism among farmers resulted. Agrarian elites also came to bring considerable pressure to bear on President Hindenburg – himself a Junker with experience of indebtedness – in the final intrigues leading to the appointment of Hitler as Chancellor.

Given its inherent weaknesses, it is scarcely surprising that Germany's economy was affected so badly by the world recession in the years after 1929.[5] Whatever the intrinsic political weaknesses of Weimar democracy even in the 'golden years', it was undoubtedly the depression which precipitated the actual collapse of Weimar democracy and paved the way for the rise of the Nazis to power.

The Grand Coalition of 1928–30, including the SPD, led by Chancellor Hermann Müller, was the last genuinely parliamentary government of Weimar Germany. Plans had already been made for its replacement by a more authoritarian alternative – essentially presidential rule through a Chancellor and cabinet lacking majority support in parliament – several weeks before its actual collapse. Having survived earlier crises, the Müller administration fell over the issue of unemployment insurance in the wider context of economic recession and rising unemployment. In October 1929 the Wall Street Crash prompted the withdrawal of American loans from Germany, and heralded a phenomenal rise in bankruptcies and unemployment in the following three years. With rising numbers out of work, unemployment insurance could no longer be paid at the level decreed in the unemployment insurance legislation of July 1927. Müller's coalition government was unable to reach agreement on the issue of whether to raise contributions or lower the level of benefits. Foundering on this issue, the last cabinet of the Weimar Republic to rely on parliamentary support was replaced by a presidential cabinet under Chancellor Brüning, which, lacking majority support in parliament, was to rule by presidential decree.

Brüning's policies have been the subject of considerable debate. He pursued austere, deflationary policies designed – at the cost of sacrificing the well-being of millions of German families – to achieve certain foreign policy aims. In particular, he consciously exacerbated a worsening unemployment situation with the intention of lifting the burden of reparations payments from the German economy. This was effected first, in the Hoover Moratorium of 1931 and then ultimately, when Brüning was no longer Chancellor, by the cancellation of all reparations at the Lausanne Conference of 1932. Brüning's deflationary policies have been defended by some historians, who suggest that there was no alternative set of economic policies either politically or technically open to him at the time. Brüning, on this view, operated in a period when there was very little room for manoeuvre (in Knut Borchardt's phrase, *Handlungsspielraum*). Others, such as C.-L. Holtfrerich, have disputed such an interpretation, suggesting that a range of other policies were open both theoretically and politically and could thus have been pursued – and indeed were being promoted increasingly by influential groups at this time.[6] Whatever the balance of argument in this debate, one thing is quite clear: the consequences of Brüning's policies were such as to produce the socio economic circumstances which provided fertile ground for Nazi agitation.

Brüning had been appointed Müller's successor, on the collapse of the latter's cabinet, without any dissolution of the Reichstag. However, when the latter demanded the withdrawal of a decree which Brüning had issued after the Reichstag's rejection of parts of the finance bill, Brüning chose to have the Reichstag dissolved in the summer of 1930. Under the constitution new elections would have to be called within sixty days. These took place in September 1930. Now, under conditions of rising economic crisis, the NSDAP achieved its electoral breakthrough. With 6.4 million votes, or 18.3% of the total vote, the NSDAP became the second largest party in the Reichstag, after the SPD (with 24.5% of the vote). At last, with 107 deputies out of a total of 608, the Nazis had a large, visible, disruptive presence in the Reichstag. The NSDAP made its greatest gains in the Protestant, agricultural regions and small towns of north and north-east Germany. In 1930, they achieved figures of 27% in Schleswig-Holstein, 24.3% in Pomerania, and 24.3% in Hanover South-Brunswick. In the mixed agricultural and small-scale industrial areas of Lower Silesia–Breslau (24.2%), Chemnitz–Zwickau (23.8%) and Rhineland–Palatinate (22.8%) the Nazis also achieved good results.[7] Most impervious to Nazi penetration were Catholic areas, where Catholics tended to remain loyal to the Centre Party, and urban-industrial areas, where the organized working class on the whole stayed with the two major parties of labour, the SPD and KPD, although, as the depression worsened, the Social Democrats lost votes to the Communists. (In 1930, when the Nazis gained 107 seats, the Communists won 77 seats.)

Presented, by skilful propaganda, as the party of dynamism and of youth, in contrast to the ageing, stolid image of the SPD, the NSDAP attracted many young voters and new voters with visions of a better future. The Nazis also benefited from the enhanced respectability and widespread publicity arising from

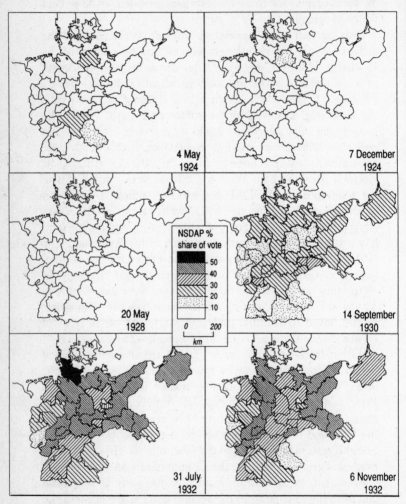

The electoral performance of the NSDAP, 1924–32

co-operation with Hugenberg's DNVP in the campaign against the Young Plan in 1929. With a more 'respectable' image, the NSDAP was able to make inroads among 'pillars of the community' – local notables such as mayors, schoolteachers, and Protestant pastors. The increasing radicalism of frightened former liberals and conservatives who had previously supported a range of parties led many more into the Nazi camp. In the closing years of the Weimar Republic the support for liberal and conservative parties shrank markedly. The share of the vote held by the DVP and DDP collapsed from 20% at the beginning of the Weimar Republic to a mere 2.2% in July 1932; the DNVP's share fell from 20% in late 1924 to 5.9% in July 1932; the Wirtschaftspartei and the agrarian parties also collapsed mainly to the benefit of the NSDAP.

Given the outcome of the September 1930 elections, the SPD chose to 'tolerate' the Brüning government rather than trying to topple it and risk new elections which might provide further support for the extreme right. In the meantime, Brüning's policies only served to heighten the misery of millions in the economic depression. Unemployment rose steadily, from 1.3 million in September 1929 to over 3 million by September 1930, to over 6 million by the beginning of 1933. This last figure represented one in three of the working population; with official underestimation of the true figures, and with widespread short-time working, perhaps one in two families in Germany were severely affected by the depression. Brüning's priority nevertheless remained that of showing that Germany was unable to pay reparations, whatever the cost in human misery, misery which could have been alleviated by public expenditure programmes and less deflationary policies. In the summer of 1931, the economic situation was further exacerbated by a financial crisis. A failed attempt at a German–Austrian customs union led to a withdrawal of French credits from Austria, precipitating a collapse of the main Austrian bank, a rush of bankruptcies in Austria and Germany, and a banking crisis, which necessitated a 'bank holiday' of three weeks duration in July 1931.

In the midst of this mounting economic chaos, politics was increasingly played out not in parliament but on the streets. Skirmishes took place between rival political gangs: most frequently, the paramilitary organizations of the KPD joined violent battle with the unruly SA units. Hitler, in an attempt to retain the air of respectability cultivated over the preceding few years, now made concerted efforts to improve his relations with conservative elites: the army, agricultural landowners, leaders of industry. While some industrialists – particularly Fritz Thyssen, and the banker Hjalmar Schacht – had for some time been sympathetic to the Nazi cause, the prevailing attitude among business leaders was on the whole one of suspicion. Weimar democracy might have been rejected in principle; but it was quite another matter to consider Hitler's Nazism as embodying a preferable alternative. Before 1933, industrialists were not important supporters, at least financially, of the NSDAP; small donations by local notables were a more significant source of NSDAP funds than any contributions from leaders of industry (with the exception of Thyssen, whose book entitled *I Paid Hitler* provided a basis for much of this myth).[8] In the early 1930s, it was clear to Hitler that he needed to woo industrialists, and convince them that he was worth backing. On 26 January 1932, Hitler addressed the prestigious Düsseldorf Industry Club, seeking to create a distinction between his condemnation of *Jewish* capital and capitalism in general. More important perhaps was a combination of increasing disaffection with Brüning's management of the economic crisis and increased willingness, in the apparent absence of viable alternatives, to view Nazism as at least acceptable or tolerable. This shift in attitude was particularly important in army circles, who began to insist that officers and civil servants should be allowed to become members of the NSDAP. An attempt at developing links between conservative parties and the NSDAP in a right-wing 'National Opposition' was less successful. In October 1931, the so-called 'Harzburg Front' – named after a rally in Bad Harzburg – consisting of Hugenberg's DNVP, the leadership of the veterans' *Stahlhelm* organization, and Hitler's Nazis, failed to develop a truly united front in opposition to the Brüning government.

In the spring of 1932, Hindenburg's seven-year term of office as President came to an end. Brüning mismanaged – from

Hindenburg's point of view – attempts to obviate the need for re-election, and Hindenburg had to face the humiliation of going to a second ballot, having failed to win an absolute majority on the first round against a powerful vote for Hitler as President. Symptomatic of the politics of this period was the line-up of candidates: Germans of a Social Democratic or liberal persuasion were constrained to choose between the conservative nationalist Hindenburg, the Nazi Hitler, the right-wing Stahlhelm representative Theodor Duesterberg, or, at the other extreme, the declared enemy of the Social Democrats, the Communist Ernst Thälmann. The anti-democratic, elderly Field Marshal, who had been working systematically to replace parliamentary democracy by more authoritarian rule, was now the only possible choice for all those genuine and committed republicans who feared that a vote for any of the other candidates would only bring 'something worse'. In the event, the re-election of Hindenburg was to effect precisely that result. From the early summer of 1932, a series of alternatives were pursued and played out, until finally the appointment of Hitler to the chancellorship seemed to the old elites and the ageing President the only viable solution to the perceived problems of the ill-fated Weimar Republic.

Hitler's Path to Power

From April 1932 to January 1933 the final debacle of the Weimar Republic unfolded through a series of intrigues and machinations, as alternative strategies were pursued, and found unworkable, in relation to the economic, political and governmental crisis. Distanced from Brüning by his management of the Presidential elections, Hindenburg was prepared to countenance the removal of this increasingly unpopular Chancellor. First the Army Minister Groener was forced to resign on 12 May, over the issue of his ban on the SA and SS in April; then, at the end of May, when Brüning gave Hindenburg an emergency decree to sign, proposing drastic measures to deal with indebted East Elbian estates, the President refused to sign and instead accepted Brüning's resignation. Brüning's proposal to dispossess

East Elbian estates overburdened with debts was the occasion, rather than the cause, of his downfall; behind it lay wider plots for alternative political scenarios.

On 2 June, the Catholic Franz von Papen became Chancellor – losing the support of his own Centre Party in the process. Papen failed in the period of his chancellorship to gain parliamentary support: his cabinet excluded Social Democrats and trade unionists, and never succeeded in securing a substantial conservative nationalist base. On 4 June the Reichstag was dissolved and new elections called for 31 July. The ban on the SA and SS was lifted on 18 June, and despite the fact that the paramilitary organizations of the KPD were still outlawed, there was near civil war on the streets as Nazis and Communists engaged in violent battles. The alleged failure of the Prussian state police to control political violence – which had in effect been legalised by the Reich government, with its unleashing of the SA – provided the justification for a coup against the Prussian state government on 20 July. The SPD leadership of Prussia (at that time heading a caretaker coalition) was ousted and replaced by a Reich Commissar – a useful precedent for Hitler's takeover of *Land* governments the following year. The SPD's lack of resistance to this coup has often been criticized; but Social Democrats still believed in the rule of law, and were unwilling to meet force with force; they also, by this time, were suffering from a certain weariness and resignation, a lack of a broader vision in the face of changing events.

In the General Election of 31 July 1932, held amidst this atmosphere of violence and crisis, the Nazis achieved their greatest electoral success in the period before Hitler became Germany's Chancellor. With 37.8% of the vote, and 230 of the 608 seats, the NSDAP for the first time became the largest party in the Reichstag. Claiming to be a 'people's party' or *Volkspartei*, transcending class boundaries and narrow interests, the NSDAP at the height of its electoral success did indeed succeed in gaining a relatively wide social spread of support, in contrast to the narrower socio-economic, regional or confessional bases of the parties of the Weimar period.[9] As before, the organized industrial working class tended to remain faithful to the SPD and KPD, with the latter gaining votes from the former, and particularly winning support among the increasing numbers of unemployed. But the Nazis actively solicited votes among the working class, and were to a limited but nevertheless significant degree successful in winning support among workers in handicrafts and small-scale manufacturing, who were not so fully integrated into the organized working class. Similarly, most Catholics remained loyal to their Centre party, which had retained a remarkably stable vote throughout the Weimar Republic. The Nazis benefited most from the collapse of the liberal and conservative parties. The NSDAP's greatest electoral successes were in the Protestant, agricultural and small-town areas of Germany, and their most stable vote from 1924 onwards came from small farmers, shopkeepers, and the independent artisans of the 'old' middle class, who felt threatened by the tensions and tendencies of modernization and industrial society. This core was augmented in periods of economic crisis by a 'protest vote' from other sections of society, including a sizeable vote from the new middle classes, and among established professional and upper middle class circles. In Childers' summary of these groups: 'Motivations were mixed, including fear of the Marxist left, frustrated career ambitions, and resentment at the erosion of social prestige and professional security. Yet, while sizeable elements of these groups undoubtedly felt their positions or prospects to be challenged during the Weimar era, they cannot be described as uneducated, economically devastated, or socially marginal.'[10] Civil servants, pensioners, white-collar workers, added their votes to those of the small farmers and shopkeepers in a rising tide of protest against the chaos that Weimar democracy, to them, had ushered in. People of all ages were in the end attracted to the apparently young, energetic, demagogic movement, which appeared to offer a new way forward out of the deadlock and disasters of the Weimar 'system'.

Armed with his electoral success – which still fell short of an overall majority – Hitler was hoping to be offered the chancellorship by Hindenburg. But the President despised this upstart 'Bohemian corporal', and snubbed him by refusing to offer anything more than the vice-chancellorship. Enraged, Hitler refused to accept second-best – and caused considerable anger and consternation among the ranks of the Nazi party, who felt he had missed the opportunity of putting the Nazis into government.

When the Reichstag reopened on 12 September, it passed a spectacular vote of no confidence in the Chancellor, Papen, by 512 votes to 42 (the remainder of deputies having abstained or stayed home). Papen was unable to command either a parliamentary base or popular support for his government; but nor was he able, in tandem with Hindenburg, to finalize plans for establishing a non-parliamentary, authoritarian regime in complete breach of the constitution. Parliament was dissolved, and fresh elections called for 6 November. By now, the worst trough of the depression was passing, and the Nazis lost some of their protest vote of the summer. With the loss of two million votes, parliamentary representation of the NSDAP after the November elections was reduced to 196 deputies. Nevertheless, the governmental crisis and parliamentary deadlock were not resolved. At the beginning of December, having been persuaded by General von Schleicher that unless matters were taken in hand a civil war was likely to break out which the army would not be able to control, Hindenburg rather unwillingly replaced Papen and appointed Schleicher Chancellor. Schleicher's brief period in office – until 28 January 1933 – was characterized by an unsuccessful and somewhat far-fetched attempt to cobble together an unlikely set of alliances, including trade unionists and the 'left-wing' of the NSDAP under Gregor Strasser. This attempt failed, and managed along the way to antagonize both industrialists – who were suspicious of Schleicher's rapprochement with the unions – and agrarian elites, who viewed Schleicher's plans for agriculture as a form of 'agrarian bolshevism', and not nearly as favourable to their interests as Papen's policies had been.

During January 1933, intrigues and machinations in high places set in motion a campaign to convince the ageing President to appoint Hitler as Chancellor. Papen came round to the view, as did leading representatives of agrarian interests in the (by now Nazi-infiltrated) *Reichslandbund*, that the Nazis must be included in a coalition conservative-nationalist government, in order to provide it with a measure of popular support; and that, in order to include the Nazis, it would be necessary to offer Hitler the chancellorship. Those pressurizing Hindenburg to take this move were of the view that, if Hitler and one or two other Nazis were included in a mixed cabinet, they would be effectively hemmed in and could be 'tamed' and manipulated. The idea was that the army, industrial and agrarian elites would be able to benefit from and subvert Hitler's demagogic powers and mass support. Finally, after a series of meetings in Ribbentrop's house in Berlin in the last week of January 1933, and through the mediations of Hindenburg's son Oskar, an acceptable set of arrangements was constructed and the President persuaded. On 30 January 1933, Adolf Hitler was, by fully constitutional means, offered the chancellorship of Germany by a reluctant President Hindenburg. With Hitler's acceptance, the process of dismantling Weimar democracy was accelerated and rapidly completed. For a while, the fateful coalition between the old elites and the Nazi mass movement survived; in the end, the last-ditch gamble by elites, who had failed to rule Germany on their own, to survive through alliance with Hitler, proved to have been a historical mistake of inestimable and tragic proportions.

Who, finally, should bear the brunt of responsibility for the failure of Weimar democracy? What factors are most important in explaining its collapse? The Left has often come in for criticism on a range of counts. The bitter hostility obtaining between the KPD and SPD has often been remarked on as a fateful split among those who should have been united in opposition to the greater evil of Nazism. In addition to the bitterness arising in the early years, when the SPD as the party of government had no qualms about using force to suppress radical Communist uprisings, the rift was deepened by the late 1920s and 1930s, when the KPD, under the influence of Moscow, adopted the theory that Social Democracy was equivalent to social fascism. Whatever one's views on these matters, in a wider sense the working class in the closing years of the Weimar Republic was scarcely in a position effectively to resist the course of events. In contrast to 1920, when a general strike had been sufficient to bring down the Kapp putsch, there was little that could be done on a mass scale in the early 1930s: it is extremely difficult to use the weapon of striking when one is unemployed or desperate to retain a job. For most ordinary working-class people, sheer material survival was all that could be striven for in the years of the depression.

More attention needs to be paid to those who were in a position to affect events – and indeed often did so, in a direction ultimately favouring Hitler. There are a number of separate strands which interrelated to produce the fateful, but by no means inevitable, outcome. The pursuit of deflationary economic policies by Brüning served to exacerbate the economic crisis and nourish the conditions in which the NSDAP was able to achieve mass support. While industrialists may not have played an important role in fostering or financially supporting the rise of the NSDAP, they certainly made little effort to sustain the democratic political system and indeed attacked its structure and fabric sufficiently to render it weak in the face of the final onslaught. The agrarian elites who had such a favourable reception with Hindenburg must also bear a burden of guilt, as must those army officers who worked to undermine democracy and install an authoritarian alternative. The Social Democrats had faced a difficult enough task in guiding the Republic through its early stages, at a time when moderate parties had greater parliamentary support and authoritarian elites had effectively abdicated their responsibility and retired to the wings of the political stage; now, when pro-Republican forces were in a minority and conservative-nationalist forces were joined by a new, popular and virulent right-wing radicalism in the shape of the Nazis, there was even less possibility for democrats of the moderate left or centre to control developments.

It was this socio-political configuration, in a country defeated in war, reduced in territory and status, subjected to a burden of reparations, rankling with revisionism, lurching from one political crisis to the next, and finally suffering major economic collapse, which ultimately spelled the death of democracy. No one factor alone is sufficient to explain the collapse of the Weimar Republic: not the provisions of the constitution, nor the implications of the Versailles Treaty, the impact of the Depression, the strategies and political abilities of Hitler and the Nazi Party, nor the decisions and actions of other prominent individuals; it was the peculiar combination, under specific historical circumstances, of a range of activities, orientations and pressures which produced the ultimate outcome. Perhaps the only comforting lesson from this complex period is that, while radical and extremist movements have arisen and may arise elsewhere and at other times (and indeed there were many in the inter-war period, of which Mussolini's Fascists were a notably successful example), such a unique combination of circumstances as occurred in Germany, opening the way for the rise of Hitler, is unlikely ever to recur in its entirety.

FOUR

A 'National Community'?
State, Economy and Society, 1933–9

Gleichschaltung and Hitler's state

Hitler became Chancellor on 30 January 1933; but he had by no means actually 'seized power', as the myth of the *Machtergreifung* (seizure of power), supported by the celebrations and propaganda of the Nazis themselves at the time, would suggest. He still had much to do to consolidate his hold over German administration, government and people; indeed, at this time many still felt that he could be harnessed and restrained, and his popular support co-opted and redirected.

However, in the course of 1933–4 Hitler systematically pursued a policy of so-called *Gleichschaltung* (literally, putting everyone 'into the same gear'; co-ordinating, or bringing into line), in order to consolidate his hold on German politics and society. Even then, however, Hitler's power was by no means absolute. His state was a complex system, riddled with rivalries among competing centres of power and influence, in which the notion of a charismatic Führer, above the fray, played a key role in maintaining a degree of cohesion. Equally important was the extent to which this system was, almost to the last, sustained by key elite groups (particularly in the army and industry) who, while not necessarily themselves 'Nazi', must bear a large degree of responsibility for the functioning and consequences of the regime.

Hitler had declared that the elections following his appointment as Chancellor would be the last free elections in a parliamentary state. In the event, the elections of 5 March 1933

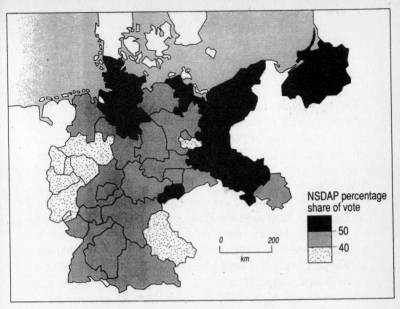

The Reichstag elections, 5 March 1933

were less than 'free'. On 27 February 1933 the Reichstag was set on fire. While uncertainty still surrounds the circumstances of the arson attack, there is no doubt that it was the Nazis who obtained the utmost benefit from the consequences of the fire. It was used as the pretext for an emergency decree on 28 February, which suspended most civil liberties and legitimized mass arrests of Communists and Social Democrats. In conditions of mounting tension, with rising violence on the streets, and left-wingers no longer able freely to express their opinions, the elections of 5 March were held under highly intimidating conditions. Nevertheless, Hitler and the NSDAP still failed to gain an overall majority: with 43.9% of the vote, the Nazis won 288 seats, while the left gained over 30% of the vote (128 votes for the SDP and 81 for the KPD), and the Centre (73 seats) and Liberals together won 18% of the vote. Even with the votes for the right-wing DNVP

67

the Nazi-dominated 'government of national concentration' could only barely command an absolute majority, and could not achieve the two-thirds necessary to pass an Enabling Law (*Ermächtigungsgesetz*) to alter the constitution and 'legalize' the destruction of democracy. Yet by 23 March, this had become possible.

On 21 March the Reichstag was formally opened in the Garrison Church at Potsdam. Much was made of this carefully stage-managed 'Day of Potsdam' by the Nazis, who attempted to emphasize continuities between Frederick the Great, Hindenburg and Hitler, with the great traditions of German and Prussian history culminating in the figure of Hitler. Somewhat relieved by these appearances, the Bavarian People's Party, the German State Party, and the Centre Party were more prepared to consider voting for the Enabling Law. The Catholics in particular were rather reassured by Hitler's insistence that the position of Christianity would be untouched in the future; and Centre Party politicians also felt that their willingness to ally with the Nazis might help to moderate the government – as had their former co-operation with Social Democrats in 1919, although in a rather different direction. The Communist Deputies were prevented from attending the Reichstag vote, as were twenty-one of the Social Democrats. In the event, when the Reichstag convened in the Kroll Opera on the evening of 23 March, the only members courageous enough to vote against the Enabling Act were the Social Democrats. Otto Wels read out their reply to Hitler, in which he stated: 'At this historical hour, we German Social Democrats pledge ourselves to the principles of humanity and justice, of freedom and Socialism. No Enabling Law can give you the power to destroy ideas which are eternal and indestructible ... '[1] With the passage of this law, Hitler was able – with all the appearance of legality – to overthrow the remnants of any form of parliamentary democracy. He no longer needed to pay attention to the views of most of the nationalist members of the government, nor did he need President Hindenburg's signature for the passage of legislation. Henceforth, 'law' could be used to justify any arbitrary act of the regime. But this garb of legality, while reassuring to moderate, middle class Germans, did not preclude the use of violence and terror; it simply accompanied it.

From the spring of 1933, the Nazis engaged in a series of moves to extend and consolidate their power. Initial measures were taken to purge the civil service in the 'Law for the Restoration of the Professional Civil Service' of 7 April 1933. Having survived the transition from Imperial Germany to the Weimar Republic relatively unscathed, the German professional civil service found itself under stronger attack in this new revolutionary upheaval. Jews were removed from the civil service, as were political opponents of the regime. The purge was, however, by no means as thorough as many NSDAP members would have liked, since considerations of administrative efficiency in some cases outweighed Nazi credentials. Furthermore, some civil servants who harboured misgivings about the Nazi regime justified their decision to stay as 'preventing something worse'. Yet the overall record of civil servants in the Third Reich remains one of compromise, rather than serious subversion of the regime. At the same time, the traditional decentralization of the relatively recently unified Germany was attacked – a continuation of tendencies already evident towards the end of the Weimar Republic. The powers of the *Länder* were reduced by the Nazi seizure of power in the regional states in March 1933. (The take-over of Prussia the previous summer, with the installation of a Reich Commissioner in place of the elected government, had provided a useful precedent.) On 7 April 1933 ten so-called *Reichsstatthalter* (Reich Governors) were appointed, usually the senior *Gauleiter* of each state, except in the cases of Bavaria (Ritter von Epp) and Prussia (Hitler). The take-over was by no means smooth: as at national level, there were perpetual tensions between party and state. Frictions varied from place to place, depending on pre-existing political configurations and circumstances. Curiously, the heavy-handed actions of local party officials were often dissociated in people's minds from the regime as a whole, and the person of Hitler in particular: people frequently asserted that 'if only the Führer knew', things would not be allowed to go on in the way they were locally.

While the Nazis made strenuous efforts to woo economic elites – many of whom had been belatedly persuaded to give financial support to the Nazi election campaign in the spring of 1933 – they had no such tender consideration for the bulk of the German people, the workers. Giving the appearance of populism by proclaiming 1 May a national holiday on full pay, the Nazis rapidly proceeded to dismantle and destroy the autonomous workers' organizations. Trade unions were wound up and replaced by a body spuriously claiming to represent the interests of all German workers in the new 'national community', the German Labour Front (DAF) under Robert Ley. Walther Darré took control of the Reich Food estate (*Reichsnährstand*), dealing with the peasantry and agriculture, while small traders were organized into the HAGO (*Handwerks-, Handels- und Gewerbe-Organisation*). While in appearance developing a form of corporatism, in practice this was a coercive system in which none of the Nazi organizations actually represented the real interests of their 'members'. At the same time, there was an assault on political parties. In the course of the spring and summer of 1933 these were either outlawed (starting with the KPD) or they dissolved themselves (the Centre Party formally dissolved itself on 5 July 1933). With the 'Law Against the Formation of New Parties' of 14 July 1933 a one-party state was formally established. No longer was there any legal parliamentary opposition: the sole function of the Reichstag was to acclaim the decisions of the Nazi government. Yet this government itself became progressively more chaotic in nature: cabinet meetings were less and less frequent, eventually being so rare that they ceased to fulfil any governmental function; and political decision-making processes became more and more a matter of gaining direct access to the Führer – an increasingly difficult task as he spent more time in his mountain retreat near Berchtesgaden and became less interested in the minutiae of most aspects of domestic policy.

On 30 January 1934, one year after Hitler's appointment as Chancellor, the *Reichsrat*, or upper chamber of the Reichstag, was abolished and the federal system was effectively terminated by removing independent authority from the states. Perhaps the final major event in terms of initial constitutional change came with the death of President Hindenburg on 2 August 1934. Hitler made use of the occasion to merge the offices of President and Chancellor, and to take personal command of the armed forces. Abolishing Hindenburg's title of Reich President, Hitler now styled himself 'Führer and Reich Chancellor'. The Army and public officials now had to swear personal oaths of obedience to Hitler – oaths which subsequently proved for many to be a moral obstacle to resistance against Hitler's regime.

The Army was able to ignore or surmount its potential misgivings about Hitler in August 1934 for a number of reasons. For one thing, Hitler had made no secret of his intention to pursue an aggressive foreign policy, revising the much-hated Treaty of Versailles. Hitler's whipping-up of resentment against Versailles, and his sharp denunciations of the Jews and Bolsheviks whom he held to be the 'November Criminals' responsible for Germany's national humiliation, had been constant themes prior to his coming to power. After becoming Chancellor, Hitler lost little time in settling revisionist policies in motion: on 8 February 1933, Hitler informed ministers that unemployment was to be reduced by rearmament; in July 1933 Krupp's euphemistically named 'agricultural tractor programme' started the production of tanks; and by 1934 explosives, ships and aircraft were in production – all contrary to the provisions of the Treaty of Versailles, but greeted with approval by the Army itself.

Furthermore, Hitler had just resolved a potential source of friction in relation to the traditional armed forces. The SA, under its leader Ernst Röhm, had become a large and rather unruly organization, propagating unwelcome notions of the need for a 'second revolution', and developing into a rival not only for the elite SS but also for the Army proper. Hitler decided that the support of the latter two groups was more important to him than was the SA; so he instigated the so-called 'Night of the Long Knives' on 30 June 1934, during which the leaders of the SA were murdered along with other individuals with whom Hitler had fallen out, including Gregor Strasser, Gustav Kahr (who had been state commissioner for Bavaria at the time of the abortive putsch of 1923), and General von Schleicher. There were also a few cases of mistaken identity. Retroactively this mass murder – which continued for three days, entailing seventy-seven officially admitted deaths, although the true figure was much higher – was 'legalized' on 3 July 1934, when a law was passed simply stating that 'the measures taken on 30 June and 1 and 2 July to strike down the treasonous attacks are justifiable acts of self-defence by the state.'[2] Although few can have been genuinely taken in by the Nazi version of the terror, which they represented as a nipping in the bud of a treacherous plot against the regime, the garb of legality helped to allay disquiet in many circles; and many were also to an extent relieved that the more radical, unruly elements in the Nazi party appeared to be being put in their place. In any event, the purge certainly helped in the co-option of the Army by Hitler.

Meanwhile, the Nazi regime was bolstered by an elaborate apparatus of terror. The first concentration camp for political opponents of the regime was opened at Dachau, near Munich, with considerable fanfare and publicity in March 1933. In subsequent years, well before the radicalization of the wartime period, a network of concentration camps was set up across Germany. These camps made use of prisoners as forced labour, sending labour gangs to *Aussenlager*, or subsidiary camps, in the vicinity. Gangs of concentration camp inmates were marched through surrounding towns and villages to work long hours under inhumane conditions with very little food. Within the camps, brutality and violence were the norm. While certain methods of torture and execution were employed, these camps were not intended primarily for the physical destruction of their inmates (as were the extermination camps in the east which functioned from 1942). The SS, under the command of Heinrich Himmler, was able to arrest, detain, imprison, torture and murder, with little respect for any rule of law or putative notion of justice. Himmler, who between 1934 and 1936 took over the police powers of the Reich and State Ministries of the Interior, became on 17 June 1936 'Reichsführer-SS und Chef der deutschen Polizei im Reichministeriums des Innerns', thus effectively controlling the means of terror in the Third Reich. Fear of arrest, and fear of informers, led to public conformity and the leading of a double life for many Germans, who withheld their real views and feelings for expression only in complete privacy in the company of family and close friends.

The Nazis attempted to promote a great display of power and unity under the national Führer. The mass parades, the battalions marching past Hitler, the apparently adoring populace, hands raised in the *Heil* salute, fostered the image of a strong leader and a united people – as encapsulated in the slogan of 'Ein Volk, ein Reich, ein Führer!' ('one people, one empire, one leader') – and indeed the myth of the Führer, above all the petty everyday conflicts and frictions, constituted a powerful element of cohesion in the Third Reich. But to a certain extent the Nazis' self-promotion has been misleading. The myth of a strong leader in a one-party state, with a single official ideology and the back-up of force, fed into the concept of totalitarianism – a concept which proved particularly useful in the Cold War period after the Second World War when dictatorships of the left and right, communist and fascist, were simplistically equated. But it has become increasingly clear to serious analysts of the Third Reich that the monolithic image does not correspond to a more complex reality.

While the Nazis clearly took over the government of Germany, they never entirely took over the state: the tendency was rather to create new parallel party agencies, with spheres of competence and jurisdiction overlapping or competing with those of the existing administration, and armed with plenipotentiary powers directly dependent on the Führer's will. In this 'dual state' there was no rational means of adjudicating between the rival claims of competing agencies to represent the undisputed fount of authority on a given issue – and there were, in addition to conflicts between party and state, also disputes between different party agencies. In the final resort, recourse had to be had to the Führer, and the 'Führer's will' became the ultimate source of authority to resolve all disputes. The 'Hitler state', with the Führer the only final source of arbitration, was to some extent a structural result of this relative administrative chaos.

Since Hitler often stood aside from the fray, only to enter at the last moment to side with the emerging winner, some analysts have been inclined to see him as a 'weak dictator', with very real limits to his power. However, as others have rightly pointed out, when it mattered to Hitler he made sure his own views were predominant.[3] The degree to which Hitler was able to realise given aims, or intervene in detailed policy-making, varied with the sphere of activity, as is discussed below in greater detail with respect to economic, foreign and racial policy in both the peacetime and wartime years.

Not only was the Nazi state never as streamlined as the concept of totalitarianism suggests, German society also proved somewhat resistant to its own reformation into a harmonious national community. It is time to consider in more detail the impact of Nazi policies on the everyday life of the German people.

*Society, culture, and everyday life**

The Nazis did not only want to control the German people: they wanted to transform them into a cohesive, racially pure 'national community' (*Volksgemeinschaft*) of national comrades (*Volksgenossen*) – which would of course exclude those 'community aliens' (*Gemeinschaftsfremden*) who were deemed inferior, 'pollutants' of the social body: Jews, gypsies, homosexuals, the hereditarily diseased, and 'a-social' people. The 1939 edition of the *People's Encyclopaedia* (*Volksbrockhaus*) defined the *Volksgemeinschaft* as 'the life-community of people, resting on bonds of blood, on a common destiny and a common political faith, to which class and status conflicts are essentially foreign'.[4] After the near civil war conditions of the Weimar Republic, the notion of an organic, harmonious, biologically-based racial community, with common political beliefs and a common historical destiny, transcending and healing the wounds

*Parts of the following two sections have been previously published in slightly different form as the opening section of an article by the author in *Historical Research*, vol. 62, no. 148 (June 1989).

of the preceding years, could sound intrinsically appealing to many Germans. Every effort was made by the regime to realise this concept of society, both through overt indoctrination and through the transformation of social organization and everyday experience.

Goebbels' Ministry of Propaganda and Enlightenment, created in March 1933, sought increasing control of all media of communication and culture. A symbolic early event was the burning of books written by Jews, socialists and other 'undesirable intellectuals' on 10 May 1933. Although instigated by radical students, the book-burning was given official blessing by Goebbels' presence at the bonfires on Berlin's central street, Unter den Linden. The event did not in practice succeed entirely in eradicating books by banned authors from libraries across Germany, but it certainly contributed to the 'inner emigration' – self-censorship and public silence – as well as the literal emigration of many authors, among them Thomas and Heinrich Mann and Bertolt Brecht. Subsequent cultural life in Nazi Germany was to a considerable extent reduced to the level of 'German art', typified by a mediocre realism in painting and grandiose schemes in architecture; in the fields of music and drama, some notable individuals compromised with the regime to continue to realise peaks of artistic perfection in the performance of German classics. Britain, and, on a larger scale, the USA, were the major beneficiaries of the mass exodus of cultural talent from Nazi Germany.

Goebbels also made use of the media of popular entertainment and less highbrow culture to attempt to influence the masses. Film was a highly effective medium for propaganda, and the Nazis became adept at producing short newsreel pieces glorifying the achievements of the Führer, illustrating popular adulation of Hitler, and celebrating the achievements of the Reich as a result of its 'national awakening'. Care was taken to stress positive aspects and downplay features which would tend to alienate people and lose popular support. The press, which under the Weimar Republic had been diverse and decentralized, was gradually subjected to Nazi control. This was done partly by the Nazi publishing house gaining an increasing share in the outright ownership of newspapers, partly by increasing control over publishers, editors and journalists, partly by censorship, and partly by feeding stories through a Nazi-run news service. By the later 1930s, the news in the different newspapers was sufficiently *gleichgeschaltet* (co-ordinated) and predictable for most people to adopt a cynical approach and put little store by what was said in German newspapers. The radio was similarly co-opted to Nazi ends, and mass ownership of the 'people's receiver' (*Volksempfänger*) was encouraged – which trebled ownership in the six pre-war years, giving Germany the highest percentage of radio-owners in the world. The emphasis was placed on a combination of light entertainment and snippets of slanted 'news' coverage.

In education, there was a purge of teachers lacking the appropriate racial credentials or political views, at both school and university levels. While a large number of school and university teachers in the Weimar Republic had held conservative and nationalist views, by no means a majority were of Nazi leanings. Many leading academics were forced into emigration, including, for example, Albert Einstein. Attempts were made to influence the contents of what was taught, as well as the people who taught it. While topics such as biology, history, and German were fairly readily adapted for Nazi purposes, other scientific and technical subjects were less susceptible to Nazi distortion. Yet even at the level of school mathematics, examples could be used for exercises in arithmetic which sustained or propagated a certain world view. Pupils were asked to do sums relating to the distance covered in certain times by tanks, torpedo boats, infantry battalions; they were asked to work out, given different speeds, at what distances from a town an enemy aircraft would be met by German air defence forces, if the latter started when the former were a certain distance away; and so on.[5] The subject of *Rassenkunde* was introduced, putting across Nazi views on heredity and racial purity. Schoolchildren undertook such projects as bringing to school a photo of a relative and writing an essay describing the features characteristic of the racial group of the person illustrated. The overall balance of the curriculum was altered too. There was an increased emphasis on sport and physical fitness, with sport compulsory even at university. There was also an emphasis on community service through various work schemes – a useful means not only of attempting to inculcate a sense of community but also of obtaining cheap labour, particularly important in the later years of the Third Reich.

Attempts were also made to create a sense of national community through organizational means. On the one hand, old, previously autonomous organizations had their independence removed and their capacity for harbouring subversive views neutralized; on the other hand, people were harnessed for activities which gave them experience of comradeship and community at the same time as promoting particular Nazi aims. The luxuriant profusion of clubs, associations and societies characteristic of Imperial and Weimar Germany was pruned, coerced, and remoulded into new, Nazi-dominated frameworks. The wide range of youth organizations, ranging from conservative and nationalist through Catholic to Social Democratic youth groups, were submerged into the Nazi youth organizations under the leadership of Baldur von Schirach. Children between the ages of ten and fourteen were encouraged and expected to join groups for boys (DJ) and girls (JM), while those between fourteen and eighteen were to join the Hitler Youth (HJ) and League of German Maidens (BDM) respectively. The Nazi youth organizations were at first similar to their non-Nazi predecessors in their open air activities: camping, hiking, singing songs as they marched through the pine forests or sat by camp-fires at a lake-side. Many young people undeniably enjoyed the expeditions and comradeship engendered by these activities. But from December 1936, the Hitler Youth was given an official status alongside school and home as an educational institution which was supposed to cover all those in the relevant age groups. Children were expected to enter on 20 April (Hitler's birthday) in the year in which they reached the age of ten. Membership finally became compulsory in a decree of March 1939. Meanwhile, since 1934 there had been an increasing emphasis on paramilitary activities and attitudes.

Nevertheless, it does not seem that the Nazi youth organizations were an unmitigated success in inculcating a Nazi world-view in those who participated in them. Many young people simply conformed to the minimum extent necessary to avoid sanctions. Other young people developed their own youth sub-cultures, which the Nazis failed to suppress. Alternative youth groups included the 'Edelweiss Pirates' (spontaneous groups of youngsters who waged war on the Hitler Youth), as well as the Leipzig *Meuten*, the Dresden 'Mobs', the Halle *Proletengefolg-schaften*, the Hamburg 'Deathshead Gang' and 'Bismarck Gang' and the Munich *Blasen*. While these groups were in the main working class, the swing movement was largely supported by upper middle class enthusiasts for 'decadent' jazz music. It is quite clear, not only from isolated autobiographical accounts of individual alienation from the Hitler Youth (such as that by Heinrich Böll) but also from these more visible subcultural groups – members of which ran considerable risks, and did not always escape Nazi retribution for their nonconformity – that Nazi attempts to bend the minds of a whole generation were at best only partially successful.[6]

While youth was an obvious focus for investment in the future of Nazi Germany, so too were the progenitors of future generations: women. In this area, Nazi ideology was clear in principle but less than consistent in practice. As is well known, the Nazis promoted the view of women's role being confined to 'children, kitchen, church' (*Kinder, Küche, Kirche*). The birth rate had been declining in early twentieth-century Germany, and the Nazis wanted to reverse this trend and replenish the 'racial stock'. A variety of means were attempted, many of which were not specifically Nazi but represented more widespread attitudes at the time. In the depression of the late Weimar years there had been much criticism of 'double earners', and the effective expulsion of women from sections of the labour force was underway before the Nazis came to power. After 1933, the pattern of female participation in the labour force was a partially contradictory one. While Nazi prejudices had deep impact in some areas – the exclusion of women from practising law or becoming judges is an example – in other areas, such as the caring professions and primary school teaching, female participation increased slightly. By the later 1930s, the pressures of rearmament and labour shortage encouraged a higher female employment rate. There is some dispute among historians as to whether, during the war years, ideology or economic necessity took precedence in policies on female employment.

At the same time, birth control techniques were discouraged, and the benefits and virtues of having a large family were promoted. Attempts were made to propagate a view of marriage as being for the purpose of producing healthy, racially pure stock, with the state having a clear interest in the reproduction of a 'superior' species. As in other areas, Nazi views were dressed up to appear scientifically respectable: the expert – the doctor – had a role to play in giving a medical blessing to what might otherwise have been seen as purely the intimate, private affair of an individual couple. The decision to reproduce was not a matter solely for individuals, but an affair of the state, responsible for ensuring healthy future stock – and for sterilizing those people deemed unfit to pass on their genes into the genetic pool of the next generation. Such views were insidiously put across in such seemingly non-propagandistic publications as popular dictionaries of health and medicine, such as *Knaur's Gesundheitslexikon*.[7] Financial incentives were given to those having numerous children, and symbolic rewards in the form of a 'mother's cross' (*Mutterkreuz*) were awarded to those having eight, six or four children (gold, silver and bronze crosses respectively). Courses in motherhood and domestic science were run by the Nazi women's organization, the *Deutsches Frauenwerk* (DFW), which had been established in September 1933 to co-ordinate the various women's organizations of pre-Nazi Germany. Along with the original NSDAP organization, the National Socialist Frauenwerk (NSF), the DFW attempted to organize and mobilize women. Like Nazi youth organizations, Nazi women's organizations had a limited impact: working class and rural women proved relatively impervious to their supposed attractions. Moreover, Nazi women's policy was in any case subject to intrinsic contradictions: while attempting to emphasize the woman's role as wife and mother, it simultaneously tended to take her away from the family through time-consuming organizational activities. As it turned out, the essentially private sphere of family life proved relatively resistant to Nazi infiltration and 'co-ordination'.[8]

In the sphere of work, similar attempts were made to foster a sense of community. Programmes such as 'Strength through Joy' (*Kraft durch Freude*) and 'The Beauty of Work' (*Schönheit der Arbeit*) made a pretence at fostering the health and well-being of workers. Although a few benefited from well-publicized holidays, such as pleasure cruises, many were not taken in by the propaganda about the 'factory community' in which individual effort served the good of the whole community. On the other hand, with the demise of independent trade unions the experience of collective solidarity was lost; and with the introduction of individual wage negotiations for individual advancement, working class collective identities and bonds began to be eroded. Nazi policies may not always have had the effects intended; but they were not without impact altogether.

Not all organizations and ideologies were equally susceptible to Nazi co-ordination, penetration, or subversion. Catholics had initially proved more resistant to the attractions of pre-1933 Nazi electoral propaganda than had Protestants. The *Reichskonkordat* of 1933 appeared to establish a *modus vivendi* for Catholicism with the Nazi regime, but Catholics were concerned to preserve a strict separation between the spheres of religion – which remained their preserve – and politics, which could be left to the state. When the latter encroached on the former, Catholics were prepared to resist, as in the campaigns waged against the Nazi attacks on confessional education and attempts to remove crucifixes from schools.[9] The Protestant churches, lacking the transcendent loyalty to a higher authority equivalent to the Catholic focus on Rome, initially appeared more vulnerable to Nazi incursions. But Nazi attempts to co-opt Protestantism, with the appointment of a 'Reich Bishop' and the formation of a movement of pro-Nazi 'German Christians', soon led to a serious rift among Protestants. Those who recognized the essential criminality of the Nazi regime came to sympathize with the 'Confessing Church', associated with theologians such as Dietrich Bonhoeffer and Martin Niemöller. A majority of Protestants sided with neither the German Christians nor the

Confessing Church, and the latter two groups were in the event subject to internal divisions and disputes. The Nazis eventually gave up their attempt to co-opt Christianity, and made little pretence at concealing their contempt for Christian beliefs, ethics and morality. Unable to comprehend that some Germans genuinely wanted to combine commitment to Christianity and Nazism, some members of the SS even came to view German Christians as almost more of a threat than the Confessing Church.[10]

Clearly there was a wide range of opinions among Christians of different confessions, political perspectives and social backgrounds, and different issues took precedence for different individuals at various times. For many lay people, the 'pastors' squabbling' (*Pfarrergezänk*) must have seemed at best an irrelevance to the pressing concerns of everyday life. For some members of the laity, the singing of hymns with deeper meanings may have helped them to retain a sense of the transience of contemporary oppression, while not galvanizing them against the regime, and may hence have aided regime stability.[11] On the other hand, it was also possible to hold what would otherwise have been forbidden political gatherings under the guise of church meetings or Bible study groups. But insofar as it is possible to generalize on a complex issue, it must be said that, whatever the diversity of opinion and action, the record of most Christians (Protestant and Catholic) was at best a rather patchy and uneven one. With the notable exception of those religious individuals and groups who stood out for their principled resistance to the regime – of whom more in the next chapter – it seems that, for many Germans, adherence to the Christian faith proved compatible with at least passive acquiescence in, if not active support for, the Nazi dictatorship.

Economy and society

Undoubtedly of major impact on most people's attitudes and perceptions was their economic experience. Weimar democracy had been associated, for millions of Germans, not only with national defeat and a humiliating peace treaty, but also with economic disaster. Many had survived the inflation of 1923 only to be buffeted by the slump which started in 1929. Despite the increasing political repression, for a large number of Germans the Third Reich appeared to give new hope of prosperity and stability. Small retailers looked forward to the suppression of their rivals, the big department stores; peasants looked forward to a rightful place in a country proclaiming the importance and glory of 'blood and soil'; industrialists welcomed the suppression of trade union rights in the hope of regaining power for the employers, eroded under the Weimar system. While socialists and communists, Jews, and other committed opponents of the regime viewed it with foreboding, for many apolitical Germans the 'national awakening' appeared to offer hopes of a brighter future.

What actually happened to German economy and society in the Third Reich, and what were the relationships between economics and politics under Nazi rule? Controversies over these questions are far from settled. The Nazis themselves proclaimed that they were effecting a 'national revolution', although the hopes of more radical Nazis were rapidly dashed after they attained power, leading to pressure from the party ranks for more radical action and a 'second revolution'.

It is clear that Hitler's overriding interest lay in the preparation for the conquest of *Lebensraum* and not primarily in the transformation of the economy. In his view, everything must be directed towards the ultimate goal of rearmament. As Hitler put it in a speech to his cabinet only a week after becoming Chancellor, on 8 February 1933: 'The next five years in Germany had to be devoted to rendering the German people again capable of bearing arms. Every publicly sponsored measure to create employment had to be considered from the point of view of whether it was necessary with respect to rendering the German people again capable of bearing arms for military service. This had to be the dominant thought, always and everywhere.'[12] Insofar as there was a coherent, specifically Nazi economic programme, it had two main features: the notion of self-sufficiency, or 'autarky', and the notion of expanded living-space in central Europe, encompassing particularly lands to the south-east and east of Germany. These notions were, of course, integrally related to the development of a self-sufficient war economy sustained by territorial expansion and exploitation of the raw materials and labour of conquered territories. At the same time as giving priority to rearmament, however, the Nazis were concerned to retain popular support, which meant paying attention to consumer pressures and not imposing severe levels of austerity on the people. These different objectives were not entirely compatible, and periodic strains and crises resulted from attempts to pursue mutually contradictory strands of policy. Such crises also had effects on, for example, the timing of certain foreign policy moves, such as the remilitarization of the left bank of the Rhine in 1936.

Initially, the economic policies of Nazi Germany were controlled by the relatively orthodox former President of the *Reichsbank*, Hjalmar Schacht, as Minister of Economics. Deficit financing began in 1933 with the issue of so-called "Mefo Bills", which served to disguise spending on rearmament under the cover of the spurious 'Metallurgische Forschungsgesellschaft m.b.H.'. On 1 June 1933 the first 'Reinhardt Programme' was announced with the 'Law to Reduce Unemployment', followed by a second plan on 21 September 1933; and on 27 June 1933 there was a law initiating the construction of autobahns. While the economy had already begun to turn around in 1932, prior to the Nazis' participation in government, economic recovery up to 1936 was certainly aided – perhaps speeded up – by Nazi work-creation schemes, motorization and construction works, and their willingness to engage in deficit financing. Many of these early schemes were of an infrastructural nature, facilitating later mobilization for war without being directly war-related themselves. While autobahns would later be highly useful for the rapid movement of troops, they could also serve more immediate ideological ends, symbolizing the rebuilding of the community and the integration of its different parts into one future-oriented national whole.[13] Schacht's New Plan of 1934 marked the first stage in the planned development of autarky, (although Schacht himself was an opponent of out-and-out autarky) with bilateral trade agreements between pairs of countries not relying on certain international foreign currency exchanges.

By 1935, however, it was becoming clear that, despite the return towards full employment, Germany's economic problems were by no means resolved. With a shortage of foreign exchange reserves, a choice had to be made between the import of raw materials for the rearmament programme or of foodstuffs for consumers. Moreover, there were splits within industry: while some industries, most notably the great chemical combine I. G. Farben, supported the manufacture of synthetic materials and an economy of autarky, others, more export-oriented, were opposed to such policies. In August 1936 Hitler issued a key memorandum stating that Germany must be ready for war within four years, and that economic activity must be geared towards this primary end. On 18 October 1936 the Four Year Plan was announced, with Goering in charge. Yet despite the precarious economic condition of Germany, and the overriding priority given to rearmament, there was to be no drop in the standard of living of consumers. From then on, in attempting to pursue both these objectives, economic policy became less and less orthodox and increasingly unbalanced.

The Four Year Plan involved close collaboration between members of certain industries – again, particularly I. G. Farben – and Nazis in high positions. It represented to some extent a clear illustration of the proliferation of spheres of competence and institutional rivalries in the Nazi state, as the powers of Goering conflicted with those of the Ministers of Labour (Seldte), Agriculture (Darré) and Economics (Schacht). Schacht in fact resigned his post in November 1937, partly because of these conflicts. Not only were there party–state conflicts, but also conflicts between different sections of the party. There were, for example, conflicts between party agencies concerned with rearmament, and those more concerned with aspects of consumer satisfaction or popular opinion, such as the DAF.

These developments have been variously interpreted. While rearmament has often been held up as one of the prime factors in German economic recovery in the 1930s, R. J. Overy suggests that it was only increasingly important after 1936, and that in fact attempts to orientate the economy towards war actually slowed down the rate of recovery and growth, partly because of the resistance of some cartelized industries to Nazi policies. Yet Overy plays down Volker Berghahn's emphasis on what the latter calls a deliberate 'unhinging' of the economy from 1936, when traditional economic considerations were discarded and ultimate economic salvation was predicated on a successful war of conquest.[14] The relationships between industry, party and state are also more complex than sometimes assumed. Although the older orthodox Marxist interpretation of fascism as the last ditch stand of a capitalist state in crisis is untenable, it is by no means clear either that a pure 'primacy of politics' was achieved. Some industries benefited from close collaboration with the state; others attempted to resist interference; and while the Nazis attempted to control the direction of economic policy, they were by no means always successful; nor could they be, given their own partly mutually contradictory aims. Moreover, the successes of economic recovery and a return to full employment by 1936 had by 1939 generated a shortage of skilled labour, necessitating the conscription of workers into compulsory labour service on certain projects. There were also conflicts between aspects of Nazi ideology and the demands of reality: women, for example, despite Nazi views of their proper place being in the home, in fact participated in increasing numbers in paid employment outside the home, even before the more acute shortages of (literally) manpower in wartime years.

What is quite clear is that, far from achieving a social revolution, the effects of Nazi economic policies on society represented in large measure a continuation and perhaps exacerbation of previous socio-economic trends. Realities under Nazi rule by no means corresponded with pre-1933 election promises. While the return to full employment did mean jobs and a steady income for many, the associated withdrawal of trade union rights and collective bargaining, as well as the very variable rates of pay and conditions, rendered the experience at best an ambiguous one. Despite attempts by the All-German Federation of Trade Unions (ADGB) to reach a compromise with the new regime in April 1933, autonomous trade unions had been unequivocally smashed; and although many workers were prepared somewhat cynically to enjoy any holidays or outings offered to them by organizations such as Strength through Joy, few really swallowed much of the propaganda about the 'harmonious factory community' and the like. While concessions were made to small businesses, insofar as they did not conflict with major political aims, other demands of small retailers were not met; in particular, big department stores continued to flourish. While peasants were praised in Nazi ideology, the measures taken under Darré (who had replaced Hugenberg as Minister of Agriculture in June 1933) were by no means universally popular. The control of the production, distribution and pricing of foodstuffs by the Reich Food Estate and the control of the inheritance of farms under the Entailed Farm Law met with the hostility of considerable numbers of peasants in different areas, varying with local conditions. It is clear that, while there were certain fundamental changes – particularly in the increased political direction of the economy, with the attempt to control and subordinate economic development to the goal of preparation for war – Germany continued to be an industrializing society with certain endemic conflicts and strains. The 'national community' was created neither in reality nor in popular social perceptions.[15]

The radicalization of the regime

Hitler had two main aims, expressed in *Mein Kampf* and the later *Second Book*: to create a 'pure' racial community in Germany; and to expand Germany's living-space, dominating central Europe and, eventually, seeking world mastery. Hitler's anti-Semitism, while finding resonance in the widespread prejudices against Jews, clearly went way beyond existing concepts of discrimination in its eventual practical implications. Hitler's grandiose visions of the future of his Thousand Year Reich, while having much in common with conservative-nationalist desires for revision of the Treaty of Versailles, also went some considerable way beyond them in terms of global aspirations. While Hitler lost little time in jettisoning the political framework of the Weimar Republic, it took rather longer to transform the relationship of the Nazis to the old elites, whose miscalculated support had brought Hitler to power and who were essential for the effective use of that power. Moreover, Hitler had simultaneously to play to a number of galleries: to public opinion, dependent as his charisma was on repeated popular acclaim; to the Nazi Party activists, who were often frustrated at the apparent stalling of momentum and the incompleteness of the 'national revolution'; and to the established economic and military elites whose co-operation was vital to the realization of Hitler's ends. Added to these sometimes conflicting pressures was Hitler's distinctive style of leadership, which allowed the duplication, indeed proliferation, of state and Party offices and functions, and blurred the lines of leadership and responsibility. But on issues which mattered to Hitler, he pursued his aims with ruthlessness and appropriate brutality. While Hitler's intentions alone are not sufficient to explain the pattern of developments in the Third Reich – after all, Hitler had to attempt to realize his intentions under given circumstances and not always welcome conditions – the chronology of Nazi Germany reveals a progressive radicalization of the regime in line with Hitler's pursuit of his overriding aims.

Anti-Semitic policies in peacetime were powered to a considerable degree by Nazi Party radicals, and Hitler sought to distance himself somewhat – at least as far as his public image was concerned – from the consequences of the more extreme or less successful of their actions. The attempted boycott of Jewish shops in April 1933 was rapidly called off. Systematic discrimination against Jews continued, however, in the removal of Jews from professional and cultural life. In 1935 the so-called Nuremberg Laws – announced in a last-minute way at the Nuremberg Party rally – sought to give legal validity to racial discrimination. Under the *Reichsbürgergesetz*, two categories of citizenship were introduced, with Jews given second-class citizenship, in that they could not become *Reichsbürger* with full political rights. Under the Law for the Protection of German Blood and German Honour, Jews were no longer permitted to marry those of German or related extraction, nor – a deliberate affront in its moral implications – to employ German women under the age of forty-five in their households. Consideration was given to the vexatious question of *Mischlinge* – those of mixed extraction who, in Nazi eyes, might be deemed to 'pollute' German blood. The milder view of excluding 'half-' and 'quarter-Jews' from the Nuremberg Laws was finally adopted, while 'three-quarter Jews' were included. For many Germans, the Nuremberg Laws were welcomed as an apparent legalization of the rather *ad hoc* measures of discrimination against Jews.

But, far from being the culmination of Nazi anti-Semitic measures, the Nuremberg Laws marked but a stage in the systematic exclusion of Jews from 'normal' life. With a brief, partial respite in deference to international opinion when Berlin hosted the Olympic Games in 1936, a series of *Verordnungen* consequent on the *Reichsbürgergesetz* in the following years systematically continued to exclude Jews from their professions, from education, and from public and cultural life. From 1938, discrimination became more severe, with the 'aryanization' or confiscation of Jewish property, and the effective removal of the means of material existence in a variety of ways. The effect, as a Nazi article of 24 November 1938 remarked with glee, would be to reduce the Jews to dependence on crime – which would 'necessitate' the appropriate measures on the part of a state committed to law and order, ending in the complete extermination (*restlose Vernichtung*) of German Jewry.[16]

Commitment to law and order was scarcely evident in the actions against Jews on the *Reichskristallnacht* (Night of Broken Glass) of 9 November 1938. Ostensibly precipitated by the murder of a member of the German Embassy in Paris by a young Jew, a supposedly 'spontaneous uprising' was incited by a speech by Goebbels on the occasion of the annual anniversary celebration of the Beer Hall Putsch. Party radicals burned synagogues, and attacked and looted Jewish property across Germany. Official party figures reported ninety-one deaths of Jews, and subsequently around thirty thousand Jews were arrested and detained in concentration camps for a period of time. Jews had to pay compensation for the destruction of property themselves, and hand over any payments from insurance policies to the state. Many Germans, far from having spontaneously perpetrated attacks – as the Nazi propaganda would have it – were actually appalled at the wanton destruction of property and evident lawlessness of the *Reichskristallnacht*. But they did little to protest against the continued series of measures discriminating against the Jews – the removal of their driving licences, the withdrawal of their passports (which were returned stamped with the initial 'J'), the enforced adoption of the first names Israel or Sara, the ban on visiting museums, theatres, concerts, swimming-pools, the forced surrender of gold and silver objects and all precious jewellery with the exception of wedding rings, the systematic reductions in status and livelihood. Most Germans simply acquiesced in the piecemeal process by which Jews were identified, defined, stigmatized, segregated, and stripped of the status of fellow citizens and even human beings to become an oppressed community in their own homeland. These peacetime measures of discrimination were a precondition for the subsequent preference of many Germans to ignore the later, more tragic fate of these people who had already been effectively removed from a normal status in civil society.

On the foreign policy front, desires for the revision of the Treaty of Versailles were, as indicated above, widespread among Germans. Already in the closing years of the Weimar Republic, after the death of Stresemann, less cautious, more strident tones had been evident in German foreign policy. These revisionist tendencies were unleashed with vigour by Hitler. In 1933, he made clear his preference for bilateral rather than collective security arrangements, and soon withdrew from the League of Nations. With the approval of the Army, by 1934 rearmament was in full swing, with the production of aircraft, ships and explosives. In January 1935, after a plebiscite, the Saarland was returned to German jurisdiction. In March 1935 the rearmament programme, the existence of a German air force, and the introduction of one year's conscription (raised to two years in August 1936), were made public. These clear breaches of the Treaty of Versailles were censured by the so-called Stresa Front of Italy, France and Britain, and by the League of Nations, in April 1935, but to little effect. By June of that year, Britain and Germany had concluded a Naval Agreement under which Germany was permitted to increase her navy to one-third the strength of the British navy. The 'Stresa Front' was in any case less than solid. Hitler on the whole tended to admire Italy's fascist leader Mussolini, and, despite tensions between Italy and Germany over Austria after the attempted coup by Austrian Nazis in 1934, Hitler was concerned to foster good relations with his fellow-dictator. Hitler was also a prime opportunist. Taking advantage of British and French preoccupation with the Italian invasion of Abyssinia in October 1935, and under some pressure from domestic discontent over a deteriorating economic situation, Hitler took his first major foreign policy risk in March 1936. German troops marched over the Rhine to reoccupy the demilitarized left bank, in clear defiance of the Versailles Treaty. This served to boost Hitler's domestic popularity considerably, and occasioned only very limited criticism from abroad.

From then on, foreign policy moved into a new gear. Under the Four Year Plan, presided over by Goering, rather unorthodox economic policies were initiated, which marked a clear break with Hjalmar Schacht's notions of economic management. Schacht's resignation as Minister of Economics in November 1937 came partly as a result of conflicts between the Economics Ministry and Goering's office. There were similar conflicts between Nazis and more traditional conservative nationalists on the diplomatic front. For some time, Ribbentrop had been running a diplomatic service in rivalry with the Foreign Ministry. In 1936, Ribbentrop became Ambassador to Britain. The Spanish Civil War, which broke out in July 1936, fostered closer relations between Italy and Germany (with both supporting Franco), and helped to bring about a new alignment. The emergent 'Rome–Berlin Axis' was strengthened as, in the course of 1936, it had become clear to Hitler that he would have to abandon his ideas about an alliance with Britain; and, in 1938, under Ribbentrop's influence, Hitler opted for Japan as the third member of the 'Axis'. The Tripartite Pact was finally signed in September 1940. Meanwhile, it was becoming increasingly clear that the attempt to combine preparation for war with domestic consumer satisfaction was in the long run economically impracticable and that it was essential for Germany to go to war sooner rather than later. This realization occasioned a new rift between the increasingly radical Nazi regime and the old elites: Hitler's clash with army leaders in the winter of 1937–8 marked a further step in the gathering momentum of the Nazi regime.

In November 1937, at a meeting with leaders of the army, navy and air force, together with the Foreign Minister and War Minister, Hitler delivered a lengthy harangue on Germany's need for *Lebensraum*. Notes of this meeting were taken unofficially by Hitler's military adjutant Colonel Hossbach, in what has become known as the 'Hossbach memorandum'. Some of Hitler's audience were not convinced by his ideas, which were greeted with grave reservations. Notwithstanding criticisms, in the following weeks Nazi military planning became offensive. Rather than responding or listening to criticism, Hitler simply removed the critics from their strategic positions. By February 1938 a significant purge had been effected: Blomberg's post of War Minister was abolished; the old *Wehrmacht* office was replaced by the *Oberkommando* (High Command) of the *Wehrmacht* (OKW) under General Keitel; Fritsch was replaced as Commander-in-Chief of the Army by General von Brauchitsch; fourteen senior generals were retired, and forty-six others had to change their commands; and, in the Foreign Ministry, Ribbentrop officially replaced Neurath as Foreign Minister. Hitler, who was already Supreme Commander of the Army by virtue of his position as head of state since the death of Hindenburg, now also became Commander-in-Chief of the Armed Forces. The regime was now more specifically Nazi, less conservative-nationalist, in complexion.

The overthrow of Hitler was first seriously contemplated by members of the elite during 1938–9. Army leaders including Beck and Halder, as well as the head of the Foreign Ministry Ernst von Weizsäcker, considered the possibility of a coup. Their ideas were conveyed to the British government, but ignored. Similarly, any prospect of success for Adam von Trott's visit to Britain in June 1939 was marred by suspicions of his real intentions: while Trott was seeking to buy time for a military coup to be successful, his official reports back to the German Foreign Ministry and his proposals for further concessions to Hitler, as well as his sincere German nationalism, sufficiently opened his aims to misinterpretation and misrepresentation for the Americans as well as the British to choose to take little notice of his mission.[17] But these early attempts at resistance in high places were deflected, first by the apparent success of Hitler's foreign policy – and the 'appeasement' with which he was met – and then, after the final outbreak of war in September 1939, by the combination of rapid early military success and unwillingness to commit an act of treason against the head of state when the fatherland was at war.

In the course of 1938–9, Hitler achieved certain major foreign policy goals without igniting an international conflict. In March 1938, after considerable exertion of pressure on the Austrian chancellor Schuschnigg – who attempted to organize a plebiscite which would avoid German takeover, but was outmanoeuvred and replaced by the Nazi sympathizer Seyss-Inquart – the peaceful invasion of Austria by German troops and its annexation into an enlarged German Reich was effected. Later myths of 'the rape of Austria' and being 'Hitler's first victim' notwithstanding, the entry of German soldiers was greeted by many Austrians with considerable enthusiasm. While those Austrians of left-wing and liberal opinions viewed the *Anschluss* with foreboding, others gave a rapturous welcome to the triumphant return of Adolf Hitler to his native land, in which, over a quarter of a century earlier, he had collected his ideas and fomented his rag-bag of prejudices while a drifting failed art-student in Vienna. Austrian Jews had good reason to be worried: a virulent anti-Semitism was unleashed, soon making their situation even more demoralizing and unpleasant than that of the Jews in Germany, against whom discriminatory measures had unfolded more gradually and legalistically. As far as international responses were concerned, the reaction was muted. For one thing, since Austria had been a dominant force in 'German' affairs for centuries, and had only recently been excluded from Bismarck's small Germany (and forbidden any union under the Versailles Treaty), it did not seem entirely unnatural that Germans in the two states should be united under the Austrian-born leader of Germany. For another, the major powers were at this time not prepared for military confrontation with Hitler. The USA was adopting an isolationist, neutralist stance with respect to European affairs; the

Soviet Union under Stalin was preoccupied with domestic purges of perceived internal opposition; neither France nor England was ready for a military challenge to Hitler, although rearmament had been underway since the mid-1930s.

In the summer of 1938, Hitler turned his attention to Czechoslovakia. The Sudeten German Party under Henlein, with help from the German Nazis, had been cultivating unrest among ethnic Germans in the border areas, the Sudetenland. There was a heightened sense of crisis as misperceptions of German mobilization led to an actual Czech mobilization, and for a week in August 1938 it appeared that war was about to break out. By September, the threat of war had been averted, and attempts were made to resolve the Czech crisis by diplomatic means. The British Prime Minister Neville Chamberlain, braving the novelty of airborne diplomacy, returned from the Munich conference of September 1938 – at which Czechoslovakia, whose fate was to be decided, was not represented – waving the famous piece of paper with Hitler's signature and proclaiming 'peace in our time'. The western powers felt that, by ceding portions of the Czech border territories, they had fulfilled legitimate ethnic demands and averted the threat of a war for which they were not yet ready. Whether or not their policy of appeasement was justifiable, it certainly served to buy further time for rearmament. Hitler, for his part, felt cheated out of war by the Munich Agreement.

Czechoslovakia's loss of the western border territories also meant loss of key border defences – and the will to defend herself, after the debacle of the summer. When, in March 1939, Hitler's armies invaded Prague, there was little the Czechs could do to resist German takeover. Bohemia and Moravia became a German protectorate, while Slovakia became a satellite state of the German Reich. As far as Britain was concerned, it was prudent to allow this 'far-away country' of which they knew little (as it was put in September 1938) fall without western military intervention.

Emboldened by the feeble western response to the invasion of Czechoslovakia, Hitler now turned his attention to Poland and the Baltic states. Lithuania ceded Memel to Germany, but the Poles stood firm on Danzig. At this point, the British took

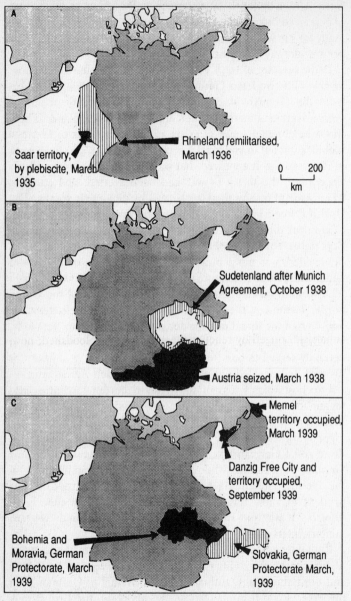

A

Saar territory, by plebiscite, March 1935

Rhineland remilitarised, March 1936

0   200
km

B

Sudetenland after Munich Agreement, October 1938

Austria seized, March 1938

C

Memel territory occupied, March 1939

Danzig Free City and territory occupied, September 1939

Bohemia and Moravia, German Protectorate, March 1939

Slovakia, German Protectorate March, 1939

Territorial annexation, 1935–9

a stronger stand, issuing a guarantee of Polish independence. Hitler chose not to take too much notice of this, given the British record of appeasement. In August 1939, in a surprise move – and putting an end to parallel British negotiations with the Russians – Hitler concluded a pact with his ideological arch-enemy, the Communist leader Joseph Stalin. In conjunction with a further agreement in September, Hitler and Stalin mutually carved up the Polish and Baltic states, and achieved certain strategic aims; while Stalin bought time for further rearmament, Hitler sought to avoid the possibility of war on two fronts.

On 1 September 1939, German troops used the pretext of incited border incidents for a well-organized invasion of Poland. By 3 September, Britain and France had concluded that this clear act of German aggression now meant that they were, at last, at war with Germany. The precarious attempt at stabilizing European affairs and achieving a new international order after the First World War had collapsed. Germany under Hitler was again unleashing war in Europe. But this time – unlike the mood of August 1914, however exaggerated by nationalist mythology – there was little enthusiasm for war among the German people. The peaceful gains of the preceding years had been greeted with an acclaim tinged by relief at the avoidance of bloodshed; now, in the main, the Germans took up arms in sombre mood, with considerable foreboding, clinging to the hope that Hitler was right in his predictions of an assured and early German victory. But, as it was to turn out, Hitler's aims for the 'master race' were so ambitious as to pave the way for eventual total defeat.

FIVE

War, Extermination and Defeat

The early experience of the war seemed to prove Hitler right. An ill-prepared Polish army was defeated within three weeks by the combined might of Germany military forces. By the end of September, Poland had been dismembered. The western parts were incorporated into the Greater German Reich; eastern Poland and the Baltic states were annexed by the Soviet Union; and what remained became the 'General Government' under German occupation Agreements between Hitler and Stalin led to the first major enforced movements of population, as ethnic Germans were resettled into the newly incorporated territories of the Reich, while Poles and Jews were expelled eastwards into the area of the General Government. Under the civil administration of Hans Frank from the end of October 1939, the population of Poland was soon to experience the terroristic practices of police and SS power. SS units systematically rounded up and killed those whom they considered potential enemies or undesirables: members of the Polish nobility, left-wingers, and many Polish Jews, were simply murdered after the invasion of Poland. Murmurings by army officers, and even sharp protests in the lower ranks, led to the understanding that the army should turn a blind eye to SS transgressions of the normal 'morality' of warfare. Other Poles were drafted into becoming slave labourers for the victorious Nazis. Meanwhile, as far as the western powers were concerned, the rapid *Blitzkrieg* or lightning war was followed by the *Sitzkrieg* or 'phoney war' of relative inaction in the winter months.

Despite the rapid success of the Polish campaign, there was dissent between Hitler and certain army and intelligence leaders, including Canaris, Oster and Halder. The latter realistically

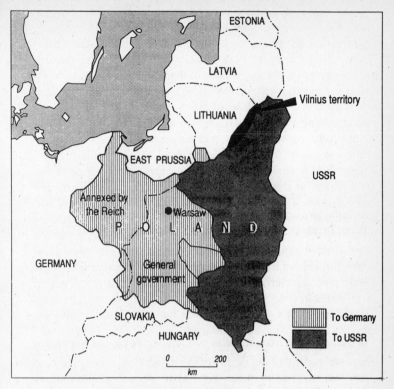

The partition of Poland, 1939

considered that Germany was not equipped for a sustained
military campaign, and wanted to enter into negotiations with
the western powers. But their considerations were ignored by
Hitler, and their own delays and disagreements rendered their
embryonic opposition ineffectual. In the event, active military
opposition was delayed so long that it could salvage neither
millions of lives nor German honour. In the meantime, more
decisive – but unsuccessful – action was taken by a lone,
courageous individual, with neither political backing nor a
personal stake in any future, non-Nazi state. A Swabian carpenter

by the name of Georg Elser had come to the conclusion that Hitler was an evil who must be eliminated. Alone, Elser carefully planned his attempt to kill Hitler. He prepared to install a time-bomb in a pillar in the Munich Beer Hall where Hitler annually commemorated the anniversary of the failed 1923 putsch. Night after night, Elser waited in the Beer Hall until after closing time, then got down on hands and knees to work on hollowing out the pillar, taking the wood shavings away with him in a briefcase. Unfortunately, when Elser had successfully installed a bomb timed to go off during Hitler's speech, the particular night of November 9 1939 happened to be foggy. Hitler decided not to fly back to Berlin as planned, but rather to leave early and take a train. The bomb went off as planned – but Hitler had left shortly beforehand. Elser was later apprehended crossing the border into Switzerland. Despite hysterical Nazi assertions that a wider plot – including the British secret services – must have lain behind Elser's assassination attempt, no such contacts were ever discovered. Elser was held under relatively favoured conditions in concentration camps throughout the war. In April 1945, on Hitler's orders, Elser was forced to stand against the wall in Dachau and was shot dead.[1]

Meanwhile, in the winter of 1939–40, Hitler had taken personal control of the details of the military campaign, and paid ever less attention to the cautious advice of more senior military advisers. With Russia gaining control over Finland, Germany's attention was focused on securing Scandinavia against the British. Denmark was rapidly occupied, and by the summer of 1940 a compliant regime under the pro-Nazi politician Vidkun Quisling had been established in Norway. In the West, a careful campaign of advance through Luxemburg and the Belgian Ardennes permitted rapid invasion of France in May 1940, and by 14 June the German army had entered Paris. On 17 June, the French leader Marshal Pétain capitulated to the Germans. France was divided, both geographically – with a rump French government based in Vichy, in the south, while northern France was taken under German occupation – and politically, between collaborators and those committed to resistance.

The British army had been forced to retreat from Dunkirk, unable to withstand the bombardments of the advancing German army. In Britain, a governmental crisis had precipitated the formation of a war cabinet under the bullish leadership of Winston Churchill, who replaced the relatively conciliatory tones of his predecessor Neville Chamberlain with a public commitment to fight – and win. Churchill nevertheless had to contend with appeasing voices in his cabinet – notably in the guise of his Foreign Minister, Lord Halifax – and it was by no means clear in the dark hours of the summer of 1940 that the island kingdom would succeed in its attempt to hold out alone against the apparently invincible Germans. In August 1940, Germany mounted a major operation soon to be known as the Battle of Britain, bombarding London and major industrial centres in southern England day and night. By mid-September, however, it became clear that an invasion of Britain (under 'Operation Sea-Lion') was not practicable, and this plan was postponed for the spring. But after a few weeks' lull in the air raids, bombardment was renewed with the massive destruction of Coventry on the night of 13–14 November 1940. Night air raids continued through the winter, sending the British population running for cover in air-raid shelters or clustering in the London underground, while the RAF gained a reputation for bravery and expertise in combating the German onslaught.

In the summer of 1940, Hitler appeared to be at the height of his power, as the German public applauded his victories and had yet to feel the real pinch of economic strains on the domestic front. Faced with extraordinary military successes, elite opposition to Hitler evaporated or fell silent. Yet the war was proliferating, and the expansion of the military arena was soon to reveal the degree to which the German war machine was in fact overstretched. Even with the gains in materials and labour made by plundering the resources and exploiting the populations of defeated and occupied territories, the German economy increasingly felt the strain of escalating armaments production. Having ignored early warnings that the war should be strictly limited in time and territorial scope, Hitler proceeded to expand the range of fronts without waiting for a decisive victory against Britain. Within a year, this expansionism was to sow the seeds of Hitler's ultimate defeat.

The Soviet Union, having annexed the Baltic states in June 1940, was now turning its attention to the troubled region of south-east Europe. What concerned Germany most was Russian pressure on Romania, the main source of German oil supplies. In the course of the autumn of 1940, Hitler made up his mind that Russia must be neutralized or knocked out of the war; and that if it were not possible to invade Britain itself, then the fight against Britain must be displaced to an attack on British colonies and interests overseas. This entailed co-operation with other powers with similar interests, in particular Italy and Japan. On 2 September 1940 Ribbentrop's notion of a 'world triangle' was realized in a Tripartite Pact between Germany, Italy and Japan, each of which felt the others could be used in pursuit of their own particular ends. While Italy had interests in the Mediterranean – particularly north Africa, Yugoslavia and Greece – Japan could be encouraged to take over French and attack British colonies in the Far East, and to tie up the USA – which had both pledged support in principle for Britain and sent a considerable amount of equipment – thus keeping America fully occupied in Pacific conflicts and out of the European arena. Ribbentrop even contemplated including the Russians in this scheme; but soundings on this matter were taken just as Hitler was formulating plans for an invasion of Russia to take place the following summer, and hence came to nothing. On 18 December 1940, Hitler issued a directive for what was to be code-named 'Operation Barbarossa': the invasion of Russia.

The transformation of what might have remained a limited, European war – from which Germany might well have emerged the victor – into a World War which was to bring total defeat and unconditional surrender came in 1941. After a diversionary invasion of Yugoslavia and Greece in the spring of 1941 – following earlier attacks, not co-ordinated with Hitler, by Germany's Axis partner Italy – the invasion of the Soviet Union finally went ahead on 22 June 1941. The Russians, who had not taken serious action on being warned of the proposed attack, were initially unprepared, and the three invading German Army Groups were able at first to make rapid advances. However, Russian resistance quickly stiffened; and, unknown to the Germans, the Soviet Army had undergone considerable reform and strengthening since Stalin's purges of officers and since the rather poor Soviet performance against Finland in 1939–40. The Germans were thus unable to inflict the rapid defeat on the Russians for which they had been planning, and soon started to suffer from overextended lines of communication and inadequate reserves. Disputes arose between Hitler and the High Command of the Army over priorities in the Russian campaign. By October, the German troops were being seriously affected by the autumn rains, and were bogged down in mud; soon, the mud and mire gave way to an early winter. The German army had been prepared only for a blitzkrieg; it was not equipped to contend with the icy winds, deep snows, and frozen wastes of the Russian winter. Attempts to mobilize resources on the home front – through donations to the WHW (winter relief fund), giving up fur-coats, boots, skis, and eating 'one-pot' meals – proved pitifully inadequate to protect the freezing German soldiers on the eastern front. At the same time, incensed by the Nazi proclamation of all-out ideological warfare against Communism (with the infamous 'Commissar Order' instructing that Bolshevik political commissars should be shot on the spot rather than taken as prisoners of war), and with the escalation of brutality and transgression of the normal rules of warfare, Soviet determination to resist the Nazis and defend their homeland solidified. A long drawn-out struggle ensued, characterized by increasing stridency and fanatic exhortations to self-sacrifice on the part of Nazi propagandists, combined with serious errors of military strategy and tactics under Hitler's leadership. Despite all attempts to gloss over losses and setbacks, no amount of Nazi propaganda or biased newsreel coverage was in the end able to disguise the scale of German defeat at the battle of Stalingrad in the winter of 1942–3.

Having involved Germany in a war on two fronts – a situation which he had always been explicitly at pains to avoid – Hitler

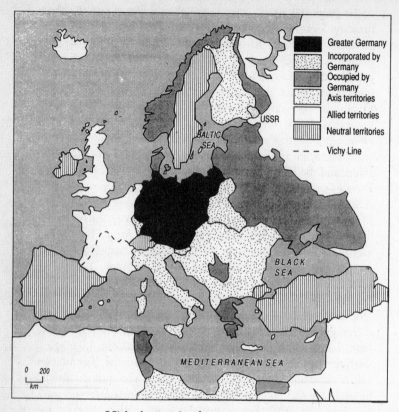

Legend:
- Greater Germany
- Incorporated by Germany
- Occupied by Germany
- Axis territories
- Allied territories
- Neutral territories
- – – – Vichy Line

Hitler's empire by autumn 1942

made a further move which was to seal the fate of the war he had launched. On 7 December 1941, Japan attacked the American fleet at Pearl Harbor. While Germany's pact with Japan committed Germany to aid Japan if the latter were the victim of attack, there was no need for Germany to come to Japan's assistance in an act of aggression. Yet Hitler used this opportunity to declare war on the USA, thus finally bringing America out of its isolationist stance and decisively turning the European war into a World War. A combination of strategic miscalculation – thinking the USA would remain tied up in the Pacific conflicts – and sheer megalomania and desire for 'world mastery' brought Hitler into making this ultimately suicidal move. No longer would America merely support Britain with supplies from the sidelines; now the full force of the world's leading industrial power was entered into the military equation.[2]

By 1942–3, war was being waged on a number of fronts: there were conflicts in south-eastern Europe, desert campaigns in north Africa (with the Germans led by General Rommel), a resistant Britain supported by the USA in the west, and a protracted struggle against the Soviet Union in the east. Relentless air raids were being carried out over Germany itself by the British and American air forces, and fighting continued in Italy even after the fascist leader, Mussolini, had been deposed in July 1943. The burden of war was beginning to tell ever more heavily on the German people, as rations were shortened, labour and housing conditions deteriorated, and menfolk left for the front, often to return with serious injuries – or from whom there might be no news other than, eventually, a black-edged card proclaiming that they had fallen for the Führer and the fatherland. German women and children lived through air raids, surviving in ruined cities, or running their farms with foreign labourers from the occupied territories. While Nazi propaganda continued to proclaim the inevitable victory of the Thousand Year Reich, many Germans lost their faith in their erstwhile apparent saviour and charismatic Führer, and longed merely for a return to 'normality' and peace. Life for many ordinary people at this time was simply a sheer struggle for survival marked by private, familial concerns and personal worries. Insofar as they were aware of the escalating scale of atrocities perpetrated by the regime, they preferred to ignore, suppress, blank out from consciousness what their leaders were co-ordinating and executing in their name.

For it was at precisely this time, as the war was raging on all sides, that Germany entered its darkest hour. It was after the invasion of Russia that the policy of systematic extermination began: the 'Final Solution', which has inevitably coloured all subsequent perceptions and interpretations of German history.

Mass extermination and the Holocaust

From the late summer of 1939, a systematic 'euthanasia' programme had been underway in Germany. This was based on eugenic theories and the alleged need to weed out those deemed to be hereditarily diseased in order to build a 'healthy racial stock'; it was also premissed on the view that a state need not support 'unproductive' or 'worthless' life (*lebensunwertes Leben*). Involuntary sterilization of such people had already begun in January 1934; 'mercy killing' of the mentally handicapped and incurably disabled took this one step further. An order signed by Hitler in October 1939, but dated 1 September (the date of the invasion of Poland), permitted the selection and removal of patients from asylums and sanatoriums, and their transportation to places of execution. Killing was effected in a number of ways: gassing and lethal injections were the most frequent means of administering death. Children with congenital abnormalities might be used first for 'scientific' experiments, with no consideration for their safety since they were in any case to die. Known as the T4 programme, after the Berlin address (Tiergartenstrasse 4) of the section of the Führer's Chancellery which was responsible, the whole operation was conducted in a manner designed to deceive relatives and others concerned. There was a bureaucratic process of informing sanatoria of selections, and later sending certificates to relatives notifying them of some appropriate alleged cause of death (pneumonia, asphyxiation during an asthma attack, or whatever) and offering to forward the urn containing the ashes of the victim, who had been cremated before any post-mortem could be requested. But suspicions began to be aroused, and soon many people were well aware of what was happening to their relatives – some of whom, far from being 'insane', merely suffered from, for example, occasional epileptic fits and were well capable of accurately assessing their situation. There was a growing wave of protest, until finally, on 3 August 1941, an outspoken sermon was delivered by the Bishop of Münster, Clemens August Count von Galen, thousands of copies of which were printed and circulated. Under pressure from this and other protests, Hitler called a halt to the main euthanasia programme on 24 August 1941. But those deemed 'unworthy to live' were still, in smaller numbers and less systematic ways, encouraged or allowed to die in asylums in the following years, through enforced malnutrition, administration of inappropriate medication, or heightened susceptibility to the inadequate treatment of disease. In all, over seventy thousand people were directly killed as a result of the 'euthanasia' programme.

If Germans rallied in protest against the selection and murder of members of their own families and communities, they were less vociferous about the fate of those with whom they felt no such close bonds. Widespread indifference characterized the response of many Germans to the fate of the European Jews and others killed in the extermination camps after the formal termination of the euthanasia programme. Those whom the Nazis deemed, on the basis of certain spuriously scientific quasi-biological theories, to be unfit to live included categories of people other than Jews: Jehovah's Witnesses, homosexuals, and those considered to be subnormal, were also despised, and although far smaller in numbers than the Jewish community, the European gypsy community suffered proportionately greater losses, being nearly obliterated. In numerical terms, the largest number of victims were Jews. The name given by the Jews to Hitler's Final Solution, *Shoah* or Holocaust, refers to a sacrificial burnt offering. While essentially a misnomer, it has come to stand for the whole policy of mass extermination for which Hitler's Germany has attained its place of historical infamy.

Hitler's anti-Semitism had been evident throughout his political career, and had formed a major part of NSDAP ideology, although it was given varying degrees of public emphasis at different times.[3] That Jews were 'not desired' in the 'New Germany' after 1933 had become quite clear, with the escalating series of measures stripping Jews of their citizenship rights and making life increasingly uncomfortable in the pre-war years. But there is a major difference between anti-Semitism as expressed in policies of exclusion from the 'national community' – however vile and inhumane – and the almost unimaginable qualitative leap to the bureaucratically organized mass killing of millions of children, old people, women and men.

The precise number of those killed will probably never be known with certainty. But in any event, to speak in terms of statistics – was it nearer four million or six million, under or over six million, sixty per cent or seventy per cent of the previous population? – cannot convey the enormity of the phenomenon, the unthinkable nature of the Nazi programme of genocide. It is clearly almost impossible to write about, to seek to summarize and 'explain'. Any attempt at brief description will inevitably be inadequate; but an attempt must be made.

For those fortunate enough never to have witnessed the Holocaust at first hand, or to have had close acquaintance with the sufferings of those affected, it can only be conceived if one attempts to imagine it in concrete, small-scale terms: one train arriving in Auschwitz station, shunting off down the siding into the extermination camp of Auschwitz-Birkenau, entering through the infamous watch-tower gate; passengers falling exhausted from the train, half-crazed with thirst, covered in excrement, among them those who had died on the journey; being lined up for 'selection' for work duties or immediate death, being whipped and insulted along the platform, jostled, cajoled and hit into the 'showers' for disinfection; the kicks, screams, cries, tears, fainting, bravado, farewells; the undressing in faint hope and widespread disbelief in the stories about showers and delousing; the crowding into the gas chamber and brief struggle in the dark against the unavoidable death with Zyklon B gas; the crematorium and disposal of the ashes. The whole process, with the tumultuous, noisy arrival of a train carrying hundreds of people, through its emptying, cleaning and silent return on the tracks back to the west, need last only three hours or so; it is described in terrifying detail by eyewitnesses and survivors in Claud Lanzmann's film *Shoah*. Polish peasants working in the fields nearby, with horses pulling carts of hay – as they still do today – would see the trains go in full, hear the cries, see the smoke from the chimneys, smell its stench for miles – and see the trains leave empty. To attempt to imagine it in this way – the sudden, complete, final end of a particular train load of people, and the endless repetition of this process, camouflaged in the language of objectivity and heroism of the perpetrators – can help to begin to make the statistics more real. To see the piles of discarded clothes, spectacles, shoes, cooking implements, human hair, all carefully collected by the SS, gives some inkling of the realities of lives that had been truncated, terminated. To see the drawings of children from Theresienstadt is to apprehend the nature of young life that recorded, in all the simplicity of children's drawings, everyday experiences: festivals at home, butterflies and family scenes – and gallows and corpses that were the current reality. And to read, below each drawing, the dates of the child artist's life – 'Born —, 1935; died Oświęcim (Auschwitz) 1944' – is to choke on the criminality of the Nazi policy of extermination.

It is necessary to confront these realities if attempts to explain Nazi genocide are not to be reduced to an intellectual game, a dry debate among academics or a political curiosity belonging to another era. It is necessary, however, also to rise above a mere contemplation of these realities – accompanied by emotions ranging from an infinite sadness for all those unknown people whose lives and futures were taken away so brutally, to anger and bafflement in relation to the perpetrators of the evil – and to go beyond simply denouncing and abominating this crime. For simply recounting the evil does not attribute causality or explore responsibility: or, insofar as it does, there is the implication that the culprits were a small band of criminals, and no further analysis is required. It is notable that many West German popular histories of Germany treat the Holocaust in this way: a sad story, we raise our hands in horror or hang our heads in shame, this exonerates us, and fortunately it is all over now.[4] But the Holocaust demands more serious analysis and raises a series of questions which must be confronted rationally, however unanswerable they may ultimately prove to be.

Among the many questions associated with the Holocaust, perhaps the following are the most important. How did it come about that the Nazis embarked on a policy of radical physical extermination, an extraordinary attempt simply to kill every single person they considered to belong to a particular category? Was it intended all along, or was it in some way the consequence of general radicalization in wartime? How was it actually possible to execute such policies: how was the co-operation or compliance of both perpetrators and victims achieved; and why was there not more public outcry and opposition, both in Germany and abroad, no serious attempt to halt the mass extermination of people? First, however, a brief factual account must be given.

The concentration camps which had been set up in Nazi Germany from March 1933 onwards had been camps for political prisoners and other 'undesirables' in which there was forced labour (with a range of satellite camps or *Aussenlager*) and in which conditions were by any standards terrible. There was overcrowding, inadequate food, poor sanitary facilities, and cruel and harsh treatment which might often result in intended or unintended death. Disease, starvation, torture, shooting and hanging were all common. But before 1941 there were no camps primarily devoted to killing people. The qualitative leap came in 1941 with the invasion of Russia: following the Army were four *Einsatzgruppen*, special task forces whose job it was to round up Jews and kill them. The Jews would be collected together and taken to a suitable spot, usually in woods near the place of collection, where they would dig their own mass grave and then, in groups, undress and line up in front of the grave to be shot. The first mass killings took place in the forest of Rumbuli near Riga. There were problems with this method of killing: those who did the actual shooting often required considerable quantities of alcohol before they could begin, and it was a relatively public spectacle, with many unintentional witnesses (such as engineers working on nearby road construction projects) as well as partial collaboration, and sometimes also conflict, with local Army units. Nor could the numbers killed, although large, begin to add up to a total 'solution' of the 'Jewish question', if complete removal of Jews from occupied territories were the aim.

Actual physical extermination of the Jews had not necessarily been intended all along – a question we shall return to in a moment. On 24 April 1940 a directive of the Reich Security Main Office (RSHA) attempted to encourage Jewish emigration. After the defeat of France in June 1940, plans had been seriously considered for resettlement of the Jews in Madagascar. In preparation for this, Jews were deported from Alsace and Lorraine to southern France. However, the attack on Russia in June 1941 made the Madagascar plan appear unrealistic, as there seemed no prospect of an early end to the war, and the idea was dropped. In the mean time, there had been moves to create a Jewish reservation in the territory of Lublinland, south-east of Warsaw, in Poland. Jewish ghettoes had been created in Łódź (April 1940), a large industrial city (frequently said to be Poland's Manchester) now incorporated in the Warthegau, and in the autumn of 1940 the Warsaw ghetto was established. Jews from western areas of Poland and from the Greater German Reich were deported to these ghettos and to the Lublin area. By the summer of 1941, the situation of overcrowding, malnutrition and disease was dreadful. Formerly civilized, cultured human beings were reduced to shivering, starving, ailing bundles of rags, a living caricature of the way in which the Nazis attempted to portray and dehumanize the objects of their persecution. At the beginning of October 1941 *SS-Brigadeführer* Dr Friedrich Übelhör, who was in charge of the Łódź ghetto, protested to Himmler about further deportations from the Reich, claiming that he could not cope with any more Jews.

There is some debate among historians about whether Hitler gave an order for the physical extermination of the Jews some time in the course of the summer or autumn of 1941. No written order has been found as yet, and in any case such an order from Hitler would be more likely to have been given orally, making known to associates what was 'the Führer's wish'. We shall return to the question of debates over the genesis of the Final Solution in a moment. What is clear is that by the end of 1941 death was no longer a matter of overwork, malnutrition, disease, or mass shootings. The euthanasia programme had been at least formally terminated in response to public outcry from relatives, church people and others. But the techniques learnt on the euthanasia programme of 1939–41 were transported to the death camps in the east.

The first camp to use gassing for systematic extermination was at Chełmno (Kulmhof), north-west of Łódź. Jews were transported there, collected for 'delousing' in an old castle, herded into vans which had the exhaust pipes directed back into the van, and then driven around until they died from carbon monoxide poisoning. Their bodies were dumped in mass graves in nearby woods. This process started on 5 December 1941. By the end of May 1942 at least fifty-five thousand Jews had been deported from the Łódź ghetto and gassed at Chełmno, as well as around five thousand gypsies. But this operation was nevertheless on a comparatively small scale, and technically inefficient. In the course of 1942, a number of camps were set up specifically to kill large numbers of people as quickly and unobtrusively as possible. Under the so-called 'Reinhard Action' (retrospectively named after Reinhard Heydrich, who was assassinated in Prague in May 1942), camps were established at Bełżec (starting operations in March 1942 and continuing until December 1942), Sobibor (in operation from the end of April 1942 until 14 October 1943) and Treblinka (July 1942 until August 1943). Prisoner uprisings precipitated the already planned closures of the latter two camps. Between them, these camps 'achieved' the liquidation of the vast majority of Polish Jews deported from the ghettoes; a further forty thousand remaining in labour camps in the Lublin area were summarily slaughtered in November 1943 in the so-called 'Operation Harvest Festival'. The Reinhard Action made considerable use of both the expertise and the personnel of the euthanasia programme, with T4 staff being transferred straight to the east. As Gerald Fleming puts it:

A straight path leads from the built-in gas chambers of the euthanasia institutes in Brandenburg, Bensburg, Grafeneck, Hartheim, Hadamer, Sonnenstein, and Eichberg to the extermination camp in Sobibor, under SS-Major Christian Wirth, formerly of the euthanasia institute

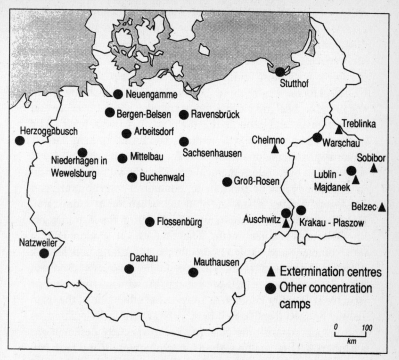

Major concentration camps, including extermination centres

in Brandenburg. In the euthanasia institutes German victims – chiefly mental patients – were 'quickly and quietly' eliminated with carbon-monoxide gas; and already in June 1940 the practice of pilfering gold-filled teeth from the corpses of Jewish victims among them had begun. At Sobibor, identical liquidation procedures, along with the same despoliation of Jewish corpses, were the order of the day.[5]

The camp whose name has become the most infamous international symbol of the Holocaust was of course Auschwitz. An Austrian army barracks existed in the Upper Silesian town of Oświęcim (Auschwitz), which became incorporated in the Greater German Reich, and was not part of the General Government (as were the extermination camps further east). This barracks was used as a prison and labour camp, largely occupied by Poles, from 1940, under Camp Commandant Rudolf Hoess. From these beginnings, the Auschwitz camp expanded to become an enormous complex spread over several kilometres in and around the town of Auschwitz itself. The original camp, which was named Auschwitz I, held largely political prisoners (of whom Jews formed a minority) and was the scene of horrendous medical experiments, including surgical interventions without anaesthetic, compulsory sterilization, and Dr Josef Mengele's studies of twins which often culminated in killing them and examining the effects of the experiments on their organs after death. The first use of Zyklon-B as a more efficient and easily obtainable gas for killing people took place in Auschwitz I. Its use was to be hideously extended with the construction of a new camp, Auschwitz-Birkenau, or Auschwitz II, a few kilometres away on the other side of the main railway line. Killings started here in 1942; gradually techniques were improved, with the construction of specially designed gas chambers and crematoria, the largest of which, it was boasted, could 'process' up to three thousand people a day, although individual transports were never quite that large. When all the gas chambers and crematoria were in operation it was possible to kill over nine thousand people within twenty-four hours – a figure achieved one day in the summer of 1944.[6] 'Selections' of those fit to work, and those designed to go straight to the gas chambers, initially took place on the main Auschwitz station, and then, when the side line had been constructed, on the long platform or 'ramp' in Auschwitz-Birkenau itself. A third camp in the Auschwitz complex was at Monowitz, whose inmates worked for I. G. Farben's new Buna plant at Dwory. The Auschwitz camps also supplied labour for a number of other German firms, including Krupp, Borsig, and Siemens. The area covered by this complex of camps was large, interpenetrating the local industrial and residential areas, and the fields worked by Polish peasants lay alongside the barbed wire and watchtowers of the factory of death. This was no isolated, hidden extermination centre in the less populated east, outside the German Reich, but rather was a major enterprise straddling the main railway line from the west: a large-scale organization for exploiting human labour, experimenting on human subjects, and killing train-load after train-load of people, whose trains, organized by hundreds of bureaucrats in the German railway system, arrived full and departed empty, according to timetable. The smoke and the stench from the chimneys could not be ignored by inhabitants or passers-by for miles around. The myth that mass killings took place so far from human civilization that the news could not have filtered out cannot be sustained.

The Reinhard Action camps had killed most of the Polish Jews; Jews from Germany and western Europe and other occupied countries were in the main transported to Auschwitz. A major staging-post was in the Czech town of Terezin, or Theresienstadt. This eighteenth-century fortified town, with its walls and fort, (named after the then Austrian ruler, Maria Theresa), provided both a political prison (in the fort) and a ghetto (in the main town). In the latter, the Jews were allowed a large degree of self-government, extending even to their own postal system, and there was a considerable level of artistic and cultural activity. Despite the overcrowding, malnutrition, and repression by terror, this transit camp helped to sustain the fiction that the deported Jews were simply being 'resettled' in the East. Many Jews from western Europe, despite apprehension, went to the deportation trains in the hope and belief that stories of resettlement were true – clinging to arguments such as that the Nazis would not have given such precise instructions about what possessions to bring for their new life if there were to be no such life. These shreds of hope were given forlorn nourishment when a group of families from Theresienstadt were taken to Auschwitz and held under relatively favourable conditions in the 'family camp' at Birkenau, where they were forced to write misleadingly happy postcards to friends and relatives at home. Even the arrival of a few postcards led people in the west to continue to hope for the

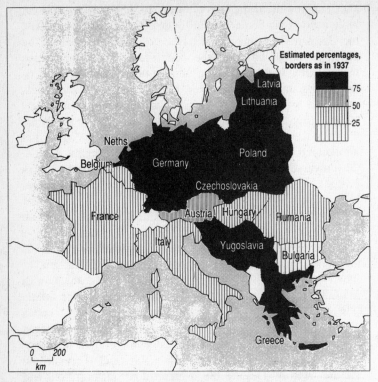

Proportion of Europe's Jewish population murdered in the
Final Solution

silent survival of many more who had, in actuality, long since
perished.

What were the final statistics of the Final Solution? This is
almost a meaningless question, but statistics must be attempted.
Estimates vary, but at least 4·2 million and probably over 6
million Jews were killed; the latter figure is probably nearest
the truth. (In the Nuremberg trials, the figure of 5·7 million
was given.) On the highest estimates, perhaps 80–90 per cent
of the pre-war Jewish populations of Poland, Czechoslovakia,
Lithuania, Latvia, Yugoslavia, Greece, Holland and Germany
were exterminated.[7]

What role did Hitler and Hitler's rabid anti-Semitism play in the genesis of the Final Solution? This question is closely related to debates about the structure of the Nazi state.

On the one hand, the so-called intentionalists perceive the Holocaust as the straightforward outcome of Hitler's ideological world-view. In the words of Gerald Fleming, 'the line that leads from these early manifestations [of Hitler's congenital hatred for the Jews] to the liquidation orders that Hitler personally issued during the war . . . is a direct one.' Fleming perceives a 'single, unbroken and fatal continuum'.[8] According to Lucy Dawidowicz, the 'mass murder of the Jews was the consummation of [Hitler's] fundamental beliefs and ideological conviction'. She continues: 'The nexus between idea and act has seldom been as evident in human history with such manifest consistency as in the history of anti-Semitism . . . [N]ot until Hitler's accession to power in Germany and his domination over Europe had the abstract idea of Jew-hatred assumed so terrible a concrete and visible reality . . . For Hitler's ideas about the Jews were the starting place for the elaboration of a monstrous racial ideology that would justify mass murder whose like history had not seen before.'[9]

On the other hand, the so-called functionalists query this line of interpretation. Rather than seeing the Holocaust as the direct, logical outcome of a system of pre-existing ideas and intentions, historians such as Hans Mommsen and Martin Broszat emphasize rather the fumbling, improvisational way in which anti-Semitic policies developed. As Hans Mommsen put it: the development of anti-Jewish measures was 'not . . . a result of a single plan but . . . a consequence of a combination of uncoordinated strategies. While Hitler supported this process ideologically, he never designed it . . .'[10] In Mommsen's view, 'intra-party rivalries as well as those between the party and state agencies contributed decisively to what can be described as a process of cumulative radicalisation.'[11] While Martin Broszat agrees with Lucy Dawidowicz that Hitler's 'fanatic-pathological' ideological views are indispensable to the explanation, he argues that the historian must still examine the actual ways in which ideology was transformed into reality, and the ways in which the constraints of circumstances and the mediation of institutions and individuals affected, even distorted, this translation from theory into practice.[12] Broszat sees mass killing as an 'improvised' solution which was not set in motion by a single Hitler order but rather emerged, bit by bit, as the only way of disposing of the increasing numbers of Jews collected up in Eastern Europe. Granted that the basic aim was to 'cleanse' Germany's empire of Jews (make it *Judenrein*), a number of different possible means could be considered, including the Madagascar plan mentioned above. It was only the combination of factors in the winter of 1941–2 which rendered mass killing the 'solution'. The reversal of the war's fortunes meant that vast areas for resettlement in the east would not be available; at the same time, however, the violence of wartime, the transgression of moral norms incurred by the mass shootings, and the deteriorating conditions in the ghettos, made the purging of the 'Jewish bacillus' by physical liquidation more possible to contemplate. Local initiatives were finally co-ordinated into a more coherent overall policy at the Wannsee conference of January 1942.

The debate has proceeded on a number of levels: the level of interpretation of available empirical evidence; the more general level of overall modes of interpretation of the regime's dynamics as a whole; and the moral level of the implications for allocation of guilt and responsibility. It is perhaps the latter which has rendered the debate so acrimonious. Yet neither side seeks seriously to downplay the role and responsibility of Hitler. Broszat, for example, stresses the intense personal interest of Hitler in the progress of the Final Solution. He also argues that, since aspects of the extermination of the Jews (such as their transportation, and the loss of Jews from the labour force engaged in war industries) were against the interests of the Army, policies could only be forced through against Army protests with Hitler's backing. There is no attempt to exonerate Hitler from blame; on the other hand, the shift of emphasis away from ideology to conditions of execution of policy does involve the implication of other groups and individuals in a measure of guilt. At the empirical level, historians by and large agree that the search for a written Hitler order to resolve the issue is probably a waste of time, since it is in any case unlikely

– given both Hitler's work habits, and his known desire to camouflage the Final Solution, even linguistically – that such an order would ever have been issued in written form. There is probably little more light to be shed on the question of whether and when Hitler might have either set in motion, or given his blessing to, the policies of killing Jews in large numbers in Eastern Europe in the late summer and autumn of 1941.[13]

What is quite clear is that Hitler's fanatic anti-Semitism provided the context, motivation and legitimization for the mass extermination programme; and that while, for purposes of public popularity, he might have downplayed his fanaticism for long periods of time, his oft-repeated 'prophecy' made in a speech to the Reichstag on 30 January 1939 that a war would bring the destruction of the Jewish race in Europe was undoubtedly a manifestation of earnest intent. Obviously the precise manner of execution of this policy depended on unfolding circumstances.

Hitler's role is far from the only serious question associated with the Holocaust, and the intentionalist–functionalist debate has probably exhausted all relevant aspects. As important are the roles of others involved – or failing to be involved – with the process. After the war, there were reactions of shock and horror as pictures of liberated concentration camps began to be published. For Americans, 'Dachau' came to symbolize the evils of Nazism, while the word 'Belsen' to describe extreme degrees of emaciation entered the English language simply because the camp of Bergen-Belsen happened to be the first to be encountered by the British. The world threw up its hands in supposedly innocent horror; the Germans, forced to confront the criminal acts committed in their name, professed to have known nothing of it. But were these protestations of innocence and expressions of horror merely the belated cover-up for previous sins of omission?

It is quite clear that very many people in Germany did know, if not the details, then at least the general thrust of anti-Semitic policy in wartime Germany. There were enough witnesses on the eastern front, enough couriers and postal services, enough avenues of communication even in wartime Europe, for a large number of Germans to have been reliably informed that exterminations were taking place. Even if, as Walter Laqueur points out, those Germans who knew that the Jews were being killed *en masse* constituted only a small percentage of the population, this small percentage would still amount to several million people. In Laqueur's view, 'by the end of 1942, millions in Germany knew that the Jewish question had been radically solved, and that this radical solution did not involve resettlement, in short, that most, or all of those who had been deported were no longer alive.'[14] Similarly, it is clear that news of the extermination of the Jews was reaching foreign governments from a wide range of sources. While details and numbers might have been inaccurate, the general picture that Hitler was systematically killing as many of the Jews of Europe as he could emerged quite clearly. In June 1942, the British newspaper the *Daily Telegraph* was the first to report the gassing of 700,000 Jews; by the end of 1942 the knowledge of techniques and aims, if not actual numbers of killings, was widespread in the occupied countries, among the neutrals, and the allies.

There was however a difference between receiving factual information, and believing in its reality, not to mention acting upon it. For one thing, the propaganda stories about alleged atrocities in the First World War predisposed people to a certain scepticism in relation to these new stories. For another, the very nature of the Final Solution is almost beyond imagining. Sheer doubt about the literally 'incredible' news might be compounded by a more moderate anti-Semitism on the part of the recipient of the news; in Laqueur's view, this played a role in the British Foreign Office's unwillingness to publicize the news of the Holocaust.[15] Moreover, it must not be forgotten that in wartime, there were other, more immediate preoccupations: mere daily survival, and wartime strategy, took priority. In the end, there were many reasons why the news of the Holocaust did not produce action. In Laqueur's summary:

> The failure to read correctly the signs in 1941–2 was only one link in a chain of failures. There was not one reason for this overall failure but many different ones: paralysing fear on the one hand and, on the contrary, reckless optimism

on the other; disbelief stemming from a lack of experience or imagination or genuine ignorance or a mixture of some or all of these things. In some cases the motives were creditable, in others damnable. In some instances moral categories are simply not applicable, and there were also cases which defy understanding to this day.[16]

No doubt that aspect of the Final Solution which proves most resistant to understanding is the question of how the perpetrators were actually able to carry it out. Again, there can be no one simple and all-encompassing answer to this question. Different groups, with different constraints and considerations, were involved in different aspects of the process. For those Jewish prisoners who had to empty the gas chambers and load the corpses into the crematoria, the alternative to compliance was of course immediate death. One survivor speaks with retrospective horror, in Claud Lanzmann's film *Shoah*, about the way in which his own survival depended on the continued deaths of others. It was known, too, that convicted criminals were used to help staff concentration camps; and there was inevitably considerable coercion exercised over the lower levels of organizational personnel. Perhaps more problematic are the mentalities of the bureaucrats who made the machinery function, and the leaders of the SS and others who spearheaded the programme. On the one hand, there was an attempt both to 'objectify' and dehumanize the process, making use of technical language not only to camouflage the real nature of what was happening, but also to make it psychologically possible to continue the operations. (Terms such as 'special treatment' and 'processing' stood in for killing.) There was also an attempt to dehumanize the victims, both linguistically, describing Jews in medical terms as dangerous bacilli which would infect the healthy community, and in actuality, by reducing them to gaunt bestiality with few remnants of individual humanity. Despite such techniques, it is still clear that the process was by no means one with which even Himmler could be comfortable: he returns again and again in his speeches to the problem of the deed whose history must not be written; his reiterated attempts at justification reveal the need for reassurance about the long-term historical importance of the action, and the moral qualms which had repeatedly to be suppressed by members of the SS.[17] (Himmler himself vomited when he witnessed gassings.) The shaping of the ethos of the SS itself, with its stress on notions such as *Härte* (hardness), and its techniques of inculcation of obedience, was itself complex and problematic.[18] The long-term psychological legacies of the Holocaust, for perpetrators as well as bystanders, survivors, and their children, have by no means been exhaustively examined. As we shall see, the process of 'denazification' after the war bore little serious relation to the realities of what took place in Germany during these years.

Resistance and defeat

While Jews, gypsies, homosexuals, Christian and political opponents of Nazism were being killed, the war was raging across Europe, north Africa, and the Pacific, claiming the lives of millions more, whether active soldiers or civilians at home. With the defeat of the Germans at Stalingrad, the truth became clear even to the most fanatical Nazis: Germany was not destined to become master of the world, and the Thousand Year Reich was rapidly heading for its *Götterdämmerung*, its collapse in ruins. The war-weary German people turned in on themselves; and Hitler himself became more and more of a recluse, refusing to make public appearances, and increasingly retreating to the relative isolation of his 'Wolf's Lair' in East Prussia, surrounded only by a small circle of sycophants and trusted advisers.

There were courageous individuals who attempted, in one way or another, to protest against and even sabotage the ever more evil regime. Even in the peacetime years, around a quarter of a million Germans, largely of left-wing sympathies, had been imprisoned or forced to emigrate because of their political opposition. At least 150,000 German Communists and Social Democrats had been put into concentration camps; about 40,000 had emigrated for political (rather than racial) reasons; around 12,000 had been convicted of high treason, attempting to overthrow the government; and perhaps 40,000 had been sent to prison for lesser political crimes – and all this *before* the outbreak of war and associated radicalization of brutality.[19] Sometimes such opponents of the regime acted as individuals; others were associated with small opposition cells, such as the left-wing group known as 'New Beginning'.

Most of this clandestine resistance was limited to such activities as the publication and circulation of subversive newspapers; there was little that ordinary opponents of the regime could do, far as they were from the centres of power and influence. The one left-wing group with members in high places was the so-called Red Orchestra, including Harro Schulze-Boysen and Arvid Harnack, who were able to pass military and economic intelligence reports to the Russian secret service after the invasion of the Soviet Union. Other left-wingers, such as the trade unionist Julius Leber, or the Social Democrat Wilhelm Leuschner, sought to foster contacts with army and conservative opponents of the regime. Many could simply hope to keep a flame of morality alive amid the indifference, the compromises, and acquiescence in evil. In Munich, a group known as the 'White Rose', associated with the Catholic students Hans and Sophie Scholl, produced and distributed large numbers of leaflets intended to arouse public opposition to Hitler's dictatorship. Idealistic quotations from Goethe and Schiller were interlaced with urgings to their fellow citizens to rise against the system, or at least to help the resistance by duplicating and spreading as many leaflets as possible. These young people – apart from Professor Huber, members of the White Rose group were in their twenties – risked their lives to protest against an evil regime. Their activities lasted from the summer of 1942 until February 1943, when the Scholls were arrested and executed. Others – Probst, Schmorell, Graf and Huber – were also put to death later in the year for their part in the group. Even individual acts might be of some limited effect: in Berlin alone, for example, some four thousand Jews were able to go into hiding and survive the war through the help of their 'Aryan' German friends. Despite widespread indifference and apathy, many Germans retained a certain decency and civic courage on a personal level. But, unfortunately for the fate of millions, these individuals remained mostly an isolated minority:

there was no broad, co-ordinated mass movement against the Nazi regime.[20] Nor, by and large, did many ordinary Germans have much hope of even coming close to Hitler, let alone toppling him and replacing the Nazi regime with any realistic alternative form of government.

Those in elite positions in the army and government were, however, in such a situation; and it is the rather belated attempt at resistance to Hitler in the 'July Plot' of 1944 which for decades was celebrated in West Germany as *the* opposition to Hitler, and as evidence of 'another', democratic, Germany. Clearly the personal courage and moral integrity of those involved in this plot is not in question. It took considerable bravery on the part of Colonel Claus Schenk Count von Stauffenberg – who had been seriously injured on the Russian front, incurring the loss of an eye and his right hand – to play his role in transporting a bomb to Hitler's headquarters at the Wolf's Lair, and placing it in a briefcase by the table where Hitler was involved in discussing military strategy. Had subsequent events gone otherwise – had the full quantity of explosives been prepared for detonation, had the briefcase not been pushed under what turned out to be an extremely solid table – Hitler might have been killed by the blast rather than coming away with minor injuries and a ruined pair of trousers. Then the subsequent course of German history might have run rather differently. As it was, Stauffenberg returned to Berlin under the impression that all had gone according to plan, and plans for the governmental coup were set in motion before it was realised, too late, that Hitler had indeed survived the blast. Those closely involved in the conspiracy were shot the same night; others were arrested and executed later; a couple were able to commit suicide. In the ensuing reprisals, there was what can only be described as an orgy of generalised political repression. In the winter of 1944–5, around five thousand people were executed after 'trials' in the so-called 'People's Court' under its notorious President, Roland Freisler. And the slightest muttering of discontent, refusal to believe in inevitable victory, listening in to foreign radio broadcasts, or repeating of low political jokes against prominent Nazis, was sufficient to occasion arrest and even death. The individual case histories at Berlin's Plötzensee jail provide chilling evidence of this final phase of Nazi terror.

Those involved in the July Plot, for all their individual integrity and courage, have come under belated posthumous criticism on a number of counts. For one thing, despite all earlier discussion of resistance, in the event plans had been postponed and shelved until very late, when it was quite clear that the war was lost. Against this, it might be said that by this stage the Allies would have accepted nothing less than unconditional surrender whatever the nature of the regime; but it still seems clear that members of the conservative resistance were hesitant about attempting a coup at a time when German military fortunes were on the ascendant. For another, for all the differences of view represented among the conspirators, on the whole these conservative opponents of Hitler were not committed democrats. Clearly there were variations. For example, the nationalist Carl Goerdeler distanced himself from the ideas being elaborated by the so-called 'Kreisau Circle' (named after the Silesian estate of Count Hellmuth James Moltke, where it met). This group, which first met in 1940 and continued with a series of meetings in 1942–3, encompassed a fairly broad spectrum, including Christian and socialist reformism as well as conservative-nationalism, with links ranging from Adam von Trott to the socialists Adolf Reichswein and Julius Leber. But what plans were provisionally formulated for the post–Hitler government suggested little sympathy for notions of pluralist democracy, and little perception of the need for any popular legitimation of the new government. As Hans Mommsen has put it, the July Plotters 'saw themselves as a political leading caste, and their claim to represent "the whole" as legitimate simply by reason of their social position and concomitant political responsibilities.'[21] Under the conditions in which they were operating, the most important thing was to oust Hitler: to restore a state of law and justice, and to put an end to the corruption, inhumanity and fanaticism of Nazi rule. It was less easy to provide clear guidelines for what sort of constitutional arrangements should ultimately be put in place in any post-war regime – and with their sympathies for German soldiers fighting on the front, the plotters felt these too should have a say in their future. As far as foreign policy was concerned, there was desire for peace – but this had to be a 'just and lasting' peace, unlike the Treaty of Versailles.[22] For all the differences of opinion, the prevailing political orientation of those involved in the July Plot can be said to have been a form of traditional conservative authoritarianism, rather than any preview of Bonn democracy, however much the latter may have laid claim to the July Plotters as celebrated forebears.

In the event, however, the July Plotters had no chance to develop any sort of post-Hitler government. Hitler survived to preside over the devastation and ruin of the succeeding months. Following a successful landing in Normandy by the western Allies on 6 June 1944, combined with decisive advances by the Soviet Army on the eastern front, the Germans were increasingly beleaguered. Hopes were raised by talk of new, secret weapons, and by a German counter-offensive in the spring of 1945. But, with the Allied crossing of the Rhine and the Red Army coming ever closer to Berlin, it became increasingly clear that all was lost. While thousands fled their homes in the east, starting the treks westwards in advance of the dreaded Soviet troops, those who had profited from the Nazi regime attempted to salvage their booty and hide the traces of their misdeeds. Concentration camps were cleared and the half-starved inmates forced into long marches to other locations, while Nazi bigwigs tried to conceal their stolen works of art, gold and jewellery, casks of wine and other luxury goods. Amidst all the devastation and destruction, the loss of life and tragedy, with the clear realization that the end was near, Hitler proclaimed the 'scorched earth' policy: Germans must never surrender, but fight to the last. If the Germans were not strong enough to be victors, then they deserved to be vanquished, annihilated – Hitler was true to his Social Darwinist views to the last. The depleted German troops were replenished by old men and young boys, hastily thrown into uniform and sent as sacrifices to Hitler's fanaticism. Finally, as the Red Army closed in on the ruins of Berlin itself, Hitler took his own way out of the catastrophe he had brought down on Germany. On 29 April 1945, in his bunker in Berlin, Hitler married his long-time faithful friend Eva Braun; on 30 April, the two of them committed suicide, and their remains were partially incinerated by members of Hitler's entourage.

The Thousand Year Reich lay in ruins. The Germans surrendered to the western and Soviet victors on 7 and 8 May. A short-lived government under Hitler's allotted successor, Admiral von Dönitz, was finally wound up on 23 May 1945, when the victorious powers took over control of the defeated country. As the Allies explored the terrain they had overcome, the scale of problems facing them appeared ever more immense: lack of housing, communications, sanitation; displaced persons on the move, whether refugees, returning soldiers, foreign labourers, released concentration camp inmates, or prisoners of war; malnutrition, disease, disorientation; a population in a state of physical and moral collapse. And the wartime alliance of convenience between western democrats and Soviet communists was by no means a firm base for securing a united set of consistent policies to deal with this extraordinary situation.

Far from resolving the tensions which had troubled the short-lived democracy of the Weimar Republic, Hitler had exacerbated them. Internal social divisions had been 'solved' by radical displacement: 'national renewal' could only be attempted by removing those who disagreed, imprisoning them and killing them; the united 'national community' could only be sought for by stigmatising, separating, and ultimately murdering those who were deemed to pollute its 'purity'. Divisions within were displaced also by the ultimately catastrophic division without of war, engulfing the world in a conflict of unprecedented scale. Hitler's 'achievement' ultimately lay in total destruction and total defeat. A cycle appeared to have run its course, and many of the protagonists in the previous drama had been, or were about to be, written out of the script. In the following four years under military occupation, international events were to impose a new form of division, and one that for nearly half a century seemed to solve the problem at least of domestic political stability: the division of the German nation and the formation of two quite different German states.

PART TWO

THE DIVIDED NATION

The Two Germanies,
1945–90

SIX

Occupation and Division, 1945–9

When Germany was defeated in May 1945, a demoralized population was living among ruins. The big cities that had suffered bombardment from the air were reduced to piles of rubble between gaunt, hollow shells of bombed out buildings, lone walls with empty windows forming a jagged skyline, the occasional intact building standing out starkly amidst the ruins. People eked out an uncomfortable existence in cellars. In towns and villages which had escaped the worst attacks of the Allies, conditions were nevertheless comparably demoralizing, as women worried about husbands and sons at the front, and about the need for food and clothing for the children and old people at home. Enthusiasm for Hitler, and for his war, had been waning steadily since the turn of the war's fortunes with the Russian campaign, and faith in the omnipotent Führer had given way to weariness and a longing for the end of war. Yet there was no knowing exactly what the post-war period would bring. Some Germans longed for 'liberation' and the possibility of a radical transformation of Germany; others felt fear and ambivalence about future retribution. When hostilities ceased in May 1945, few could have predicted what the future would bring. Yet in the following four years patterns were developed and set which were to stamp their mark on the next four decades of German – and international – history.

The Allies and the framework of political life

Initially the Allies themselves were not at all certain what to do with post-war Germany. There were differences of opinion both between the Allies – particularly between the Soviet Union and the Western powers – and within each Allied regime. In practice, the developments following the defeat of Germany laid the foundations for the double transformation that subsequently occurred: the establishment of a divided nation, with a relatively conservative, arguably 'restorationist' state in the West, and a hardline communist state in the East. In neither Germany was the 'Third Way' taken, for which many democratic, anti-fascist Germans had hoped – the transformation which would combine democracy and socialism, while also permitting German unity and neutrality. While the division and remilitarization of the two Germanies – and their relative 'conservatism', although of differing political complexions – only became crystallized in the course of the 1950s, the initial steps in this bifurcation can be seen even in the very early stages of the occupation period.

During the war, a range of options for the future of Germany – pending what all agreed should be an unconditional surrender – were mooted. Some advocated relatively mild treatment, others harsh and punitive handling; some sought the retention of a relatively centralized, if federal, state, others radical dismemberment and division into a number of smaller countries which could pose no threat to the balance of power in central Europe. There were differences of opinion between, for example, American President Roosevelt and his State Department; British Prime Minister Churchill and the British Military and the British Foreign Office; as well as, more obviously, between the Soviet Union, the Americans and the British. One of the few decisions which emerged from wartime planning which was however to have decisive long-term significance was the agreement on zones of occupation. A map (emanating from the Post-Hostilities Planning Subcommittee in September 1943) was put before the European Advisory Committee in London in January 1944, and accepted by the Soviets in February 1944. This proposed three zones of occupation – and in the event drew the line of what was subsequently to become the East–West division of Europe and the international system. In September 1944 it was agreed that Berlin should be under four-power control, and a little later a Control Commission

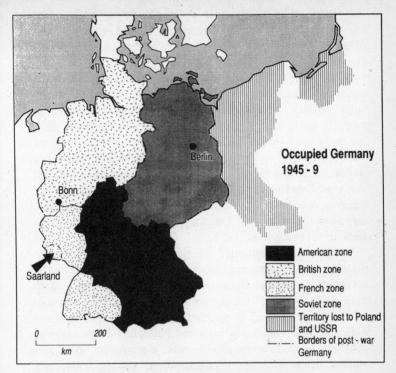

Occupied Germany 1945 - 9

- ■ American zone
- British zone
- French zone
- Soviet zone
- Territory lost to Poland and USSR
- Borders of post - war Germany

Berlin

Bonn

Saarland

0   200
km

The division of Germany after 1945

for the co-ordination of Allied occupation policies was decided upon.

At Teheran (28 November – 1 December 1943) and Yalta (4 – 11 February 1945) there was vague and general agreement in principle on the need to demilitarize, denazify and democractize Germany. It was also agreed at Yalta that France should have a zone of occupation. There was by now some friction and unease over this question: the original zones had been drawn to give rough parity of population numbers in each of the British, American and Soviet zones – thus in effect giving the Soviets a much larger land area, since much of their zone was less densely populated agricultural land. The early agreement over zones had been facilitated by Western fears that the Red Army might in fact have overrun most or all of Germany by the end of the war, and would then be committed or forced to retreat to its previously determined occupation zone. However, in fact by the war's end it was the western allies who had advanced deeper into Germany than they had expected; and it was western troops who eventually had to withdraw from areas that were to form part of the Soviet zone. By the spring of 1945, this position had become clearer, and the western powers hoped that France would gain her zone at the expense of the Soviets. This was however opposed, and France's zone was carved out of western territory in south-west Germany. Disagreements between the Allies also continued over questions concerning the form and level reparations should take, the eastern boundaries of Germany with Poland, and the future shape of Germany itself.

These problems continued to bedevil the Potsdam Conference of 17 July – 2 August 1945. Although the war was over, with the surrender of German troops to the Allies on 7–8 May 1945, there could be no Peace Treaty since there was no German government with which to conclude one. The eventual Protocol of Proceedings emanating from the Potsdam Conference was a vaguely worded compromise – again assenting to broad and laudable aims, such as demilitarization, denazification, and democratization – which left many areas open to a variety of interpretations.

Most potent sources of friction were again the questions of reparations and Polish–German frontiers. The western Allies refused Stalin's demands on reparations, and an agreement was reached by which each power would take its own reparations from its own zone. In addition, the USSR was to get ten per cent from the western Allies, and a further fifteen per cent was to be provided by way of exchanges for food supplies and the like. The reparations agreement both consolidated the relative independence of the zonal administrations, despite the mouthing of assent to the notion of central co-ordination of policy, and provided the basis for subsequent disagreements and divisions between East and West. As the British put it at the time, 'It is inconceivable that a Germany which is not treated as an economic unit could very long be treated as a political unit.'[1]

On the Polish boundary question, a decision had been largely pre-empted by the de facto Soviet interpretation of Poland's western boundary as lying along the western, rather than eastern Neisse river. Poland was to be compensated with additional former German land on the west for losses in the east to the Soviet Union, which expanded westwards, and retained territory (including the Baltic states) taken under the Nazi-Soviet Pact of 1939. While British and American leaders agreed with the moving of Poland's borders in principle, they had understood the eastern Neisse river to be the limit. But under Stalin's interpretation, German inhabitants of the relatively rich Silesian territory between the two branches of the Neisse had already been expelled and Poles settled on the contested land. Given this circumstance, the Oder and western Neisse rivers were provisionally agreed as Poland's western border; but a final decision in principle (rather than simply a *de facto* movement of population) was postponed until a peace conference – which in the event never occurred. (It was only with the unification of the two Germanies in 1990 that the western border of Poland was officially confirmed.) Some commentators have suggested that the bargaining power of the western powers in relation to Stalin was weakened by the fact that Churchill was replaced by Attlee in the course of the Conference, as the results of the British General Election were made known and a Labour administration replaced the Churchill government. A further problem lay in the fact that France, although it was granted a zone of occupation, did not attend the Potsdam Conference and made little subsequent attempt to co-ordinate French occupation policies with those of the British and Americans.

In practice, after the end of hostilities the four zones of occupation were treated in very different ways, with even British and American policies diverging in certain respects. Moreover, there were not necessarily clear or consistent lines of policy within any one zone of occupation. Not only were there differences of opinion among different factions and agencies within (or influencing) the governments of each power; there were also major shifts of policy as the military governments experienced unforeseen difficulties and constraints on policy on the ground; and there was the wider question of changing priorities in the context of changing international relations. In the American zone, for example, the initial policy document – the so-called JCS 1067 – represented the hybrid outcome of a number of divergent policy directions. It retained elements of the brief influence of Morgenthau's draconian proposals for a 'pastoralization' of Germany as well as reflecting other sources of opinion. General Lucius Clay found it open to a wide latitude of interpretation in practice in the American zone, and some of its measures, particularly concerning economic policy, were in any case overtaken by the Potsdam Agreement. JCS 1067 was finally formally jettisoned after major shifts in subsequent American policies (described further below). There were comparable ambiguities and changes in British policy. While American views constituted a major influence on British policy, on many matters of purely British concern the views of the British military government on the ground tended to prevail over those of British politicians at home.[2] In any event, in the period from defeat and occupation in 1945 to the division of Germany in 1949, the aims and practices of all the occupying powers shifted dramatically. While the French were somewhat unwillingly brought to toe the western line, the Soviets initiated quite distinctive policies in their zone. In the unfolding story of transformation and division, it can perhaps be suggested that the attitude of the western powers to western Germany changed more markedly, with 1947 representing a key turning-point. It is time to explore certain aspects of this crucial period of transition in more detail.

The democratization of German politics?

What did the reorganization of German domestic politics look like in the early months after the end of the war? The war's end had been greeted with a range of responses among Germans. On the whole, the political attitudes of most Germans may be characterized in terms of apathy, a weariness in relation to 'politics' and what it brought with it, and an overriding concern with sheer physical survival from day to day. Only a minority at either end of the political spectrum were ideologically committed and active. Certain Nazi diehards were determined to follow Hitler's 'scorched earth' policies and defend their strongholds to the last; other Germans, equally loyal to the defence of their fatherland, felt that it was better served by an orderly handover to the Allied forces, thus protecting life and property. Some feared the consequences of German defeat; others welcomed the prospect of release from oppression and the chance of making a new beginning. A wide spectrum of political tendencies started to emerge from the silence of the Third Reich, with varied hopes for a possible future. In the different zones of occupation, the aspirations of these groups were suppressed, subverted, facilitated or transformed in different ways, as the politics of occupiers and occupied began to interact.

In the closing months of the war, a number of anti-fascist groups had emerged, determined finally to oust the Nazis and take control of local government in order to facilitate what they perceived as their liberation, rather than defeat, by the Allies. The 'non-defence committees' (*Nichtverteidigungs-komitees*) had varying degrees of success in different areas. In some, they were captured and summarily shot by the SS. In others, they were able to have some impact on the course of events. In Bavaria, for example, the *Freiheitsaktion Bayern* (FAB) was a military resistance group linked with conservative resistance circles, with the *Demokratische Bewegung Deutschlands*, and with the Bavarian separatist movement *Bayerische Freiheitsbewegung*, (BFB) as well as with cells in industrial concerns in Munich. Although ultimately unsuccessful in its Munich uprising of 28 April 1945, the FAB was able to avert late Allied bombings of the city and while in control of the local radio station sent out the order of the 'pheasant chase' (*Fasanenjagd*). As a result, the BFB in other areas of Bavaria chased the Nazi 'gold pheasants' (*Goldfasanen*), and although the SS retaliated in some instances, in others the hunt was successful.[3] Such actions were to be important in the formation of a post-war democratic identity, as indicated by the celebration of the FAB by the *Süddeutsche*

Zeitung in the winter and spring of 1945 and 1946; but despite the anti-Nazi credentials of these spontaneous movements the western Allies were to treat them with considerable caution and to suppress their organizational forms while co-opting certain individuals into service under the Military Government.

This disbanding of 'antifas', or indigenous German democratic groups, was symptomatic – in both the western and Soviet zones – of the way in which the Allies sought to impose their own, differing, conceptions of the reorganization of German political life. There has been considerable debate subsequently about notions of 'missed opportunities', suppressed historical alternatives, and avoidable 'restoration'. On some views, the anti-fascist groups, if given appropriate encouragement and support, might have provided the basis for a democratic socialist transformation. Against this, some historians (such as Rolf Steininger) have argued that these groups were insufficiently strong or united to have achieved much by way of positive policies.[4] In any event, the question remains hypothetical, since such organizations were suppressed and disbanded by the Allies, in both west and east. This was a source of considerable disillusionment and disaffection among members of these groups, a disaffection which was later compounded by the political climates of both East and West Germany in the 1950s.

The impact of the occupying power on the reorganization of German political life was most marked in the Soviet zone. Already before the end of the war, in April 1945, a group of Moscow-trained German Communists under the leadership of Walter Ulbricht had been flown in to the area which was to be under Soviet occupation. One of the first measures of the Soviet Military Administration (SMAD) was the licensing of political parties, in order to legitimize the existence and activities of the KPD. The KPD, under Soviet direction, rapidly sought to take control of all key positions in local administration – often choosing a non-Communist, such as a respected member of the local community with impeccable 'non-political', 'bourgeois' or moderate credentials, for the formal figurehead position (such as mayor), while a Communist wielded the real power in a secondary post. This is not to suggest that the KPD did not encounter problems. There were tensions and differences of view both between the German Communists and their Soviet masters, as well as within the KPD itself. Those members of the KPD who had weathered the Third Reich in exile in the west, or underground in Germany, or who re-emerged from imprisonment, often subscribed to a humanistic version of communism which differed considerably from the Stalinist variant propagated by the Moscow faction. Nevertheless, the KPD certainly enjoyed a privileged position in the emerging political life of the Soviet zone, and at first felt strong enough to resist overtures towards unification from the Social Democratic Party (SPD), which had lost little time in re-founding itself.

Other parties soon founded in the Soviet zone included the Christian Democratic Union (CDU), a German-wide party of former Catholic Centre party members and former conservative and nationalist Protestants – thus seeking to form a conservative party with a wider constituency of support than the narrow confessional basis of the earlier Centre party. Similarly, the liberal LDPD sought to bring together a variety of liberal views. Initially, these parties were independent; in the event, their members and leaders were subjected very soon to immense pressures, such that by the time of the foundation of the GDR in 1949 they had become more or less puppets of the Communists. Two further parties in the Soviet zone were actually founded as Communist puppet parties: the NDPD to encompass people of right-wing, nationalist sympathies, and the DBD as the peasants' party.

In the course of the summer and autumn of 1945, particularly as the results of local elections came in, it became clear to the KPD that they could never win mass electoral support in competition with an independent SPD. Even though the KPD was unfairly advantaged in the provision of such materials as paper, election posters, the availability of rooms for meetings – and even electricity for lighting those meetings – the Communists simply did not win enough votes to convince anyone of their democratic right to rule. Accordingly, in the winter of 1945–6 immense pressure was put on a now less than willing SPD to enter into a merger with the KPD. Many Social Democrats now chose to leave for the western zones rather than continue in what they saw as the dictated political circumstances of the Soviet zone. A forced merger with the rump of the SPD, hammered out in a deal still not fully understood, was finally ratified at a unification meeting in April 1946.[5] The KPD and SPD merged to become the Socialist Unity Party of Germany (SED), with formal parity between former Communists and Social Democrats. Over subsequent years, the latter were increasingly pressurized and purged, so much so that the Communists came to exert clear control in the SED. Under Soviet occupation, the SED was to spearhead Soviet policies in its zone of Germany, and the 'democratization' of East German politics became increasingly predicated on the Marxist–Leninist interpretation of democracy as 'democratic centralism'.

The impact of the western powers' political views on the reorganization of West German political life was more muted, but nonetheless important. The decision to license the re-foundation of political parties was taken later, in response to the Soviet initiative and the energetic activities of the Communists. The western Allies believed in a grass-roots approach, with the foundation of political parties first at a local level. Groups of individuals wishing to form new political parties were invited to apply for licenses in the autumn of 1945. Licensing was strictly controlled to ensure the democratic character of the new parties.

The re-founded SPD in the west, under its leader Kurt Schumacher, was bitterly hostile to the activities of the Communists. Despite the merger to form the SED in the Soviet zone, in the west the SPD and KPD remained very firmly separate and opposed organizations. As in the east, a new conservative grouping of both Catholics and Protestants formed the CDU; in Bavaria, this retained a separate identity as the Christian Social Union (CSU). With the 1947 Ahlen programme, the CDU/CSU initially adopted a relatively radical – or at least progressive – social programme as part of official party policy. This was later downplayed and replaced by the more conservative views of the individual who was to dominate the CDU – and West Germany

– for the next decade and a half: Konrad Adenauer. Several liberal parties sprang up over the western zones of Germany, which eventually merged to become the Free Democratic Party (FDP). This grouping had a strong, right-wing, pro-business emphasis, in addition to more obviously 'liberal', individualist elements. There also existed a large number of very small parties, some never transcending the level of local politics, others laying more serious claim to wider representation of regional or special group interests (such as the *Bund der Heimatvertriebenen und Entrechteten* representing refugees and persons expelled from their eastern homelands). Many of these were separatist in aims; some were quite right-wing. In the occupation period – and even at the beginning of the 1950s – the party system in the western zones looked very like that of the Weimar Republic, with a relatively large number of small parties which under a system of proportional representation might bedevil attempts to find stable governmental coalitions. It was only in the course of the 1950s that the configuration of two main parties with a third small party holding the balance of power began to emerge.

The British and Americans were determined to give the Germans an experience of democracy working in practice at the level of local government. They wanted to install a basic framework, including rules of fair play, but encountered a number of difficulties in the process. Local studies have indicated that some obstacles were of the Allies' own making: Barbara Marshall's detailed study of Hanover, for example, has indicated that the British Military Government tended to favour – and give unfair advantages to – conservative groups rather than Social Democrats. The traditional penumbra of SPD youth, sporting and special interest groups was forbidden, depriving the SPD of one of its main organizational means of gaining and sustaining support.[6] Other studies, such as that by Rainer Schulze of the Chambers of Commerce and Industry, have shown how British support of these employers' organizations allowed them to secure advantages in influencing the policies of, and placing individuals within, emerging right-wing political parties.[7]

There were also more politically neutral difficulties: the British, for example, set great store by the attempt to separate 'politics' from 'administration', politicians from civil servants, which in German traditions of local government had been conflated (as in the office which combined the functions of chief executive and mayor). There were also attempts in the British zone to replace the proportional representation voting system with the British system of 'first past the post', resulting in the hybrid compromise found in the later voting system of the Federal Republic (which combines both, as discussed further in Chapter Seven). Unforeseen problems were encountered with some of the aspects of democracy in post-Nazi Germany in practice. The Americans were somewhat taken aback when in one town a former Nazi mayor was re-elected, by democratic majority vote, as the new mayor. It was not immediately clear whether the most 'democratic' thing to do would be to reject the democratic vote for an undemocratic person, or to install, undemocratically, a democratic candidate against the wishes of the majority. What was clear, however, was that many Germans had little conception of what was meant by 'democracy': it was associated for those who were old enough to have experienced it as adults in the Weimar Republic with national defeat and humiliation, economic crisis, and political chaos. Now it was associated for many with the undemocratic imposition by victors on vanquished, and again with national defeat, humiliation and economic devastation. Concerted efforts had to be made to try to convince Germans that the ruins around them were the harvest of the Nazi tyranny and its consequences, rather than the necessary concomitants of political democracy. Many saw the occupation by the Allies as a 'Fourth Reich', no better than the Third. Even despite all these factors, however, in the course of the spring of 1946 local governments were formed in the western zones, and local German politicians who had been elected by Germans, rather than appointed by the Military Governments, were able to start co-operating with their erstwhile enemies in the rebuilding of post-war Germany. They played what was certainly a subordinate, but by no means unimportant, role in the reconstruction of German life.

Denazification and re-education

The problems facing the Allies in 1945 were immensely complex. They had to administer a war-torn country, attempt to get basic transport and communications functioning again, feed and house the hundreds of thousands – eventually millions – of refugees fleeing or expelled from former eastern homelands, and combat problems of homelessness, malnutrition and disease among the native population. At the same time, they had to be extremely suspicious of those Germans who were in a position to help administer affairs; they had to deal with the problem of taking over a society which had been run by Nazis and immersed in Nazism for over a decade.

Along with democratization, denazification was an agreed aim of all the occupying powers. It was generally accepted that in some way Germany must be cleansed of Nazis, that those guilty of sustaining Nazi rule must be punished, and that it was essential, if future peace was to be secured, that Germans should be convinced of the error of Nazi views and persuaded to assent to more democratic and peaceful values. Yet it was not at all clear how these various goals should be effected. In practice, the Allies in different ways stumbled through a series of changing conceptualizations and policies which produced their own quite curious and frequently wayward effects. Neither the negative tasks relating to denazification, nor the more positive programmes of re-education, could be said to amount to a straightforward success story in either the western or eastern zones.

The only part of these processes in which all the Allies collaborated was that of the Nuremberg Trials of the major war criminals. These lasted from 20 November 1945 to 1 October 1946. The war guilt of individuals was investigated, as well as that of the German government, the General Staff of the Army, the SA, the SS, the SD, the Gestapo, and leaders of the NSDAP. The government and the Army General Staff were cleared in general terms, but the other organizations mentioned were declared to be criminal. Three individuals were acquitted of charges of war crimes: Franz von Papen, Hjalmar Schacht, and Hans Fritzsche. Death sentences were pronounced on, among others, Joachim von Ribbentrop, Generals Keitel and Jodl, and Gauleiter Julius Streicher and (in his absence) on Martin Bormann. Goering committed suicide after being sentenced; Rudolf Hess was sentenced to life imprisonment, and remained in Spandau prison until his death in 1987; Walther Funk and Admiral Raeder also received life sentences but were released early because of ill-health. Others received shorter sentences: Admiral von Dönitz was released in 1956, Baron von Neurath in 1954, Baldur von Schirach in 1966, and Albert Speer also in 1966.

The Nuremberg trials raised a host of questions, legal, moral and political. To what extent could people be punished for actions which were not at the time a crime? Had war atrocities only been committed on the German side, and was it not simply a case of 'might makes right', with the victors claiming a spurious moral superiority over the vanquished? Would the German public not simply gain sympathy with their leaders who were on trial, and not really believe – or become immune to – the evidence of the atrocities that had been committed in their name? Despite initial war-time discussions about possible vengeance on a mass scale, the Allies finally agreed that it was important to restore a sense of the rule of law and justice in Germany; but in some respects the Nuremberg trials did not adequately fulfil these tasks. Nevertheless, these and succeeding war crimes trials did serve to raise a host of questions about the nature of guilt in Nazi Germany, such as that concerning the relative importance of giving orders from behind a desk far removed from the actual scene of the crime, or the implications of following orders and committing acts of the utmost inhumanity under threat and duress.

Individuals continued to be investigated and tried for alleged war crimes by the Germans and other affected governments for decades after the end of the war. The German statute of limitations, which set a limit of twenty years in prosecutions for murder, was lifted in 1969 to allow continued prosecutions for war crimes. Many criticisms have been raised about the Nazi war crimes trials. At first, it seemed that the Germans were less than energetic in pursuing prosecutions. A Central Office of *Land* Justice Departments was established at Ludwigsburg, near Stuttgart, in 1958 to co-ordinate investigations. By the end of 1964 – two decades after the end of the war – it had just over seven hundred cases in hand, leading to the trials of the later 1960s. Much of the credit for tracking down former Nazis must be given to the Simon Wiesenthal Centre, set up by a Jew who was determined neither to let the perpetrators of atrocities retire into happy civilian life nor to leave the nature of their crimes unrecorded. In the process of acquiring testimonies and accumulating evidence of the post-war fates and whereabouts of former Nazis, uncomfortable facts were discovered about the Allies' own treatment of some of them after the war. In particular, certain Nazis had been found very useful by the US government in its efforts to combat Communism in the Cold War, and had therefore been protected and aided in their disappearance in the post-war period. But despite both this sort of revelation, and the mounting and perpetually disturbing evidence of Nazi atrocities, later war trials gave rise to a range of criticisms. Elderly, pathetic figures were being brought to account for deeds committed in their youth, and while it could be fairly said that the disturbance to their health, reputation, tranquil retirement or family life was totally incommensurable with the appalling deeds for which they were being tried, legal aspects of some of the trials gave rise to concern. War crimes trials were increasingly hampered, too, by such problems as the reliability and availability of eye-witness testimony and of other evidence, decades after the events which were alleged to have occurred. They could however be justified in a number of ways, including the importance of educating a younger generation.

In the immediate post-war period, trials of individual war criminals could hardly help to deal with the far broader question of what to do with, and how to transform, a society which had been imbued with Nazism at all sorts of levels and in a variety of ways. At the more general level, that of the transformation of

German society, what denazification meant in detail depended on a variety of factors: on theories of the nature and roots of Nazism as a sociopolitical system; on assumptions about German society, about the bases of certain beliefs and behaviour, and the social determination or social location of political guilt; and on considerations about the exigencies of post-war reconstruction. The major difference was between the Soviet interpretation of Nazism as rooted in certain socio-economic conditions, with the correlate that the eradication of Nazism required major structural change, and the more individualistic, psychological western interpretations of the problem.

Even within the western camp there were considerable differences of interpretation. Some held the extreme view that all Germans were bad Germans, and endorsed the notion of 'collective guilt' – which initially informed at least American policy in Germany. Others wished to distinguish between real Nazis, nominal Nazis, and non- and anti-Nazi Germans. Once the principle of distinction was accepted, the problem arose of the criteria by which people could be thus classified. Left-wing and Marxist-influenced intellectuals in Britain and America held the view that certain prominent social groups bore a greater burden of responsibility than others. But, in practice, after the initial period when automatic arrest categories were employed (for example, for SS personnel), the question was refocused at the individual level, and the task became one of trying to find appropriate external indices or evidence for internal predispositions and states of mind. The complications proved to be immense. For example, Party membership might indicate commitment to Nazi ideals; it might indicate (as for those joining after it became compulsory for certain professional groups in 1937) a desire to support one's family by retaining one's job; it might even indicate a desire to work against Nazism from within, or to fill a position for fear of replacement by someone worse. More problematic, membership could subsequently be represented as having been motivated by the highest ideals, there being no real means of checking claims about inner state against ambiguous external evidence. Most people could in any case persuade themselves of the acceptability and justifiability of their actions, and produce appropriate testimonies to their character, forgetting the ambivalence, the compromises, and the baser considerations of the past. Important, too, were the practical problems of implementation, the unintended effects, and the other considerations which arose to alter the subsequent course of denazification. In no zone did denazification present a simple, clear, consistent story.

In the Soviet zone, given the primarily structural and socio-economic interpretation of Nazism which prevailed, major efforts were devoted to the radical transformation of social and economic organization. Apart from the land reform which served to abolish the Junker class, the resources of certain Nazi industrialists were expropriated, and there were reforms of industry and finance which had not merely reparations as their aim. The Soviets were concerned also to oust individual Nazis from important positions. They carried out purges not only in the political and administrative spheres, but also in the teaching profession and the judiciary. The degrees of thoroughness varied in different areas. By October 1945, only 26% of remaining teachers in Mecklenburg and 24% in Brandenburg had been members of the NSDAP, while in Saxony and Thuringia the figures were 67% and 68% respectively.[8] The office of the US High Commissioner for Germany produced a report on the 'Sovietization of the Public School System in East Germany' in 1951 which estimated that by 1949 over 80% of lower school staff in the Soviet zone were new teachers, and that in 1948 two-thirds of schoolteachers were under thirty-five years of age.[9] The Soviet purge of the *Land* bureaucracies produced comparably variable results, with Thuringia again notably lagging behind. More lenient attitudes appear to have been adopted in relation to the medical profession, given the concern about public health.[10] Distinctions had been made between 'nominal' and 'activist' Nazis as early as November 1945, and from 1947, there was something of an amnesty for 'small Nazis' who were prepared to join in the building of a new society. Restrictions on the activities and rights of former Nazis were removed in stages in 1948 and 1949, and in 1952 full rights as citizens of the GDR were granted to all former Nazis insofar as they were not war criminals.[11] On the positive side of re-education, strenuous efforts were devoted to changing the content of education in schools, to the production of newspapers proclaiming the Soviet line, and to evening classes and Party schools expounding the tenets of Marxism–Leninism as currently interpreted.

Denazification lurched along in curious ways in the western zones. It was not quite clear whether the aim was to punish or to rehabilitate former Nazis; and whether the intention was to cleanse the political, administrative and economic spheres of their presence, or to cleanse former Nazis of the taint of Nazism in order to reinstate them in their former areas of expertise. In contrast to the Soviet zone, which effected a major restructuring of society, along with a replacement of old elites by new personnel, as well as permitting individual rehabilitation, the western zones tended towards rehabilitation rather than transformation. In this respect, the charge of certain radical critics that West German history represents a case of missed opportunities, and restoration rather than transformation, may with qualifications be upheld.

By the early summer of 1945, there were at least four directives, partially mutually contradictory, concerning denazification in the American zone. These gave way to the directive of 7 July 1945, which decided on the notion of 'guilt-by-officeholding', with 136 mandatory removal categories.[12] This was followed by General Lucius Clay's Law no. 8 of 26 September 1945, which extended denazification into the economic sphere, decreeing that Nazis should be employed only in menial positions. (This gave rise to considerable re-labelling of jobs, to make elevated jobs appear more mundane.) Law no. 8 marked the first shift away from an emphasis on structural location and towards a focus on individual beliefs and private predispositions. This shift was consolidated when on 5 March 1946 the compromise Law for Liberation from National Socialism (*Befreiungsgesetz*) came into force. The automatic arrests of the previous year had produced, by the winter of 1945–6, full internment camps and empty offices (in Niethammer's formulation), with associated problems both of injustice to individuals and loss of expertise in administrative and public life. Under the new law, individual cases were to be considered in detail by tribunals, staffed by Germans but supervised by the Allies, on the basis of previously completed detailed questionnaires (*Fragebögen*) with 131 questions on all aspects of political orientation and activity during the Third Reich. The information provided in these questionnaires was intended to permit the classification of individuals into one of five categories: (1) major offenders; (2) offenders; (3) lesser offenders; (4) followers or fellow-travellers; (5) exonerated. Appeals could be made to the tribunals, on production of appropriate evidence, to achieve an amelioration of classification. On the basis of final classification, individuals might be imprisoned, or fined, or restricted in their activities and employment, or given a clean bill of political health and permitted to return into the community as free citizens. The whole procedure was immensely cumbersome, producing vast and unmanageable quantities of paperwork and ever-increasing backlogs of unprocessed cases. 'Easy' cases were dealt with first, with the result that those who were more compromised by their political past were left until later, when greater lenience prevailed, or even managed to escape the net altogether. There were gross differences in implementation across the zones: while in the British zone nearly ninety per cent emerged as 'exonerated', only just over a third were similarly exculpated in the American zone and just over a half in the French zone. Equally, only one-tenth were deemed to be 'followers' in the British zone, compared with over half in the US zone and a little under a half in the French zone.[13]

The denazification process involved manifest injustice, giving rise to assorted criticisms from different sections of society. In Bremen, for example, it was reported that while the middle classes were maintaining that denazification was too severe, and bemoaning the loss of expertise because of the penalization of purely nominal and professionally necessary party membership, the working classes were by contrast complaining of lack of sufficient severity and that, as usual, the really big Nazis were getting away free.[14] Many felt that the 'small fry' were being caught and punished while the 'big fry' escaped the net. The need for paper credentials led to the mass production of 'Persil certificates' (*Persilscheine*), as people sought testimonials from worthy and respected members of the community, such as priests and pastors, affirming that they had always been good Christians and only nominal Nazis. The tribunals soon came to be likened to laundries: one entered wearing a brown shirt and left with a clean starched white shirt instead. Denazification had finally become, not the cleansing of German economy, administration and society of Nazis, but rather the cleansing and rehabilitation of individuals. Gradually, as practical problems mounted and other preoccupations began to take precedence, denazification processes were wound up, at different dates in the different *Länder*, such that by the early 1950s they were all terminated. There was even a swing in the other direction; under a law based on Article 131 of the Basic Law, former civil servants were granted their jobs back, or retired on full pensions.

The actual effects of denazification procedures appear to have been somewhat wayward. Apart from the failure to effect a general purge or a far-reaching replacement of old by new elites, the ultimately rehabilitative focus of western denazification efforts did not even appear to provoke much serious soul-searching or confrontation with one's past on the part of most Germans who went through it. The major concern was for individual survival: for self-justification, a whitewashing of the past, the production of testimonials reinterpreting former activities in a favourable light. Most Germans now attempted to represent themselves as always having been (at least secretly, whatever their outward behaviour) 'against it' (*immer dagegen*), and as having had the best of motives for having done, or belonged to, whatever they did. Some observers bitterly commented that, the way Germans were talking now, Hitler must have been the only Nazi in Germany. Moreover, the manifest discrepancies in the treatment of different individuals, and the general sense of injustice at the crudities of Allied conceptualization and approaches to denazification, arguably served to create a 'community of the aggrieved', a sense among Germans of a common fate and a common hostility against the occupying powers. These were hardly appropriate conditions in which to attempt to transform German political attitudes in democratic directions.

Denazification was the negative aspect of the attempted transformation process; re-education represented the more positive side. Yet the story of re-education attempts is similarly one of policy confusion, difficulties in implementation, and minimal, irrelevant, or wayward effects. At school level, the western Allies failed to restructure the education system in any radical manner, giving way to German conservative and Christian insistence on retaining the tripartite selective system and the confessional schools. Within the old, pre-Nazi school structure, the main problems were those of adequate staffing, the provision of politically acceptable textbooks, and the finding of suitable accommodation among the ruins. That the schools functioned at all, and kept ill-clad and hungry children off the streets, is in itself something of an achievement. But there is little evidence to suggest that at this most direct of levels, the education system managed to inculcate much in the way of democratic attitudes. In higher education, there were persistent complaints of collusion among senior university administrators and academics to protect former Nazis, and accusations that these institutions had failed to denazify themselves adequately. There was also considerable evidence of the persistence of right-wing and racialist attitudes among students.[15] The impact of explicitly propagandist films, like *Todesmühlen*, on concentration camps, is hard to ascertain; but it appears not to have been very deep or widespread. Perhaps the most successful organ of re-education was the licensed press: newspapers produced by politically acceptable Germans do appear to have had a wide and receptive readership and may arguably have played a notable role in some transformation of attitudes in the early post-war years. In the Soviet zone, however, the overtly propagandistic and ideological line of the newspapers was so patently belied by personal experience that it is likely they had little impact.[16]

Probably more important than the explicit denazification and re-education programmes in the remoulding of German society in the eastern and western zones were the social and economic transformations of the occupation period. In the west, the change from the initial punitive measures to a focus on economic recovery set West Germany on the path to becoming a flourishing capitalist economy; in the east, the radical socio-economic reforms in agriculture, industry and finance started the process of transformation into a Soviet-style society. In each case, such measures played a major role in the reshaping of the political attitudes and perceptions of the population. But the fact that West Germany ultimately developed into a stable democracy, to a considerable degree as a result of post-war economic success, should not serve to obscure the shortcomings of the denazification and re-education processes of the occupation period. 'Nazism' may not have survived, for other reasons; but the effects of the western Allies' policies were to feed the collective amnesia evident in much of post-war West German history and to compound the difficulties many West Germans experienced in coming to terms with their past, just as surely as the Communists' failure to confront the German legacy together with their assumption of a clean bill of political health formed part of the historical distortions and difficulties which hampered the creation of a new national identity in the truncated state of East Germany.

Economic revival and transformation

The economy was the key arena for the transformation of Germany into a divided state and diverging societies. Differences in economic policy between the occupying powers both precipitated and symbolized their wider political dissimilarities; and differences in economic policy in the different zones set the pattern for long-term contrasts in the social and political structures of the two Germanies. In the east, despite no initial Soviet commitment to staying in Germany, the measures taken nevertheless radically altered East German socio-economic structure and were consistent with the subsequent sovietization of the zone; in the west, the initial fairly draconian attitude gave way to a focus on reconstruction, under the broad aegis of the Marshall Plan, which facilitated West Germany's renowned economic growth, material prosperity, political conservatism and western integration. On both sides, economic circumstances were probably far more important than directly political measures (such as re-education) in affecting the political attitudes of the people.

The beginnings were scarcely promising: a devastated, war-torn country, with few functioning means of communication, little fuel, food or resources, appalling housing conditions particularly in the cities, and, by the winter of 1946–7, the serious danger of famine. An additional problem was the mass movement and resettlement of around ten million people. Apart from the problem of returning prisoners of war, there was the massive problem of refugees. Those from the eastern provinces who had not joined the treks westwards fleeing before the advances of the Red Army in the closing months of the war now found themselves being expelled from their homelands as a result of Germany's changed boundaries agreed at the Potsdam Conference. Taking what few possessions they could carry, they were herded onto trains for the west; in the course of the journey, frequent ambushes plundering the trains meant that many arrived only with the clothes in which they were dressed. Although some settled in the Soviet zone, others saw this as only a transitional stop on the way to resettlement in the western zones. Agricultural and less populated areas which had escaped the bombing inflicted on the towns and cities bore the brunt of housing the refugee population. In some areas in north Germany, refugees formed as much as fifty per cent of the population, and there were inevitably frictions between natives and refugees. Conflicts were based not only, and obviously, on resentment over differential distribution of scarce resources (food and fuel), but were rooted also in differences of culture, religion, dialect and life-style. Furthermore, it was not only refugees who were facing immense problems of adaptation to changed circumstances: natives as well had to come to terms with the radically changed conditions of post-war, occupied Germany.[17]

Social and cultural problems compounded the more purely economic and material sources of stress. Overcrowded, cramped living conditions, with several families sharing rooms, cooking and washing facilities, and widespread exhaustion and illness in addition to psychological disorientation, were exacerbated by prejudices and misunderstandings. For both natives and refugees, there were breakdowns of 'normal' family life, with the loss of many husbands and fathers, and women bearing the brunt of what has been called 'survival work' in the 'hour of the women'.[18] Women took a large share, not only in feeding and caring for their own families, but also in the hard physical labour of rebuilding from the rubble and ruins of post-war Germany. The concept of *Trümmerfrauen*, bands of women passing stones and bricks from one to the next in the reconstruction of ruined buildings, encapsulates and symbolizes the circumstances of the time (*see* plate 12). In what was barely a subsistence economy, money became almost meaningless. The severely restricted calories nominally available on ration cards had to be supplemented with the products of bartering, 'hamstering', and the exchange of goods and services on the black market. It was more profitable to go out foraging in the countryside, or to engage in 'trading upwards' through a succession of goods, cigarettes, drink, chocolate, and services (including prostitution), than to labour in a paid, full-time job precluding such activities. Archbishop Frings unwittingly gave his name to a new activity, *fringsen*, when in a sermon he implied that stealing coal to keep one's family warm was not a heinous offence in these circumstances. Many took this to legitimize their – or their children's – activities. The black market became an essential sector of the economy, and one which had eventually to be conquered in order to restore more orthodox life.

The Allies were torn between, on the one hand, concerns for both punishment of the Germans and reparations for themselves, and, on the other, the desire to avert widespread starvation and associated social unrest. Particularly in the west, it was feared that Communism would spread rapidly if economic conditions were bad. Moreover, each of the Allies was also attempting, in however confused and tentative a fashion, to reshape its part of Germany in a new image, appropriate to varying visions of a future political and economic order in Europe. Hence there were inconsistencies and changes in policy, although Soviet policies can perhaps be seen as the most consistent combination: the exaction of maximum reparations alongside maximal restructuring, throughout the occupation period.

The Soviet zone of occupied Germany had certain initial economic advantages. Although its population was about 40% of that of the western zones, its fixed industrial capital was about 48% of that of the western zones. The northern parts of the area were largely agricultural, but in the south, particularly in Saxony and Thuringia, there were major industrial centres. The Soviet zone had been less badly affected by war damage and bombing than the western zones (with notable individual exceptions, such as Dresden): its loss of productive capacity through war damage has been estimated at approximately 15%, compared with 21% in the west. However, it did suffer from certain disadvantages. The area covered by the Soviet zone had been a rather specialized, non-self-sufficient economy: in particular, it was dependent on the west for raw materials. It had, for example, produced only 2% of the Reich's hard coal and pig iron, and 7% of the Reich's steel, by the end of the war. It was also to some extent dependent on lost provinces further to the east for agricultural imports and some coal. Thus, while it was intrinsically a highly productive area, it was dependent on a particular network of trade links in the former Reich, and would suffer particularly adverse consequences from a severance of these links. Furthermore, it had a relatively unfavourable demographic structure. Partly owing to the war losses of young males, there was a preponderance of the old and of females. Initially there was an influx of refugees fleeing from territories further east, and exacerbating shortages of food and housing; before the advantages of the increased labour force could be realized, however, there were subsequent losses of population through further movements to the western zones.[19]

Whatever the initial disadvantages and advantages of the economic situation in the Soviet zone, matters were undoubtedly worsened by Soviet occupation policies. Soviet dismantling reduced the productive capacity of the zone by about 26%, compared with a figure of 12% for the western zones. By the spring of 1948, the Soviets had dismantled over 1900 plants, almost 1700 of them completely. Including war damage, the total loss of productive capacity was about 50% compared to 1939 (although according to some economists, productive capacity was still greater in the late 1940s than in the mid-1930s, due to the increased productivity of the last pre-war years). The scale of dismantling was one indication that the Soviets had no initial firm intention to remain on German soil in the long term; they at this time appeared to want to get in, take what they could, and get out – although only on certain terms. However, even from this point of view, their dismantling policies – which were obviously detrimental to the economy of the area – proved problematic. Much of the equipment became rusty or was damaged during its transportation to the Soviet Union; and more complex equipment, once dismantled, could not be successfully reassembled in the USSR. One solution was to ship out German experts along with their machinery, in order to reassemble and operate it in the USSR. Another was to leave equipment in Germany but appropriate the product. In June 1946 twenty-five Soviet joint-stock companies (SAGs) were formed, with 213 firms, producing thirty-two per cent of the total production of the Soviet zone, taken over into Soviet ownership. These were gradually phased back into German state ownership in the period 1949–54. The Soviets also exacted considerable reparations and occupation costs. Up to 1953, about one quarter of the zone's national product was spent on occupation costs and reparations payments (compared with a figure for the west of perhaps 11–15% in the period up to 1949). It has been estimated – although precise calculations are highly contested – that by 1955 the total value of goods and services taken by the Soviets was in the order of $30 billion, as against an agreed figure of $10 billion.

Quite apart from their attempts to gain some form of compensation for the enormous material and human losses imposed on them by German aggression, the Soviets implemented certain economic policies designed so to transform the socio-economic structure of their zone that there could never again, in the Soviet view, be the material basis for a

Nazi/capitalist militarism. They sought to eradicate the Junker class and the large capitalists in a stroke.

In September 1945, about seven thousand large estates (those over 100 hectares, approximately 250 acres) and those belonging to former 'Nazi activists' were expropriated. This amounted to about thirty per cent of the agriculturally fruitful area of the zone. Some of the land was redistributed to form peasant smallholdings; the rest was taken into state-owned farms (*Volkseigene Güter*). The small peasant land-holdings were too small to be economically viable, and lacked adequate equipment to be farmed properly. This cunningly produced a situation in which those in receipt of land might be both grateful for what they had been given, and yet dependent on state support to make any use of it.[20] This strategy aided the later development of co-operative forms of organization (such as the introduction of tractor-lending stations) and facilitated the first collectivization of agriculture in 1952.

In July 1945 there was a move from private to centralized state banking, and private insurance companies were merged into five public insurance corporations, one for each *Land*. In industry, there were comparable moves. Thuringia started transferring mines and minerals into state ownership in September 1945, followed by other states in the next two years. In October 1945 ten thousand individual enterprises owned by 'Nazi activists' were sequestered. In June 1946 there was a plebiscite on expropriation in Saxony. This produced a high turnout, with an overwhelming majority in favour of expropriation. (There was a 93·7% turnout; 77·6% voted in favour, 16·5% against, with 5·8% of the votes cast invalid.) It is notable that some of the economic measures of the Soviet occupation were at least initially welcomed by sizeable numbers of the populace, despite their hostility towards Soviet politics. This was taken as a general mandate legitimizing expropriations in other *Länder* in the zone without prior plebiscite. In April 1948 expropriated enterprises became *Volkseigene Betriebe* (VEBs). Along with the Soviet-owned SAGs they accounted for about 60% of industry's gross product. Between 1949 and 1955 remaining private enterprises suffered detrimental tax, price and planning measures. By 1955, the private sector accounted for about 15% of industrial production; by 1970, as little as 2%, frequently in the form of part ownership with the state.

The western Allies were not initially clear about their economic plans for post-war Germany. Just as in the sphere of denazification there was a switch from drastic notions of collective guilt to an eventual policy of rehabilitation, so in the sphere of economic policy there was a radical change in approach. It was obvious that a primary aim of the Allies must be to prevent a resurgence of German militarism as a threat to peace, but it was not clear as to how best this was to be achieved. The early Morgenthau plan for the deindustrialization of Germany, despite its mixed reception, found some echoes in the economic proposals in the Potsdam Agreement, as well as in the Level-of-Industry Plan of March 1946. According to this, Germany's standard of living was to be reduced to the 1932 level, and was not to exceed that of other European countries; industrial capacity was to be reduced to about 50–55% of the 1938 level; about 1546 plants were to be dismantled in the western zones; and there were limits on the output of almost all industries, with some (armaments and war-related) banned entirely. Only coal output was to expand. This plan was related to reparations agreements which, because of the deterioration of East–West relations, were not in practice effected; in particular, after a couple of months the agreement on partial exchange of food and raw materials from the Soviet zone for products of western dismantling was terminated. While opinion in the USA had been divided, Britain was always strongly conscious of the problems that a deindustrialization of Germany would bring, particularly with respect to feeding the German population. However, it was not only for practical reasons (the attempt to prevent mass starvation) but also because of the developing Cold War, that western approaches to the German economy changed.

The change was signalled in the speech by US Secretary of State James Byrnes in Stuttgart on 6 September 1946, when the German public learned for the first time explicitly that it was to receive more lenient treatment. In the spring and summer of 1947 the shift in policy was confirmed. On 1 January

1947 the Bizone was created out of the British and American zones, ostensibly to allow for a more efficient joint economic administration, but to all intents and purposes actually creating a new, West German political unit in which the Economic Council acted as quasi-government. In March–April 1947 the Moscow Conference of Foreign Ministers saw a breakdown in East-West relations and the Truman doctrine enunciated the American policy of containing the advance of Communism. Associated with this shift in priorities, away from anti-Nazism and towards anti-Communism, was a major shift in economic policy. On 5 June 1947 US Secretary of State George Marshall, in a speech at a Harvard graduation ceremony, called for a European Recovery Programme. This was rejected in July by the USSR and by the East European states, because it was predicated on a market (rather than state-controlled and centrally directed) economy which would benefit American exports. Effectively the USA was now to support the economic recovery of western Europe, and in particular of western Germany, both for the economic benefits it would bring to the American economy which was seeking overseas markets, and for the political motive of seeking a bulwark against the expansion of communism in central Europe. The USA now officially supported the view that 'an orderly and prosperous Europe requires the economic contributions of a stable and prosperous Germany'.[21] In late August 1947, the revised Level-of-Industry Plan permitted increased production in the American and British zones to approximately 70–75% of the 1938 level.

Subsequent developments in economic policy in the western zones were closely linked with the political division of Germany. Both to facilitate the introduction of Marshall Aid, and to combat the problems of the black market, a currency reform was introduced in the western zones on 20 June 1948, in which the new Deutschmark accomplished an effective devaluation of the old Reichsmark and achieved, in conjunction with the lifting of price controls on many items, a stabilization of the economy in the western zones and a return to money as the unit of currency (rather than cigarettes or direct barter and exchange of goods and services). The currency reform in the west was soon followed by both a comparable currency reform in the Soviet zone, and by an attempt by the Soviet Union to cut Berlin off from communications with the western zones. The 'Berlin Blockade' lasted from 24 June 1948 to 12 May 1949, when the road, rail and water routes to Berlin were blockaded, and the western powers flew supplies into Berlin by air routes, dropping food to Berliners from so-called 'raisin bombers'. As Grosser has pointed out, this transformed Berlin overnight from being perceived as a bastion of Nazism and Prussian militarism to being the symbolic last outpost of freedom and democracy in the western sense, to be protected at all costs.[22] The end of the airlift – which amounted to 277,000 flights – came when the political division of Germany was effectively accomplished, as will be seen below.

It is notable that, in contrast to the Soviet zone, there were no radical transformations in economic structure in the western zones of occupation. In the case of land reform, the argument could be made that there were in any event few large estates to be divided in the west. The Soviets had in their zone the main areas of the Junker estates. Nevertheless, what land reform there might have been in the west was deflected, partly by the representations of interested German land-owners, partly because of lack of clarity and forcefulness in Allied policy-making in this area. In some areas, there were moves for a serious restructuring of the German economy – moves which were often met with considerable German resistance, and which did not always achieve lasting changes. In banking and industry, attempts were made to break up trusts and cartels. The Deutsche Bank, Dresdner Bank and Commerzbank were to be split into thirty successor institutions with geographic limits; I. G. Farben was broken up into four successor companies in 1953; the twelve largest coal and steel concerns were turned into twenty-eight independent successor companies, and the links between coal and iron were broken. But despite Allied pressures for decartelization, and the eventual passing of a watered-down decartelization law in 1957, the concentration of the West German economy continued in the post-war period.

Nevertheless, it can be argued that in more subtle, less immediately obvious ways, there was in fact a major socio-economic reorientation taking place in the western zones of Germany. In the immediate post-war period, many people thought the way was open for a socialist transformation of Germany. The Allies' decision to suppress indigenous anti-fascist groups and support moderate and conservative political parties was paralleled in the sphere of economic policy. Indigenous demands, for example, for the socialization of mines, were peremptorily dealt with by the Americans. Socialization measures proposed by the *Land* governments of Hesse and North-Rhine-Westphalia were suppressed by the Americans and – under American pressure – the British respectively. Subtle pressures were exerted by the Americans to split communist and socialist trade unions, to isolate the former and moderate the latter. A frequently overlooked aspect of the Marshall Plan was its influence on what might be called the political culture of the economy. Beyond the giving of Marshall Aid with attached conditions and constraints, there was a great emphasis on exporting a notion of an 'American way of life'. This stressed the importance of enhanced productivity and the reduction of political disputes to technical problems of producing a greater shared abundance.[23] A potential 'Third Way', to which many Germans had looked with hope in the later 1940s, was as much suppressed in the West – channelled into an American-influenced mould – as it was in the East by the obviously and visibly radical sovietization of the economy.

This is not to suggest that American views were simply imprinted on West Germany. The so-called 'social market economy' which emerged under the guidance of Ludwig Erhard – a former Professor of Economics who became West Germany's first Economics Minister, and eventually Chancellor from 1963 to 1966 – was a complex product of American influence and German interest group pressures, on the part of both employers and employees. There was considerable resistance and opposition by German political and economic elites, as well as by trade unionists, to different aspects of American economic policies. Initial measures by the Americans – such as those relating to decartelization – were met with hostility, and subsequent developments tended to reverse, water down, or amend certain aspects so as to deflect their impact from original intentions. It can also be argued that the strength of radicalism in late 1940s Germany was not as great as some interpretations of 'missed chances' suggest: for example, the depoliticization of strikes – which narrowed their goals to purely economic demands on wages and conditions – was evident already in 1947. Yet, however difficult to quantify, a certain weight must be given particularly to American influence in setting West Germany on the course of a moderate, liberal-conservative form of western capitalism. And the importance of the economic success of that form of capitalism for the subsequent political stability of West Germany can scarcely be overrated.

The Cold War and the division of Germany

In 1949, two German states were founded, dividing German soil. Between them lay the border that Winston Churchill, in a famous speech in Fulton, Missouri, on 5 March 1946, had dubbed an 'iron curtain' dividing west from east, the free world and democracy from dictatorship and communism. West Germans and the western allies effectively jettisoned the Germans living in the Soviet zone in the east, in favour of integrating a partial state into a new order in western Europe.

Who was responsible for the division? Debates continue over interpretations of the Cold War more generally – was it the Soviet Union or the USA which was the primary aggressor? Did the Americans misjudge and exaggerate Soviet expansionism, or did they simply act appropriately to contain a real Soviet threat? These wider debates obviously have relevance to attempts to understand the division of Germany, but further factors are also of importance here. For example, whatever the origins of the Cold War, it is conceivable that Germany could have remained united, as a neutral power (as was in the end the case with Austria), with the Iron Curtain running along a different frontier. Moreover, in asking who was responsible for the division of Germany, one must focus not only on the superpowers, but also on the role played by the Germans themselves. While the chronological stages of division may relatively easily be recounted – with the west appearing to take the initiative at almost every turn – the balance of interpretation must remain somewhat more tentative.

Elements of a post-war division into 'spheres of influence' had already been mooted in informal 'friendly agreements' between Churchill and Stalin in 1944. But while recognizing the legitimacy of spheres of influence in an informal way, no decisions had been reached on Germany in particular before the end of the war. An important factor after the cessation of hostilities was the zonal, rather than central, level of effective administration, as we have seen above. This inevitably led to the *de facto* divergence of socio-economic and political conditions in each zone. But a major factor was the increasing concern of the Americans with a perceived Soviet threat.

It was the British who first seriously considered, not the dismemberment of Germany into a number of small states (as had been mooted in some wartime plans) but rather division with a western partial state corresponding to the western zones of occupation. In April 1946, amidst growing fears about Soviet intentions, the British Foreign Office decided that the West German *Länder* would have to be strengthened and made able to resist any communist-dominated central government; and that if it were to come to a division of Germany, the Soviet Union would have to be made to look responsible.[24] The dissolution of the former province of Prussia, and the founding of North-Rhine–Westphalia as a large state encompassing the industrially important and politically contentious Ruhr district, must be seen in this context. So must the discussions between the Americans and the British which led to the fusing of their two zones into the Bizone, coming into effect in January 1947. The British had quite pragmatic considerations: their economy was suffering badly after the war, with bread rationing being introduced for the first time in July 1946, and the British having to borrow American dollars to feed the Germans while their own people – who had 'won' the war – were suffering economic hardships in peacetime. For a range of different reasons the Americans came round to the view that German economic recovery was to be encouraged. The Stuttgart speech by James Byrnes in September 1946 was the first official signal that the punitive approach to post-war Germany had finally been dropped.

In 1947 the Cold War became public. On 12 March 1947 American President Harry Truman made his famous speech to the American Congress enunciating what became known as the Truman Doctrine. Initially arising as a specific response to a specific crisis – the situation in Greece – Truman's emphasis on the 'containment of communism' was generally interpreted as having wider, indeed universal, implications. America was formally committed to a world policy of stemming what it saw as the tide of Soviet expansionism, wherever it might occur. With the failure of the Foreign Ministers Conference in Moscow, the British and Americans set in train moves to transform the economic administration of their new Bizone into a quasi-political structure, providing the embryo of a new western state. The new Economic Council of the Bizone prefigured the immediate political future of the Federal Republic in more than purely formal respects. The SPD delegates, failing to obtain the position of *Wirtschaftsdirektor* for their party, opted to sit in 'constructive opposition', renouncing the chance of fundamentally affecting economic policy and foreshadowing their role in the best part of the next twenty years of West Germany's history. In June 1947, the Marshall Plan for the recovery of post-war Europe was announced on terms which made it impossible for Soviet-occupied East European states to accept. As the economic division of Germany became more apparent, so the political division – the need for political institutions to administer economic policies in the west – became more inevitable. It was clear even before it began that the Foreign Ministers Conference in London of November–December 1947 was doomed to fail. France still proved a recalcitrant partner for the British and Americans, having designs on the coal-rich Saarland (which was in fact administered separately from the Federal Republic until it rejoined West Germany after a plebiscite in 1957) and disagreeing with British and American policies on the Ruhr. But in 1948 the latter pair went ahead with their plans for the political reorganization of the Bizone into a shadow state; and finally, recognizing the inevitable, France joined to form a 'Trizonia' in the spring of 1949.

By the summer of 1948, with the currency reform and the Berlin blockade in full effect, the division of Germany appeared more or less a fait accompli. There was one last-minute attempt to consider alternatives, in a plan put forward in May 1948 by the British Military Governor in Germany, Sir Brian Robertson; but this was rejected by a sceptical British Foreign Office. In the West German zones, a Parliamentary Council formed of representatives from the West German *Land* parliaments met to draw up a new constitution for a West German state. This, a document deemed to be sufficiently impermanent – and committed to reunification – to warrant the term 'Basic Law' (*Grundgesetz*) rather than 'constitution', was formally approved on 8 May 1949 and, with the signature of the Allies, came into effect on 23 May 1949, four years to the day after German capitulation and the dissolution of the government of the German Reich. On 14 August 1949 the first national elections were held in the new Federal Republic of Germany; and, after some bargaining with the FDP, Konrad Adenauer of the CDU became West Germany's first Chancellor four weeks later. The Federal Republic had been launched onto a particular course; and, under Adenauer's leadership, it was to set its face firmly towards the west in the coming decade, suppressing both memories of the past and concern for the lost Germans in the east.

In response to, and lagging behind, developments in the west were the steps towards the establishment of an East German state in the Soviet zone. The radical socio-economic measures in the Soviet zone had been paralleled by increasing Communist control of political life, with the Stalinization of the SED and increasing coercion by the SED of the other parties. Given what was occurring under Soviet influence elsewhere in Eastern Europe (particularly Poland and Czechoslovakia), there was good reason for the western powers to fear Stalin's ultimate designs in respect of the Soviet zone of Germany. Attempts at co-operation between the former war-time allies had clearly broken down. Yet the formal stages in the foundation of the GDR arose as responses to western initiatives. On 14 June 1947 the Soviets founded the German Economic Commission (*Deutsche Wirtschaftskommission*) in response to the western foundation of the Economic Council. The German Economic Commission took over central administration of the economy in the Soviet zone in March 1948. The German Democratic Republic was formally founded on 7 October 1949, after the foundation of the FRG. The first constitution of the GDR was in principle very similar to that of the FRG, so as not to prejudice the possibility of reunification; as we shall see, it was subsequently amended in 1968 and 1974 to conform somewhat more accurately to the realities of East German political life. Wilhelm Pieck was elected first (and only) President of the GDR, with Otto Grotewohl as Prime Minister; the real power, however, lay with the SED and its leader, the Moscow-trained Walter Ulbricht, who was to consolidate his power in the coming decade.

Who, then, was primarily responsible for this division of Germany? The most obvious first answer to this question must be one which is in fact frequently overlooked: the Germans themselves. Had they not unleashed a World War, had they not declared war on the Soviet Union and the USA, and involved these powers in the affairs of central Europe, there would have been no post-war reorganization of the international system. This simple fact should not be forgotten – and particularly not by self-pitying Germans who want to place the blame on one or the other superpower. However, even beyond this obvious point, there is a further degree of responsibility to be apportioned to the post-war Germans themselves, particularly in the west. West German political elites, whatever their lip service to the goal of unity, were prepared to contemplate with some equanimity the prospect of material prosperity and political and military security at the price of jettisoning their East German relatives. They participated actively, and co-operated efficiently, in the establishment of a new economic order and a new political framework for a partial nation, a western state, and did remarkably little to attempt to hinder or alter the course of division. Even on the one occasion when it appeared that all German politicians were hoping to discuss frankly among themselves the consequences of Allied policies – the meeting of German Prime Ministers in Munich in June 1947 – the western politicians were not prepared to keep open channels of communication between themselves and their eastern counterparts, or explore the extent to which the latter really were dominated by Moscow. They showed intransigence in refusing even to let the East German politicians read out a prepared statement prior to the start of proceedings. As will be seen in the next chapter, the determination of certain West German politicians to achieve western unity at the expense of the east was even more apparent in 1952, when reunification for a moment appeared a possibility. So while many Germans might have been longing for unity, certain West German politicians in key positions were acting to undermine whatever formal noises they were making about national reunification.

In relation to the respective contributions of the superpowers, analyses of Soviet policy must remain partly a matter of guesswork. It does however seem clear that western integration of part of a divided Germany, and the reconstruction of the West German economy in the wider framework of West European economic recovery, was very much in both the political and the economic interests of the USA. Politically, a strong, well-integrated, materially prosperous western Europe would provide an effective military defence against communist aggression, while also being less susceptible to communist infiltration or subversion from within. Economically, American capitalism required the sort of international market which a flourishing western Europe could provide. So it was clearly a realignment of the international system which would operate to America's advantage. Whether the American perception of the Soviet threat was exaggerated must remain an open question. The Soviet Union, with its war-ravaged economy, and its experience of invasion by western powers – in 1919 and in 1941 – was clearly concerned to have a defensive belt of compliant satellite states between itself and the west. The extent to which it wanted to have an East Germany as one of these satellites is however another matter, and it seems likely that for a considerable period of time Stalin was keeping his options open on this. It might have suited Soviet interests just as well to have taken what was possible by way of reparations, and then left a united, neutral Germany in central Europe, in a position rather like that of Austria. The British and French were influenced by consideration of possible future alignments of a united Germany: the 'Rapallo complex', or fear of an arrangement between Germany and Russia, undoubtedly played a large role, particularly in French thinking. In any event, both superpowers made the best of the final outcome; and the communist bloc certainly benefited from the inclusion of industrialized, productive East Germany in its economic camp.

What then did Germany look like in the year of the foundation of the new Republics? In the West, an economic upswing was already becoming evident: the black market had disappeared almost overnight after the currency reform and a return to, or a development of, 'normal' life seemed to be possible – even for the many refugees who were beginning to find jobs and new lives in what was essentially a new country. Moreover, the people of West Germany were beginning to be valued by the western powers as good democrats, partners in the international freedom fight against the evils of communism. With the foundation of the North Atlantic Treaty Organization (NATO) in April 1949, following the Organization for European Economic Co-operation (OEEC) one year earlier, the western world was becoming reorganized militarily and economically. At first, West Germany's western neighbours – particularly France – treated her with some caution, and measures such as international control of steel and coal production in the Ruhr were designed to contain any future German threat. In the longer term, these developments were to feed into closer West European economic co-operation and in particular into the European Community – even in 1990 seen as a means of binding a by then powerful and wealthy Germany into a wider set of containing structures. In 1949, many West Germans saw a potential new role in a new Europe. They could set their sights forward, and try to forget – or repress – the traumas of the recent past. In the East, things did not appear nearly so rosy. Economic conditions were by no means as favourable as in the West; and political repression was increasingly evident, particularly after 1948. Yet even in the East it had been made clear to former 'small Nazis' that they could find a role for themselves in the new state if they were prepared to participate and help in the new tasks of building socialism. In the East as well as in the West, many Germans wished simply to forget the past, and lived day-to-day, seeking to make the best of current circumstances and harbouring their respective hopes for the future. Yet the foundations which had been laid by 1949 set the pattern for paths followed in the future: diverging paths which shattered the hopes of many for another kind of new Germany after the defeat of Hitler's Reich.

SEVEN

Crystallization and Consolidation, 1949–61

The period from the foundation of two separate states in 1949 to the erection of the Berlin Wall in 1961 is one in which the division of Germany was confirmed, and in which the peculiar characters of the two new states were consolidated. While in 1949 much still appeared open, by the beginning of the 1960s patterns had been laid which were to shape the next quarter of a century of German history.

Before considering the historical development of East and West Germany in this crucial decade, we must briefly consider certain features of their constitutions and political systems. The very different political systems – liberal democracy in the West and a 'democratic centralism' based on Marxist-Leninist theory in the East – provided the framework for the very different patterns of political, social and economic development in the two German states which succeeded the Third Reich.

The constitution and political system of the Federal Republic

The Federal Republic of Germany represented Germany's second attempt at a liberal parliamentary democracy in the twentieth century. The writers of the constitution in 1948–9 had an ever-present regard for the failures of the Weimar Republic, and although the Basic Law (*Grundgesetz*) was the result of many positive considerations, it was also a document written with an eye to perceived weaknesses in the Weimar constitution. But a simple comparison of the constitutional and political frameworks of the Bonn and Weimar democracies can only serve to open the question of the bases of the stability and longevity of Bonn democracy in contrast to that of Weimar. Just as the Weimar constitution cannot be blamed as the total explanation of Weimar's failure, so too there is more to the explanation of Bonn's success. The constitutional framework could not in itself guarantee the success of Germany's second attempt at democracy, but it at least provided certain safeguards and provisions to protect the new democracy against some of the problems experienced on the first attempt.

There were a number of key differences between the Bonn and Weimar constitutions. In the Federal Republic, the role of the President – remembering the fateful actions of President Hindenburg – was weakened considerably. The President of the Bonn Republic was to be more of a ceremonial figurehead, a head of state in the symbolic sense with few real powers. He was not to be elected by popular plebiscite, as in the Weimar Republic, but rather – reflecting a certain mistrust in the voice of the people – indirectly by an electoral college. Chancellors could only be ousted by what was called a 'constructive vote of no confidence'. This meant that parliament could not simply indicate its lack of support for a particular Chancellor; it had at the same time to vote in, 'constructively', an alternative who could command majority support in parliament. If no majority could be found for a successor, then a General Election was to be called. (Normally there was no leeway for deciding to call an 'early' election, as in Britain: the standard term of office of West German governments was to be four years.) Thus the President could not simply appoint his own Chancellor and promulgate laws by emergency decree. The notorious article 48 of the Weimar constitution, with its dubious history, had gone.

The voting system was to be a rather complicated one based on the so-called 'd'Hondt' formula. According to the Electoral Law of 1956, each West German elector was to have two votes: one for a named local representative (the equivalent of the British constituency MP), and one for a party. The political parties were to draw up lists of candidates and take as many representatives from these lists as their proportion of the vote entitled them to. The system of proportional representation was however modified by the five per cent hurdle: in order to receive parliamentary representation, a party must receive at least five per cent of the popular vote, or win one constituency outright. This provision was intended to hinder small parties from gaining a national platform for their programmes, as the NSDAP did with only 2.6% of the vote in 1928, and to avoid the problem of having numerous small parties rendering complicated post-election coalition bargaining necessary before a government could be formed. In the event, the fairly numerous small parties active in the early years of the Federal Republic soon became absorbed into the main larger ones, with a couple of important exceptions (the FDP throughout, and from the early 1980s the Greens). There was also a restriction on the type of party that would be permitted to compete for a share of the popular vote: parties deemed to have aims and ideals at odds with those embodied in the 'free democratic basic order' of the constitution were to be banned from organization and activity. The Federal Republic was to be formally a 'party state'. Article 21 of the constitution explicitly stated that 'the political parties shall take part in forming the political will of the people. They may be freely established. They must publicly account for the sources of their funds.'[1]

Elections were to take place also for regional (*Land*) governments. The Federal Republic was to be, as its name implies, a federal state: the separate regional states were to have considerable powers over their own internal affairs. Locally elected *Land* parliaments (*Landtage*) were to control such matters as cultural policy and education. Federalism was an extremely important feature of West German politics, with local elections being matters of considerable importance, and local personalities and issues having high profiles. (The most notable example for much of West Germany's post-war history until his death in 1988 was the 'uncrowned king' of Bavaria, and leader of the Bavarian CSU, Franz-Josef Strauss.) The *Länder* were to send representatives to the second chamber in Bonn, the *Bundesrat*. This was to have certain powers of veto (when the issues directly concerned the *Länder*) and some powers of amending and delaying legislation. The party which commanded a majority in the lower house, the *Bundestag*, need not necessarily command a majority in the *Bundesrat*, given the variable election dates and different political complexions of the local states. The West German upper house thus had a rather different composition than the (historically peculiar) British House of Lords. As a city under Allied control with special status (and not able to elect members of the Bonn parliament directly), West Berlin's city government was also able to send representatives to Bonn.

The West German constitution, as adopted in 1949, subsequently underwent a number of amendments and alterations, both with respect to specific issues (such as remilitarization) and with respect to broader questions, such as the balance between the central *Bund* and the regional *Länder*, and the nature and location of emergency powers. Originally, the constitution stressed a representative, rather than participatory, form of democracy (as in, for example, the indirect election of the President): few Western democrats in 1949 were prepared to trust the German people, so soon after the war, with the degree of democratic freedom that had allowed them, in the Weimar Republic, to bring Hitler to power. The question of the degree to which the constitution of the Federal Republic contributed to its political stability, in contrast to the Weimar Republic, is one to which we shall return below.

The constitution and political system of the GDR

In 1949, when the first constitution of the German Democratic Republic was proclaimed, its status and future prospects were by no means certain. The constitution, which was not ratified by popular vote, was designed to be compatible with that of the Federal Republic, providing the basis for possible future reunification.

Nominally, the German Democratic Republic was to have a multiparty political system with a two-tiered parliament. The lower house of parliament, the *Volkskammer* or People's

Chamber, was the equivalent of the West German *Bundestag* although its actual role and make-up were in practice somewhat different. The upper house, the *Länderkammer*, was to represent the interests of different *Länder* in the GDR, being the equivalent of the West German *Bundesrat*. The *Volkskammer* included representatives of all the permitted parties – CDU, LDPD, NDPD, and DBD – as well as members of the mass organizations, including the Free German Youth (FDJ) and the Confederation of Free German Trade Unions, the FDGB. However, according to Marxist-Leninist principles, elections were held on the basis of single lists of candidates, and each party or organization had a previously determined number of allotted seats in the *Volkskammer*. Thus, given both the fact that the SED had the largest number of seats, and that it dominated the personnel and policies of the other parties and groups which were only nominally independent of communist control, the real character of East German democracy was rather different from that in West Germany.

Formal similarities existed in 1949 in other respects too. But the constitutional similarities between the two systems disappeared as the realities of political, social and economic divergence developed over the decades after the founding of the two Republics. In 1952, the five *Länder* of the GDR were abolished and replaced by thirteen *Bezirke*. These rather smaller regions aided the SED's attainment of its goal of the centralization of politics, and the suppression of regional political strongholds for alternative power bases. In 1958 the *Länderkammer* was abolished.

Another initial similarity with the Federal Republic was the position of the ceremonial head of state, the President. In 1960 the first President of the GDR, Wilhelm Pieck, died; and with his demise went that of the office of President. In its place the *Staatsrat*, or Council of State, took over as a collective head of state, chaired by the leader of the SED, Walter Ulbricht. But the pre-eminence of the *Staatsrat* was similarly short-lived. When Ulbricht was replaced by Honecker in 1971 as First Secretary of the SED, Ulbricht retained the chairmanship of the Council of State; but this was shortly thereafter demoted in importance in favour of the *Ministerrat* or Council of Ministers. In 1968 and again in 1974, there were major amendments of the East German constitution, to take account of changed political realities. In 1968 the 'leading role' of the SED was enshrined in the constitution, rendering any remaining apparent similarities to the West German constitution devoid of all real significance, since the Marxist-Leninist party was able to interpret the formal 'rights' of citizens in any way it chose. In 1974 the constitution was again changed in response to the new status of the GDR under *Ostpolitik* (*see* Chapter Eight).

In theory, the state structure of the East German political system consisted of a pyramid. At the top was the formal head of state – first the President, later the collective head of state, the *Staatsrat*. Below this was the Council of Ministers, to which the different ministries were responsible and where important decision-making in such areas as economics and state security took place. Below this was the People's Chamber, (*Volkskammer*), which met infrequently, effectively to ratify and promulgate legislation decided upon at a higher level. Its functions were therefore very different from those of the West German parliament. There were bodies for local government at regional, district and local levels. At all levels of government, the leading role of the SED was evident – and, indeed, after the 1968 revision, enshrined in the East German constitution until the revolution of 1989.

The SED was itself organized hierarchically, according to the principle of democratic centralism. Lower levels of the hierarchy, while able to have a say in any formulation of policy, were bound ultimately to accept and execute the decisions taken by superior bodies. Ultimately, power lay with the leadership in the Politburo and its secretariat, with the party leader (General Secretary or First Secretary) *primus inter pares*; below the Politburo, the next most important body was the Central Committee, with its specialist subgroups, although membership of the Central Committee might imply more of an advisory than a decision-making role. This was particularly true of so-called 'candidate members' of the Central Committee, who did not have voting rights. Membership of these bodies was, particularly from the 1960s, increasingly predicated on a level of technical expertise in some important area – whether the economy, military matters, or culture. But political commitment to party goals and methods remained the decisive factor. The Central Committee was elected by the Party Congress, which met about every five years (although it was also possible to convene extraordinary party congresses under certain circumstances). At lower levels, there were regional and district party organizations comparable in organizational structure to those at the national level, with their own executive, secretariat, and conference. At the most basic level, party membership was organized in work-based branches, or, where this was not possible, in branches based on place of residence.

As with the West German, so the East German constitution provides only a partial insight into the realities of political development in the GDR. More dramatically than in the West, East Germany actually adopted new constitutions in 1968 and 1974, prior to the more fundamental upheavals of 1989. These were intended partly to reflect more accurately changed political circumstances; and it is in the political realities, rather than the constitutional provisions, that clues to the development and longevity of the GDR must be sought. We shall return to a discussion of the political structures and dynamics of the two German states in more detail in Chapters Ten and Eleven, below; first, however, we must establish a basic chronological framework for the political and socioeconomic development of the two Germanies, and for their relations with the wider world and with each other.

The problem of missed opportunities, 1949–61

A number of open questions concerning the future of Germany remained, even after the formal foundation of the two Republics in 1949. For one thing, it was still quite possible that some means would be found to facilitate reunification. For another, even if Germany remained divided into two states, incorporated into different international spheres of influence, there were a number of possible options available for the internal political development of each Germany. Many Germans, returning from exile or emerging from 'inner emigration', still hoped that a means would be found to develop a democratic, socialist Germany. In the event, in neither East nor West were their hopes to be realized.

In 1949, Adenauer was elected Chancellor by a majority of only one vote, supported by a coalition which had been put together only after considerable politicking and pressurizing. It seemed quite possible that the CDU-dominated coalition government could soon be ousted by an SPD-led government, or at least a coalition of the two major parties (an option which had been seriously canvassed). Had this indeed been the case, the whole future course of West German history – and then also that of both Germanies – might have been quite different. Under Adenauer, the rump state formed out of the British, American and French zones of occupation was to be transformed into a western-orientated, liberal-conservative, materialistic form of 'Chancellor-democracy'. The price paid for the Federal Republic's rapid economic and political rehabilitation was the jettisoning of fellow-countrymen to their fate in the east – and Adenauer deemed it a price worth paying. The Adenauer era poses many problems of evaluation: many criticize Adenauer's policies on a range of grounds while recognizing that the early economic success of the Federal Republic – and its importance to western defence strategies in the Cold War – were vital to the successful establishment of Bonn democracy. Debates about 'missed opportunities' and 'suppressed historical alternatives' are also debates about the likely consequences of alternative policies; and evaluations are frequently complicated by confusions between the immediate effects or acceptability of certain policies on the one hand, and their long-term consequences on the other. These points will be considered in detail in connection with the economic and foreign policies of Adenauer's Germany, as well as the inevitably controversial question of the integration of former Nazis into the new democracy.

Similarly, the dominance of Walter Ulbricht and his particular brand of hardline communism was by no means predetermined in the GDR. Indeed, his authority and position were seriously in question at the time of the June Uprising of 1953; and it was an ironic outcome of this event that Moscow decided to confirm Ulbricht in power rather than topple him, purging Ulbricht's opponents instead. Ulbricht was able in the course of the 1950s to deal with further factional dissent of one sort or another, and from the late 1950s until the 1980s the SED was marked by relatively little internal factional strife. The form of communism which became established in the GDR was a variant of Stalinism which was anathema to humanistic Marxists of the 'Third Way'. Curiously, this too had as a consequence a relative stabilization of the political system in East Germany. In contrast to those communist states where reform communists retained a hold or developed factions within the ruling party, and which subsequently experienced major revolts (Hungary in 1956, Czechoslovakia in 1968, Poland in 1980–1), East Germany was relatively stable for four decades, before the revolutionary year of 1989. While the longevity of the GDR as a communist state cannot be explained solely in terms of the relative cohesion of the ruling party, this was undoubtedly an important factor; and one which Ulbricht's early hardline policies and purging of dissent did much to create.

In neither Germany, then, were democratic socialists or humanist Marxists able to impose their vision of what they thought post-Nazi society should be like; in the course of the 1950s and 1960s very different patterns emerged and crystallized. And in different ways, the two new Germanies repressed their past. The issue of Nazism was ignored, suppressed, or argued away, as new realities and new struggles took precedence in contemporary life.

Associated with the consolidation of new patterns was the question of non-reunification. As with internal politics, certain key turning-points – or missed opportunities – can be discerned. One such is the Stalin overture of 1952. By 1955, when the Soviet Union made another gesture towards reunification, it was clearly too late. In August 1961 the division of the two Germanies was literally cemented, with the building of the Berlin Wall, which closed the last means of escape from East to West.

While the two Germanies had been radically ripped apart in the 1950s, and energetically pointed in different directions, there had yet been a lingering sense of impermanence; but in the 1960s, with division sealed, the two societies witnessed changes of generation and internal divergences as they more gradually, but no less fundamentally, proceeded to grow apart.

Foreign relations

In October 1949, only a few months after the foundation of the Federal Republic, West Germany became a member of the Organization for European Economic Cooperation (OEEC); in March 1951 the Occupation Statute was revised; in April 1951 West Germany entered the European Coal and Steel Community (ECSC) and in May became a full member of the Council of Europe. In 1957, in the Treaty of Rome, West Germany became a founder member of the European Economic Community. Curiously, what began as an attempt to contain the German threat eventuated ultimately in a strong German economy becoming one of the pillars of emerging West European integration in the later post-war period, in contrast to the declining economic power and European influence of Britain, which tended to lag behind as far as European affairs were concerned. Meanwhile, in July 1951 the western powers declared the state of war with Germany to be at an end, although there could still be no peace treaty, as there was no all-German government with which to negotiate it.

Along with West German economic integration went plans for western European defence. In 1950 France began planning the European Defence Community. In the event, considering the proposal for 'mixed units' from different states participating in a supranational force to be an inadequate safeguard against potential future German aggression, the French Parliament in the summer of 1954 failed to ratify the participation of a French army in this Defence Community, following earlier British refusal. (It is curious that a form of this was later revived with a small joint German-French defence force in January 1988.) However,

Eden's plan for Germany to become a full member of the North Atlantic Treaty Organization (NATO), which had been founded in 1949, was agreed in the Paris Treaties, including the German Treaty, of autumn 1954, which took effect on 5 May, 1955. On this date, the Occupation Statute lapsed and the Federal Republic of Germany became a fully sovereign state. The Saar, following a plebiscite, was returned to Germany in 1957. Political and economic rehabilitation of the partial state appeared to be well underway.

But this western integration was not without considerable opposition, both from within West Germany and from the East. As far as the western alliance was concerned, the strategic dimension was crucial: forward troops had to be stationed on German soil to make NATO effective. But within West Germany there was widespread opposition to remilitarization. In the light of the disasters of recent history, many Germans adopted the so-called '*ohne mich*' attitude (literally 'without me', or 'count me out') in relation to rearmament. The refoundation of a German army and the introduction of conscription were highly contentious issues, by no means unanimously supported by the populace of Adenauer's new Germany. (We shall consider the nature and political implications of the army further in Chapter Ten, below.) As far as the USSR was concerned, western integration of the Federal Republic appeared extremely threatening, and to be averted if at all possible.

The year 1952 was a key turning-point which has provoked debates about responsibility for 'lost chances' for reunification. In March 1952, at a crucial stage of negotiations between Paris and Bonn over the European Defence Community, Stalin sent a famous note in which, in return for the abandonment of the West German rearmament process, he proposed a united, neutral, unoccupied Germany. Western historians have spent considerable time speculating on whether or not Stalin's motives were genuine at this time – a debate which reflects the puzzlement of contemporaries, who were also divided and uncertain as to how to react to Stalin's initiative. The most plausible explanation appears to be that at the time of the first note on 10 March, Stalin was indeed genuinely pursuing what was for him a relatively risky course in the interests of averting West Germany's absorption into a western military alliance. By the time of the third note, however, when the western powers had made it clear that they were not amenable to Stalin's overtures, Stalin was simply making propaganda and clarifying to the Germans themselves exactly what options were being closed by the policy of western integration. There is also the question of the responsibility for the failure of this last serious reunification attempt. Many have castigated Adenauer, who – despite compulsory lip-service to the cause of reunification – was firmly committed to a CDU-dominated, western capitalist democracy, and who viewed the prospect of a united, neutral, SPD-dominated state with a predominance of Protestants with little enthusiasm. Whatever the strength of Adenauer's personal views, however, it also seems clear that his ideas ran in the same vein as the perceived interests of the western allies. The American and British plans for western defence were too far developed for them to consider the Soviet offer seriously at this time. To official policies of 'containment' and 'roll-back' of communism, and the importance of negotiation from strength, the western allies could add the 'democratic' argument – against Stalin's view that a peace treaty imposing neutrality should be signed before any elections – that only a democratically elected all-German government could accord binding status to a peace treaty and it would have to be free to determine its own foreign policy, its own neutrality or alliances. Whatever the contribution of different considerations, different individuals and policies, the outcome was that Stalin's reunification initiative of 1952 failed. A subsequent Soviet attempt made in 1955 was viewed as a propaganda gesture with little if any credibility.[2]

In partial response to the integration of the Federal Republic in the west, the German Democratic Republic entered into a comparable set of economic and military alliances in the east. In 1950 East Germany was integrated into the eastern bloc's economic system in the Council for Mutual Economic Aid (COMECON). In 1952 the 'building of socialism' was announced, making it clear that East Germany was now embarking formally on a path of development quite divergent

179

from that of West Germany. In March 1954 the Soviets made a declaration on East German sovereignty, granting the GDR the rights of an 'equal people's democratic state'. The 'People's Police in Barracks' (*Kasernierte Volkspolizei*), which had been set up in 1946, was renamed the 'national armed forces' in 1952; in January 1956 the 'National People's Army' (*Nationale Volksarmee*, NVA) was formally established, and become an integral part of the Warsaw Treaty Organization (or Warsaw Pact) forces. It consisted of 100,000 regular troops, which with additional security and border guards, made a total force altogether of somewhat under 200,000 men.

By the mid-1950s, far from a united German people being viewed with hostility by allied Soviet and western powers as a decade previously, a divided German people now faced each other in hostility, with their respective armed forces representing the wider opposition of the western and Soviet blocs. This dramatic transformation had much to do with the changed international system, and in particular the changed interests of the USA and the USSR in a Europe which they had divided into spheres of interest; but it also reflected the ways in which domestic politicians in each Germany responded to opportunities and constraints during this period. And, whatever the causes of the failure of reunification attempts, in practice both sides consolidated the division by the institutional embedding of the two partial states into two very different systems and spheres of influence.

Adenauer's Germany

When Adenauer came to power, the CDU/CSU held thirty-one per cent of the vote. He had to rely on the support of a number of small parties in addition to the liberal FDP. In many respects, the situation looked comparable to that of the Weimar Republic: larger parties were dependent on coalitions with small, frequently single-issue or regional, parties. Despite the transformation from a purely Catholic party into a more broadly-based Christian Conservative one, the CDU/CSU was not simply assured of a majority; and it seemed quite possible that the instabilities of Weimar politics might bedevil the Federal Republic also. Two extremist parties which were deemed to be hostile to the constitution were outlawed: the right-wing SRP (Socialist Reich Party) in 1952, and the Communist KPD in 1956. At the same time, many adherents of small permitted parties (such as that representing refugees and expellees) began to be won over to the CDU/CSU. In 1957, the CDU/CSU gained over fifty per cent of the vote, achieving an absolute majority for the first time.

A number of factors are relevant to any explanation of the success of Adenauer and the CDU in the 1950s. Probably the single most important factor was the vigorous rate of economic growth. Pragmatic, material considerations undoubtedly played a major role in sustaining and increasing popular support for the CDU. The so-called 'economic miracle', with the astonishing leaps in West Germany's productivity, an economy growing at around eight per cent a year, and rapid improvements in living conditions, made many Germans willing to accept a regime that seemed to be delivering the goods. Adenauer's election slogan of 'No experiments!' (*Keine Experimente!*) symbolized the cautious, pragmatic approach to politics of many people who had been through too many ideological and socio-economic upheavals in recent years to want to commit themselves in a wholehearted, idealistic way to a new political orientation. They were prepared simply to assent, relatively passively, to the system that appeared to be working for the time being. This benefited both the political system in general – democracy was at last being associated, not with economic crises, as in the Weimar Republic, but with economic success – and the CDU-led government in particular, since it was Adenauer's Economics Minister, Ludwig Erhard, who was presiding over the economic miracle. Few were willing to risk or jettison this fragile, recent success in order to experiment with Social Democratic theories or policies.

The economy of the western zones of occupied Germany was already beginning to pick up before the full impact of the Marshall Plan, or European Recovery Programme, was felt. The role of Marshall Aid in furthering an economic recovery which was already underway was not only financial – it has been estimated that in the western zones the total occupation costs and reparations may have exceeded the amount of actual aid received – but also, perhaps more importantly, it was a stimulant to economic activity and a psychological prop, lending credence to the Deutschmark and encouraging investment in an economy which had American backing. The Marshall Plan also had consequences for the psychology of industrial relations, and the political organization of the economy, which are more nebulous and difficult to quantify but in the long term just as important for German economic recovery. The fostering of a managerial climate of opinion, and the depoliticizing of industrial relations, with a focus on enhanced productivity rather than social redistribution, were certainly important factors in post-war economic growth. Low wage demands, a low strike record and a relative lack of militancy characterized the conduct of federal German trade unions. The refugees' urgent desire for jobs even at low wages was an obvious factor but other factors too, including the exclusion of communist influence, were important. And as the economy grew, people were even less inclined to rock the economic boat, subscribing rather to the psychology of 'rebuilding' ('*Wir bauen wieder auf*').[3]

The structure of the West German economy has often been labelled 'social market', a term that became current among neo-liberal economists in the late 1940s. (Whatever the relevance of the label at first, the Western German economy turned towards neo-Keynesianism in the mid- and later 1960s, and changed again in the 1980s, but the original label has tended to stick.) To some extent the revival of neo-liberal (or so-called Ordo-liberal) ideas represented an understandable desire to mark a break with the state-directed economy of the Nazi period, and to give a freer rein to market forces, with the state merely guaranteeing the conditions for productivity but not playing too interventionist a role. Some analysts have suggested however that the West German economy of the 1950s and 1960s was neither 'social' nor 'market'. Interventions, steering, and control by the state made the notion of a 'free market' into at best a half-truth. The qualification 'social' was intended to deal with this, since the state was not only to ensure the conditions for economic growth, but also to protect the weaker members of society from the full ravages of market forces. Conservatives and Social Democrats differed in their interpretations of the extent and character of such protection. It was quite clear to both supporters and opponents of the conservative government in the 1950s that its economic policies would serve to increase the gaps between rich and poor, would increase disparities in wealth and lead to a more unequal society. High profits, tax incentives, and squeezes on domestic credit encouraged investment, while workers' wages were kept low, with only modest increases. By the mid-1960s, a large proportion of the nation's wealth was concentrated in a small minority of hands. But the assumption was made that overall growth would be of a sufficient scale and speed that *all* members of society would benefit from increased shares in a larger national cake, even if some benefited more than others. And the 1952 Equalization of Burdens Law was intended to compensate those who had suffered disproportionately as a result of the war, particularly refugees from the east.

In the event, the average disposable income of West German households grew by four hundred per cent between 1950 and 1970. People compared their own situations, not with the degree to which other people's prosperity had increased, but rather with their own past: and they were for the most part able to register an extraordinary change from the ruins and devastation of the immediate post-war period. Being well-fed and well-housed mattered more to most West Germans than the seemingly more academic question of whether theirs was becoming a more unequal society. Interestingly, the percentages supporting democratic – rather than monarchical or Nazi – political views in opinion polls of the 1950s and early 1960s grew in close correlation with the increase in the average weights of ever more satiated West Germans.[4]

A number of factors are relevant to explaining West Germany's rapid growth, in addition to the direct and indirect effects of the Marshall Plan mentioned above. It was uniquely adapted to benefit from the Korean War which broke out in June 1950, and from subsequent defence policies (in favour of nuclear, rather than conventional, defences, as favoured by Defence Minister Franz-Josef Strauss). The structure of unions was simplified, with one union per industry, and the unified unions belonging to a single umbrella organization, the DGB. A myth soon grew up of 'social partnership' between employers and employees. 'Co-determination' in industry (*Mitbestimmung*) was in fact only introduced, against considerable employer opposition, in a limited fashion in 1951, so that all joint stock companies in the coal and steel industries with over a thousand employees had to have representation of workers' views at the managerial level. (It was extended, again against considerable employer opposition, in 1976 to cover *all* joint stock companies with over two thousand employees.) In 1952, the Works Constitution Law provided that there should be works councils for enterprises with more than twenty employees. West Germany had a relatively low strike record. It also uniquely benefited, in the first decade or so after its foundation, from a supply of cheap and mobile labour: the refugees from the German Democratic Republic. Initially these people represented a burden of extra bodies to be housed and fed; and in 1950 the unemployment rate stood at 8.1%. But the rapidly expanding economy was soon able to absorb them (with early help from the Korean War boom), and by the mid-1960s the unemployment rate stood at a mere 0.5%. During the 1950s, around three million people fled from the east, and a large proportion of these were young, skilled people in search of better career prospects than they could find in East Germany. Many of the attempts by the Allies to restructure and decentralize the economy were successfully resisted by West German industrialists: there was fairly rapid reconcentration and recentralization, and the revised Law on Decartelization which was passed after many amendments in 1957 left sufficient loopholes as to be little impediment to West German industrialists.

Whatever the reasons, in the course of the 1950s West Germany was becoming a prosperous society. By the later 1950s, writers such as Heinrich Böll were beginning to pour scorn on what they saw as a bourgeois, self-satisfied materialism which lived only for current comforts and suppressed the past; but rapid economic success was certainly a powerful factor in ensuring the early commitment of vast numbers of formerly undemocratic Germans to the new democracy which had been in large measure thrust upon them in an hour of national humiliation and defeat. The contrast to the early years of Weimar democracy is striking.

Despite the relative lack of positive ideological commitment to democracy, there was nevertheless a powerful transitional ideology in the 1950s: that of anti-communism. Anti-communism had long been a prevalent orientation among the German middle classes, and it had played an important role in the rise of Hitler. It was not something new which had to be inculcated in the Germans by foreign powers. Yet it took on new flavours during the Cold War, and was stimulated by the anti-communism in particular of the Americans. Fear of the 'bolshevist threat' provided powerful support for Adenauer's policies of western integration, outweighing the natural desire of most Germans to see their country reunified. At the same time, the example of Marxist-Leninist practice in the East was used to cast aspersions on the West German SPD, which, despite its constant and genuine avowal of commitment to democracy, was adversely affected by slur campaigns from the right.

The SPD itself was somewhat in disarray in the 1950s, and did not present a powerful and united opposition to Adenauer and the CDU. There had always been tensions within the SPD since its foundation, and we have seen the way in which splits among socialists facilitated the rise of Hitler. In the 1950s, there were debates on a number of issues, including the fiercely divisive question of German rearmament and remilitarization. But by the late 1950s, under the rather drab leadership of Erich Ollenhauer who had succeeded Schumacher as leader on his death in 1952, the issue was less one of principle than of pragmatic politics: how, with its electoral support static or even declining, could the SPD ever hope to present a serious challenge to the broadly-based and recently triumphant CDU? The SPD's solution to the conundrum of being seen as a working-class and radical party in an increasingly middle-class, affluent, and materialist society, was contained in the Bad Godesberg programme of 1959: the SPD simply abandoned the electorally damaging Marxist rhetoric it had inherited from its pre-Nazi past, and aimed instead to become a 'catch-all people's party' (*Volkspartei*). No longer did the SPD profess the revolutionary aim of transforming and overthrowing the capitalist socio-economic order; rather, like the CDU, it aimed to improve its functioning so that inequities could be alleviated by growth in the national cake.[5] Differences in domestic socio-economic policy between the parties were subsequently to be more differences of method, rather than of principle or goal. Nevertheless, certain key differences between the two major parties remained, particularly in the sphere of foreign policy before the completion of *Ostpolitik*.

In West Germany in the 1950s, many people were able to find a new way of life and to forget or repress unpleasant memories of the recent past. People were able to find jobs and live in relatively comfortable homes; they obtained enough food to eat, and increasing numbers were able to afford luxuries and durable consumer goods such as fridges and cars. Under Adenauer's leadership, West Germany was beginning to be able to assert itself as a responsible and necessary partner in a number of transnational activities, both economic and political, in the western world. The Nazi past could be ignored, except insofar as the privations of recent years of war and occupation were contrasted with the modest but increasing prosperity of the present. Former Nazis, both the committed and the conformists, were able to fit relatively easily into Adenauer's Germany. Although in the immediate post-war period about 53,000 civil servants had been dismissed for membership of the NSDAP, only about 1000 were excluded permanently from any future employment. Under the 1951 Reinstatement Act, many were reemployed in the civil service, and obtained full pension credits for their service in the Third Reich. By the early 1950s, between forty and eighty per cent of officials were former NSDAP members. Similarly, only a very few members of the judiciary were permanently disqualified.[6] Former Nazis were even able to gain prominent positions in public life: Adenauer was quite prepared to include former Nazis in his cabinet, such as former SS-member Oberländer as Minister for Refugees. Perhaps the most controversial of Adenauer's appointments was that of Hans Globke, the author of the official commentary on the Nuremberg Race Laws of 1935, as Adenauer's chief aide in his Chancellery. (Subsequent apologists for this appointment have tried to suggest that Globke's interpretation of the Nuremberg Laws was a milder one than others might have written.)[7] Past misdemeanours in different circumstances were ignored in favour of current attitudes and expressed changes of heart. If the Hitler-period was considered at all, it was more or less dismissed as an isolated aberration in German history when a madman unfortunately took over the country and misled the poor German people, leading them into war and committing atrocities in their name about which they had known nothing. (On the other hand, many West Germans still assented to the statement that Hitler would have been one of the greatest statesmen there had ever been, if only he had not lost the war.) For the most part, however, working for the present and the future was more important – and certainly more productive – than raking over the ashes of the past. The main point was to rebuild, not sort through the ruins.

The period is an exceedingly difficult one to evaluate – if indeed it is part of the task of historians to evaluate. It is a period which has provoked heated debates among Germans. A number of facts are clear, and lead to somewhat contradictory conclusions. From one point of view, it can be pointed out that many former Nazis received minimal, if any, punishment for their crimes or complicity in an evil regime. It can even be shown that entrepreneurs who built up vast personal fortunes on the basis of Nazi 'aryanization' policies (forcible expropriation of Jewish concerns) and exploitation of slave labour, working Poles and Jews to the bone before their death by exhaustion, starvation or gassing, were able to use the capital thus amassed to continue successful entrepreneurial careers in the Federal Republic – and to influence prominent politicians in their favour.[8] It can be pointed out that there was a massive wastage of talent, as thousands of courageous people who had refused to compromise with the Third Reich found their paths to post-war careers in the Civil Service blocked, as positions were retained or re-filled by Nazi time-servers.[9] It can be pointed out that the chance of a fundamental restructuring of German society was missed, as neither structure nor personnel were radically changed in an era of conservative 'restoration'. Against all this, it can be asserted that without the integration of former Nazis, and without the startling economic success, Bonn democracy might have had as little chance of survival as Weimar democracy. Radical anti-system opposition on the part of a few activists would have combined with mass discontent based on economic misery and uncertainty to provide powerful forces for political destabilization. The argument can be mounted that the end, retrospectively, might have justified the means: actions which can be criticized on moral grounds might have had consequences which even the critics would applaud. In any event, the ambiguities which are contained in these historical reflections were ambiguities which were to explode into the West German public arena in the 1960s, although not always in a manner characterized by rational discussion.

Ulbricht's Germany, 1949–61

Meanwhile, a comparable if rather more fragile consolidation – based more on repression than success – was taking place in the GDR. In 1948, the SED had become a 'party of a new type', in line with the general Stalinization of East European Soviet satellite states. The proponent of the notion of a 'German road to socialism', Anton Ackermann, was subjected to a process of 'criticism and self-criticism' and forced to recant.[10] Stalin was introduced as a new idol, and party schools forced the Stalin cult onto party members. Although the word *Volksdemokratie* (People's Republic) was not formally used until the Second Party Conference of July 1952, in practice the GDR was already in 1949 comparable to other Soviet satellite states.

At the Third Party Congress of the SED, 20–4 July 1952, Walter Ulbricht was elected General Secretary of the SED (a title which was changed to First Secretary in 1954, when the

Soviet Union moved to a more collective form of leadership after Stalin's death), thus gaining a position of dominance which he succeeded in retaining until 1971. The late 1940s and early 1950s saw the transformation of the structure of the SED, with the introduction of a Central Committee and Politburo in 1950 and the development of cadre politics, as well as the 'cleansing' of the party with the purging of individuals with social-democratic or western leanings or associations. At the Second Party Conference of 9–12 July 1952, the 'building of socialism' was announced.

A combination of methods were employed to ensure the compliance of the East German populace, including terror as well as attempted ideological indoctrination, as the SED sought both to control the state means of administration, policing and justice, and to exert its influence in education, the media and all avenues of opinion formation. Schoolteachers were supposed to teach the new political principles, and those unwilling to do so were likely to be replaced. Christians were subjected to coercion, with the secularization of schools, and the squeezing out of religious education – although curiously, given the radical measures of expropriation taken in other areas, church property had been left intact in the occupation period, and the churches had been left to denazify their own personnel (which, it might be noted in passing, they had accomplished in a less than energetic manner). While Christian institutions remained relatively unscathed – and at this time retained their all-German links – individual Christians were subjected to considerable harassment. The young Christians' organization *Junge Gemeinde* was tarnished as an 'illegal organization' of political opposition, supposedly harbouring enemy agents and spies. The introduction in 1954 of a secular state 'confirmation' ceremony, the *Jugendweihe* (*see* plate 15), which Christians viewed as incompatible with confirmation in church, was used as a means to identify and discriminate against the children of those not fully committed to the state ideology.[11] Members of the 'bourgeoisie' and their children were also systematically discriminated against, in favour of the ideologically committed and the politically sound members of the working classes and peasantry. Life was less than comfortable for many previously relatively privileged people in the new GDR of the 1950s.

Admittedly, it could be claimed that this coercion was in a good cause: that of greater social equality. But it appeared to many that it was merely replacing one form of privilege by another, and one form of dictatorship by another. Yet no-one could foresee how long the current situation was likely to last. Moreover, the particular, hardline form of communism which developed in the GDR in the 1950s was not inevitable – alternatives seemed possible to many socialist humanists – and the dominance of Ulbricht as party leader did not go unchallenged.

There were serious differences of opinion within the higher echelons of the SED in the summer of 1953, which to some extent reflected differences in Moscow after Stalin's death in the spring of that year. In some conflict with Ulbricht over certain areas of policy were Rudolf Herrnstadt (editor of *Neues Deutschland*) and Wilhelm Zaisser (Minister for State Security). They were supported in Moscow by Beria, and Moscow was seriously considering the ousting and replacement of Walter Ulbricht, who was not an entirely convinced supporter of Moscow's 'New Course'. Differences of opinion within the SED played a key role in the origins of the only major uprising in the GDR's history before the revolution of 1989, that of June 1953.[12] While productivity goals (or 'work norms') were being increased for industrial workers, causing an exacerbation of already existing discontent with living conditions in the 'Soviet zone' (as it was still called by those who refused to concede legitimacy to the GDR), concessions were being made to other groups, including the middle classes and the peasantry. These somewhat contradictory policies in relation to increased work norms were announced suddenly, and not only was there no prior warning to the general population, there was also inadequate prior discussion and preparation for those party functionaries who would have to justify the new line. Remarkably for a communist state, quite different official views appeared in the press. On 14 June an article in *Neues Deutschland* (which was of course edited by Herrnstadt) criticized the SED's hardline policies; while on 16 June an article in the official trade union

(FDGB) newspaper *Tribüne* came out in support of the raised work norms.

On 16 June workers in the Stalinallee, who were employed on the massive construction of this imposing street as a monument of Stalinist architecture, decided that rather than sending two representatives they would together down tools and go as a group to the central union building to protest against this measure. Soon the workers from the first site were joined by others. A series of accidental circumstances turned this spontaneous protest against a specific measure into a more general political demonstration. On arrival at the FDGB house, no-one in authority appeared; so the crowd moved on to the *Haus der Ministerien*, where they shouted down Minister Selbmann and Professor Havemann (who was later to gain a reputation as a dissident humanist Marxist, placed under house arrest for most of his life). The situation became further confused as a result of contradictory announcements. While Selbmann proclaimed the retraction of the raised work norms, a Politburo announcement simply said that the decision of the Council of Ministers would have to be reconsidered. There was an increasing sense of power among the crowd, who began to make political demands for the resignation of the regime; but they remained lacking in central direction and leadership, and there was no strike committee to take overall direction of the protest. Nevertheless, one enterprising worker seized a loudspeaker and pronounced a general strike for the following day, 17 June. In the event, on 17 June there were uprisings and demonstrations in a number of places spread across the GDR, with between 300,000 and 372,000 workers going on strike – an estimated 5.5% to 6.8% of the work force. Most of those demonstrating were industrial workers, with little or no participation from the middle classes, the intelligentsia or the peasants.

Despite this evidence of widespread popular dissatisfaction among the workers, who were now supposed to be an emancipated proletariat, and despite the obviously quite serious challenge to his authority, Ulbricht came out of the June Uprising with his power augmented rather than decreased. The protestors had failed to develop an adequate organization or leadership, and their movement was already losing impetus and direction before it was finally suppressed by a display of force by Soviet tanks on the afternoon of 17 June. Twenty-one people were killed, and shots were fired mainly in the air as a warning: the level of violence was relatively low in comparison with conflicts on German streets earlier in the twentieth century. Although Ulbricht had to back down on work norms, and workers thus obtained an apparent concession, ironically the main result of the uprising was the confirmation in power of the hardliners and Ulbricht himself. Herrnstadt and Zaisser were removed from their positions in the Politburo, and in January 1954 they were expelled from the SED for 'factionalism'. This was made easier by the downfall of their supporter in Moscow, Beria. The Justice Minister, Max Fechner, who had been inclined to lenience towards the strikers, was removed from his position on 16 July, and harsh sentences were imposed on many 'ringleaders' who were convicted on political charges (since there was under the GDR's first constitution a right to strike). In the course of the following months, the SED was purged throughout its ranks, with the denunciation of approximately twenty thousand functionaries and fifty thousand ordinary members as 'provocateurs'. Former Social Democrats were particularly affected in this way.

There were still challenges to Ulbricht's views in the course of the 1950s. Ulbricht himself had considerable difficulty with the de-stalinization initiated in Eastern Europe by Khrushchev's speech at the Twentieth Party Congress of the Communist Party of the Soviet Union in February 1956. In the end, he was again more or less saved by another uprising – this time in Hungary. In the context of political instability elsewhere in Eastern Europe, it seemed too risky to the Soviet leadership to open the opportunity of destabilization in the GDR by a change of leadership there.

Ulbricht also had to deal with a number of individuals and groups in the GDR who hoped for a real destalinization and liberalization of East German socialism. A curious and eclectic set of political demands from a group of critical Marxists associated with Wolfgang Harich was published in 1956. Their programme implied a general liberalization and democratization and even, in the context of possible reunification with West Germany, suggested that the SED would have to step down in favour of the SPD if this were the democratic majority will of the people in free all-German elections. Harich was himself in communication both with the West German SPD and the Polish reform communists. Ulbricht was understandably less than enthusiastic about Harich's proposals and activities, and Harich was sentenced to ten years' imprisonment (but released in 1964 after an apparent change of heart). His associates received varying lesser sentences. Politics as such was not the only area in which Ulbricht had to contend with vocal, explicit differences of opinion. Fritz Behrens, Arne Benary, and other revisionist economists were advocating economic reforms implying decentralization. They too were at this time attacked and silenced (although some of their ideas were subsequently resurrected in the New Economic System of the 1960s). Finally, in 1958, certain rivals or opponents of Ulbricht in the Central Committee and Politburo – Karl Schirdewan, Erich Wollweber, Gerhart Ziller, Fritz Selbmann, Paul Wandel and Fred Oelssner – were removed. By the end of the 1950s, Ulbricht had effectively consolidated his political hold and eradicated the presence of 'Third Way', humanistic Marxists, at least from the higher echelons of the SED.[13]

Ulbricht had not however gained the kind of pragmatic support among the population that was evident in Adenauer's Germany. The differences were partly political, partly economic. People resented the repression, the existence of the security police, the harsh measures imposed on those with differences of political opinion, the constraints on the activities of Christians, the uniform world-view which was being inculcated in the schools and the media, the sense of fear and the pressures towards conformity in every area of life which necessitated the continuous leading of a double life (to which many Germans had become all too accustomed, in different ways, under the Nazi regime). At the same time, there were few material advantages to be enjoyed in the GDR, particularly for skilled people who could potentially be high earners in the West. The East German concentration on heavy industrial production rather than consumer goods, and the extraordinary difficulties experienced in transforming and centralizing the economy led to difficulties in the supply and quality of basic necessities such as food and clothing. People simply did not like the standard of living in the GDR in the 1950s, particularly in comparison with the ever-improving living conditions in West Germany.

Throughout the 1950s there were attempts at central state control of the economy launched via major 'plans' on the Soviet model. These were perpetually being subjected to revision in order that at least some measure of fulfilment might be seen to have been achieved. There were numerous problems associated with central planning. The aim in industry was the production of *quantity*, with little concern for the quality – or saleability – of goods. Prices were fixed, in order to aid planning, and did not represent any true measure of supply and demand. The time lag of plans meant that they were generally out-of-date before they were implemented; and the one-year focus of plan-fulfilment meant that managers would either produce 'soft' plans that were easily 'overfulfilled', or, if difficulties were experienced in fulfilling a plan, use up stock and not replace capital equipment in order to achieve the appropriate balance at the end of the year. The lack of managerial responsibility for investment also led to a wastefulness in the use of resources.

Initially the emphasis was, in line with the Soviet Union, on heavy capital goods industries. Following the death of Stalin in 1953 and the introduction of the 'New Course' under Malenkov, there was in theory a shift towards greater consumer orientation in production (also related to the impact of the 1953 Uprising). However, in 1954 the New Course was abandoned in the USSR, and the GDR now adopted the dual aim of combining consumer orientation with the production of capital goods. The need for greater inter-regional specialization within the COMECON states was recognized, and reflected in the second Five Year Plan announced for 1956–60. However, considerable problems were experienced in the reorientation of the East German economy towards its eastern neighbours and partners. The Five Year Plan was abandoned, and a Seven Year Plan was announced for 1959–65 to synchronize the GDR's economic development with that of the USSR. The end of the 1950s actually saw an upturn in the GDR's economy, coinciding with a brief period of economic difficulty in the Federal Republic. The GDR now proudly proclaimed that its goal was to overtake the West Germans in material as well as moral terms. It was even suggested that those considering flight to the West would be better off staying in the East. However, the beginning of the 1960s saw renewed economic problems, and the Seven Year Plan had been dropped by the summer of 1962. A second Seven Year Plan was announced for 1962–70, but was never enacted, as other developments intervened (on which more below).

The 1950s also witnessed the collectivization of East German agriculture. In 1952–3 agricultural production co-operatives (*Landwirtschaftliche Produktionsgenossenschaften*, LPGs), were set up. Initially, only the land was tilled together, and use was made of machine and tractor-lending stations. (These were known as 'Type I' collectives.) By 1959, LPGs accounted for about 45% of the agricultural sector. In 1959–60 there was a further wave of enforced collectivization, raising the proportion of co-operative farms to about 85%. By the end of the 1960s, most co-operatives were of the so-called Type III, where there was total collectivization including livestock and machinery. Initial collectivization of agriculture was associated with decreased productivity. Just as the first wave of collectivization was associated with economic and ultimately political problems in 1952–3, so the second wave in 1960 saw the flight of farmers to the west, and of townspeople as the food position worsened, necessitating the reintroduction of rationing in 1961.

There was still one simple means for people to escape from East Germany, provided that they did not want to take too much by way of possessions: they could travel to East Berlin, proceed to West Berlin, and then leave for West Germany from there. Figures of refugees adopting this route varied from year to year, with particularly bad figures in years of economic crisis, as in the wake of the rapid collectivization of agriculture in 1959–60. Up to 1961, an estimated three and a half million people left the GDR for the West (with a counter-traffic of perhaps half a million, implying a net loss to the GDR of three million). Given the predominantly skilled, educated nature of these refugees – who, according to some surveys, gave economic considerations and better material and career prospects in the West as their primary motives for leaving – it was a drain of talent and labour that the post-war economy of the GDR could ill sustain. It served only to exacerbate the problems which were also the main cause of the haemorrhage. In 1961 Ulbricht terminated this flow with the building of the Berlin Wall. On August 13 1961, Berliners stood amazed and aghast as barbed wire, bricks and concrete rapidly divided their streets, and neighbours and families living only a few yards from each other were separated as finally and effectively as if they had been resident in Moscow and Washington. The building of the Wall was an admission that the population had to be contained by a form of national house arrest, imprisonment within its own country; but also, in some ways, it created the conditions for a subsequent process of coming to terms with, and finding an acceptable way of life in, that country. From 1961, there were very clearly two Germanies; and, with such different political and economic structures, they increasingly grew apart in their social and cultural patterns also. The 1960s proved to be a decade of divergence and inner transformation in East and West Germany alike.

EIGHT

Transformation and the 'Established Phase', 1961–88

At the time of Adenauer's stunning election victory of 1957, and the SPD's dispirited change of course at Bad Godesberg in 1959, it appeared that the CDU was in an almost unbeatable ascendancy. However, a mere decade later, in 1969, West Germany had an SPD Chancellor for the first time since the Müller cabinet of 1928–30. And, within three years of taking office, Willy Brandt had negotiated a series of agreements in his so-called *Ostpolitik* which fundamentally altered the relationship of the two divided Germanies. By this time, the climate on both sides of the Wall was quite different from that of the 1950s.

Adenauer's position began to wane in the late 1950s, his authority in his own party being seriously weakened by the crisis in 1959 over his vacillating and ambivalent candidacy for the position of President. He was persuaded to stand, then ultimately withdrew, partly because he was unable to resolve to his own satisfaction the question of who should succeed him as Chancellor, and partly because he realised the Presidency's lack of real power. But Adenauer delayed his departure from the national political stage too long; when he finally went, after having presided over West Germany's phenomenal early resurrection from the ashes of the Third Reich, he departed under a cloud. In 1962, Adenauer was seriously discredited by what is known as the *Spiegel* Affair. NATO autumn manoeuvres had revealed that West German civilian defences and conventional arms were essentially inadequate. It had been in the interests of West German industry in the 1950s to have a defence policy oriented towards potentially profitable nuclear armaments rather than conventional defence forces, which would have been manpower-intensive in a period of labour shortage. The weekly news magazine *Spiegel* published a highly critical article, which was in fact but one in a long series seeking to discredit Adenauer's Minister of Defence, Franz-Josef Strauss, through accusations of improprieties, misconduct and corruption. *Spiegel*'s offices were raided (recalling methods employed by the Nazis) and eleven members of the journal's staff were arrested and charged with leakage of defence secrets (one was even hauled back from holiday in Spain for this purpose). In the ensuing controversy, the article itself became infinitely less important than issues relating to freedom of the press in a democratic state. Nor did the politicians always act with integrity: Strauss himself at first lied over his role in the Spanish arrest, and it was revealed that Adenauer and Strauss had seriously misled Parliament. After considerable pressure (including the refusal of FDP ministers in the coalition to work with Strauss), Adenauer was forced to accede to Strauss' resignation and to confirm that he would himself retire in 1963. The 'affair' was thus significant, less for what *Spiegel* had actually printed, than for the sea-change in German politics which it helped to inaugurate.

Adenauer was succeeded as Chancellor by the mastermind of the economic miracle, Ludwig Erhard. Unfortunately, Erhard was less adept at politics than at economics – and even in the latter field his Chancellorship ran into difficulties. The FDP had been in alliance with the CDU-CSU since the elections of 1961 (when the CDU/CSU lost 28 seats, the SPD gained 21 and the FDP gained 26); this alliance was reconfirmed after the 1965 election (when the FDP lost 18 seats, the CDU/CSU gained 3, and the SPD gained 12). However, difficulties in the West German economy by the mid-1960s led to serious problems in attempting to balance the budget. In October 1966 Erhard's proposals, which included higher taxes, were not accepted by the FDP, and the FDP cabinet ministers resigned. At the same time, increasingly vocal currents in the SPD were arguing that it was time to show that the Social Democrats were capable of taking governmental responsibility, rather than remaining permanently in opposition.

A powerful government appeared all the more desirable because of a worrying rise in right-wing activities in the shape of the neo-Nazi NPD, as well as considerable criticism from left-wing quarters. Shades of Weimar appeared to loom on the horizon. In the event, responsible politicians decided to take effective action to ensure stable majority government: in November 1966 a 'Grand Coalition' between the CDU/CSU and the SPD was formed, with the CDU's Kurt Georg Kiesinger (a member of the NSDAP from 1933 to 1945) as Chancellor, and SPD's ex-Mayor of Berlin, Willy Brandt (who had an impeccable anti-Nazi record and was accused by some nationalists of having been a 'traitor' for having fought against the Germans in the Second World War), as Foreign Minister. This participation of the SPD in government opened a new period in West German political history.

Neo-liberal economic policies were replaced by neo-Keynesian policies (a transition which had begun already under Erhard). The 1967 Law for Promoting Stability and Growth in the economy gave the government new tools to intervene in the economy. Tax concessions were reduced and a programme of investment in the economic infrastructure (particularly in expanding education and improving motorway and rail networks) was introduced. Co-operation among workers, employers and the state was encouraged in the so-called 'Concerted Action', which was held to be a means of dealing effectively with policy formation in periods of economic crisis. Particularly after 1969, when there was a coalition government between SPD and FDP, there was what has been termed a veritable 'planning euphoria', with a new Research and Technology Ministry established in 1972.

The supply of refugee labour had dried up with the building of the Berlin Wall. The West German economy in the 1960s became increasingly reliant on cheap 'guest workers' (*Gastarbeiter*), who were encouraged to come to Germany from the Mediterranean countries. While in 1960 foreigners represented 1.1% of the workforce, by 1973 they constituted nearly 10%. These foreigners were brought in with little thought for their future status or the well-being of their families. They were in the main simply seen as a supply of labour which could be exploited in low-paid, unskilled, temporary and frequently dirty or dangerous jobs which unionized German workers were unwilling to take on. Moreover, they had incurred no previous costs to Germany by way of education or training, and their tax and insurance contributions helped the German welfare system considerably. Insofar as thought was given to the future of these workers, it was by and large simply assumed that young men would come and work for a few years, without dependents, and would send money home to their families, to whom they would eventually return. In the event, however, many families came and settled, and inevitably, too, many children of *Gastarbeiter* were actually born in Germany, which was more 'home' to them than an unfamiliar country which they rarely visited. The *Gastarbeiter* were to find that they were less than welcome guests in West Germany when oil crises and world recession in the 1970s and 1980s were accompanied by rising unemployment and economic difficulties.

After the startling rates of economic growth experienced in the 1950s, the German economy began to come into line with the performance of other western economies in the 1960s. It also began to be westernized in other ways. With a change of generations, younger entrepreneurs began to adopt American attitudes and patterns of industrial organization.[1] Importantly for the firm anchoring of the new democracy, economic elites found that they could use the political system to their advantage – in contrast to the Weimar Republic, when it was viewed as a hindrance. Under the form of corporatism which developed in West Germany, employers' organizations, unions, and the farming lobby were able to meet and hammer out compromise policies which then informed the legislative process in the *Bundestag*. From one point of view, this could be argued to be a less than democratic influence on the parliamentary decision-making process; from another, it could be seen as an efficient means of policy-formation which sought the views of a range of organized interests in advance of any detailed legislation.

West Germany became, visibly, a very different place in the course of the 1960s. Old, ruined town centres were rebuilt, with modern buildings and pedestrian shopping precincts. Transport was improved, with rapidly expanding networks of autobahns bringing formerly isolated communities into a more modern, fast-moving society. Fewer people were working on the land, and in the old heavy industries: more were beginning to work in the service sector and in new electronics and other high-tech industries. The image of affluence was spreading: the 'typical' West German was no longer an emaciated ex-POW, a person lacking an arm or a leg, a prematurely aged widow in black, but rather a bloated, cigar-smoking businessman, an efficient banker or industrialist, or a fashion-conscious, smartly-dressed woman. The 'toytown' image of new, freshly-painted housing, clean streets, pleasant facilities, was developing. The charge that Germany was an 'economic giant, but a political dwarf' might have been partially justified; but new generations were growing up who would radically change the face of German politics. The passage was to be a stormy one.

As we shall see further (in Chapter Eleven, below), the 1960s was a decade of political polarization: it saw increasing antagonism between comfortable conservatives and the idealists of an emerging New Left. This was partly also a polarization of generations: between the older generation who had lived through the Third Reich, with their baggage of compromise and expediency and their rationalizations and repressions, and younger people who challenged the role, conduct and values of their parents' generation. Numerous factors were involved in the cataclysmic clashes of the 1960s: wider trends in the western world (the emergence of a youth culture characterized most succinctly by the slogan 'make love not war'); the expansion of higher education; political issues such as American involvement in Vietnam; and in the German case the reaction against the lack of effective parliamentary opposition during the Grand Coalition, necessitating – so it seemed – the development of extra-parliamentary opposition. The clashes came to a head with the shooting of a student on a demonstration in Berlin in the summer of 1967, and the year of student revolt in 1968.

In the following years, left-wing protests diversified and became more sectarian; one notorious group was to be the terrorist Red Army Faction, active throughout the 1970s.

East Germany in the 1960s

By late 1961, Ulbricht appeared to have secured the future of his form of communism in East Germany. Mass dissent had been suppressed; revisionists had been purged from the SED; the building of the Berlin Wall had ended the damaging drain of skilled manpower to the west; and the lack of effective intervention of the western powers, both in 1953 and 1961, indicated that no-one was willing to make an international issue, involving violent confrontation, of the German question. Although not formally recognized as a legitimate separate state by the Federal Republic of Germany – whose 'Hallstein doctrine' also meant refusing diplomatic relations with any other country which did recognize the GDR – to all intents and purposes East Germany was now an established state. It was moreover one of considerable economic and military importance to the Soviet empire in eastern Europe. And to the people of East Germany, after the building of the Berlin Wall it seemed that they would simply have to make the best of a life to which there was no longer any alternative.

There was even something of an upturn in the East German economy in the 1960s, although interesting experiments in the economic sphere were not given long enough to prove themselves. There had been discussions in the later 1950s by certain GDR economists such as Professor Fritz Behrens and Dr Arne Benary about possible economic reforms, but in 1956–7 they had been officially attacked and denounced as 'revisionists'. In 1962 discussion started in the USSR of ideas officially associated with the name of Liberman. At first, these Soviet discussions were merely reported without comment in the GDR; then they were taken up for discussion there too. On 15 January 1963, at the Sixth Congress of the SED, Ulbricht suddenly revealed reform proposals which showed the influence of the Liberman debate. The spring of 1963 saw small-scale experiments; these were discussed in the Central Committee of the SED in June 1963; and on 11 July 1963 the Council of Ministers approved the 'Principles for the New Economic System of Planning and Management of the National Economy'. This was defined as 'the organic combination of (a) scientifically based leadership in the economy, and (b) scientifically grounded central state planning of the long term, together with (c) the comprehensive use of material interest in the shape of the consistent system of economic levers'.[2]

The New Economic System (NES) differed somewhat from comparable experiments in other Eastern European states in the 1960s. It did not represent a simple adoption without alteration of the Liberman principles in the USSR: profit was not to be the only economic indicator. Overall central state planning was retained; the NES in the GDR did not imply a form of market socialism along Yugoslavian lines, nor the sort of economy introduced in Hungary and attempted in Czechoslovakia. The state retained the functions of forecasting, long-term planning, and overall control of the economy. There was however some devolution to intermediate and lower levels of economic organization, and increased flexibility. At the top stood the Central State Planning Commission (Ministry of Planning) and eight industrial ministries, which retained overall control. At the intermediate level there were eighty so-called *Vereinigungen Volkseigener Betriebe* (VVBs) which were organizations combining clusters of individual enterprises, and which were given considerable powers of decision-making. These VVBs had general directors who co-ordinated the production of all the individual enterprises – the *Volkseigene Betriebe* (VEBs). Profit was to become the main criterion of performance of each production unit; hence enterprises had to manufacture products of a quality which could be sold, and to keep a close eye on production costs. Profits were to be reinvested, but there was to be a certain flexibility in reinvestment, with stimulation of research and development technology. Bonus incentives and wage differentials were introduced. Banks were given an entrepreneurial role: credit was to be given to encourage the technologically advanced sectors of industry. Market research accompanied the so-called 'scientific-technical revolution'.

In many respects this all seemed very promising. Along with the introduction of the New Economic System went the development of what has been called an 'achievement-oriented career society'.[3] Since the building of the Berlin Wall, aspiring young technologists and managers could no longer leave to seek more promising careers in the West. The New Economic System and the stress on the application of technical expertise in production appeared to offer prospects of advancement and professional fulfilment in the East. The 1960s saw members of the technical intelligentsia increasingly being solicited for professional advice, and enjoying a relatively high social and political status. At less elevated social levels, a new generation was coming to maturity who had achieved upward social mobility through state policies to sponsor the children of workers and peasants. Many of these felt they had something of a stake in a system which had facilitated their rise.[4]

It nevertheless remained the case that professional technical advice was not able to outweigh entirely political considerations: the introduction of the economically unfavourable Soviet trade agreement of 1966–7, for example, was a result of political pressures which overrode economic considerations. It was also clear that there were considerable intrinsic difficulties which the New Economic System would have to overcome before it could function smoothly. Three sets of price reforms were required in the period 1964–7. There was a failure to develop an adequate long-term plan, despite the emphasis on forecasting. The lack of managerial and business administration expertise among managers, who had not been used to bearing such responsibilities, was soon revealed; yet they were not given enough time or opportunity to acquire relevant training and experience. The fixed pricing system continued to cause problems, and all sorts of dislocations in the economy emerged. There were problems associated with the hoarding of raw materials to overcome log-jams in the supply of materials from other countries in the socialist bloc. Even the introduction of wage differentials and the profit incentive did not seem to be working very well, particularly when the range of consumer goods on which income could be spent was rather limited and of inferior quality.

Many of these problems might have been overcome, had the New Economic System been given time to develop. But external political developments intervened. In particular there was a change of political climate in the USSR, and following the upheavals of the Prague Spring and the subsequent invasion of Czechoslovakia in 1968, and the Polish troubles of 1970, a recentralization process started throughout the Eastern bloc countries. Although Ulbricht had made it quite clear throughout that, unlike the Czechoslovakian reform communists, he had no intention of allowing political decentralization or democratization to be a concomitant of economic decentralization, the Soviet Union was no longer willing to countenance further experiments in this line. Already in 1967 changes had been inaugurated with the Economic System of Socialism (ESS) which superseded the New Economic System, and in the late 1960s a process of recentralization began. The New Economic System was quietly dismantled with none of the fanfare which had accompanied its inauguration.

Meanwhile, account had been taken of the changed realities of political life in the GDR. In 1968 a new constitution was proclaimed, and presented as a 'socialist' replacement of the earlier 'anti-fascist' constitution of 1949. This new constitution of the 'socialist state of the German nation' held that power no longer derived simply from 'the people' but rather from the 'working people' under the leadership of the Marxist-Leninist Party. Thus the leadership of the SED was for the first time explicitly enshrined in the constitution. Its leading role was justified ideologically by the notion that Marxist-Leninist theory alone provided a guide to the laws of history, and that the Party was thus uniquely placed to lead the people through the necessary – and sometimes uncomfortable – transitional stages to achieve the final goal of history, truly communist society.

Other amendments ensured that 'liberal' aspects of the 1949 constitution, such as the right to strike, and rights of free speech and assembly, were effectively abolished or formally restricted by clauses further empowering the party to decide what was or was not permissible under socialism. The differences between Ulbricht's conception of developed socialist society, and other Marxists' vision of the transition to the perfect communist society (the ultimate stage of human history) were marked – not to mention the differences between official ideology and non-Marxist views.

But for the time being, whatever criticisms people might privately harbour about the East German state, dissenting voices – as that of Robert Havemann – remained largely isolated and subdued. Many who were not committed Marxists now felt they had to try to work within socialism, and to confront and make the best of the constraints within which they had to operate. During the 1960s, less emphatic attention was paid by the state to trying to convert people ideologically, or to repress them with overt coercion, and there was a realization of the need to achieve a 'minimal consensus' or at least to 'neutralize' those of different views.[5] New modes of 'dialogue' were introduced, as for example with certain church leaders – who were, however, regarded with suspicion by many Christians as not genuinely representative of church views.[6] However forced and limited such attempts at 'dialogue' were, they indicated a degree of willingness to accept lack of wholehearted commitment so long as people were prepared to conform and not undermine the system. Limited concessions were made: while conscription was introduced in 1962, in 1964 a form of alternative service was made possible for those whose consciences would not allow them to bear arms. But the course was a rocky one: a brief period of seeming cultural liberalization was again followed, from 1965, by a renewed clampdown in the cultural sphere. Whatever the gestures towards economic improvements, career incentives, and less overt repression, East Germany in the 1960s was a place which many of its citizens would not freely have chosen to live in, had they had the choice. And at the beginning of the 1970s, with the normalization of relations between the two Germanies, it increasingly looked as if the initially impermanent division was one which was there to stay.

Ostpolitik and mutual recognition

The relations between the two Germanies were transformed by the so-called *Ostpolitik* of Willy Brandt's SPD-led government after 1969. Against strong conservative opposition, Brandt pushed through negotiations which regularized relations between the two Germanies, entailing mutual recognition and an amelioration of conditions for furthering human contacts between the two parts of the divided nation. These efforts were criticized, both at the time and subsequently, as a form of 'appeasement' towards communists, from which the latter benefited while giving very little, if anything, in return. The argument ran that the boundaries produced by aggression were being accepted, that money was being sent which in improving people's conditions merely served to prop up an illegitimate state, and that supposed concessions on the human rights front were basically ignored in practice. Against this, supporters of the policy saw it as merely a realistic acceptance of an essentially unalterable situation, and as a means to improve relations and make the borders more permeable for individual human contacts, by a policy of 'little steps'.

The groundwork had already been laid when Brandt was Foreign Minister in Kiesinger's government. In the West German elections of September 1969, the CDU/CSU won a total of 242 seats, the SPD 224, and the FDP 30. The FDP had taken a somewhat leftwards move when at the end of 1967 Walter Scheel had replaced Erich Mende as leader. After three weeks of bargaining, in 1969 a coalition was formed between the SPD and the FDP, with Willy Brandt as West German Chancellor. This marked a major step in West German political history: after two decades of conservative dominance, a Social Democrat was in charge of government in a social-liberal coalition.

Brandt was also in many respects a unique individual for West Germany to have as Chancellor. Born illegitimate, as a young man Brandt had opposed Nazism, fled Nazi Germany and fought in the Norwegian resistance. With his modest social origins and anti-Nazi record, he marked a real break with the compromised pasts of the former NSDAP member, Chancellor Kiesinger, and of President Lübke (who resigned early and did not stand for a second term of office because of stories about his role in the construction of Nazi concentration camps, or slave labour barracks). A former Mayor of Berlin, Brandt also had experience of divided Germany's position in the front line of Europe, and had been forced to witness the construction of the Berlin Wall. A man of strong moral convictions, Brandt was arguably more successful in his foreign policies than he was on the domestic front. Whatever the controversies surrounding the end of his chancellorship in 1974, as well as the end of his period chairing the SPD (in 1987), Brandt's moral stature introduced a new chord to the difficult politics of post-Nazi democracy.

Brandt's period in office is chiefly noted for his drive to achieve some sort of 'normalization' of relations between the two states in divided Germany. This initiative coincided with a period of detente between the superpowers, in which it suited both the Americans and the Russians (who both had preoccupations in Asia) to defuse the previously volatile situation in central Europe. Preliminary meetings were held between Willy Brandt and East German Prime Minister Willi Stoph in Erfurt in the GDR (where the East German public greeted Willy Brandt with notable enthusiasm) in March 1970, and in Kassel in West Germany in May 1970. In August 1970 West Germany signed the Moscow Treaty with Russia, and in December 1970 the Warsaw Treaty dealt with relations with Poland. In 1971 the ageing Ulbricht, who was far from being a convinced supporter of *Ostpolitik*, was prematurely removed from office and replaced as leader of the SED by the more obliging Erich Honecker. In September 1971 the erstwhile allies of the Second World War were able to reach agreement in a Four-Power Accord on Berlin, in which they regularized certain arrangements with regard to Berlin's status and agreed to resolve future disputes by negotiation rather than resorting to force. The way now seemed to be clear for a treaty on the relations between the two Germanies.

There was however a problem of serious opposition to *Ostpolitik* in West German conservative circles. To them it appeared to be an unconstitutional acceptance of the permanent division of Germany, given the explicit commitment in the Basic Law to work towards German reunification. Some FDP members defected from the coalition to vote with the CDU/CSU, and CDU leader Rainer Barzel moved a vote of no confidence in Brandt's Chancellorship. This was lost by two votes, and various rumours were rife concerning scandalous bribes and corruption. In September 1972 Brandt made the second use of this constitutional measure, engineering the dissolution of parliament and the calling of new elections by instructing SPD members to refrain from supporting his government in his own vote of no confidence. This tactic duly succeeded, and elections were called for 19 November 1972. The elections were fought largely on the *Ostpolitik* issue, and saw an unprecedented ninety-one per cent turnout. It was clear that the electorate were more interested in recognition and improvement of German-German relations than in taking a principled stand on reunification. For the first time, the SPD won more seats than the CDU/CSU, with 229 and 225 respectively – and this despite a vilification campaign partially funded by far-right circles determined to oust Brandt from the Chancellorship. The FDP rose from 30 to 42 seats; and the NPD, which had loomed so alarmingly in recent local state elections, revealed its essential irrelevance on the national scene by polling only 0.6% and failing to gain national representation. With a slightly more comfortable parliamentary margin, Brandt was able to go back into Parliament and conclude, in December 1972, the Basic Treaty between what West Germany now recognized as the 'two German states in one German nation'. This Treaty was ratified (again in the face of considerable opposition) in May 1973. In September 1973, both Germanies were accepted as full members of the United Nations.

Although the Hallstein doctrine (of breaking off diplomatic relations with states which recognized East Germany) was renounced with the signing of the Basic Treaty, West Germany still refused to view East Germany as a completely foreign state. There was to be, for example, an exchange of 'representatives' rather than 'ambassadors'; and East Germans leaving for the west still could automatically claim West German citizenship. Constitutionally, West Germany viewed the border between the two Germanies as in principle no more than a border between two West German *Länder* – although in practice, of course, this highly fortified frontier was of a very different order. The West German constitutional commitment to reunification was not abandoned, but the focus switched to working for an increased permeability of the two states, with improved human contacts and communications between citizens of each Germany, to keep alive the sense of a shared national identity. By contrast, in East Germany, as the physical barriers changed, so there was a conscious policy of cultural *Abgrenzung* and stressing of differences in GDR national identity from the identity of the West German capitalist state. In the period after mutual recognition relations between the two Germanies developed a certain dynamic of their own, but so too did the divergences between the two Germanies become more apparent. Until late 1989, few thought that the issue of reunification would return to become a serious question of contemporary politics. Rather, it was simply a sacred cow to which lip-service could be paid while recognizing the reality, and likely permanence, of division.

West Germany in the 1970s and 1980s

Recognition of the division of Germany meant a twofold development: on the one hand, the two Germanies diverged further as societies, as their common historical past receded ever further; on the other hand, they in some ways came closer together, as communications between the two states improved, and as the dynamic of inner-German relations developed in ways sometimes at odds with the interests of the superpowers.

Willy Brandt remained Chancellor of West Germany until 1974. In this year, a serious spy scandal became the immediate occasion for his resignation. One of his senior aides, Günter Guillaume, was revealed as an East German spy. Brandt was forced to resign – although many suggested that there may have been additional personal or health reasons behind this decision. Brandt was succeeded by Helmut Schmidt, a smooth Chancellor with excellent English, a certain distrust of and independence from American policy, and a generally conservative approach within Social Democracy. Schmidt's Chancellorship, in coalition with the FDP (with elections in 1976 and 1980) was confronted with difficulties on several fronts.

The left-wing movements of the 1960s had partly dissolved, and partly diversified. While many former radicals became mainstream citizens, others retired into retreatist subcultures or sectarian squabbles; but a few became terrorists. The Red Army Faction, or Baader-Meinhof gang (named after two of its prominent members, Andreas Baader and Ulrike Meinhof), organized a series of physical attacks on the West German 'system'. These began with offences against property – such as the bombing of department stores, as a statement against capitalist materialism – but developed into the systematic murdering of individuals prominent in economic and political life. Just as the Federal Republic appeared to be gaining a new reputation as a politically stable, 'model' democracy, which could begin to develop more of an independent role on the international political stage, a small minority of people were challenging the very essence of the system and provoking it into measures which would justify their criticisms of repression. While their acts of assassination could in no way be justified, new controversies flared as some liberals attempted to criticize the state's responses to the terrorist threat. With wider (and initially unrelated) measures to weed out 'radicals' from public service employment, there remained a degree of uneasiness about the nature of West German democracy.

Terrorism was not the only domestic problem for the Schmidt government. The 1970s saw energy crises, occasioned by the spiralling of oil prices internationally. The attempt to replace oil by nuclear power had political implications, and Schmidt's relatively right-wing form of Social Democracy came under attack from left-wing Social Democrats. Nuclear power was not the only issue provoking protest: the stationing of nuclear missiles in Germany became a major bone of political contention in the late 1970s, with the USA in 1979 deciding to station nuclear missiles in Europe (including Britain). Protest movements in favour of peace and disarmament, as well as about environmental concerns and the dangers of destruction from methods of production, began to proliferate.

While the Schmidt government was having problems with its left-wing and grass roots, it was also experiencing strains with its more right-wing coalition partner, the FDP, largely because of problems in the economy. An ageing population, in which relatively fewer people of working age were having to support the pension schemes of relatively more retired people who were living longer, gave rise in any case to problems in relation to the benefits system; these were exacerbated by the general economic recession which set in during the 1970s. Although the West German economy performed relatively well in comparison with, for example, the British, there was nevertheless some increase in unemployment and inflation, giving rise to serious frictions in the coalition over the budget. In 1982, the FDP decided to switch its allegiance away from the SDP to the CDU/CSU. In a constructive vote of no confidence, Schmidt was voted out as Chancellor and Helmut Kohl of the CDU/CSU voted in.

There was considerable unease in the country that a small party, commanding only a minimal fraction of the popular vote, should be able to change so radically the complexion of the government without reference to the general will of the people. After considerable debate and consideration (including reference to the constitutional court at Karlsruhe) a new vote of no confidence was engineered which the new Chancellor, Helmut Kohl, arranged to lose, such that the President could dissolve Parliament and call new elections in the spring of 1983. The election was won by the conservatives, and the coalition of FDP with CDU/CSU was confirmed in office. This change of government in 1982–3 was generally known as *die Wende*, the turning-point: after thirteen years of social-democratic government, Germany entered a new phase of conservative dominance, confirmed by a second election victory in the 1987 elections.

With the accession of the CDU government came a jettisoning of Keynesian economic policies. Once the budgetary deadlock of the SPD-FDP government had been broken, the CDU-FDP government introduced measures to control inflation and stimulate investment while allowing unemployment rates to remain relatively constant at an uncomfortable figure of around 8–10%. This was exacerbated by the continuing problem of the now very much less than welcome *Gastarbeiter*. Although the overall proportion of foreign workers fell slightly to around 8% in 1980, in some areas – such as the traditionally working-class Kreuzberg district in Berlin – they constituted as much as 50% of the inhabitants. Furthermore, in the course of the 1980s a stream of ethnic German refugees came into the Federal Republic from eastern European countries and the Soviet Union – even before the stream became a flood, with hundreds of thousands of East Germans entering West Germany in the summer and autumn of 1989. While the budgetary deficit was successfully cut, growth rates in the 1980s remained relatively low (around 2.5% in 1984). Nevertheless, with low inflation, the West German economy certainly performed a great deal better than the British economy in the 1980s. There was a continuing shift in emphasis away from the old heavy industries of the Ruhr to a new stress on the microelectronic industries, concentrated notably around Stuttgart, Frankfurt and Munich. Furthermore, West Germany was at the forefront of initiatives with respect to closer European economic and monetary integration in the context of the European Community. While Mrs. Thatcher's British government dragged its feet with respect to European union, Germany played a key role. This was of course to be complicated by the reopening of the German question in late 1989, only two years before the projected institution of a single European market in 1992.

During the 1980s, the SPD was provoked into considerable rethinking of its position. This re-evaluation was related to the fact that some people who formerly supported the SPD, as well as many new young voters, were switching their allegiance to the new ecological and environmentalist party, the Greens. In 1983, the Greens gained national representation, and even held the balance of power and participated in government in some *Länder*. They had, however, their own internal dissensions, with splits between 'realists' (*Realos*) and 'fundamentalists' (*Fundis*), as well as differences of aims and emphasis between the 'green Greens' (ecologists), 'brown Greens' (right-wing defenders of the German *Heimat*) and 'red Greens' (anti-growth socialists of a 'small is beautiful' persuasion). The conservative and free-democratic government parties were also not without their own problems. They were beset by a series of scandals, ranging from serious allegations of financial corruption in party finances (in the so-called Flick Affair which necessitated the resignation and trial of certain prominent politicians), through the puzzle of the murky election campaign and mysterious death in 1987 of the CDU Minister-President of Schleswig-Holstein, Uwe Barschel, to the series of more mundane political banana skins to which Helmut Kohl was prone. At the same time, widespread, vocal concern for such issues as the 'death of the forests' due to acid rain, the implications of the national census, the scandals relating to nuclear waste disposal, and American and Soviet policies towards nuclear weapons in Europe, continued to dominate the public agenda in the 1980s.

East Germany under Honecker

The period from Honecker's taking office in 1971 up to the mid-1970s was in many ways promising. *Ostpolitik* had resulted finally in international recognition for the GDR, which was now able to take up formal relations with many foreign countries, including the USA. In the sphere of culture, Honecker announced a policy of 'no taboos' under socialism, which helped promote a ferment of new cultural activity (or the release of previously suppressed energies). On the economic front, while the economy was recentralized and while political ideologists regained predominance over technical specialists, pragmatic

varian women around the chapel in Bad Tölz on the annual St Leonard's Day
cession of this patron saint of prisoners and horses (hence the chain on the cart).

men working in a munitions factory in the First World War, when many men were
ay at the front.

Spartacists man the barricades in the newspaper quarter of Berlin during the January 1919 uprising.

A member of the German bourgeoisie finds it cheaper to paste up bank notes than to buy wallpaper, in the great inflation of 1923.

(Opposite top) In the depression of 1932, impoverished peasants from the Thuringian village of Deesbach apply to the local mayor for official permits to go begging.

(Opposite bottom) Human billboards for the presidential elections of 10 April 1932. The choice was between the elderly military hero and conservative-nationalist, Paul von Hindenburg, the Communist Ernst Thälmann, and the Nazi Adolf Hitler.

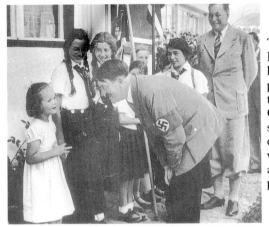

The sunny side of the Third Reich: *(top)* Hitler professes his love for children; *(middle)* a propaganda picture emphasizes the importance of healthy German mothers and babies, supported by state education in childcare; and *(bottom)* the Nazi women's organization celebrates a traditional children's Christmas party.

Those who were not so lucky: *(above)* the invasion and occupation of Poland, which was followed by acts of the utmost brutality; and *(below)* Jews in the Warsaw Ghetto, who, if they survived the misery, hunger, and sickness of ghetto life, would ultimately be transported and murdered in an extermination camp.

Reconstruction after the war: *(above) Trümmerfrauen* work to rebuild from the ruins; and *(below)* a newly independent peasant gratefully receives his plot of land, a result of the expropriation of large estates in the Soviet zone of occupied Germany.

Coercion and socialization in the GDR: *(top)* Soviet tanks suppress the uprising of June 1953; *(middle)* SED leader Walter Ulbricht addresses young people at the secular state 'confirmation' ceremony, the *Jugendweihe*; and *(bottom)* schoolchildren, on their weekly 'day in industry' in the 'people's own factory' with which their school is twinned, admire the progress board in the 'competition for fulfilment of the plan'.

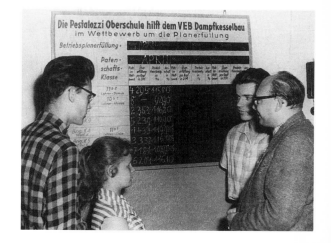

West German Chancellor Konrad Adenauer looks uncomfortable on a visit to Berlin's Brandenburg Gate, in August 1961, a week after the Berlin Wall was erected.

East Berliners hack out mementoes from the now defunct Wall, in the spring of 1990.

consumer-orientation and concern with material satisfaction began to prevail. Utopian ideas of 'jam tomorrow', prevalent in the Ulbricht era, gave way to attempts to ensure more bread and butter, and even cake, today. The phase of 'actually existing socialism' was recognized to be a relatively long-lasting one, and not a brief transitional stage; moreover, it was one with certain social tensions which could not be resolved by being ignored or denied, but which had rather to be faced, examined, and dealt with in an appropriate manner.

Economically, after the recentralization which took place in Ulbricht's last years as leader, further shifts took place under Honecker's regime in the balance between overall central planning and direction of the economy on the one hand, and a flexibility of decision-making utilizing steering mechanisms at a more decentralized level on the other.

Following economic difficulties in the mid- and later 1970s, the 1980s saw the replacement of VVBs by combines. These linked production processes with technological research and development and with market research, in order to enhance overall efficiency and productivity. While ultimate control and supervision remained with the central state organs, both direct and indirect steering mechanisms, including the use of profit incentives, operated at the enterprise level.

Further changes also took place in the sphere of agriculture, with reorganization starting in the early 1970s. Larger, more specialized units were created, and specialization continued in the 1980s, with different units focusing on crop-farming or animal husbandry, for example. Planning and inter-farm co-operation was aided by co-operation councils, which operated at an intermediate level between district councils and individual farms. Farming in the GDR was relatively productive and advanced in its degree of mechanization: the contrast between serried ranks of tractors or combine harvesters moving in efficient formation across East German fields and the lonely horse-drawn carts and ploughs ubiquitous in the small peasant agriculture of neighbouring Poland, was striking. East Germany achieved a high degree of agricultural self-sufficiency; its principal imports were grain and animal feed.

Despite certain difficulties, the economy under Honecker was relatively successful, at least in comparison with certain of its East European neighbours. There were advantages and disadvantages in the GDR's economic situation in the 1970s and 1980s. The GDR was heavily reliant on foreign trade, particularly for imports of fuel and raw materials. It was thus highly sensitive to world energy prices, and was adversely affected by the energy crises of the 1970s. Although about thirty per cent of the GDR's total foreign trade was with the developed market economies of the West, it imported a considerable proportion of its energy at unfavourable prices from the USSR, particularly oil, coal and gas. The main source of energy was lignite ('brown coal', which emits an unpleasantly dusty and characteristic smoke) although there were moves in the direction of developing nuclear energy supplies. Lignite supplied around seventy per cent of the GDR's primary energy requirements in the mid-1980s. Conversely there were also advantages associated with the GDR's reliance on foreign trade. Nearly a third of the GDR's trade with developed western market economies was with the Federal Republic of Germany, including West Berlin; and this trade was based on very favourable conditions. As a result of agreements between the two Germanies there were no trade barriers or external tariffs; hence the GDR was in practice a secret extra member of the European Economic Community (EEC). There were automatic credits for trade deficits, and the GDR was often able to overcome East European bottlenecks in supplies with efficient deliveries of material from West Germany. West Germany also made sizeable loans available to East Germany. The arrangements were favourable economically to the GDR, while the Federal Republic sought political gains (for example in ease of visiting, or for improved human rights) from its close economic links with the GDR. The Federal Republic was affluent enough to want to pay for improved relationships with the GDR and for improved conditions for its people (who were officially considered by the West German government to have 'German' citizenship, valid also in West Germany); the East German economy benefited sufficiently from its links with the West for the East German government to be prepared to pay the political price of some dependency. As a result of its unique links to West Germany, the GDR was able to weather relatively smoothly some of the economic storms experienced in the early 1980s by other East European economies.

In the 1980s, the emphasis was on such fields as micro-electronics, electrical engineering, computer production, in addition to traditional strengths in such areas as the chemical industry and vehicle manufacture. However, in all these fields the GDR lagged significantly behind western developments, in both quantitative and qualitative respects. Moreover, it paid little attention to its serious pollution problems and the consequent adverse effects on public health and on the environment. While voices in West Germany were increasingly strident in their complaints about the death of the forests, the problems of pollution were downplayed in the infinitely more polluted East. The true extent of the problem was only revealed in 'Round Table' discussions, after the East German revolution, at the beginning of 1990. There were also signs that despite its relatively good performance in East European terms, the GDR economy was in deteriorating shape: growth rates fell from 5.5% in 1984 to 2.8% in 1988 – well before the deleterious effects of mass emigration in the latter half of 1989. But the implications of economic performance varied with political circumstances; until the collapse of the Iron Curtain in 1989, most East Germans were prepared to put up with their situation, contenting themselves with the thought that things were not as bad as elsewhere in Eastern Europe.

Honecker made a concerted effort to establish the GDR, not merely as a viable economic entity, but also as an accepted feature of the political landscape. The foundations had to a considerable degree been accomplished by *Ostpolitik*, but this opened new risks and opportunities. A new constitution introduced in 1974 was characterized by a determined emphasis on a GDR national identity, a symbolic separation from notions of Germany and German. The GDR was proclaimed to be linked in undying friendship with its partner (and big brother!), the Soviet Union. This special relationship was formally sealed by a friendship treaty between the GDR and the USSR in October 1975. At the same time, the role of the Party became more prominent, against Ulbricht's more pragmatic approaches. And with the new broom in charge, there initially appeared to be a promise of liberalization on the cultural front. International recognition could perhaps permit an easing of domestic repression, and coaxing as well as coercing people into having greater pride in what now seemed a securely established state.

From the mid-1970s, however, it became apparent that tensions and strains had not been successfully resolved. In 1976 a renewed period of cultural repression was inaugurated with the exile of Wolf Biermann, a guitarist and singer who, late in 1975, was refused permission to re-enter the GDR after a permitted concert tour in the West. A number of writers, artists and intellectuals protested against this enforced exile, only to find repressive measures directed against them as well. In the later 1970s a number of GDR writers left for the West. At the same time, the energy crises affecting western economies were having a comparable impact on eastern bloc countries. Rises in the standard of living faltered, and the East German economy appeared to stagnate. Moreover, in the late 1970s and early 1980s a new era of frosty relations and even a second Cold War appeared to be developing between the superpowers, the USA and USSR. Following the American and Soviet decisions to station nuclear missiles in Europe, the GDR regime had to agree, reluctantly, in 1984 to the stationing of Soviet nuclear missiles on East German soil. The one area in which domestic politics appeared to be becoming more relaxed and tolerant was in relation to the church. Following a meeting between leaders of the Protestant churches and the state in 1978, a new accord was reached which permitted Christians greater latitude of activity and practice in the GDR. The relative toleration of dissenting views, at least until the mid-1980s, may have made a considerable contribution to the political stability of the GDR in the early 1980s.

The pragmatism and the odd combinations of repression and relative toleration which had characterized the Honecker era were by the mid-1980s looking vulnerable. The accession to the Soviet leadership in 1985 of the active reformer Mikhail

Gorbachev, with his ideas of *perestroika* and *glasnost*, posed challenges to all the countries of the eastern bloc. The initial official responses in the GDR ranged from the cool and relatively dismissive to the formally friendly and assenting. Yet among certain groups in the East German population expectations were raised of a further democratization of East German politics and society. Instead, the events of late 1987 and early 1988 – with arrests and imprisonment or exile for certain activists – suggested the start of a period of renewed repression.

Meanwhile, relationships between the two Germanies had been developing with a certain dynamic of their own, partly independent of, partly related to, the dynamics of superpower relations. In the period of superpower hostility – partially provoked by the Soviet Union's invasion of Afghanistan – the two Germanies were nevertheless pursuing a form of mini-*détente* and *rapprochement* of their own. Yet a visit to West Germany planned by Honecker for September 1984 had to be called off at the last minute, following certain blunders in the West and pressures from the USSR. In the changed international context of 1987, when, under Gorbachev's leadership, relationships with the USA had markedly improved, the postponed visit of Honecker was finally able to take place. The relationship between the two Germanies in the 1980s was designed to reduce tensions and improve conditions for all Germans. Favourable loan, credit and trade agreements were reached, benefiting the East German economy. There were improvements in travel and communications between the two states, although there was a fifty per cent drop in the number of visitors to East Germany after the compulsory currency exchange was increased following the Polish disturbances of 1980.[7] In 1987, there was an amnesty of prisoners in the GDR. After a wave of officially sanctioned emigrations in 1984, 1987 witnessed an unprecedented number of permitted short visits to the West by East Germans. According to the official 'Address on the state of the nation' by Helmut Kohl, there were five million visits by East Germans to West Germany in 1987, of which approximately one million were by citizens under pensionable age, travelling on 'urgent family business'. A few years earlier, the figures had been 1.3 million visits by pensioners and only 40,000 family visits[8]. (The concept of 'urgent family business' was also reinterpreted with some considerable elasticity.)

In the context of international negotiations on the stationing or removal of certain nuclear missiles from Europe, the two Germanies had very specific and unique interests in common. Both were particularly vulnerable as front-line states in a divided world. In both Germanies there were strong movements for a nuclear-free central European zone. But the events which were to change fundamentally the relationships between the two Germanies – and the very existence of the German Democratic Republic – occurred with the revolutionary upheavals of the autumn of 1989.

Before considering these dramatic developments, the following chapters will analyse in more detail the socio-political dynamics of the two Germanies, and assess the degree to which their societies and cultures had diverged. In this way, a deeper understanding can be gained of the conditions upon which each country's stability was predicated for over forty years, the factors contributing to the ultimate demise of the East German communist state, and the nature of the two rather different Germanies which in 1990 were to embark on a process of unification, with all its attendant tensions and difficulties.

NINE

Diverging Societies

As the streams of Trabant and Wartburg cars bumped across the newly opened borders from East to West Germany in the winter of 1989–90, it was quite clear that there was a considerable disparity between the quality of life of Germans in the two states. East Germans stared amazed at the wealth of consumer goods available in West German shops, and rapidly stocked up on bananas, oranges, and other delights which had been rarities for so long. Conversely, visitors from West to East experienced with less pleasure the bumpy, pot-holed roads, often still cobbled, the crumbling plaster on the unpainted houses, the pall of pollution, belching yellow-grey factory fumes hanging over the sky, and the ubiquitous, dusty smell of brown coal. It was clear that East Germany had suffered from numerous disadvantages in terms of economic development, and that her modest successes in comparison with other East European economies in themselves constituted something of an economic miracle, though never on the same scale of that of West Germany. But to what extent had the two Germanies developed into different societies in the period before 1989?

Let us start with an attempt to compare the two Germanies in a number of different empirical respects. There was an obvious difference in the question of ownership of the means of production: in West Germany, capital remained predominantly in private ownership, while in East Germany between 1945 and 1989 private ownership of the means of production was to a major extent abolished. According to the GDR's official statistics, in 1983 out of 8,445,300 economically active persons, only 397,100 were engaged in privately owned concerns.[1] This effect was achieved in stages over the years; while, as we have seen, there were radical changes in socio-economic structure in the occupation period, in 1952 over forty-five per cent of the economy was still in private hands.[2] In this fundamental respect, then, capitalist West and communist East were – by definition – quite different. In other respects, however, the similarities and differences were more muted. Both Germanies participated, to varying degrees, in the general shift of industrial societies away from manual towards white-collar occupations, giving rise to similar proportions of blue- to white-collar workers.[3] The developments in the West were, however, more 'advanced' (in terms of theories of development of industrial societies) than in the East. According to the 1983 West German publication, *Zahlenspiegel*, while in the FRG only 5.9% were employed in agriculture and forestry, the GDR still had nearly twice as many in this sector. (*Zahlenspiegel* gives a figure of 10.1%; the official East German statistical yearbook gives 10.7%, as compared with 27.9% in 1950). More were employed in trade in the West (12.6%) than in the East (9.6%); and significantly more were employed in the service sector in the West (16.4%) than in the East (6.9%). There were other interesting differences too: 17.6% of the East German working population were employed in a category covering state, education and health, in contrast to a slightly but significantly lower 14.8% in the West.[4]

West Germany in the 1980s was a more urbanized society than East Germany. While in 1950 in both East and West 29% of the population lived in communities of less than two thousand inhabitants, by 1980 only 6% of West Germans lived in such small communities, in contrast to a surprising 24% of East Germans. Of West Germans, 74% lived in communities of over ten thousand in 1980, compared to 57% of East Germans. The figure for both East and West in 1950 was 48%, indicating the extent to which urbanization in West Germany outpaced that in East Germany. The main growth in West Germany was of communities of between ten and a hundred thousand inhabitants, whose representation doubled from 21% to 40% of the population between 1950 and 1980; in East Germany the comparable figures rose only from 27% to 31%. It is easy to see why pre-1989 East Germany had such an archaic, old-fashioned feel to it: the profile of community sizes was not so dissimilar to the immediate post- and even pre-war period, whereas the urban/rural configuration of West Germany had changed quite dramatically. There was an interesting change, too, in the overall population numbers in the two Germanies. In 1939, the area which subsequently became East Germany had 16.7 million inhabitants; in 1980, it had the identical number, 16.7 million (after a brief rise in 1950 to 18.4 million, declining to 17.2 million in 1960 and 17.1 million in 1970). By contrast, in 1939 the area which was to become West Germany had 43 million inhabitants; in 1980 – despite fears in the 1970s about the declining birth-rate, and claims that the 'Germans were dying out' – the population had risen to 61.7 million.[5] These figures, and the corresponding statistics concerning numbers of inhabitants per square kilometre, again give detail to the immediate impressions of relative emptiness and sparser population of East Germany in comparison to the West.

Discussions of ownership or non-ownership of the means of production, and of the distribution of population among agrarian, industrial and service sectors of employment, or levels of urbanization, do not tell us very much about social structure, however. Central questions about stratification and social inequality must be addressed also. The German Democratic Republic was grounded in a political theory committed to the eradication of class differences; yet East German theorists admitted that social inequalities persisted, and certain inequalities of status, privilege and income were variably condoned or encouraged in East Germany. Comparisons in this area are problematic. Nevertheless, it seems clear that there was greater disparity of incomes in the West than in the East; fewer people had high incomes in the East, and the difference between the top and the bottom of the hierarchy was greater in the West. Other features than income are also salient in considering social hierarchy and inequality in the East: privileges such as freedom to travel to the West, access to western currency (and hence hard currency shops), preferential treatment for the purchase of new cars (particularly western cars), might be far more important than additional income in East German

Marks. The degree of privilege enjoyed by members of the political elite – private hunting lodges with relatively luxurious facilities, personal fortunes in western currency – were to shock the masses when they were revealed in the aftermath of the 1989 revolution.

Patterns of social mobility in the two societies showed differences which reflected their different socio-political systems. In the East, political conformity was a prerequisite for career advancement and upward social mobility; or, put differently, political nonconformity would actively block chances of advancement, while political conformity was a necessary but not sufficient prerequisite for promotion prospects. In addition, in East Germany levels of education and qualifications were increasingly important. Even in that sphere which is primarily political – politics itself – educational credentials became more and more important further up the political hierarchy. Political commitment was obviously central to a political career; for a career in other areas where technical expertise mattered, such as medicine, science, engineering, economics, it was sufficient to conform passively. Those who in any way stepped out of line, or had politically suspect backgrounds – such as the children of pastors, who might have refused the *Jugendweihe* or opted for alternative military service as *Bausoldaten* – might find it exceedingly difficult to gain entrance to the university course or training of their choice, however brilliant their performance at school might have been. There were, however, some changes in patterns of social mobility in the GDR. The politically determined preference given to the children of workers and peasants in the early years gave way, in the late 1960s, to the fostering of talent irrespective of social background; and this led in practice to a tendency towards the reproduction of status across generations by the 1980s.

Political conformity was not such an important factor in West German social mobility (although nonconformity might still be a hindrance, as evidenced in the *Berufsverbot* cases discussed further in Chapter Ten, below). From the 1950s to the 1980s there was a considerable amount of structurally-induced social mobility, related to the shift from heavy industry to light electronics and service industries, but there was at the same time a marked tendency for class status to be inherited across generations. Educational qualifications tended to serve as credentials legitimizing the inheritance of social status in a society based explicitly on the principle of individual achievement and aptitude rather than birth and wealth.

How salient were social inequalities and perceptions of social structure and mobility in the two Germanies, and how did Germans in East and West view their societies? Some commentators suggested in the 1970s that the Federal Republic was a 'classless' society: regional differences and accents did not have the same class connotations as they did in Britain, for example, and there was, supposedly, no entrenched 'them and us' two-class mentality in West Germany as in Britain. This interpretation is somewhat dubious on a number of counts. Leaving aside changes in perceptions of class in Britain, it is clear that to describe West Germany as a 'classless' society is misleading. Old aristocratic families continued to lead a distinctive life-style and to assert a certain social superiority. Considerable social inequalities continued to persist, despite the relatively high standard of living of at least those working class Germans in employment. Ironically, however, the existence of the ethnically and culturally distinct *Gastarbeiter* as an underclass served to make West Germans appear rather homogenously 'middle class'.

East Germany was frequently held to be a 'working class and petty bourgeois' society, with a predominantly working class or lower middle class way of life and outlook. There was not the obvious survival of the aristocracy and elite business entrepreneurs in East Germany; merely the thin layer of the politically privileged. How far did the people in this self-proclaimed 'workers' and peasants' state' feel themselves to be 'emancipated'? Marx's theory of alienation, as outlined in his *Economic and Philosophical Manuscripts* of 1844, had several aspects (alienation from the object of labour, from oneself, from fellow human beings, and from one's 'species-being'), each of which was directly rooted in the capitalist mode of production; by definition, these should have been overcome with the abolition of the private ownership of the means of production in East Germany. Subsequent non-Marxist sociological research has tended to depart from Marx's strict definition of alienation and to interpret it rather in psychological terms. On this view, workers in East German factories appeared to feel as dissatisfied with, and powerless in relation to, their work as did workers in many western capitalist factories. Moreover, social envy and grumbling about differential privileges were manifestly not overcome in the actually existing socialism of the GDR in the 1980s.

It seems clear that, whatever their similarities in terms of technological, industrial development – measured in terms of ratios of white-collar to blue-collar workers, proportions employed in different sectors of the economy, and the like – the two Germanies had developed into rather different forms of society by the 1980s. How far then did they illustrate an arguable 'convergence' of advanced industrial societies, and how far were their divergences based in differences of economic and political structure? On the one hand, despite their different economic principles and patterns of ownership, they did seem to play remarkably comparable economic roles within their respective economic contexts: both were productive industrial economies highly dependent on the import and export of goods, and although East Germany lagged somewhat behind West Germany in these respects, their positions in relation to COMECON and EC countries respectively was similar. On the other hand, their differences in political organization and ideology did seem to have made considerable impact on differences in social structure, social mobility, and perceptions of society.

Standards of living

How did people actually experience life in these two societies? Quite obviously the degree of consumer satisfaction was much higher for most people in the affluent West. Increasingly high average earnings, a decreasing working week, generous holiday provision, a very low inflation rate by the standards of other countries, a stable currency, and a safety net of a welfare system which survived even the more stringent conservative governments of the 1980s, combined to make the Federal Republic of the late 1980s a very comfortable place to live. West Germans became renowned as hard workers who were also able to enjoy relaxing – whether tanning themselves on Mediterranean beaches, or escaping to the mountain air of the Alps for skiing in winter or walking in summer. Obviously, given the range of social inequalities in West Germany, such an image does not describe everyone; nevertheless, life for large numbers of West Germans certainly was materially preferable to conditions for East Germans.

Assessing the situation in East Germany cannot simply be reduced to a comparison of average incomes. Whatever the clear superiority of West German standards of living, a number of factors must be added in connection with the GDR. For one thing, while East German workers had no right to strike, they also did not need to fear unemployment. Everyone was guaranteed a job – whether or not it was commensurate with abilities, training and aspirations. Given the high proportion of employed women, there was a high proportion of two income families. The problem for many was not so much lack of money, as lack of goods to spend it on. Nevertheless, despite a time lag, particularly in the Honecker era East German households began to catch up with their West German counterparts in the possession of at least some consumer durables. A comparison between average four-person middle-income households in West and East Germany reveals that by 1988, 99% of East German households had a washing machine and a fridge, 96% had a television (although only 52% in colour), and 52% possessed a car. West Germans were relatively saturated too, with 99% having washing machines, 98% televisions (94% in colour), and 97% having cars. In 1970, the corresponding figures for East Germany had been 54% owning washing machines, 69% televisions (no colour), and 16% with a car. The major numerical differences remained in possession of telephones: by 1988, while 98% of West German middle income households had a telephone, only 9% of East Germans did.[6] It might also be apposite to add that numbers do not reveal everything: even the most committed East German Communists would admit the superiority, in qualitative terms, of a Mercedes or BMW over a Wartburg or Trabant.

Basic foodstuffs were extremely cheap, being subsidized, in the GDR: there need be no actual hunger. On the other hand, nor was there much choice. By the mid-1980s, East Germans were consuming on average more calories than their West German counterparts, with higher levels of meat, eggs, and dairy produce but lower levels of fresh fruit and vegetables.[7] Food queues were not a daily event of normal life in the GDR as in Poland, but rather reflected the sudden appearance of some much-desired item, such as the arrival of a consignment of bananas.

The East German economy was complicated by lack of widespread availability of certain goods and produce, accessible only to the privileged, and the existence of waiting lists for certain desired goods, such as new cars. It was also a two-tier consumer society, divided between those with access to western currency and those without. The former could shop in the Intershops, selling western goods (such as instant coffee) at high prices in western currency, which were first opened for westerners in 1962 and then made available to East Germans in 1974. So-called Delikat and Exquisit shops also sold more luxurious or desirable items at relatively high prices in East German currency.

Apologists for the GDR liked to point to the notion of 'collective consumption' as further complicating the comparison. Relatively high state expenditure on health and social welfare was held to offset lower incomes, since private money was not necessary to fund these services. As we shall see, the GDR certainly provided very generous maternity benefits and comprehensive child-care provision. Pensions too were adequate, given the low cost of living. The GDR was also held to have a good health service, although hospitals were not as well equipped as in the West, and the best facilities were to be found in church-run hospitals which were supported by funds from the West German churches, with western machinery and maintenance. Housing was subsidized, with very low rents, although the quality was not always very high. Housing the population became a priority under Honecker, when the policy of rapid building of pre-fabricated high rise dwellings was complemented by renovation of old city centre housing which had been becoming increasingly dilapidated. As with jobs, although people might not like their accommodation, at least they could be sure of actually having a home.

What were the implications of this rather depressed, but essentially adequate, life-style? Given that the majority of East Germans tuned in to western television every night, they were well aware in theory of the much better living standards in the West – although knowledge was not quite the same thing as direct personal experience of western consumer choice, as many found when they first visited the West in 1989–90. On the other hand, there seemed little that could be done about this situation beyond private grumbling. A more salient comparison might be with the far worse living standards of their eastern neighbours, in Poland. On this front, the East Germans could indulge in a little national pride. As far as political implications were concerned, the provision of a modest minimum meant that there was no revolutionary groundswell to support the dissent of intellectuals when there appeared no prospect of a successful revolution. While many East Germans would leave for the West if they had a chance – and many did so in droves after the opening of the borders – they were not, before 1989, for the most part prepared to rise in a clearly hopeless revolt just because the choice in their fruit and vegetable shops was between cabbages and more cabbages, while the West Germans ate peaches, oranges and grapes.

Education and socialization in the two Germanies

One of the major tasks to be faced in both East and West Germany was that of the reconstruction of the educational system. The Nazis, as we have seen, attempted to subvert the German education system: they sought to produce physically fit, politically indoctrinated exemplars of the 'Aryan' master race. In both East and West Germany the Nazi system was rejected; but the introduction of new systems, new teachers, new textbooks, new aims and ethos, proved problematic. The two Germanies developed rather different solutions.

In West Germany, Allied attempts to reform the school system were initially resisted by the *Länder*. There was a return to pre-Nazi educational traditions. At primary school level, there was the *Volksschule*. At secondary level, the *Gymnasium*, or traditional grammar school, which had been such a prestigious vehicle for elite education in the nineteenth century, was retained, along with vocational schools and general schools (*Realschulen* and *Hauptschulen*) for the majority of children. While different *Länder* retained control over their own school systems, there were certain moves towards rationalization in the 1950s. Hamburg, Bremen, and Schleswig-Holstein were pressurized to come into line with the four-year primary education current in other *Länder* instead of the postponement of selection until six years after starting school which they had initially preferred. In the 1955 Düsseldorf Agreement of the Kultus-Minister-Konferenz, there was generally traditionalist agreement not to experiment with education. The theory that the distribution of intellectual ability broadly conformed with the existing social structure, and that in any case the working classes 'did not want culture', underpinned the tripartite selective system.[8] The failure to achieve early reforms of the education system, and the generally conservative reaction against the democratizing aims of Allied education policies, has since been subjected to considerable criticism in the Federal Republic.[9] Nevertheless, certain inherited inequalities were slowly dismantled. By 1958–9 school fees had been abolished or were being phased out in almost all *Länder*. The *Rahmenplan* was introduced, aiming at reforms particularly of the *Gymnasium* curriculum.

In East Germany, by contrast, early measures were designed to overthrow such social selectivity. The 1946 Education Act (the Law Relating to the Democratization of German Schools) abolished the tripartite system and replaced it with co-educational *Grundschulen* for all six to fourteen-year-olds, with a subsequent transfer to *Oberschulen* for more gifted pupils. Private schools and confessional schools were abolished. There were attempts to reduce urban–rural inequalities by setting up

Zentralschulen in rural areas.[10] The notion of common schooling for all children survived a subsequent sequence of changes in the structure of the system. The *Zehnklassenschule* (ten-class school) was introduced in 1950. Although *Oberschulen* continued to exist, it was still possible to gain eventual access to higher education via the alternative routes of *Berufsschulen* and *Fachschulen* (vocational and technical schools). From 1953 there was discussion of 'polytechnical education', with a day a week spent in industry. This was introduced gradually from 1956, with a concerted effort to introduce such a system of combining practical experience of work with theoretical learning in school universally in 1958–9. The 1959 Law Relating to the Socialist Development of Education replaced the *Grundschule* with a *Zehnklassige allgemeine polytechnische Oberschule* (Ten-year general polytechnical schools, POS), followed by two years at an *Erweiterte Oberschule* (extended upper school, EOS) for the academically gifted.[11]

There were considerable differences of opinion on education in the GDR in the 1950s: the SED was somewhat at odds with the Ministry of Education, first under Education Minister Else Zaisser (wife of Wilhelm Zaisser, of the anti-Ulbricht Herrnstadt-Zaisser faction) and then under Fritz Lange (dismissed in May 1956 for 'revisionist opinions' associated with the Schirdewan, Wollweber and Ziller group).

There were difficulties with finding adequate replacement teachers, and with reconciling SED (and Soviet) views of education with the reform-pedagogical ideas of many genuinely left-wing educationalists in the GDR who wanted to latch onto some of the progressive ideas of the Weimar period. Yet one of the basic aims of East German political ideology was to a considerable extent achieved: the promotion of equality of educational opportunity. By the mid-1950s, 53% of university students in the GDR were from the working class (which constituted 69% of the population), in contrast to only 4% in West Germany in 1950 (when 57% of the population were deemed to be working class) rising to a mere 7.5% in West Germany by 1970.[12]

In both Germanies, there was considerable rethinking concerning the aims and structure of the respective education systems in the 1960s. In the East, it was realized that promotion of equal opportunities had to be compatible with the production of skilled workers required for an efficient economy (particularly after the introduction of the New Economic System in 1963). In the West, the glaring social inequalities of the educational system became a matter of public concern, and it was realized that they might be disguising a wastage of talent. To some extent the two systems then converged in the decade which was characterized by an emphasis on technological advance in a number of industrial societies (including British Prime Minister Harold Wilson's emphasis on the 'white-hot heat of technological revolution' and the explosion of higher education in Britain after the Robbins Report).

In the early 1960s, special schools and special classes were introduced in the GDR for specially gifted children. Ironically, old elite schools with strong nineteenth-century traditions were still being used as elite schools in the communist East Germany of the 1980s, but now for children in theory selected according to ability and talents rather than social background. (One such school was Schulpforte, earlier attended by such notable pupils as the Chancellor of Imperial Germany, Theobald von Bethmann Hollweg.) Special schools only accounted for about 2–3% of the education system, but were very important in training certain elites – such as the future sports champions of the GDR. The 1965 Law Relating to the Unified System of Socialist Education stressed the importance of achievement, and the goal of promoting equality of opportunity gave way to that of fostering talent, from whatever social background it might come. Quotas for children of peasants and workers at universities were dropped, and the 'Workers' and Peasants' Faculties' abolished. While in 1958 there was a peak of 52.7% of university students of working class origin, by 1962 this had dropped to 48.7%, dropping further to 39.1% in 1966 and 38.2% in 1967.[13] At the same time, there was considerable expansion in the higher education system, from the mid-1960s to the mid-1970s. The proportion of those with higher education among the employed more than doubled (from 2.18% to 4.86%) in the decade from 1961 to 1971.[14]

In West Germany, a comparable concern for the production of qualified manpower for the economy was combined with a newer concern over social inequalities. It was revealed that there were gross differences in educational opportunity and achievement according to region, religion, class and gender in West Germany. The industrial working class, Catholics, girls, and children in rural areas were all at a disadvantage; and despite attempts by the Kultus-Minister-Konferenz to co-ordinate the educational policies of different *Länder*, it was revealed that in 1962, for example, only 19% of sixteen-year-olds in the Saar were in full-time education as compared with 39% in Schleswig-Holstein, and only 4% obtained the intermediate leaving certificate in the Saar compared with 24% in Schleswig-Holstein. It was also revealed that the GDR had been devoting a higher proportion of its national income to education than had the Federal Republic (a GDR average of 6% per year from 1954 to 1962, as compared with 3.5–3.7% in the FRG, according to the UNESCO statistical yearbook of 1964).[15] The fear of being overtaken by the GDR in educational planning for the needs of the economy helped to provoke changes in the system.

In 1965 the *Bildungsrat* was created (partly in response to publication of H. Picht's *Die deutsche Bildungskatastrophe* in 1964); in 1970 the *Bund-Länder-Kommission für Bildungsplanung* was set up for consultation and co-operation among *Länder*; and in 1973 the *Bildungsgesamtplan* was introduced. In 1969 the *Berufsbildungsgesetz* increased state control of vocational education (which had been largely under the control of Chambers of Industry and Commerce and industrial firms). The 1970 *Strukturplan für das Bildungswesen* attempted to reform secondary education, with certain core compulsory and other optional courses. In the tripartite system, *Gymnasien* and *Realschulen* were expanded at the expense of *Hauptschulen*. The relative proportions of thirteen-year-olds at each type of school changed in the period from 1955 to 1980 from 12% to 27%, 6% to 25%, and 79% to 39%, respectively.[16] Attempts were made to make a Gymnasium education more relevant to current economic concerns, and to introduce different types of Gymnasium (with emphases on science, or modern languages, rather than classics, for example).

Neither Germany had solved the problems of its educational system by the 1970s. In East Germany, there had to be a reduction in university places because of over-production of qualified graduates who were forced to take employment in jobs below the level of their qualifications.[17] There were constraints on freedom of choice of study, because of restricted numbers of places. Reproduction of inherited status began to reappear and increase, as the goal of positive discrimination in favour of working-class and peasant students had been dropped. Meanwhile, in West Germany, attempts at introducing comprehensive schools in certain areas (such as Hesse) were greeted with mixed reactions and considerable suspicion. The fact that two to three times as many working class children managed to obtain the *Abitur* (the German equivalent of British A levels) in comprehensive schools (*Gesamtschulen*) as in the selective system, and that only ten per cent of working class children attended a Gymnasium in 1979, was generally disregarded.[18]

On the whole the West German system continued to operate in a relatively conservative fashion to perpetuate the transmission of class status from one generation to the next. Differences in opportunity and equality were also evident in the sphere of higher education. In West German universities an attempt to solve the problem of overcrowding by introducing a so-called *numerus clausus* (restricted numbers of places for study in particular faculties) was eventually dropped for all but medicine. The limited nature of student grants, however, and the introduction of a system of student loans in 1982, made university study in any case the prerogative of young people from financially secure backgrounds. This discrimination was compounded by the extended nature of university study in West Germany, by movement from one university to another, and by the flexibility of studies. Despite the drop in the number of places available in East Germany's higher education system (which included well over fifty institutions of higher education, including the universities of Berlin, Halle-Wittenberg, Leipzig,

Dresden, Rostock, Greifswald, and Jena, as well as the Technical University of Dresden), there was at least relative financial equality of opportunity, with grants according to parental income. There was also good provision for further education, and a number of possible routes to university other than the orthodox academic route via the EOS. Pupils going on to vocational and technical training could also through one route or another ultimately enter university, as could mature students in later life.

On comparing the respective education systems in the two Germanies as they stood in the early 1980s, some curious similarities and differences emerge. Both Germanies, as advanced industrial societies, laid considerable emphasis on vocational and practical training. While the West German system was structurally the more conservative, and there appeared to be greater equality of opportunity in the East German system, the roles were reversed as far as the ethos of education in the two states was concerned. West German education was characterized by authoritarianism and hierarchical relations between teachers and those they taught for much of its first two decades, but there were signs of internal democratization particularly from the late 1960s onwards. In the GDR, however, despite the more egalitarian structure, the internal atmosphere was much more authoritarian: conformity was encouraged rather than intellectual curiosity and debate. Pupils were taught to repeat approved positions rather than develop independent points of view. In neither case should one over-generalize, and there were changes in both Germanies. (In the GDR, for example, in the later 1980s – even before the revolutionary upheavals of 1989 – it was becoming possible to discuss unorthodox thinkers such as Antonio Gramsci in the Marxist-Leninist weekend schools for medical students and doctors.)[19] Nevertheless, the general effect seemed to be that West German youth learned to be democratic within a framework of social inequality (which might be accepted as 'natural' and legitimized by theories of ability and the gaining of educational credentials according to merit rather than social background), while East German youth learned to become at least outward conformists and gained little experience of genuine debate and the toleration of alternative points of view except in a rather formal sense. Curiously, while the West German educational structure was the more traditional, the East German educational ethos was the more conservative, operating to produce obedient subjects rather than participatory citizens. This was not entirely in line with the regime's desire to produce active socialist personalities, and also ran somewhat at odds with other influences on the outlook of young people in the GDR, as we shall see.

Women and the family in the two Germanies

We have seen that in some ways the GDR developed a more egalitarian society – although evaluations of that relatively greater equality (including equality in a lower standard of living and less freedom of choice) might be negative. A comparable picture emerges on examination of the position of women. While there remained structural differences in the role of women, as compared with men, in both Germanies by the 1980s, these differences were less in the East than in the West. Whether one interprets this as implying greater 'emancipation' for women in the East than in the West is another matter. The analysis of the position of women in the two Germanies reflects and illustrates wider problems of comparison of the two socio-political systems.

More women were in paid employment outside the home in East Germany than in West Germany. In 1984, 50% of the East German work force was female, compared to 39% in West Germany.[20] In both Germanies, women worked in predominantly lower-paid, lower-status jobs. Despite the fact that in 1955 in West Germany the 'women's wage groups' (*Frauenlohngruppen*) were legally abolished, in fact the so-called 'light wage groups' (*Leichtlohngruppen*) took their place, and in the 1980s the average woman's wage was 30% lower than the average man's wage in the West. Many West German women worked part-time: in 1984, 32.2% of female workers worked for less than a forty-hour week, and – significantly – 93% of all part-time workers were women. Women in West Germany constituted in effect a 'reserve army of labour', entering the economy in times of expansion and being easily excluded in times of recession. While official figures give an unemployment rate for women of 10.6% in autumn 1986 – a rate one-third higher than that for men – diverse pressures and psychological resignation leading to withdrawal from the labour market meant that the true figure of women who would in principle like to work but had no job was nearer to 16%. In East Germany, there was in theory no unemployment; but East German women shared with West Germans the problem of working in lower-status jobs, frequently failing to gain appropriate promotion and working below the level of their qualifications. For example, in 1978 East German women made up 65.8% of teachers, but only 20% of heads of schools.[21]

In both Germanies, women were rare figures in the higher echelons of politics, with only an occasional female minister (usually for a 'domestic' area having to do with education, health, and family affairs) and moderate rates of party membership. In the West, the Greens had the highest proportion of women members, party activists and MPs, followed – at a distance – by the SPD; in the East, there were relatively high numbers of women at the grass-roots and lower levels of the SED, thinning out markedly higher up the hierarchy (with the notable exception of Margot Honecker, whose career as Education Minister collapsed with that of her husband, SED leader Erich Honecker, in 1989). Interestingly, women made up more than half the membership of the East German trade union organization, the FDGB.

Such statistics could be elaborated endlessly. More and more illustrations could be adduced to emphasize the obvious: that despite the fact that the constitutions of both Germanies proclaimed the formal equality of women and men, and despite the considerable quantity of legislation that was enacted to attempt to secure such equality in reality, women in the two Germanies did not occupy positions in society equal to those of men. A number of factors are relevant in attempting to explain the differences, and the failure to realize constitutional principles in practice.

The debates centre on a number of issues: whether there are innate differences of interest, aptitude and ability between men and women; whether observable differences in aspirations and achievements are more the result of differential socialization than of biological differences; and what the implications are – or should be – of the one very obvious and undeniable gender-specific difference, namely the fact that women become pregnant and give birth to babies whereas men do not.

This is not the place to embark on detailed analysis of studies of child development and gender differentiation. It will be sufficient merely to mention that there are observable differences of development between male and female children at a very early age: for example, females – on average – develop communicative skills more rapidly, while males progress more in the area of spatial ability. However, it is not clear what interaction of biological differences and socialization patterns is responsible for these differences: some studies have shown, for example, that mothers tend to talk more to girl babies than to boy babies, thus encouraging early language development. Adults undoubtedly interact with babies of different sexes in different ways, even from the earliest days after birth. Whatever the balance between genes and environment – and any observable development is the result of a combination of influences – one fact is undoubtedly clear. Just as the weight and height distributions of males and females show a large area of overlap, so do other distributions. In other words, while there may be a difference in overall *averages*, there are many women who are taller and heavier than many men. In the sphere of intellectual abilities, putative average differences in aptitude or interest are in no way sufficient to explain the extraordinary disparities in social location, with the astonishing paucity of top women scientists, politicians, businessmen (note the word!) and the like. Attention must therefore be paid to cultural aspects of development, and the limits imposed by childbearing, to explain the differences.

Both Germanies made efforts to increase the equality of opportunity for girls in the education system. In East Germany, there was by the 1980s approximate equality in numbers: about half the schoolchildren leaving with the *Abitur* (the equivalent of A levels) were female, and half of all students in higher education were female. In the West, the figures were not so impressive; while the average percentage of girls in *Gymnasien* rose from 43% in 1970 to 50.5% in 1984, the percentage of women students in higher education rose only from 30% in 1968 to 37.9% in 1985–6. Higher up in the academic world, proportions of women declined, until only 5.2% of professors were female.[22] Both Germanies attempted to change the attitudes conveyed about appropriate career aspirations for boys and girls, by looking critically at the sex role stereotypes in school textbooks, and by ensuring full equality in lessons offered (rather than directing girls towards cookery and needlework while boys did woodwork, for example). Some advances were undoubtedly made, but surveys suggested the persistence among schoolchildren – and their parents! – of traditional attitudes about the appropriate sexual division of labour.

Undoubtedly a major factor explaining differences in the structural location of adult males and females is the fact that women bear children while men do not. This has attracted considerable attention in terms of social policies, ranging from questions concerning contraception and abortion to provisions for maternity leave and child care facilities. Both Germanies suffered a declining birth-rate, with a long-term tendency for the indigenous population to fail to reproduce itself (offset in the West by the immigration and, initially at least, the differential fertility rate of *Gastarbeiter*). While East Germany in 1972 introduced abortion on demand for women in the first twelve weeks of pregnancy (the only vote in the East German parliament prior to 1989, incidentally, not to be passed unanimously), it also adopted measures from 1978 onwards to encourage women to have two or preferably more children. By the late 1980s, maternity leave provision in East Germany was among the most generous to be found in any country: from 1984, East German women were entitled to a full year off on full pay after having a baby, with eighteen months off after a third or subsequent baby. By contrast, the West German maternity leave of six weeks before the birth and eight weeks after (or twelve weeks for premature or multiple births) seemed quite stingy. Both Germanies paid varying amounts of maternity grant and child benefit; and both Germanies instituted arrangements for taking further time off work to look after very small children – time which might be taken by either the father or the mother, or, in East Germany, by some other nominated individual such as a grandmother or a neighbour. It must be said, however, that the money paid in West Germany was not such as to excite support for the scheme or voluntary participation by most well-paid West Germans (600DM per month – about £200 – in 1986).

The major problem for most women is not so much maternity leave and childbirth as what to do with their children by way of childcare when they do wish to return to work. Shortage of labour in East Germany led to a high priority being put on the extensive provision of childcare facilities. The majority of pre-school children who needed a place in a crèche (for the under-threes) or Kindergarten (for three- to six-year-olds) was therefore provided for. In East Germany there were however indications of disquiet over the quality and benefits of crèche provision for very small children, and extensive time off work instead of use of crèche provisions undoubtedly helped to improve the quality of personal care for the under-threes. Arguments about the quality of Kindergartens tended to focus more on the contents of the 'education' offered (with doubt about the military games, and early political indoctrination) than on the effects on the child of spending a very long day away from home in the company of a large number of other small children.[23] In West Germany, the comparative lack of sufficient pre-school provision was the major problem for mothers wishing to work. In 1982, there were over 500,000 employed women with a child or children under the age of three in West Germany; yet there were only 26,245 crèche places.[24] Most working women with small children had to resort to informal arrangements with a relative (such as a grandmother), neighbour, or friend to look after the child. Child-minders and parental co-operative nurseries were gaining ground as possible childcare arrangements. Given the disparities in childcare provision, while East German women took it for granted that they would return to work, West German women found considerable obstacles and barriers to be surmounted before they could consider doing so. For East German mothers, working was the norm; for West German mothers, not working was the norm.

There are a number of other respects in which East German women's participation in the labour force was facilitated: there were provisions for staying at home with a sick child, there was a statutory day off for housework, there was extensive after-school provision, and so on. (In West Germany in 1982, there were less than two after-school places for every 100 schoolchildren – and the school day ended at lunch-time, posing enormous problems for working parents.) But the fact remains that, for all the apparent 'progress' in East Germany, East German women returned home, exhausted after a long day's work, to do most of the housework while their husbands relaxed. 'Emancipation' for East German women came to be reinterpreted as a 'double burden' (*Doppelbelastung*): doing both a man's and a woman's work. While East German feminists in the late 1960s and early 1970s were seeking to break into the men's world of work, a change of emphasis was evident in the 1980s: many articulate women in the GDR were reverting to a notion of specifically 'female' activities and endeavours, and wanting emancipation *from* competing with males in a male world.[25] When comparing 'objective facts', women in the GDR might have looked more emancipated than women in the Federal Republic – and studies have suggested that there was a genuine desire on the part of the regime to achieve greater equality for women for ideological reasons, and not simply to exploit them as part of the work force because of a labour shortage.[26] But many East German women might well have preferred to have had the choice of staying home and looking after their children, rather than working in low-paid, unfulfilling jobs all day and returning home to cope with household duties and fractious children at night.

We may conclude this section with a brief look at youth and the family in the two Germanies. Many relevant aspects have already been covered in other contexts, but a few additional points may be made here.

East Germany laid great emphasis on the socialization of youth and the development of a 'socialist personality'. To this end, East German children were organized at an early age. For younger children, there was the Young Pioneers organization (JP); for 15–25 year-olds, there was the Free German Youth (FDJ). As indicated above, although membership of these was not compulsory, there was considerable pressure to participate and penalties in terms of future prospects for those who did not. These organizations offered a range of activities, including sports, holidays and trips to places of interest (ranging from Buchenwald concentration camp to the Wartburg Castle where Luther translated the New Testament). On the other hand, there is evidence to suggest that these forms of socialization merely reinforced what young East Germans learned in all areas of experience: that they could lead a form of double life, separating outward conformity from private lives and personal spaces. West German children, by contrast, had a much freer upbringing; and despite the East German focus on childhood, it was notable that facilities for children such as playgrounds were infinitely superior in the West than the East.

Family life too showed certain differences. There was a higher divorce rate in East Germany than in the West; but there was also a higher rate of marriage. In 1985, there were 3.1 divorces per 1000 population in the GDR, compared with a figure of 2.1 in the FRG; but there were 7.9 marriages per 1000 population in the GDR compared with 6 in the FRG.[27] It could be argued that, with the greater economic independence of women in the GDR, marriage was in a sense being taken more seriously: rather than being a convenient economic arrangement, it was stripped to its essence as an emotional union of equal partners; and if this personal union failed, it was more readily dissolved. Alternatively, the figures can be interpreted quite differently: the stresses of cramped housing, poor financial circumstances, and combining paid employment and housework led to strains in marriage which caused marital break-down. There is undoubtedly some truth in both views, but the second has considerable weight. There were also high rates of illegitimacy and single-parent families in the East as compared with the West.

Bearing these rather different social conditions and profiles in mind, let us now return to the sphere of politics, and explore in more detail the nature of the two German states and the character of oppositional or dissenting forces in the two Germanies.

TEN

Politics and the State

It is quite clear that two very different political systems were imposed, and developed, in the two parts of the defeated Third Reich. That Germany was divided in 1949, and that the conditions for division collapsed in 1989, both have to do with the Cold War between the superpowers. The sustaining of the division thus has much to do with the relationships between the USSR and the USA, and with the integration of East and West Germany into the respective eastern and western defensive alliances – the Warsaw Pact and NATO. Undoubtedly the 'balance of terror' in central Europe played an important role in maintaining the status quo of a divided continent. But this does not explain everything. For one thing, even the escalating balance of terror had implications for domestic stability, with the development of peace movements in both East and West protesting against the stationing of nuclear missiles on German soil, and becoming thorns in the flesh of established governmental politics on both sides of the Iron Curtain. For another, however crucial the Cold War is in explaining the origins and the eventual collapse of the division of Germany, it does not fully explain the dynamics of domestic politics in each of the two German states.

It is worth reiterating that both East and West Germany were remarkably successful, given their unlikely origins, in sustaining and reproducing their respective systems over forty years. It is now necessary to explore some of the reasons for this relative success, and some of the ways in which the two Germanies diverged in the period of their division, before considering the origins and course of the East German revolution of 1989 and the collapse of the post-war system.

The argument to be developed below is as follows. Both Germanies, for rather different reasons and in rather different ways, were able to secure the support, the allegiance, or at least the acquiescence, of key elite groups, and avoid the development of powerful anti-system opposition of the sort that helped to bring about the collapse of the Weimar Republic. Both Germanies too – again in very different ways – managed for the most part to contain, isolate, or defuse dissent, ensuring that it remained within certain manageable limits. When popular discontent was finally expressed on a massive scale in the GDR in the autumn of 1989, it was in a situation when the regime was already in crisis as a result of changes in external circumstances. In the mean time, differences in political structure and ideology, in economy, social and cultural policy, had produced striking degrees of divergence in the profiles of the two Germanies. By the time the East Germans began, in the winter of 1989, to proclaim that they were 'one people' (*ein Volk*) with the West Germans, they had in fact developed very striking differences, not only in outward appearance but also in patterns of perception, assumption, orientation and behaviour. We shall explore these themes in turn in this and the following chapters.

The political system of the GDR

Many analyses of the East German political system assumed that a formal description of the different bodies which made up its state and governmental apparatus, along with a description of the Communist Party and its Marxist-Leninist ideology, provided the final answer to explaining the relative stability of the GDR over the previous forty years. Frequently the assumption was also made that the political systems of all the East European Communist states under the domination of the Soviet Union were broadly similar. The implicit assumption underlying both these views is that ultimately coercion, real or threatened, was the sole key to political stability in East German communism. None of these assumptions is quite adequate. There were unique aspects to the East German state, and relations between the ruling party and the state; in addition, formal analyses of the political system alone cannot provide a complete explanation of the political dynamics of the GDR more generally over the years, since factors such as the changing economic and social structure, and changing patterns of political culture among the people (considered further in subsequent chapters), must also be taken into account.

The SED was a 'mass' as well as 'cadre' party: in addition to the party activists ('cadres') there was a much larger body of passive members. In 1981 the membership of the SED was 2,069,629 (along with 102,481 candidates). This meant that 17.38% of those over eighteen belonged to the party; of the working population, the percentage was 21.9%.[1] There were periodic purges of party membership, with the recall of membership cards, and interviews with members, as a result of which many were forced or persuaded to leave the party. For the party activists, membership entailed considerable personal commitment; for the vast body of party members, it was more likely to be a matter of convenience and a sign of general commitment to the GDR than a case of enthusiastic espousal of every aspect of party ideology and policy. From the late 1970s onwards, there appeared to be a greater willingness among grass roots members to express differences from the official party line. The evidence of emigrés such as Professor Franz Loeser suggested the existence of relatively large numbers whose thinking was somewhat at odds with that of the old guard leadership.[2] Clearly a change of generations was an important factor in this process. Those who had grown up – and suffered – under Hitler's dictatorship were profoundly affected by certain formative experiences not shared by a younger generation, who might be impatient with aspects of the iron party discipline of the older members. From the mid-1980s onwards, a further crucial factor in the internal variegation of political views was the impact of Gorbachev's reform programme. Those who hoped for the introduction of a little *glasnost* and *perestroika* in East Germany were impatient with the resistance to reform of Honecker's old guard. This developing differentiation was eventually to play an important role in determining the regime's responses to the revolutionary crisis of autumn 1989.

The GDR was not in theory a one-party state. In addition to the communist SED, there were the four smaller parties: the Christian Democratic Union (CDU), the National Democratic Party of Germany (NDPD), the Liberal Democratic Party of Germany (LDPD), and the Democratic Farmers' Party of Germany (DBD). The membership figures for these parties were much lower than for the SED: between the late 1970s and 1989 they hovered between somewhat below and somewhat above 100,000 members each, with some signs of increase during the 1980s, while the CDU remained the largest.[3]

These parties all had allotted numbers of seats in the People's Chamber (*Volkskammer*, or parliament), as did the so called 'mass organizations', which in fact had larger numbers of members than did the parties. The Confederation of Free German Trade Unions (FDGB) claimed no fewer than 8,806,754 members in 1980 – slightly more in fact than the numbers of the working population, which were 8,225,000 plus 492,000 apprentices.[4] On these figures, more people belonged to the trade union organization than were actually members of the working population. The Free German Youth (FDJ) had 2,300,000 members in 1978 (and the 'Ernst Thälmann' Pioneer Organization for younger children had 1,507,211 members); the Democratic Women's League of Germany (DFD) had 1,400,000 members in 1980; and the League of Culture (KB) had 226,593 members.[5] Together, the SED, the four smaller parties (CDU, LDPD, DBD, and NDPD), and the major 'mass organizations' (FDGB, FDJ, DFD, and KB) formed the 'Block' in the 'National Front', which represented different sections of the population in the People's Chamber. Elections did not determine the proportion of seats each party or organization would hold; these were pre-allotted. Instead, elections served as a means of mass mobilization, presenting candidates and issues to the public, and advertising policies which had already been decided upon elsewhere.

This did not mean that the parties, mass organizations, and parliament had no function in the GDR. Their functions were however rather different from those of their western equivalent. From the point of view of the people, membership of a party and one or more organizations indicated a willingness to participate in the socio-political system (and the 'building of socialism'), and might be essential for career advancement and promotion prospects. (It was notable that young people who wished to gain university places to study a subject such as medicine, for example, were under some pressure to conform in all sorts of ways, and to participate actively in the FDJ.) But membership might not be purely for careerist reasons. It was possible also to give vent to personal opinions – suitably phrased – and the converse of this represented a function as viewed from above: that of the tapping of public opinion. In a state which did not have general elections in the western sense as a verdict on governmental performance, it was important to have avenues through which popular responses to policies could be gauged. Interactions between deputies and their constituents and party members could form one such channel, to be placed alongside the evidence from other channels (such as the use of increasingly sophisticated sociological techniques of investigation).

There were other functions too: policies could be widely advertised through the publicity surrounding meetings of parliament, and through the different communications systems of the parties and mass organizations; and they could be translated into the appropriate subcultural 'languages' to appeal to the different sectional interests covered by each group. This is not to suggest that what was effectively official propaganda was simply swallowed uncritically when rephrased; many Christians in the GDR, for example, treated the CDU with a certain distance and suspicion as a party more closely linked with the SED than with either the church leaderships or the opinions of grass-roots Christians. Nevertheless, a 'conveyor belt' or 'transmission function', however imperfect, did exist, and the parties and mass organizations could not simply be written off as merely a sham front providing a fig leaf for the workings of a totalitarian state.

The discussion so far has assumed the predominant role of the Socialist Unity Party (SED). This now needs further examination. In principle, there were two separate organizational hierarchies in the GDR: that of the state, with its various levels of power and decision-making; and that of the party, with its own hierarchy based on the principle of democratic centralism. Many western observers have suggested that the state was merely the means for implementation of party decisions. In practice, relations between the state and the party during the development of the GDR were somewhat more complex, and it is not always entirely clear what the parameters, constraints and tensions in the relationship were. Formally, the role of the SED was embodied in the 1968 constitution of the GDR, which enshrined the 'leading role' of the working class under its Marxist-Leninist party. In Marxist-Leninist theory, the proletariat under capitalism may be suffering from alienation and 'false consciousness'. As a result, it may not recognize what are its own long-term interests, and hence it requires a 'vanguard party' to act in its true interests. Under real communism – the 'last' stage of history, when the 'condition for the free development of each is the condition for the free development of all' and universal human emancipation will have been achieved – the state (and the party) will no longer be necessary and will 'wither away', along with such relics of false consciousness of former ages such as religion. The GDR however considered itself to be in the transitional phase of 'actually existing socialism'. This stage still needed the Marxist-Leninist party to steer and control the development of society, through the state, according to scientifically ascertained laws of history. So much for the theory. In practice, relations between party and state varied at different times during the history of the GDR. In the 1950s, the party had to intervene frequently in order to ensure that party objectives were being pursued by the state; by the 1980s, one western specialist has argued, despite the theoretical dominance of the party, the state was setting the parameters of problems, defining the political agenda and suggesting limits to the range of possible solutions and policies which could realistically be pursued.[6]

There was of course considerable overlap in personnel between the party and state organizations, particularly at the highest levels. Since 1960, the First Secretary (General

Secretary) of the SED was also usually the formal head of state by virtue of chairmanship of the Council of State (*Staatsrat*). (There was a brief period, from 1971 to 1976, when Honecker was leader of the SED but did not also chair the Council of State; until his death in 1973, Walter Ulbricht retained his position as chairman, and then Willi Stoph chaired the Council of State until 1976, when Honecker took on the chairmanship along with that of the National Defence Council, thus again uniting the most important party, state and military functions in one person.) A conscious policy was adopted of ensuring that leading Party officials (such as the Central Committee Secretaries) were also members of the Council of State, so that they could officially represent the GDR, and not just the party, when travelling abroad. The 1984 Politburo included ten members (one of whom was a candidate member) who were also members of the Council of State.[7] But overlaps in personnel cannot tell the whole story; there are additional questions concerning the interrelationships and tensions among technical specialists, dogmatists, pragmatists, humanists, and other groups. These tensions were found both within the party, and in relations between party and state.

In the 1950s, there was a general tendency in the West to dismiss the 'zone', as it was still dismissively called, as a simple instance of Soviet domination and hence of Communist totalitarianism. This arose partly from the Cold War ideology, in which Communism was portrayed as an evil equivalent to, or worse than, the recently defeated Nazism. Western political scientists also saw many similarities between one-party states with a single official ideology enforced with a back-up of terror. Whatever the bases of this analysis, its relevance to the realities of the situation in the GDR was questioned in the 1960s by P.C. Ludz. He argued that the efficient running of an advanced industrial society necessitated the rise of technical experts, forming what he called an 'institutionalized counter-elite' which provided a counterweight to the powers of the central party political clique. At the same time, Ludz discerned the development of a more pragmatic, career-oriented society, in which inner commitment was less important than outward conformity. According to Ludz, the GDR in the 1960s constituted an instance not of 'totalitarianism' but rather of what he termed 'consultative authoritarianism'.[8]

Many scholars have questioned Ludz's rather strong thesis concerning the rise of a 'counter-elite' in the GDR. Baylis, for example, pointed out that those members of the technical intelligentsia who arrived in positions of political importance were also political conformists; and that the positions which they attained were in the main advisory rather than decisive or genuinely powerful. Political considerations retained their priority over technical or professional considerations. Furthermore, whatever the partial relevance of Ludz's observations for the period of 'scientific-technical revolution' in the 1960s, the 1970s saw a clear reassertion of the predominance of party politicians over technical specialists.[9] Scholars such as Dahrendorf and Krejci have, in contrast to Ludz, suggested that the GDR was characterized by having a 'unitary elite'. Others, such as Thielbeer, even went so far as to suggest that the GDR continued to be a 'totalitarian' state, despite the relative disrepute into which that term had fallen.[10] Yet there are drawbacks to these approaches too.

It seems intrinsically unhelpful to characterize the political system of the GDR from 1949 to 1989 solely in terms of domination by a communist party with its associated ideology and power apparatus, thus by simple definition lumping all East European regimes together. A more differentiated exploration of the GDR reveals a number of ways in which it differed from its immediate neighbours in the east. These differences include not only differences in the structure of agriculture, the level of industrial development, and overall economic productivity, but also in the constitution of and relations between different elite groups. While the Czech and Polish cases cannot be considered in detail here, a couple of comments may serve to indicate important differences between them and that of the GDR. From the late 1950s until the mid-1980s, the SED appears to have maintained greater cohesion than the Czech and Polish communist parties, which had considerable reforming movements within their midst at different times.

Neither the East German technical intelligentsia nor the cultural intelligentsia posed a serious threat to SED dominance; nor did they form alliances with each other, in contrast to the Czech reformers of the late 1960s (and in partial contrast to the Ludz thesis). And the East German Protestant church occupied a unique and somewhat ambiguous position: while it provided a forum for the discussion of dissenting and unorthodox views, at the same time church leaders – particularly in the early 1980s – frequently intervened to moderate more radical opposition to the regime. This space for the articulation and yet simultaneous incorporation of dissent at certain periods of the GDR's history must in some way be included in any adequate conceptualization of East German political dynamics; and it stands in stark contrast to the very different church–state relations in Poland (and, in different ways, in Czechoslovakia). Such considerations must lead one away from both notions of 'totalitarianism' and 'consultative authoritarianism' towards a more complex model of the development of the East German political system. Emphasis must be given to a system which can be defined as relative party domination over a variety of co-opted subordinate elites. The party was also to some extent constrained in its actions by state structures, which acted both as instruments for and limits on party pursuit of political goals. Furthermore, while there was a single official ideology, Marxism-Leninism, alternative belief systems, such as Christianity, were not always in themselves actively opposed. Outward conformity was at times more important than inner commitment. When this tolerance was combined periodically with concessions to consumerism, the East German system achieved, for a time at least, a degree of stability which was based on more than solely the use or threat of force.

Perhaps the best approach is to abandon the search for a single, all-encompassing concept to summarize the East German political system throughout the period. Coercion – most often in the shape of the dreaded State Security Police, or *Stasi* – was more evident in the 1950s and again in the later 1980s than during the intervening quarter century or so. The party's degree of dominance varied, as did the insistence (or otherwise) on commitment to a single ideology. A number of distinct factors, including the international situation and the performance of the economy, together help to explain the degree of stability or instability of the East German regime at any particular time, as we shall see when considering its final collapse.

The West German political system

Unlike the GDR, West Germany did not introduce any fundamentally new constitutions. The constitution did however undergo a number of subtle shifts and alterations, through a series of amendments relating to particular issues. Appeals on contentious issues could be made to the constitutional court at Karlsruhe, the final arbiter on constitutional matters. Between 1949 and 1983 there were 34 laws to change the constitution: 47 articles were changed, and 73 new articles were added. For example, in 1956 the *Wehrverfassung* introduced military service in West Germany. In 1968 the Emergency Laws (*Notstandsgesetzgebung*) introduced provisions for a state of emergency. In the event of an emergency, powers were to be devolved to an emergency parliament, or to a 'joint committee' consisting of 23 representatives from the *Bundestag* and eleven from the *Bundesrat*. In 1967 and 1969 measures for joint financing, co-operation and equalization of conditions among *Länder* introduced a new, 'third' level of co-operation between the federal centre and the local states, effectively altering the nature of West German federalism. In the 1970s, alongside the original constitution, it has been argued that a 'shadow constitution' (*Nebenverfassung*) was developed, including increased surveillance of the population, increased police powers, and a separation of 'state' and 'constitution'. It has been suggested by radical critics that this 'shadow constitution' stands in some contradiction to certain tenets of the Basic Law, as for example in the conflict between the freedom of belief and political opinion enshrined in the latter and the actual restrictions on political expression implied by such measures as the 1972 Decree Concerning Radicals.[11]

West Germany's party system developed over time from a potentially multi-party configuration with shifting coalition possibilities into one where the two main parties – the CDU/CSU and the SPD – competed for a majority of the popular vote but usually had to enter into coalition with a smaller party. The pivotal role in determining which of these larger parties formed the government was usually played by the liberal Free Democratic Party (FDP), although there were others in the early years, and in the 1980s – particularly at *Land* level – the rise of the Greens lent variety to possible coalitions. In contrast to the party tradition of Imperial and Weimar Germany, in which parties were frequently single-issue interest groups, parties in the Federal Republic developed at least the claim to be catch-all 'people's parties' (*Volksparteien*). Nevertheless, to some extent they retained and developed distinctive programmes and social profiles of members and voters, with changes over time. More Catholics voted for, or were members of, the CDU/CSU than the SPD; and although the membership of the SPD was predominantly middle class, it still received a larger working class vote than did the CDU/CSU. Business generally made financial contributions to the CDU/CSU rather than the SPD; and CDU/CSU governments tended to be more favourable to business interests than SPD ones. The FDP was something of a chameleon party, at first rather right-wing, then going through a liberal phase (from the late 1960s), with the right-wing gaining ascendance once again in the 1980s. It also provided key elements of stability, symbolized, for example, by the long service of Hans-Dietrich Genscher as Foreign Minister.

Formally, the Federal Republic appeared to be an instance of 'pluralist' western democracy, in which citizens were free to attempt to influence the democratic process. In practice, while all citizens of course had the vote and were free to form pressure groups, some interest groups were, to paraphrase George Orwell, more equal than others. Under the West German political system, processes of negotiation among different interest groups were formalized, with considerable behind-the-scenes manoeuvring before policies were formulated and placed publicly on the political agenda. Such inter-elite negotiations were also important in amendments to legislation. The three predominant sets of economic interest group exerting pressures on government were: the employers and business interests; labour, employees, and unions; and farming interests. These have indeed been termed 'latent political elites' by virtue of their close links with policy formation.

The local associations of industrialists and employers were federated into three main national associations: the German Chamber of Commerce and Industry (*Deutscher Industrie- und Handels-Tag*, DIHT); the Federal League of German Employers (*Bundesvereinigung der deutschen Arbeitgeberverbände*, BDA); and the League of German Industry (*Bundesverband der deutschen Industrie*, BDI). The last of these was politically the most active and influential. In Edinger's summary: 'Formally and informally, directly and indirectly, individually and collectively, the leaders of big business enterprises and organizations undoubtedly exert a great deal of influence over public policy, perhaps more than any other elite in West Germany. Moreover, they form a politically more cohesive group than their counterparts in other western democracies. . . But that does not mean that they constitute a dominant power elite or homogenous ruling class.'[12]

Labour in the Federal Republic benefited, in Edinger's view, from the unprecedented 'strategic role of the labour elite'.[13] The main organization representing trade unions at national level was the DGB, which, with 7.8 million members in 1983, represented 85% of all trade unionists, members of the seventeen large unions in the Federal Republic. The German Employees Union (*Deutsche Angestelltengewerkschaft*, DAG) represented certain white-collar employees, and the German Federation of Civil Servants (*Deutscher Beamtenbund*, DBB) was the civil servants' organization. The latter occupied a rather unique position in the West German labour force, as its members were employees of the state without the right to strike, and with certain implied restraints on free expression of political opinion. Representatives of employers and labour conducted inter-elite negotiations with the government in an effort to resolve differences and disputes. On the whole, representatives of business interests proved more powerful in these talks than those of labour, with some notable exceptions such as in the extension of codetermination laws and other measures favourable to labour which occurred in the early years of the Schmidt government. Farmers still represented an important economic interest group, but, with the decline in the agricultural sector of the economy over the decades, a diminishing one in numerical terms.

There were also many independent pressure groups, including, for example, the citizens' initiative groups which campaigned on such matters as housing, environmental pollution, the building of nuclear power stations or the disposal of nuclear waste. Some of these had a direct impact on West German politics by feeding into the formation of the Green Party. But on the whole their impact was more indirect, in that the major parties were forced to incorporate or respond to environmentalist and other such concerns in their efforts to gain or retain the support of key marginal voters.

The nature of the West German political system has been subject to many and varied interpretations. These range from viewing the Federal Republic as a 'model' democratic state, whose 'efficient secret' must be ferreted out, to assorted neo-Marxist critiques both of West Germany in particular and capitalist states in general.[14] The former sort of approach generally concentrates on West Germany's orderly succession of governments, lack of serious political crises, and smoothly functioning governmental system; this success is contrasted with the failures of the Weimar Republic in the past, or the post-fascist history of Italy in the present. The focus is generally rather narrowly on features of the political system as explanatory of political stability. The latter sorts of critical approach either focus on sociological analyses of power structures and the personnel of government, or develop more all-embracing structural analyses of the modes of functioning of advanced capitalist societies. Critics of the supposed pluralism of western democratic capitalist states, for example, emphasize the disproportionate power of certain elites, the relative weight and influence of certain organizations and interest groups, and the importance of personal ties among different parts of the establishment, all tending to diminish the real powers of political participation of the average citizen, not to mention the poor and disadvantaged members of an unequal society. 'Structural' critiques of western capitalist democracies focus less on personnel, and more on the pressures and constraints of the system as such. According to one somewhat extreme interpretation, for example, it is impossible for socialist parties in capitalist states to do anything other than strengthen capitalism: for such parties are committed to high public expenditure for welfare, and must therefore ensure the profitability of capitalism in order to raise sufficient taxes for state expenditure. Thus, there is in effect little real choice between conservative and professedly socialist parties, since both must operate in a manner which allows capitalism to flourish.[15]

While evaluative elements clearly enter into these analyses, the moral-political evaluation does not always depend directly on the empirical details of the academic analysis. Some political scientists will applaud what others deplore. Edinger, for example, considers the influence of elite interest groups on West German policy formation to be beneficial, ironing out problems in legislation as it concerns interested parties prior to the formal parliamentary debates. Others consider the inequalities of influence to be more reprehensible in a system which claims to be democratic. Similarly, not everyone shared left-wingers' despair at the bleak prospects for socialist parties in many capitalist states in the 1980s. Yet, while analysis and evaluation are in principle separable – and one may have to accept the validity of an interpretation without approving of it – in practice they have been very hard to keep distinct. The problem of moral judgements has bedevilled academic attempts at comparing the two Germanies, as is evidenced in the extensive debates about 'yardsticks for comparison' carried out among Germans interested in *Systemvergleich* (comparison of systems).[16] Whatever one's views on the relative scientific and political merits of the different analyses of the West German system, some points are clear. To remain at the level of formal analysis of the West German political system is to fail to understand adequately either how it really works, or why it became established as a system capable of gradual transformation and attracting at least passive assent on the part of a majority of its citizens. Moreover, that there are critiques of the shortcomings of West German democracy paradoxically substantiates the extent of that democracy's success: it is possible for articulate citizens to analyse, debate and argue in the interests of improving the state and society in which they live. That there are diverse, often contradictory, interpretations of what constitutes 'improvement', is of course one of the problems of democracy: the winners of free elections may be those with whom one disagrees.

The state, the army, and law and order

The state, according to the German sociologist Max Weber, can best be defined in terms of its monopoly over the legitimate use of force in a given territory. Force can of course be directed both outwards – to defend the territory against foreign aggressors – and inwards – to defend the established order against threats to its stability from within. In the period before 1945, Germany had a considerable, and ambiguous, tradition of militarism; and the demilitarization of Germany was one of the few fundamental aims on which all four of the post-war occupying powers were agreed. Yet a mere decade after the collapse of Hitler's Reich, both East and West Germany regained an army – although in new and different forms. Germans have traditionally been held to be law-abiding, obedient subjects of a powerful state. Following (and even before) the foundation of the two Germanies, the police and internal security forces were built up in different ways, to attempt to ensure the compliance of the population. Definitions and treatment of socially unacceptable behaviour varied, with implications for assessments of the character and stability of each regime.

In East Germany, the 'people's police in barracks' (*Kasernierte Volkspolizei*, or KVP) was set up in 1946. By 1950, this had a strength of fifty thousand men as well as tanks and artillery. In 1952 it was renamed the 'national armed forces'. In January 1956 the National People's Army (*Nationale Volksarmee*, NVA) was formally established, and became an integral part of the Warsaw Treaty Organization forces. It consisted of 100,000 men, and additional numbers of security and border guards. Estimates suggest that in the mid-1980s there were perhaps 116,000 men in the NVA, and 70–75,000 in border, security, transport and other special formations. Additionally, about 350,000 men were involved in groups linked to their factory workplace, so-called *Kampfgruppen der Arbeiterklasse*. Of these men serving in the army, 60% were conscripts, and there was a military service of 18 months. From 1982, there was a provision that women might be called up in emergencies. About 8% of military-age males were under arms, and between 4% and 6% of GNP was spent on defence.[17]

In theory, the NVA was a nationalist army defending the socialist state of the German nation against the potential aggression of its class enemies. Great efforts were directed towards attempting to inculcate a 'friend/foe' mentality in young East Germans, so that they would perceive their West German friends and relatives as devilish representatives of capitalist imperialism, and thus be prepared to bear arms against them. This attempted militarization of values among East German youth began in Kindergarten, where toddlers played with guns and tanks. It extended through the period of formal schooling – compulsory military education was introduced as a secondary school subject in 1978 – and permeated youth and sporting organizations. The 'Society for Sport and Technology' (*Gesellschaft für Sport und Technik*, GST) was an organization offering paramilitary training alongside superior sporting facilities and the use of exclusive campsites of better quality than those available to the general public. The military forces also constituted a highly visible presence in the GDR, with tanks lurking in the fir trees behind fences along the edge of motorways, or formations of Warsaw Pact forces lumbering along on exercises in border areas.

This military pervasion of life in the GDR led to the question of whether East German society was becoming 'militarized'.[18] Leaving aside a somewhat academic debate on terminology, certain observations can be made. In the first place, attempted indoctrination did not appear to be entirely successful. Considerable numbers of GDR youth objected to military service and opted to undertake an alternative form of service as 'construction soldiers' (*Bausoldaten*), working on projects which did not require the bearing of arms. Given the pressures for conformity in the GDR, the sizeable minority who were prepared openly to make their opinions known in this way probably represented the tip of a larger iceberg of youth who were not deeply convinced by a militaristic view of the world. Secondly, at the highest levels of the state the military could not be said to have been dominant over the party either. The SED retained control of military policy, and although there was of course strong military representation in the Politburo, it was a case of symbiosis rather than rivalry between the party and the military in the GDR. The successor to Army General Heinz Hoffmann, who died in December 1985, was Heinz Kessler, who was an equally committed communist loyal to the SED line. There were debates and areas of friction – for example, over the question of whether there could be a 'just' nuclear war – but essentially, the party retained control over the East German military establishment.

Curiously, the East German army retained the old Prussian military goose step, until December 1989. This looked extraordinary when performed in the seat of Prussian militarism, the centre of old Berlin, under the banner of the new Marxist-Leninist state. The West German army had a more difficult relationship with its ambiguous heritage. It was initially established, against considerable internal opposition, in legislation amending the Basic Law (which did not at first permit an army) in the period from 1954 to 1956. While border protection forces had existed earlier, and the first soldiers were given their formal commissions in 1955, the officially celebrated birthday of the West German army was 20 January 1956. In July 1956 conscription was introduced. The Basic Law provisions for the army included the following: that it was to have a purely defensive role; that it was to be subordinated to the Minister of Defence in peacetime, and to the Chancellor in times of crisis; that parliament was to determine defence expenditure in the budget; and that the army was ultimately under parliamentary control. There were also certain provisions concerning the status of soldiers, which illustrate the lessons West Germany was attempting to learn from its past. West German soldiers were held to be 'citizens in uniform', with certain citizens' rights: the right to vote, the right to be members of political parties, and hence the right to contribute to the formation of the political will of the people.[19] They were to have, moreover, the right *not* to obey orders if obeying would mean committing a criminal act – a right obviously directly related to the defence of many that they were only obeying orders from above in the Third Reich. The notion of the soldier as simply a democratic citizen who happened to be wearing a uniform in defence of his country was also associated with an intended internal democratization of the traditionally highly authoritarian power structures of the army. A concept of *Innere Führung*, with a Defence Commissioner to investigate and arbitrate complaints, was developed. There were sharp disagreements and controversies over these democratizing tendencies in the 1960s, with traditionalists suggesting that they were simply an unimportant 'mask' to placate the SPD. Helmut Schmidt as Minister of Defence put such traditionalist authoritarians firmly in their place by insisting that democratization was a reality, not a mask, and that any individual holding views to the contrary could not hold a position of military leadership in the Federal Republic.[20] In the 1970s, Schmidt introduced certain army reforms to ensure the reality of civilian political control of the military in West Germany.

As in the East, there was sizeable opposition among young West Germans to military norms and values. There were relatively large numbers of conscientious objectors who might undertake alternative forms of service (which lasted longer than military service); there were also considerable numbers who left to live in West Berlin in order to avoid military service altogether. Because of the more tolerant political system, peace movements were large and relatively well-organized in the FRG, and there was considerable opposition to, for example, the stationing of nuclear missiles. As in the East, there was a visible military presence in West Germany. American and

British forces had their barracks, troop manoeuvres could be seen at intervals (with twig-bedecked 'camouflaged' soldiers and tanks flattening farmers' crops, for which the latter received generous compensation), and jets flew noisily overhead on summer afternoons. There were large areas of territory closed off to the public (*Sperrgebiete*). It was difficult to forget, even in this affluent, frequently picturesque tourist country of rolling hills, deep pine forests, medieval walled towns and ruined castles, that one was also in the front line of divided Europe in a period of technologically advanced warfare and superpower tension.

Both Germanies also had well-developed internal police forces. In addition to the 'People's Police' (*Volkspolizei*) in East Germany, there was the special State Security Police (*Staatssicherheitspolizei*, commonly known as the *Stasi*) which, after certain bureaucratic rearrangements in the early 1950s, was eventually placed under the control of its own Ministry for State Security, run from 1957 to 1989 by the generally hated Erich Mielke. It is estimated that in East Berlin alone the Ministry for State Security had a staff of 1500 officers and subordinates, and 1600 civilian employees; in the whole of the GDR there were perhaps 17,000 people employed by the Ministry for State Security, and in addition an incalculable number of informants.[21] The uses of the State Security Police varied over time. For a while it appeared as if the oppressive, all-pervading spying of the 1950s had given way to a somewhat more open atmosphere in Honecker's Germany, and that the time of raids in the night and long interrogations had more or less passed. However, after a period of simply monitoring developments, in the last couple of years of the Honecker regime the Stasi resumed an interventionist role in attempting to clamp down on expressions of dissent. The oppressive effects of the constant threat of Stasi surveillance, intervention, and potential ruining of people's lives can scarcely be overstated. It led to perpetual insecurity in personal relationships, and was to leave a difficult legacy for post-unification Germany.[22] East Germany also had a full complement of 'regular' police for policing against crime, regulating traffic, staffing certain bureaucracies, and of course controlling the frontiers. There was a considerable police presence and frequent occasions for contact with the police; for example, visitors had to register with the police in each location they visited (although Interhotels might do this for them), they were frequently stopped and asked to show visas and identification papers, and might be fined on the spot for such minor offences as infringement of parking regulations.

West Germany too had a range of police forces: the border protection police, the administrative police, the criminal police, and special police forces for particular crisis situations. The police in West Germany were well-equipped and carried arms. Following the terrorist waves of the 1970s the police made ample use of computers and modern surveillance apparatus to collate material on individuals which they were able to consult with speed and efficiency at any time. In 1972 a Decree Concerning Radicals (*Radikalenerlass*) essentially provided that individuals whose attitudes, activities or organizational affiliations were deemed to be hostile to the free-democratic aims of the constitution gave grounds for suspicion. Such individuals should not be appointed to, or continue in employment in, civil service jobs, a very broadly defined category in West Germany including such occupations as schoolteacher, train-driver and postman as well as state bureaucrat in the narrow British definition. This meant that many people seeking or holding jobs in such areas felt restricted in their freedom of expression and association, in contradiction to the constitutional guarantee of these rights. For if they participated in a demonstration, film of this would undoubtedly be available to the police, their names would be logged in police computers, and future employment prospects would be threatened. In some respects, then, the 'vigilant defence of democracy' in the Federal Republic served actually to limit and restrict the extent of that democracy. Although political repression in West Germany can in no sense be viewed as comparable to the extent of surveillance and intervention in East Germany, there were still grounds for concern among human rights activists about the restrictions on individual freedom of expression in the democratic West.

Having briefly surveyed at least the formal outlines of the two German states, we must now turn in more detail to the issue of domestic challenges to those states. The next chapter will consider the question of dissent and opposition in the period up to 1989.

ELEVEN

Dissent and Opposition

Two misconceptions are frequently found in accounts of democratic and dictatorial regimes. The first is that the former are essentially based on the active support of the majority of the populace; the record of Weimar democracy should serve to indicate the shortcomings of such an approach. The second is that the latter are effectively based on coercion, repression, and that, if they are indeed brought down by revolution, then this is based in the popular (and usually material) discontent of the masses. Both misconceptions deflect attention from a factor of far greater significance in regime stability or instability: the question of dissent and opposition. Clearly dissent and opposition must be viewed in connection with other factors, including the international situation, and the cohesion and strategies of response of ruling groups. We shall see in due course the particular combination of factors which together served to bring down communist rule in the GDR in 1989–90. In this chapter, the focus will be on the ways in which dissent and opposition in the two Germanies developed in the period from 1949 to the beginning of 1989.

The political systems of the two Germanies were obviously very different in the degrees to which they tolerated the expression of dissenting views. Although there were some limits on freedom of expression and political organization in the Federal Republic, people could express their views openly so long as they were not directly hostile to the democratic values of the constitution. The restriction on permissable views and activities was greater in East Germany, and 'dissent', as defined by the state, therefore covered a far wider range of opinions. What is interesting about both Germanies is that, in contrast to the unstable Weimar Republic, they were – for forty years, much longer than the twenty-seven years of the Weimar Republic and the Third Reich put together – relatively successful in incorporating and defusing dissent, and ensuring that it did not develop into serious, potentially destabilizing, opposition to the regime. This began to change in the GDR in the 1980s. While the effective challenge posed to the Communist regime in 1989 was in large measure only made possible by the radical changes in the Soviet Union and its European and global policies, the character of the 'gentle revolution' was crucially shaped by the ways in which movements for reform had been developed in the preceding decade.

Dissent and opposition in East Germany

The nature of 'dissent' and 'opposition' in East Germany changed over time, as a result of a variety of factors. Very crudely, one might propose a dual form of periodization as follows. On the one hand, there was a development from a rejection of the system as a whole, in the 1950s, to more qualified attempts to reform and improve the system from within, by the 1980s. At the same time, there was a development through three distinct phases: from widespread opposition in the 1950s, to mass accommodation combined with isolated intellectual dissent in the 1960s and 1970s, to a proliferation of principled dissent in the 1980s which was able, finally, to join with popular disaffection to challenge the regime (weakened for other, external reasons) in late 1989. We shall deal with this final phase of revolution in Chapter Thirteen, below; here, it is important to establish the earlier currents of development.

It is also important to have in mind at the outset the varieties of disagreement with the regime. We shall look at each of these in more detail in a moment, but it is worth introducing the range covered by the terms dissent (disagreement with prevailing orthodoxy) and opposition (working actively to transform the situation).

From the – actually rather limited – June Uprising of 1953 until the upheavals of 1989, there were no mass protests which might warrant the term 'opposition'. There were individuals opposing Ulbricht's and Honecker's policies from within, although these posed little serious challenge from the late 1950s to the 1980s; there were also expressions of a range of coherent world-views which differed explicitly from official Marxist-Leninist ideology and which might be categorized as 'dissent' in one form or another. These views included the humanistic Marxism of a number of intellectuals pursuing what has been called the tradition of the 'Third Way'; the religious views of the relatively large number of practising Protestants and the smaller group of Catholics living in the GDR; and, eventually, the diffuse but unorthodox views of a growing number of peace activists, environmentalists, and adherents of an 'alternative' culture in the 1980s. Although the regime tried frequently to downplay dissenting views and denounce them as Western-instigated or inspired, none of these three broad groups (each of which contained many differences of opinion within it) could be simply interpreted as supported by or supporters of the West. Frequently they were as critical of the consumerist materialism and social inequalities of capitalist society as they were of the bureaucratic authoritarianism of 'actually existing socialism' in the East. They were generally seeking, not to abandon the East for a presumed Utopia in the West, but rather to transform the East into more desirable directions from within. There were also, of course, considerable numbers of disaffected GDR citizens who simply wanted to leave.

The ways in which the regime responded to dissenting groups and individuals to a considerable degree determined the sort of political impact they were able to have. Equally, however, the extent of impact of dissent depended on the relative strength and strategies of the regime at different times.

Mass protest and isolated intellectuals

The mass strike of 1953 was largely an affair of industrial workers in particular cities and towns; it had very little bourgeois, peasant, or intellectual support. Its failure may be partly attributed to its lack of clear leadership and organization, and partly to the fact that the East German regime was at this time able to rely on the support of Moscow in suppressing it, if necessary by force. Lacking a broad social base, lacking an organizational network, and facing the prospect of forceful suppression, it remained merely an expression of discontent with no real prospect of success. As we have seen, the consequences were in fact very much the opposite of any intended outcome, with the exception of the retraction of the raised work norms – which had been the immediate cause of the strike. Until 1961, there in any event remained the escape hole through Berlin; thereafter, many workers simply came to terms with and made the best of their living conditions in the East. From 1953 until 1989, very little was heard of 'the masses' in the context of explicit challenges to the East German regime.

After the exclusion of 'Third Way' Marxists from the higher ranks of the SED in the purges of the 1950s, Marxist intellectual dissenters had in turn had very little popular support: they remained isolated figures, producing varying diagnoses of East Germany's ills and proposing assorted solutions which found little general resonance. Their lack of widespread popularity, beyond small circles of intellectuals, becomes comprehensible if one devotes a moment of attention to their ideas.

Wolfgang Harich, who was arrested with others in 1956, elaborated an authoritarian vision of a 'utopia of an ascetic police state'.[1] His views, which emphasized discipline, sacrifice, regimentation, a puritanical society concerned with ecology rather than economic growth, did not accord with the materialistic concerns of the working classes in the 1950s. He did however argue for an extension of democracy and the rather inconsistent programme of his group reflected the flurry of hurried thinking which took place in the aftermath of the Twentieth Congress of the Communist Party of the Soviet Union, which denounced Stalinism to a surprised world.[2]

Robert Havemann, who was a Professor at the Humboldt University in Berlin and Director of the Physical-Chemical

Institute from 1950 to 1964, did enjoy large and enthusiastic audiences at his lectures on general philosophical and political questions in 1963. However, his ideas and popularity were too much for the authorities, and he was removed from his positions in 1964 and his activities were increasingly restricted. He spent the closing years of his life under virtual house arrest. (He had been imprisoned by the Nazis in Brandenburg Prison, along with Erich Honecker, and it has been suggested that he received relatively lenient treatment as a result of Honecker's sympathy for a former anti-Nazi prison comrade.) Havemann was a committed communist who opposed both the Stalinist perversion of communism and what he saw as a certain legacy of Nazism in the GDR. He placed great hopes on the reforming Czech leader Alexander Dubček, and the Prague Spring of 1968, only to be disappointed as GDR tanks joined Soviet forces in suppressing the Czechoslovak reforms. Havemann was in favour of the extension of democracy, freedom of the press, and felt market mechanisms were the most efficient means of running the economy. According to Havemann, since under capitalism the market (which was in any event regulated and manipulated, not 'free') served the interests of capital, why should it not serve the interest of the whole community under socialism? Havemann viewed contemporary socialism as a case of an only half-completed revolution: the state, rather than the people themselves, had replaced capitalists and landowners; it was a dictatorship of functionaries rather than rule by the people. Havemann argued for a combination of economic democracy and democratic socialism, which he felt went together.[3]

These views were not shared by a critical intellectual of the 1970s, Rudolf Bahro. Working quietly in East German industrial bureaucracy, he secretly wrote a major analysis of the shortcomings of East German socialism, entitled *The Alternative in Eastern Europe*, parts of which were published in *Der Spiegel* in 1977. On 30 June 1978 Bahro was sentenced to eight years in prison, but left for West Germany after a deal arranging this in 1979. In West Germany he became a prominent member of the Greens in the early 1980s. Bahro's critique of 'actually existing socialism' arguably aroused more interest in the West than the East.

In contrast to Havemann, Bahro was not in favour of attaching liberal or market features to a modified form of socialism (thus differing also from Czech and Polish reform communists). Bahro argued against what he saw as unnecessary consumerism, and in favour of a 'transformed structure of needs' – again something which found little support among the East German working classes. For Bahro, the main problem in socialist societies was domination by the state and the bureaucracy. Marx and Engels failed to give adequate consideration to the problem of the state; and the fact that the first communist revolution took place in pre-capitalist Tsarist Russia, which required a revolution from above for rapid industrialization, meant that Tsarist bureaucracy and autocracy were simply replaced by communist bureaucracy and Leninist party dictatorship. Bahro also diagnosed problems with the mental and physical division of labour. Bahro's prescriptions included: a redivision of labour so that no-one would be stultified in their development; general education for all; the spread of information and discussion of alternatives; increased participation in the formation of the 'general will'; and a new 'League of Communists' which would, through public debate, reflect the emancipatory interests of all society. Bahro argued against consumerism and the definition of 'progress' as economic growth, and in favour of small-scale associations, with society as an association of communes. There would in Bahro's vision be a National Assembly arising from a Federation of Free Associations in which all could participate. While Bahro's analysis of the problems of bureaucracy and the authoritarian state had much to recommend it, few considered Bahro's prescriptions to be plausible, workable, or likely to command much popular enthusiasm.[4]

In the event, neither Bahro nor earlier dissenting intellectuals in the GDR appeared to command much popular support – or at least, there was little evidence of mass discontent in the GDR beyond a perpetual grumbling about the repressive, constrained, frequently inefficient and drab character of life under East

German socialism. Very different mass political orientations were to emerge in the 1980s.

The church and the proliferation of dissent

To understand the proliferation of principled dissent in the 1980s, it is important to analyse the role of the Protestant churches. These both provided the umbrella for the spreading of dissent, and significantly shaped the character of that dissent. Yet the churches' role was by no means a predetermined or preordained one: it only developed gradually, in the context of significantly changing relations between church and state in the GDR. To some extent, it was the state that made possible what ultimately proved to be the essentially subversive role of the church; but the state only responded to certain of the overtures and activities of a church which was redefining its role. The development is a complex and nuanced one, which can only be briefly sketched here.

The area covered by East Germany was, historically, predominantly Protestant and in 1950 it was estimated that there were approximately 14.8 million Protestants in the GDR. From 1964, official censuses did not include statistics on religion, but in 1978 the churches estimated that there were 7.9 million Protestants and 1.2 million Catholics in the GDR. Of these, perhaps one half were actually professing, personally committed Christians. The state's policies towards Christianity changed markedly over time.

Under Ulbricht, Christians suffered considerable harassment and personal difficulties, and there were violent attacks on Christian beliefs. Mention has been made (*see* Chapter Seven) of the persecution of members of the *Junge Gemeinde* and the uses of the *Jugendweihe* to discriminate against Christian children in school. But the organization and material possessions of the churches had survived the transition from Nazi to Communist Germany relatively unscathed, and church institutions continued to play an important role in society which could not be easily extinguished. Although attempts were made during the 1960s to improve dialogue between Christians and Marxists, the real transformation in church–state relations came in the 1970s.

After giving up a common organizational framework with the West German churches and setting up their own East German *Bund der Evangelischen Kirchen* (League of Protestant Churches) in 1969, East German Protestants were able to pursue new avenues in line with the famous 1971 formulation of Bishop Schönherr that they wanted to be 'a Church, not alongside, not against, but rather within Socialism'. In the course of the changed, post-*Ostpolitik* situation of the 1970s, it became clear to Honecker that there were advantages to be gained by the state from closer cooperation and better relations with the church.

A frank discussion between church and state leaders in 1978 (the so-called *Spitzengespräch*, or summit talks) regularized relations between church and state on a relatively harmonious footing.[5] Official policy was now that Christians and Marxists should work 'hand in hand', together striving to achieve a better society in the interests of humanity.

In the 1980s, the churches played a considerable role in social welfare activities in the GDR – running well-equipped and well-staffed hospitals, homes for the elderly and the handicapped, nursery and day-care centres, and the like. Additionally, there were certain legitimizing and stabilizing functions from the state's point of view. Official toleration of Christian views and stress on a harmonious partnership between Christians and Marxists helped to incorporate and harness the energies of an important minority of the population; it also looked good to human rights activists in both West and East. Partnership in certain projects with the church, such as the restoration of ecclesiastical buildings of historic importance (the most well-known being the Berlin *Dom*), or the celebration of religious-historical anniversaries (such as the Luther quincentenary of 1983) brought much needed foreign currency to the state in the form both of West German subventions and increased tourism. It also arguably helped to create a common, all-encompassing sense of national identity, defusing a potential symbolic opposition between church and atheist regime, society and alien state, as in the rather different configuration in neighbouring Poland. The church, for its part, was interested in maintaining good relations with the more powerful state, in order to be able to pursue its specifically religious activities, as well as engaging in wider social and pastoral care. In the new partnership, the church was allowed increased use of the media for religious broadcasts, and was able to build new churches and operate community centres in new housing estates. It is difficult to evaluate the overall effects of church activities in the reduction of social tensions and alleviation of social problems, in addition to the more tangible contribution made by church institutions and funds to the welfare system, but it may have been considerable.

However, this partnership – in which the state was undoubtedly the dominant partner, with the final word on the conditions and parameters, but in which the church was increasingly important – was not without risks on both sides. The church constituted the only relatively independent organization which was permitted in the GDR; as such, it provided space, both literally and metaphorically, for the free discussion of all sorts of dissenting ideas. Church buildings were made use of for unofficial peace demonstrations, and for concerts by singers with songs critical of the regime. Many of those using the church as an institutional meeting-ground were far from being Christians themselves. Thus, the state risked permitting a haven for the development of dissident views within a strong organizational framework.

On the other hand, there were also associated risks for the church; and on balance, in the early 1980s the responses of church leaders to radical unrest in fact served to moderate potential opposition and operated in the interests of the state. The church was afraid of being 'hijacked' by non-Christians, some of whose aims were congruent with those of the church – as in the question of working for peace – but whose radical actions threatened to jeopardize the fragile balance of church-state relations to the detriment of the church's overall position in the GDR. The church leadership thus stepped in on a number of occasions to influence strategy and tactics of dissenters, or to withdraw its protection if it felt actions were becoming too extreme. The church acted as a moderator between the regime and dissenters, often attracting bitter criticisms from the latter for being too conservative and cautious in its approach. Moreover, when any particular case of church pressure on the regime to influence policy, prior to 1989, is investigated, it appears to have made only moderate impact if any; for example, the introduction in 1964 of alternative service without weapons in the *Bausoldaten* units may have been a positive result of church pressure, but church opposition to the introduction of military education in schools in 1978 had no effect.

While church-state relationships in the early 1980s arguably promoted a stabilizing 'safety valve' for the regime, there was a delicate and interesting balance involved here. In the course of the 1980s, dissenting views proliferated, in conjunction with wider movements.

Mention has been made of the unofficial peace initiatives in East Germany. The decision by the Americans and the Soviet Union to station nuclear missiles on German soil gave renewed impetus to peace movements on both sides of the border, whose activities and profiles reached a peak at the time of the actual stationing of nuclear warheads in 1984. The 'new Cold War' of the early 1980s, following the Soviet invasion of Afghanistan in 1979 and fostered by the right-wing, crusading anti-communism of the Reagan administration, aroused widespread fear of nuclear catastrophe. These fears were hardly alleviated by the quite unrelated nuclear disaster at the Chernobyl reactor in the USSR in 1986.

Many East Germans were sufficiently unconvinced by the state's peace propaganda to risk their futures by demonstrating against Warsaw Pact weapons as well as those of NATO. Unofficial peace demonstrations also included prominent intellectuals, writers, and other established figures, and there were links with West German peace activists. Despite the fact that the regime claimed a monopoly over organized activities and 'movements' in the GDR, unofficial peace initiatives included a petition signed by over two hundred people, the 'Berlin Appeal' of 1982; an international writers' and scientists' meeting on peace held in East Berlin; and the 'Swords into Ploughshares' armband movement, in which peace demonstrators wore on their sleeves an armband (originally printed as a bookmark) bearing the symbol of the statue donated by the USSR to the United Nations building in New York referring to the quotation from Isaiah.[6] Large gatherings also took place in church buildings, and the church extended some protection towards many non-Christian peace activists – although it was also rather annoyed by some people using peace demonstrations as a means of rapid exit to West Germany, since one of the regime's forms of punishment was instant exile to the West.

Alternative views also began to be expressed in the GDR in relation to such matters as ecology; there was for example an unofficial 'environmentalist library' in East Berlin. Evidence of environmental pollution was becoming daily more apparent, and anger mounted at a regime which pursued production targets with no apparent concern for human health and well-being, indeed without even a willingness to recognize the existence of a problem.

With frustration mounting, there was increased criticism of the lack of freedom of speech and real democracy in the GDR. Unofficial banners with officially disapproved slogans from Rosa Luxemburg were displayed at the official demonstrations on the anniversary of Rosa Luxemburg's and Karl Liebknecht's death on 17 January 1988. (Such notions as 'Freedom is always the freedom to think differently' were unacceptable to a regime which felt it alone should be doing the thinking.) And apart from the most well-known dissenters in the cultural sphere, there was a sizeable and perhaps growing 'alternative culture' in East Berlin, including visual artists, musicians and others, who were following the process of Gorbachev's *Glasnost* with great interest.

With these growing currents of discontent, there was a differentiation of political views within the Protestant church, and more time was devoted to discussion and debate. Even before the revolutionary autumn of 1989, groups were involved in, for example, non-violence training, and were adopting increasingly active strategies to pressurize for reform from within. When the peaceful demonstrations started in the autumn of 1989, the effects of this focus on non-violence were plain to see, as was the wider context of a movement for reform partially sponsored and sheltered by the church. But in addition, dissident groups were now organising outside the framework of the Protestant church.

To discuss the role of the Protestant churches in fostering or containing dissent is not to exhaust the issue of the social role of religion in the GDR. Many people with religious commitments of whatever sort found simple solace in belonging to a community that was to a degree resistant to the demands and encroachments of the all-pervading ideology propagated by the state.

This was probably particularly the case for most of the million or so Catholics. The much smaller Catholic Church in the GDR maintained a relatively low profile, although there were signs in the 1980s that it was taking more social tasks upon itself.

The surviving Jewish community in East Germany was tiny – perhaps a few hundred – but they too were becoming more visible, with the renovation of the Oranienburgstrasse Synagogue in East Berlin and the appointment of an American Rabbi to come to work with them.[7] After the early anti-Semitism of the Ulbricht regime (in 1952–3, at the time of the Slansky trials, and until the death of Stalin) the official East German line was to tolerate Jews while opposing political Zionism. The regime did not, however, recognize any responsibility for Nazi crimes or the need to make restitution to the Jews until the end of 1989. One side-effect of the relatively repressive nature of the GDR regime was that popular anti-Semitism was rather forcefully suppressed (with only isolated incidents) until after the 1989 revolution.

It might be added that there were, in addition to the main Protestant churches, also very small numbers of other Protestant sects, such as the sixty or so Quakers, who were in the main disproportionately active in a range of social concerns. Religious dissent certainly played quite an important role in searching for the limits of freedom and the bounds of possible discussion and action in the GDR.

It may seem a little odd, in the context of discussion of dissent and opposition in a communist regime, to include mention of the official carriers of that regime. But a further, important feature of the 1980s, which has been adumbrated in the previous chapter with respect to the SED, was a process of differentiation within the SED itself. Up until the mid-1980s, the SED tended to follow Moscow's lead rather closely; but *Glasnost* evoked only the most stiff and dismissive of official responses, at least from SED leaders, up to 1989 (such as the remark that, just because a neighbour puts up new wallpaper, there is no need to redecorate one's own house). However, some elements in the GDR were placing considerable hope in the new directions taken by Soviet domestic policies – and these included many grass-roots members of the SED itself, and even some of the regional leaders, whether privately or openly.

After some years of fluctuating degrees of liberalization (varying with the sphere of endeavour) the regime itself in Honecker's later years became more repressive. Rattled by the heightened public profile and activities of dissenters, the leadership brought out the *Stasi* in more evident manner than for many years. This was illustrated in the fairly harsh treatment of the demonstrators of 17 January 1988 (including about eighty arrests, and the exile to West Germany of singer Stefan Krawczyck and his wife Freya Klier, among others). While the ultimate 'safety valve' of shipping uncomfortable subjects to the West remained, it was clear that Honecker was no longer prepared to tolerate a limited 'letting-off-steam' within the GDR. It was clear that in the forty years of its existence, the GDR had neither succeeded in converting everyone to the official point of view (no transformation of consciousness, no development of socialist personality, had been an automatic result of the transformation of the mode of production or of the education system); nor had it found an effective means of dealing with those who persisted in developing alternative views.

The regime's new repression, far from stamping out dissent, served only to galvanize the minority of active dissenters in the GDR into further, focused political activity. There was still no mass support for activities which remained relatively dangerous, with serious penalties by way of state reprisals. But in clear contrast to the workers' protest of 1953, by 1989 there was a network of people working within the system for clearly formulated aims of reform, in connection particularly with the expansion of human rights. Their chance was to come when the regime was subjected to a crisis originating elsewhere, with the effective dismantling of the Iron Curtain in Hungary in the summer of 1989 and the clear unwillingness of the USSR to use force to sustain a crumbling, reform-resistant, hardline East German regime.

Dissent and opposition in West Germany

Clearly, given the pluralistic political system in West Germany, there would be far less 'dissent' in terms of views at odds with those of the regime. Commitment to democracy is commitment to a system of rules, a manner of decision-making, and not to a substantive world-view. A variety of ideologies and belief-systems can coexist peacefully, within a relatively broad range – although West German democracy, with the experience of Weimar in the background, was clearly constituted to exclude the possibility of tolerating those who sought to overthrow the very conditions for toleration.

Given these circumstances, alternative substantive religious and political views would not be perceived in any sense as 'dissent', merely as variety within a pluralist society. Ironically, the lack of immediate salience of religion in the Federal Republic led to a greater degree of secularization there than obtained in the GDR. The churches had initially experienced a wave of popular interest, as people sought solace and a means of interpreting their situation in the confused conditions after the defeat of Nazi Germany. The churches themselves – although experiencing, in different ways, difficulties with self-representation concerning their often ambivalent roles in the Third Reich, and dragging their feet somewhat over the issue of denazification – nevertheless remained powerful and widely respected institutions. They gained and sustained a considerable public role in the formation of policy and even in the proportions of politicians of different confessional persuasions on different bodies. While the powerful institutional voice remained, over the following decades the pertinence of religion for many lay people began to decline. While Catholics continued to vote disproportionately for the CDU, and Protestants for the SPD, even these ties began to wane. So too did church attendance rates. At the level of everyday ethics and morality, secular views began to prevail over the dicta of church leaders (as, for example, in increasing popular Catholic disregard for official views on contraception). In contrast to the heightened salience of the churches in the GDR – and in contrast to the importance of religiously grounded ethical and moral principles in resisting the encroachments of the Nazi tyranny – in the tolerant society of the Federal Republic for many people religion lost some of its immediacy, its urgency as a guiding principle in everyday life. Religion, like politics, could relatively easily be ignored by the non-committed.

To point to tolerance of a diversity of views is not to suggest that, simply by virtue of the political system, the Federal Republic did not face problems of political dissent. As mentioned above, however, awareness of the collapse of Weimar democracy ensured that problems of dissent and opposition were treated with considerable wariness. A combination of reasons led to a considerable degree of success in containing, and limiting, potentially destabilizing dissent. Such success could not have been foreseen in the political circumstances of the late 1940s and early 1950s; nor was it always easy to devise means of dealing with opponents of democracy without at the same time threatening the nature of that very democracy, as we shall see.

In its origins and early years, the Federal Republic placed more constraints than the Weimar Republic on potential attacks on the system by reactionary elites. The Army was initially dissolved, and was circumscribed and firmly subjected to parliamentary control when it was refounded ten years after the end of the war. This was in notable contrast to Weimar. While West German denazification of the civil service and judiciary left a great deal to be desired in terms of the continuity of personnel, and while former Nazis gained relatively easy re-entry into political life under Adenauer, this was paradoxically a stabilizing rather than destabilizing phenomenon. Sufficiently constrained by the system not to be able to attack it openly, former Nazis were also sufficiently accepted by and incorporated into the new system not to want to attack it. Since the system appeared to be delivering the goods, both materially in terms of economic recovery and to some extent symbolically in terms of West Germany's acceptance into Western alliances as a valuable military and economic partner, these potential dissenters were in fact quite willing to accord the system a certain passive support. Many of those who had joined the NSDAP in the heyday of the Third Reich had in any case done so for a range of reasons, including the simple pressure to conform. Less than ideologically committed to the Nazi world-view, their transition to a new conformity in a new polity was relatively easy. '*Mitläufer*' will turn in whatever direction the wind is blowing, and in the first decade of the Federal Republic there were few strong reasons for former passive Nazis to stand out by opposing the new state. Rather, they mouthed its slogans of democracy and freedom with the rest. Thus in contrast to the early years of the Weimar Republic, the Federal Republic did not suffer sharp revisionist attacks on the new political system.

Right-wing dissent continued among a minority, however, and grew with the economic recession of the mid-1960s. The permitted neo-Nazi party, the NPD, had considerable electoral successes in *Land* elections in the later 1960s. It won fifteen seats in the Bavarian parliament and eight seats in Hesse in 1966, and in 1967 made gains in the local state elections in Schleswig-Holstein, Rheinland-Pfalz, and Baden-Württemberg, where it succeeded in polling nearly 10% of the vote. However, despite arousing considerable fears, the NPD was never able to break through the five per cent hurdle to achieve national representation.

While manifestations of right-wing resurgence or extremism worried liberal intellectuals in the Federal Republic, it was left-wing dissent that attracted wider popular disapproval and even hysteria. The 1960s in the western world saw a general resurgence of left-wing ideas and movements; in the German context certain unique features were evident, arising both from the particular problems posed by the Nazi past and from certain circumstances in the present. A generation was growing up within an affluent, highly materialistic society – a society which appeared to be suffering from a form of collective amnesia. There was a fairly widespread uncertainty, too, about the status of Germany itself, which in a famous phrase appeared to be an 'economic giant, but political dwarf'. There were a number of factors involved in the emergence of left-wing dissent, some general to the western world, some specific to West Germany.

The 1960s generally saw a major expansion in higher education; in Germany, because of the lack of a *numerus clausus* to restrict student numbers and access, universities rapidly became overcrowded and failed to respond adequately to students' needs. Combined with the highly authoritarian, elitist atmosphere – many elderly professors had regained their chairs after only a brief period of 'denazification' – conditions were conducive to discontent. At the same time, the 1960s were a decade of youth culture – predicated on the existence of an affluent consumer society which sought to create a distinctive youth market, as well as simultaneously provoking a reaction against that very affluence which made youth revolt possible. Hippy, flower-power idealism prevailed; interest in eastern mysticism and asceticism went along with the purchasing power of the pop music market. Politically, the Vietnam War became a major issue, particularly for American youth. It had a heightened relevance too for young Germans, particularly in Berlin, dependent as it was on American protection; for here, the superpower that had been venerated as the ideological saviour came to be criticized as hypocritical and no longer a hero of freedom, peace and democracy.

A further general feature of the 1960s context was the revival of Marxist or *marxisant* thought in western intellectual circles. In America and Germany particularly the thinking of the Frankfurt School associated with the names of Adorno, Horkheimer and Marcuse enjoyed a renaissance. 'Critical theory' – which had, in the persons of its most eminent exponents, been exported to the USA in the Nazi period, becoming institutionalized in the New School of Social Research in New York – suddenly aroused widespread interest. In the USA, the writings of the ageing Marcuse stimulated much of student thinking; in Germany, a younger scholar, Jürgen Habermas, began to develop his own brand of neo-Marxist theory. Underlying the critical theorists' critique of the heritage of the western Enlightenment was the notion that there are no eternal 'laws' of society, which can be articulated in a 'science' of society built on unassailable generalizations. Rather, they asserted that society is made by people, and can be altered by people: praxis, or action to change reality, is the true 'test' of a social theory. Theory is validated by altering society, not by replicating the results of previous research; and the theorist is a social actor, not simply a neutral observer. This approach lent a strong intellectual context and content to the left-wing politics of the late 1960s.

In terms of domestic German politics, the existence of the 'Grand Coalition' – the coalition of CDU/CSU with the SPD, 1966–9 – meant that young Germans in particular were highly concerned about the lack of a viable parliamentary opposition, and hence the need for an 'extraparliamentary opposition' (APO). The rise of the neo-Nazi NPD was disturbing; as were the implications of the emergency legislation, which had been under discussion since the late 1950s. There were failed attempts to pass an emergency law in 1960 and 1965; there were widespread fears of increasing the powers of the state at the expense of citizens (with memories of the misuse of Article 48 in the Weimar Republic), and the Emergency Law which was finally passed in 1968 was the subject of considerable public debate.

What finally sparked the explosion of left-wing unrest in late 1960s Germany was a specific incident. On 2 June 1967 there was a demonstration in West Berlin occasioned by the visit of the Shah of Persia. In the course of this demonstration a student, Benno Ohnesorg, was shot dead. The Axel Springer press, which controlled about eighty per cent of the popular daily newspapers, more or less blamed the students for bringing about this death by their provocative behaviour. At Easter 1968 the student leader Rudi Dutschke narrowly survived an assassination attempt by an individual who had apparently been spurred on by the hysteria evoked by the tabloid press. The student movement reached its height in the western world in 1968, with near revolution in

France when workers and students for a brief moment appeared to unite. The Prague Spring in Czechoslovakia aroused many people's hopes for a humanization and liberalization in the communist bloc. But with the Soviet invasion of Prague on 2 August 1968, hopes for a new form of democratic socialism in eastern Europe were crushed, and the hopes of western democratic socialists began to fade too. The League of German Socialist Students (SDS) began to dissolve, and was formally disbanded in March 1970. Henceforth left-wing dissent became more diversified and isolated.

At the time of the student unrest in the latter half of the 1960s, West German society became polarized between an older, materialistic, relatively right-wing generation – denigrated as *Spiessbürger* – and young idealists putting into question the values of their parents. In intention non-violent, they attracted rabid criticism and wild hostility from the more conservative establishment, which in turn exacerbated left-wingers' criticisms of the democracy which permitted their existence. Some even saw the Federal Republic as a repressive, quasi-fascist, regime (the word 'fascist' gained widespread and imprecise currency at this time); on this view, formal democracy was merely a meaningless facade for real intolerance.

The resurgence of a neo-Marxist writing, however, which sought to unmask and lay bare the true nature of 'late capitalist society', soon degenerated, as practised by some, into an arcane art form in itself, intelligible only to small bands of *aficionados* and not calculated to bring the mass of the working population to the barricades. However exciting and interesting for some intellectuals, theoretical developments such as Habermas' 'theory of communicative competence' were all but incommunicable to most. Critiques of critiques proliferated, structuralist Marxists and action-theorists developed a veritable industry in mutual destruction; but there was precious little praxis in evidence on the part of most academic social theorists and the 'late capitalist' western working class appeared to be proceeding in its materialistic pursuits relatively untroubled by accusations of false consciousness. Meanwhile, for those less given to the intricacies of theorizing, there was the possibility of dropping out, experimenting with communal forms of living and seeking to replace competitiveness with modes of co-operation. For all the avenues such explorations, both theoretical and practical, opened up, they did little to affect the nature of West German society more generally.

More disturbing, however, was one particular development: that of the active terrorism of the Red Army Faction (RAF, or Baader-Meinhof gang). While abstruse books can usually be relatively easily ignored, bombings and assassinations cannot. The RAF was formally established on 5 June 1970, although terrorist acts did not become a serious phenomenon until 1974. Like their leaders, Andreas Baader and Ulrike Meinhof, members were mostly middle class, well-educated, and belonged to the generation born into the chaos and disruption of the 1940s – the generation, as one analyst put it, of those without fathers and unable to mourn. Their guiding idea was that attacks on the state would serve to lay bare its true, repressive nature. At first, attacks were against property: arson attacks on department stores, bank robberies to keep themselves afloat. Then, however, began a series of murders of prominent individuals. In the course of the 1970s, terrorism was to become a serious problem for West German democracy.

The Baader-Meinhof gang assassinated a series of prominent individuals. In the particularly bad year of 1977 the banker Jürgen Ponto was shot by his god-daughter in his house near Frankfurt; the General State Prosecutor Buback was murdered, an act which was 'justified' as a response to his allegedly 'causing' the deaths of three terrorists, Holger Meins, Siegfried Hauser, and Ulrike Meinhof; the employers' leader Hanns-Martin Schleyer (who had held a high position in the SS) was kidnapped in Cologne on 5 September; and on 19 October, following the successful freeing of a hijacked airliner in Mogadishu by a special squad of the Federal Border Police, Schleyer's body was found dumped in the boot of a car in Alsace; this was one day after three terrorists in Stammheim prison, Baader, Raspin and Ensslin, were found dead, having supposedly committed suicide on hearing the news of the outcome of the hijack. It was scarcely surprising, in view of such developments, that there was considerable public disquiet about terrorism, which tended to be equated quite simply with left-wing extremism. When a bomb went off at the Munich Beer Festival in 1980, it was some time before it was generally recognized that it had been the act of a right-wing extremist.

The response of the Federal Republic to extremism was extensive and thorough. Apart from the Emergency Law passed in 1968, there were other measures which had been on the agenda for some time but which gained a new meaning in the context of the 1970s. One such was the Decree concerning Radicals (*Radikalenerlass*) of 1972. Ironically, this decree sought simply to achieve a certain uniformity and consistency in existing practice, which varied across the *Länder*, and to avoid the insensitive proscribing of a list of organizations by emphasizing the need to look at each individual case on its own merits. In practice, the result was often tantamount to a witch-hunt, and severe restrictions on the freedoms of speech and association for those many individuals having or wanting jobs in the public service sector (which included over fifty per cent of university students) were imposed. A set of anti-terrorist measures followed later in the 1970s: terrorists were no longer permitted to share a common defence counsel, or to have contact with each other after they were imprisoned; it was even made possible for their contact with their defence lawyers to be broken. They were often subjected to particularly harsh conditions, including long periods of isolation.

By the late 1970s, many who had no sympathy with the actions of the terrorists themselves were becoming highly critical of the measures taken against them. It was noted that many terrorists were serving longer sentences, under worse conditions, than had many former Nazis in the course of their denazification; and that much of the legislation impinged on Germany's desire to be seen as a state of law, a *Rechtsstaat*, in explicit contrast to its disreputable recent past. The state's response to terrorism was indeed so thorough that it gave rise to the criticism by some that, while certain measures were necessary to combat violence, the state's radical response ran the danger of itself destroying the democracy it was attempting to defend. Yet this debate was muddied by the creation of the notion of 'sympathizers', as the right-wing press attempted to conflate criticism of the treatment of terrorists with support of terrorism itself. Nevertheless, the activities of terrorists began both to subside in volume and to take new forms in the course of the 1980s, and by the second half of the decade the state was officially recognizing that new approaches by means of dialogue to defuse tension should be explored – although not at the expense of continuing surveillance. Most people were surprised as well as aghast when the banker Alfred Herrhausen was murdered in late 1989. Until the revelation, in June 1990, that many West German terrorists had been given refuge – and even new identities – under the protection of the *Stasi* in East Germany, it had been thought that terrorists had scattered far afield and no longer constituted a serious threat. (The terrorist issue had of course developed international dimensions by the late 1980s, with the IRA's frequent attacks on British military targets in West Germany, posing a rather different sort of challenge to international policing.)

The heritage of 1960s left-wing dissent in a more diffuse sense could be observed in such developments as the citizens' initiatives groups, the Green Party, and the influence of popular pressure groups and public opinion on the major parties seeking crucial marginal support among floating voters. Alternative life-styles changed somewhat in nature, however: late 1980s house-squatting in West Berlin was a rather different phenomenon from the intellectual communes of the late 1960s. West German political theory continued to be abstruse and a matter of some public debate, as evidenced by several controversies; but there was perhaps a more widespread disaffection with Marxism.

If one wants to consider the implications of left-wing dissent for the development of West German democracy, the balance is a mixed one. Some aspects were undoubtedly supportive, in that a new political culture sustaining a participatory, rather than merely representative, democracy had been emerging since the 1960s: this was clearly the case in connection with the citizens' initiative groups and the Greens. Some aspects were less beneficial, particularly the terrorist acts which provoked the state into becoming more the repressive beast it was accused of being. Equally disturbing was the way in which the press not merely reported, but actually helped to create some of the news, as in its reaction to the Ohnesorg death (as refracted in Heinrich Böll's *Die verlorene Ehre der Katharina Blum*). A particular climate of opinion was created and sustained which made life difficult both for those honestly searching for new views and supportive critiques, and for those prominent members of the establishment who found themselves having to live in ghetto-like conditions for their own security. Nevertheless, West German democracy as a system survived both the fears of the right about the effects of terrorism, and the fears of the left about undue restrictions on personal liberties, democratic freedoms, and the survival of the German *Rechtsstaat*.

Extremism was not limited to the left. Extreme right-wing views both persisted among a minority, and developed in new forms among other groups in response to changing conditions. The issue of right-wing dissent is not merely one of inadequate 'denazification', but also of the development of new modes of extremism under new circumstances. There were, for example, at intervals throughout the history of the Federal Republic, incidents indicating the persistence of anti-Semitic attitudes, such as the daubing of swastikas desecrating Jewish graves; there was also a newer racial hostility to the foreign workers in Germany, the *Gastarbeiter*, in some ways echoing the older denigration of foreign workers in the Third Reich, but representing less a persistence of old attitudes than a set of new prejudices under new conditions.

A declining phenomenon was that of open reunions of former Nazis, such as the gatherings of former SS officers. Some of these were forbidden, such as a planned reunion in Harzburg in May 1985, while others were able to take place, such as a meeting in a hotel in Nesselwang, near the Bavarian border with Austria, in December 1985. Some former Nazis, in more muted but infinitely more effective manner, had a powerful influence on West German political life up to the end of the 1970s, as documented in Bernt Engelmann's 'factual novel', *Grosses*

Bundesverdienstkreuz mit Stern. This shows the way in which economically powerful figures (whose rise to fortune started in the Third Reich) were able to sponsor and influence important political figures – including the former Prime Minister of Bavaria and leader of the CSU, Franz-Josef Strauss, and even the man who subsequently became Chancellor of West Germany in 1982, Helmut Kohl. By the 1980s many former Nazis had become rather elderly and pathetic figures, whose defence of Hitler and the Third Reich could hardly be said to pose a problem for West German democracy. Recalcitrant, unrepentant, but relatively harmless former Nazis included the former SS officers interviewed by Claud Lanzmann in his film *Shoah*, and the former leader of the Nazi women's organization, Gertrud Scholz-Klink, interviewed by Claudia Koonz at the beginning of *Mothers in the Fatherland*. There might well have been a sizeable readership for such extreme right-wing newspapers as *Die Nationalzeitung*, with its nostalgic advertisements for medals displaying former nationalist and military heroes, and its revisionist articles on such topics as the Holocaust, the treatment of Germans after the war, and German displacement from their eastern homelands. But while debates on such topics tended to be acrimonious, such views remained for the most part peripheral to mainstream West German political life. (Only when sanitized variants of such views were taken up by respected academics did they become more problematic.) Obviously, with the passage of time, the generation which had come to terms with, often even supported in principle, the Third Reich, was passing away.

In some ways more worrying from the point of view of West German democracy was the development of neo-Nazi organizations and movements which were supported by younger Germans – products of the post-war era. Members of the many neo-Nazi groups in the 1970s and 1980s were predominantly young, relatively under-educated and unskilled, and perhaps unemployed. To a certain extent, this neo-Nazism amounted to the adoption of a political *style*, rather than an ideology: wearing distinctive clothing and using the swastika as symbols of their rejection of a system which appeared to be rejecting them. These groups were small in absolute numbers, and were on occasion dealt with quite severely by the authorities, as in the disbanding of the para-military Wehrsportgruppe Hoffmann.

A more widespread form of racialism was evident in hostility directed against foreign workers. Popular fears of unemployment when facing the competition of *Gastarbeiter*, dislike of foreign cultural styles, and resentment at the apparent 'invasion' of previously homogenous communities, could be exploited by extremist organizations. The *Gastarbeiter* were targeted for attack by a new right-wing party, the *Deutsche Volksunion*, founded in 1987 and claiming to have a membership of seven thousand. Racial hostility also lay behind the rise to success of the right-wing Republican party (led by Franz Schönhuber, a man who was unrepentantly proud of his former SS-membership) in the state elections in Berlin and Hesse (particularly Frankfurt) in the spring of 1989 and in the Euro-elections of June 1989. Such racialist attitudes, and the size of the vote for right-wing parties, were indicative of serious social tensions in the outwardly prosperous West Germany of the later twentieth century.

While right-wing extremism on the whole failed to catch the headline coverage of left-wing terrorism, it nevertheless continued to exert a considerable influence, particularly at times of social strain. And this influence was wielded not only through the small, self-professedly extreme right-wing parties, which could never hope to capture a large proportion of the vote (however successful they might be locally on occasion), but also, perhaps more insidiously, by pressures exerted on the major parties, particularly of course the CDU and CSU. Minority pressure groups such as the League of Refugees and Expellees (*Bund der Heimatvertriebenen*) were able to exert revisionist pressures on conservative politicians, who were fearful of losing crucial marginal votes to the more right-wing parties. In the 1980s, mainstream conservative politicians, in playing to the nationalist gallery, helped to create a climate in which the expression of more extremist views began to appear acceptable. And in 1990, when German unification was on the agenda, such posturing to the right led to serious prevarications and delays on the part of Chancellor Kohl on the issue of guaranteeing Poland's western border, the Oder-Neisse Line.

Yet, while there were a wide range of dissenting opinions of one form or another in the Federal Republic, there was nothing which remotely resembled the extent of anti-system opposition to parliamentary democracy in the Weimar Republic. The reasons for this are various, but one key factor has to do with the relative material success of West German capitalist democracy. For the Federal Republic's first forty years there was no mass discontent to provide a popular basis for extremist parties or for the criticisms of intellectuals. On the other hand, it is quite clear that social tensions – particularly in relation to *Gastarbeiter* – and fear of the impact of immigrants (including, in 1989–90, East Germans) on unemployment and housing, could quite easily lead a substantial minority of West Germans to sympathize with or support right-wing views and groups.

TWELVE

Diverging Cultures
and National Identities?

The question of 'national identity' has been a particularly problematic one for modern Germany – and has indeed been so at least since the beginnings of modern nationalism and nation-states in the late eighteenth century. It was obviously particularly difficult after 1949, in a severed nation. Not only did the two German states have to deal with the complex problem of defining a partial, legitimizing identity while dealing with the wider issue of attitudes to division and reunification; they also had to deal with the problem of their relationship with the immediate past, the Nazi era and its legacy. But apart from the (rather major) problem of coming to terms with the Hitler period, the division of Germany in 1949 might have represented simply a reversion to an older 'German' pattern; that of a multiplicity of German-speaking states in central Europe, with regional variants in culture and identity. Switzerland and Austria are illustrations of this pattern, of greater or lesser historical longevity in their present state forms.[1] Particularly after the 'normalization' of relations between the two Germanies at the beginning of the 1970s, concerted efforts were made to establish separate 'national identities' – at least in the GDR – or to define or come to terms with a difficult historical legacy and problem of identity, as it was seen in the Federal Republic. There is also a wider question connected with these issues: that of the extent to which, given the physical separation, conscious efforts on the parts of the regimes and the multiple influences of different social experiences were combining to produce diverging profiles of culture (and particularly political culture) in the two states.

Aspects of cultural life

The conditions for cultural life in the two Germanies differed in predictable ways. There were obvious political constraints on publishing in East Germany, although the degree and severity of these constraints varied at different times in the GDR's history. In the West, the main constraints were those of a capitalist society: the need to be profitable, and the danger of certain proprietors gaining a major share of the market (particularly in the case of newspapers). Commercial success is not always the primary criterion for either quality or truthfulness. Apart from these obvious differences, literature and culture developed in interestingly divergent ways in the two Germanies from 1945 to 1989. These differences were both conditioned by and reflected the different socio-political systems of the two states.

The East German regime's policies towards literature, and the concerns of writers, changed markedly in the period up to 1989. The late 1940s and early 1950s saw the return of a number of committed left-wing writers from their enforced exile during the Nazi period. They had high hopes for the foundation of the first truly socialist state on German soil – hopes and expectations which were not always fulfilled. These writers returning from exile included Anna Seghers and Johannes Becher, both of whom in one way or another became East German establishment figures, as well as the less orthodox Bertolt Brecht. Brecht came to occupy an ambiguous position: his work was partly lauded by the regime, and partly suppressed. Brecht's Berlin theatre was restricted in the performances it could offer, and students and the general public were restricted in the range of Brecht's works which were made available for them to read.[2] Nor was Brecht himself entirely enamoured of Ulbricht's interpretation of communism. Brecht's comments on the GDR had a critical edge, as in his poem relating to the 1953 uprising which ended with the comment that, if the people did not like the government, it would be simplest to dissolve the people and elect another one. Official literary policy at this time was one of socialist realism. There was a failure to come to terms in any genuine sense with the past: accounts of the Nazi period, with communist resistance figures fighting lone battles, were over-simplistic and unconvincing; and major efforts were devoted instead to the contemporary tasks connected with the building of socialism. It was later generally recognized, by regime as well as readers, that this literature neither had great intrinsic merit nor any measurable success in transforming the attitudes of the post-Nazi East Germans. (In the later 1960s, in fact, it dawned on the regime that television might be a more appropriate medium for influencing public opinion, and attempts to use imaginative literature to this end were demoted.) Although there was a brief thaw after the death of Stalin in 1953, this did not last very long or go very far.

In 1959 there was a conference at Bitterfield, emphasizing the importance of relating intellectual and practical work to each other. Workers were urged to 'grasp the pen', while writers were encouraged to gain practical experience of manual labour and life in the factory. One notable novel to come out of this period was Christa Wolf's *Der geteilte Himmel* (1964), which, although not entirely convincing to a western reader in certain respects (such as the final preference of the heroine for life in the East rather than following her boyfriend to the West), was certainly a work of some literary merit. As a rising female writer committed to socialism, Christa Wolf gained a place as a candidate member of the Central Committee of the SED; however, she lost this position with the publication of the rather pessimistic *Nachdenken über Christa T.* in 1967. Wolf remained a critical but important figure in East Germany in the 1970s and 1980s, in some ways symbolizing the development of GDR culture while making her own unique, and internationally recognized, contribution.

Honecker started his period of office with the promising statement that 'if one proceeds from the firm position of socialism there can ... be no taboos'.[3] For a brief period in the early 1970s there was indeed a certain latitude for experimentation, with the publication of such works as Ulrich Plenzdorf's *Die neuen Leiden des jungen W.*, portraying a youth whose blue jeans, colloquial language, and general attitudes were hardly those models upheld officially. The increased consumer orientation of the Honecker regime was reflected in a greater willingness also to tolerate certain forms of popular culture and music, and a greater variety of entertainments. Emphasis was laid, in the post-*Ostpolitik* period, on a GDR-specific culture separate from the class-biased culture of capitalist West Germany. The new atmosphere encouraged an enhanced feeling of freedom among many writers, and certain self-imposed restraints began to dissolve. Difficulties in writing appeared to relate more to the inherent problems of the subject-matter. In 1976 Christa Wolf's superb exploration of the normality of the Nazi past, its impact on the formation of personality and its legacy for the present, in *Kindheitsmuster*, was published. This complex, semi-autobiographical novel is also an exploration of the nature of memory, of modes of retrieving and reconstructing the past, and a reflection on the creative process of writing itself.

1976 was however also a turning point in official cultural policy: the singer and guitarist Wolf Biermann was involuntarily exiled while on a concert tour in the West late in 1975, evidence of a new harder line on the part of the authorities. Although many writers protested – and suffered penalties, often including the loss of party membership, as a result – the protests neither helped Biermann nor changed the course of cultural policy. The later 1970s saw increasing repression, and new constraints on writers attempting to publish their work in the West (who could now be prosecuted for tax offences even if they evaded censorship regulations.) Many writers were either forced or chose to leave the GDR for the West, including Jurek Becker, Günter Kunert, and Sarah Kirsh. Others, with major reputations in the West and partially critical of their own regime, chose to stay – such as Stefan Heym, author of *Fünf Tage im Juni*, which was originally banned and only later published in the GDR, and of more recent works such as *Collin*, also semi-critical. As some commentators pointed out, a major theme in the late 1970s and 1980s was that of 'keeping silent'.[4] There was also a heightened interest in and reflection on authentic personal experience, and the relationships between individual personality development and social circumstances. Particularly interesting for western observers attempting to gain some understanding of life in the GDR was the so-called protocol literature: attempts to capture authentic accounts of experience by means of tape-recorded interviews, as in Gabriele Eckart's *So sehe Ick die Sache: Protokolle aus der DDR*.[5] Much East German women's writing in the 1970s and 1980s was devoted to reconstructing personal experience in what was still in many ways a male-dominated society.

Most western observers were aware of a considerable pressure on GDR writers in the 1980s, with a degree of self-constraint and self-censorship as well as actual censorship. The official line as late as 1988 was that, in a period of Soviet-inspired *Glasnost*, constraint and restriction was minimal.[6] Problems of accessibility (or lack of it!) of certain works allegedly had more to do with mechanical production problems than with any officially determined restrictions on the reading matter available to the general public. But when pressed by a British audience, even the apparently genial and urbane Klaus Höpcke, GDR Deputy Minister of Culture, became agitated on the topic of alternative cultural productions on the part of some more dissident GDR citizens. In his view, there was plenty of scope for experimentation for young poets, writers, singers and painters in the GDR; but certain contributions (such as the songs of Stefan Krawczyck before his arrest and exile at the beginning of 1988) had 'nothing to do with culture' – according to the official definition, of course. It was evident that whatever the regime's formal pronouncements, there were still considerable limits to freedom of cultural production in the GDR.

In contrast to other eastern bloc countries, the East German cultural intelligentsia did not however lay claim to spearheading opposition to the regime. Prominent writers, however critical they might be of aspects of life in the GDR, nevertheless occupied a privileged position, with considerable freedom of travel to the West and the opportunity to earn enough western currency to secure a comfortable life-style, as well as gaining an international reputation. Most major writers saw it as their task to contribute to the transformation of consciousness and the gradual development of a better society than to make any claims for political power. In this respect, they did not unduly trouble the regime, while not being as supportive as the politicians might have liked. Anyone who transgressed certain limits could relatively easily be exported to the West, by permission, persuasion or pressure.

For straightforward transmission of official ideology and propaganda, however, the regime had plenty of available channels. Newspapers ranged from the official daily *Neues Deutschland* through the variants oriented towards different readerships, such as *Junge Welt* for youth, to the various technical periodicals for different professional groups. East German television was also officially controlled – and generally recognized to be for the most part so profoundly boring as to be ignored by the vast majority of East Germans in favour of watching West German television (which transmitted such masterpieces of American culture as *Dynasty* and *Dallas* as well as more serious news and current affairs programmes rendering East Germans exceptionally well-informed among East European populations). Music in the GDR ranged from the highly serious performance of classical music – in good German bourgeois tradition – to a more subversive interest in pop and rock music among youth, under the considerable influence of the West.

Cultural production in West Germany was distinctive in a number of respects. As mentioned above, the constraints were less directly political than commercial. Enormous criticisms have been directed by left-wingers against the Axel Springer press, for example, with its control and alleged distortion of the news in papers such as the mass circulation daily *Bild-Zeitung*. On the other hand, considerable subventions from a number of sources permitted the development of many experimental forms, such as in the West German film industry, which produced films rarely possible in Hollywood. Moreover, there was a wide diversity in what could be published and marketed in West Germany, with a flourishing 'alternative scene' in addition to mainstream market-oriented production. At the same time, there was a continued interest in 'high culture' and serious theatrical and musical productions, with many small towns boasting their own flourishing theatres and opera houses. The West Germans remained a nation of culture-lovers, with wide middle-class interest in art exhibitions and the like. West German cultural life was far more regionally based and decentralized than that of countries like France and Britain where capital cities had long been dominant. Given such diversity, only a few features of the development of culture in West Germany can be selected for brief mention here.[7]

There was arguably an earlier serious confrontation in the West than the East with at least some of the problems posed by the Nazi past. After the Americans banned the left-wing journal *Der Ruf* in 1947, a group founded by Alfred Andersch and Hans Werner Richter formed the so-called *Gruppe 47*. There were concerted attempts to purify the German language from the taint of Nazism and, as the writers saw it, to make 'clearings in the jungle' (using notions such as *Kahlschlag*), evidenced in such works as Borchert's *Draussen vor der Tür*. While the 1950s saw the prolific production of what has been dismissed as *Trivialliteratur*, by the end of the decade four very promising writers had emerged. In 1959 and 1960 works were published by Heinrich Böll, Günter Grass, Uwe Johnson and Martin Walser which aroused international interest and suggested the potential for a serious West German literature that was not merely a pale shadow of that of the Weimar period.

In the 1960s, there was a continuing confrontation with the Nazi period, evidenced in new forms and in relation to new topics, such as Rolf Hochhuth's play challenging the role of Catholics in the Third Reich, *The Representative*. Increasingly critical views of the bourgeois, materialist, affluent present also appeared. Narrative was widely regarded as a vehicle for critique. While it is generally accepted that Heinrich Böll's greatest literary achievements were in the short story form, such as in the collection *Ansichten eines Clowns* (1963), his longer works provide an insight into the developing problems of West German society – ranging from the critique of the consequences of investigative journalism and media methods in *Die verlorene Ehre der Katharina Blum* (1974) to the observations on society's response to terrorism in *Fürsorgliche Belagerung* (1979). Günter Grass produced works which have achieved an immense international reputation such as the *Blechtrommel* of 1959 and *Der Butt* (1977). Works such as *Katharina Blum* and *Blechtrommel* were turned into widely successful films. The 1970s and 1980s also witnessed increased interest in investigative reportage, such as Günter Wallraff's

Ganz Unten (exploring the work experiences of *Gastarbeiter*), as well as an explosion of alternative, experimental, and feminist writing. There is not space here to mention the many West German writers who achieved greater or lesser international reputations. It must suffice merely to point out that, while they did not have the parlous status of East German writers, in some ways their work was of less acute interest to many of their readers: literature did not play the same role in the relatively open society of West Germany, with its diverse channels for discussion and debate, as it did in the communist East, where the impact on readers' sensibilities and perceptions was more immediate and the interest in potential – often only thinly veiled – criticisms of society more intense. On the other hand, West German writers did tend to play a critical role in public debate that was less evident in, for example, Britain.

West German newspapers and magazines also illustrated the diversity of West German cultural life. Unlike Britain, West Germany produced no major national daily (of the sort represented by the *Independent*, *The Times*, or the *Guardian*). If any paper fulfils this role, it is the (Frankfurt-based) *Frankfurter Allgemeine Zeitung*, a leading serious paper widely read across Germany. Most readers however will read their local or provincial newspaper: in Bavaria, the most important regional paper would be the *Süddeutsche Zeitung*, while many readers might also – or instead – buy their local town newspaper (such as the *Pfaffenhofener Kurier*, a paper which would not aspire to wide circulation outside the immediate vicinity of Pfaffenhofen). Important national weeklies include the newspaper *Die Zeit* and the news magazine *Der Spiegel*. There is a similar mixture of national and regional communication channels in radio and television broadcasting. Interestingly, academic debates on matters of considerable general interest – such as the controversy over interpretations of the Holocaust in the so-called *Historikerstreit*, which raged before and after the election campaign of 1987 – were carried out in the press in West Germany, in some contrast to Britain in the 1980s where the voices of academics tended to gain less of a popular audience in general.

It is clear that there was a considerable divergence in cultural life in the two Germanies, although they had certain themes to contend with in common. This is particularly the case with questions such as the confrontation with the Nazi past, and with the more general issue of building new national identities and political cultures in two very different parts of a divided nation. It is to these broader questions that we now turn.

The divided nation: national identities and historical consciousness in the two Germanies*

The German Democratic Republic and the Federal Republic of Germany, formally founded in 1949 as cold war images of their respective occupying powers, faced several key problems in the attempts to develop new national identities. There was that of being a partial state, a severed limb of a defeated and divided nation, with a political regime in the main imposed by the will of the occupying powers and not representing an indigenous development from the people. There was that of coping with the horrific legacy of the Third Reich, where racialist doctrines had led to the bureaucratically organized mass murder of over six million Jews and of others deemed unfit to live. There was that, finally, of attempting to impose drastically new forms of regime – communism and liberal democracy – on populations lacking, by and large, appropriate political values and attitudes. It should be remembered that, whatever their rather wayward actual effects, the denazification and re-education programmes of both the western and eastern occupying powers did not succeed in producing a majority of convinced democrats or communists, respectively. (If anything, they succeeded in creating a certain sense of national community where Hitler had failed: a so-called *Sympathiegemeinschaft* of aggrieved Germans, carping and grumbling about the injustices being meted out to them

*A slightly different version of this and the following sections of this chapter has been published in *Historical Research*, vol. 62, no. 148 (June 1989), pp. 193–213.

by the occupation authorities.) It has frequently been said that the Weimer Republic failed in part because it was a 'Republic without Republicans'. If there was any truth in that analysis, then the prospects for the two Germanies could hardly be said to have been much better: in the West, a democracy with precious few democrats in the immediate post-war era; in the East, a communist state with a minority of communists. Over time, it can be argued that political culture in the two Germanies became more appropriate to the divergent political forms – even if it was not entirely what the earlier occupying powers or the later respective German governments would necessarily have desired. There were shifts and changes in official interpretations of national identity; there were changing historiographical fashions and evaluations of the place of the present in relation to the past; and there were also some notable transformations of popular political culture in each state, arguably arising less from official attempts to build new national identities than from other features of the socio-political environment.

It should be noted that history was of vital importance in East Germany in attempts to represent (and hence legitimize) the present as the inevitable culmination of the past, the goal towards which all of German history had been tending. East Germany after *Ostpolitik* developed, moreover, a class theory of nation which suggested that while there were now two German nations (as well as two German states), it was the East German nation which was historically the more progressive, according to the Marxist view of historical progress. There were, during the course of the GDR's development, various official views and periodizations both of the GDR's history and of the long sweep of German history. The major shift came with the change from the Ulbricht regime to that of Erich Honecker. In the 1970s and 1980s, the GDR no longer conceived of itself as being in a brief transitional phase in which undesired elements simply represented hangovers from the past. Rather, 'actually existing socialism' would last a long time, and contained its own intrinsic contradictions and difficulties, which had to be recognized, analysed, and dealt with, rather than dismissed as the debris of past history which would eventually wither away. In terms of conceptions of national identity in relation to German history, what is of note is the two-fold development in the 1970s and 1980s of an emphasis, both on a specific GDR national identity – part of the policy of cultural *Abgrenzung* (demarcation) following the lowering of real barriers after *Ostpolitik* – and, almost paradoxically, the simultaneous revival of interest in certain previously suppressed aspects of the German past. This can be seen in a number of areas.

In the field of architecture, attention began to be paid to the rehabilitation of old houses in city centres, the renovation of churches and other notable public buildings, the restoration of historically significant areas and their upkeep as being of national importance. This stood in some contrast to earlier policies of permitting the crumbling and dilapidation of such buildings while throwing up new housing estates on the outskirts of cities and favouring Soviet-style architecture or cheap concrete prefabricated flats – which of course had the laudable utilitarian aim of ensuring rapid adequate housing provision but did little to preserve the German architectural and cultural heritage. Not only old houses but also old heroes were resurrected, symbolically and sometimes also physically. Frederick II (Frederick the Great) was to ride his horse again – on his statue re-erected on East Berlin's Unter den Linden; Luther was rehabilitated in the history books as a figure of major importance in East German history. Anniversaries and historical exhibitions flourished, although not quite on the scale afforded by the Federal Republic; in 1987 East Berlin mounted its own Berlin 750-year anniversary bonanza.[8]

The academic writing of history – which was of course somewhat circumscribed by the official line, although at times a wider latitude of interpretation was evident – partly reflected these changes. Without analysing specific works in detail, it may be noted here that there were some remarkable general changes between the mid 1970s and the late 1980s. Marxist history writing is generally characterized by a focus on the succession of modes of production, the progressive role of the exploited and oppressed classes, and the importance of revolutions in the transition from one stage to the next. While these broad emphases remained, new features emerged. There was a new focus on the historic role of individuals, such as Bismarck and Frederick the Great. Certain traditional German themes, for a long time taboo, made their reappearance, such as militarism, the Army, and the legacy of Prussia (now more positively evaluated and laid claim to). The development of a certain idealism was notable, as for example in the reinterpretation of the Lutheran Reformation as the 'essential ideological precondition' for the German Peasants' War, held up since Engels as Germany's 'early bourgeois revolution' with its hero Thomas Münzer. To outside observers, this looked like a return to non-Marxist modes of history writing in the GDR, alongside continuing materialist currents. The one area which saw little serious change, at least as officially presented, was that of the recent Nazi past: the Nazi-Soviet pact was glossed over, and the working people of Germany were represented as having simply been 'liberated' from Nazi oppression, rooted in monopoly capitalism, by the Red Army. This was evident both in such official publications as the 1985 pamphlets commemorating the fortieth anniversary of the end of the war and in the kinds of historical exhibition shown in former Nazi concentration camps such as Buchenwald. However, it was now acknowledged that there were forms of resistance other than, and in addition to, that of communists. The 20 July Plotters, for example, were accorded some belated respect. On a more general level, it has been suggested that East German historiography from the 1970s onwards broadened its scope, laying claim to the *whole* of German history, rather than selected highlights, while at the same time maintaining a distinction between *Tradition* and *Erbe*, the aspects of tradition and legacy which were or were not to be used as sources of inspiration for the present.[9]

What impact did official representations of history have on the population of East Germany? There is some evidence to suggest that the younger generation did begin to think in terms of 'GDR citizenship', 'GDR culture' and so on, rather than the notion of 'German' which appeared more natural to the older generation. In this respect, it was simply part of the passage of time which made what was once new and strange into the taken-for-granted. It also seems that East Germans assented to the respect for the German national heritage which was in evidence in the 1970s and 1980s. The state co-opted Luther not only as a religious hero but also as a national hero, thereby successfully averting a symbolic confrontation between, on the one hand, people, religion and nation, and, on the other, alien imposed atheist state, as had happened in Poland, the example of which was not lost on the East German leadership at the time of Solidarity's birth in 1980–1. On the other hand, East Germans retained an intense interest in the West German state, watching West German television and cultivating links with West German relatives and friends. Effective imprisonment behind the Wall also made East Germans perpetually aware of the consequences of war and division, which remained a continuing source of pain. Moreover, it will be argued below that there were other, more important influences on the formation of political culture in East Germany than the officially promoted views of the past and of GDR national identity.

Views of the past were much more diverse in West Germany. About the only valid generalization is that history was extremely controversial, with major national arguments raging not only over obviously contentious topics, such as the Holocaust, but also over ways of teaching history in schools, and representing history to the public in museums and exhibitions. These debates were carried out not only in academic journals, but also – with considerable acrimony – in the national press, on the radio and on television. History was a highly political matter in the Federal Republic.

In the 1950s there was a certain repression of the immediate past, a 'collective amnesia', while at the same time many prominent figures were cashing in on a ready market with the publication of their memoirs. Utilitarian rationalizations were employed to justify a certain obliteration – often physical and literal – of the less pleasant aspects of the Nazi period, as in the destruction of Nazi concentration camps to 'avert the spread of disease', or the demolition of the former Gestapo headquarters in Prinz-Albrechtstrasse, Berlin. (The reconstruction of certain sites, such as an exemplary block in the 'Garden of Remembrance' which is what Flossenbürg concentration camp was turned into, hardly give an adequate picture of their former horrific nature; the sites in Austria, Czechoslovakia, and Poland are infinitely more compelling in atmosphere.) The acknowledged general political apathy of the 1950s was supplemented by the official unease with any form of German nationalism, and a desire to seek new forms of political identity, such as absorption into wider European economic and political organizations. Both these orientations underwent changes over time.

By the 1980s, a new desire and willingness to confront the past had developed – symbolized, for example, by the popularity of films such as *Heimat*, which sought to reappropriate and 'normalize' twentieth-century German history. In a more sombre vein, the cellars of the Gestapo building in Berlin, surprisingly uncovered, were used for part of a historical exhibition on resistance. (Even this, however, and the future use of the area, became the subjects of heated public controversy.)[10] At the same time, there was a renewed willingness in conservative circles to revive nationalist themes, to speak more openly and frequently of the 'fatherland', and to call for renewed pride in the German nation and an end to feeling guilt and shame for being German.[11] All these trends were controversial: there was much public debate, both over specific issues such as whether to redevelop significant sites or retain them intact as memorials (for example, the Jewish quarter in Frankfurt), and over general issues such as renascent German nationalism. The issues did not divide simply along party-political lines: left-wing anti-Americanism, environmentalism, and right-wing nationalism had many elements in common, despite the disavowals of some commentators that left-wing anti-American and anti-nuclear, neutralist sentiments had anything to do with nationalism.[12]

The range of views expressed in public debate was found also in academic history-writing in West Germany. The conservative orthodoxy of the 1950s was shattered by the publication in 1961 of Fritz Fischer's controversial reinterpretation of German responsibility for unleashing the First World War, provoking a long-running debate which renewed focus on domestic social tensions in Wilhelmine Germany. In the later 1960s and 1970s, new forms of social and societal history began to gain ground, with the rise to prominence of such historians as Hans-Ulrich Wehler and Jürgen Kocka. While the approach of the 'Bielefeld School' (where several such historians worked) was becoming an established trend – if only among a minority of the still largely conservative West German historical profession – it was being challenged by a fresh wave of younger historians in the 1970s and 1980s, seeking to open up 'history from below'. By the late 1980s, there was a profusion of approaches to history, including the rapid spread of amateur involvement in history workshops, the proliferation of regional and local studies and exploration of the history of everyday life, the expansion of feminist history and the pursuit of other previously neglected areas and themes, often by people marginal to the academic world. While the mainstream of the West German historical profession might have retained its institutional predominance, there was certainly an enhanced liveliness in German historical debates.

The so-called *Historikerstreit* (historians' controversy) of 1986–7 about the uniqueness and comparability of the Holocaust was also indicative, less of disputes about facts, than of new modes of attempting to assimilate the past to present political consciousness. The attempt by largely conservative historians to pose certain questions (often rhetorical, particularly in the case of Nolte, and implying unsubstantiated answers) about Hitler's Germany in a wider perspective was geared towards a general desire to reassert a modicum of pride in being German again. On this view, Stalin's crimes both predated and may in some (never very clearly specified or documented) way have actually helped to cause Hitler's crimes. Those who sympathize with victims of the Holocaust, or who profess empathy with the underdogs of history, should also feel sorry for the millions of Germans expelled from their homelands in the eastern territories after the war, or with the brave German soldiers fighting on the eastern front – and so on. The debate was characterized by a high degree of acrimony, mud-slinging, misrepresentation and misquotation, and participants frequently resorted less to rational argument about the facts than to ill-founded assertions about opponents' political positions. In the end, the debate largely subsided as a public issue, being overtaken by the more immediate questions posed by the East German events of 1989. It ultimately served more to illustrate the contentious, problematic, and political nature of perceptions of history in the Federal Republic than to shed any new light on the genuinely difficult questions of the past.[13]

What impact did perceptions of the past have on popular political consciousness in West Germany among those not directly contributing to the reappropriation of history? For all the West German agonizing over *Vergangenheitsbewältigung* (coming to terms with the past), certain studies and incidents revealed a startling ignorance of, or set of misapprehensions about, the past on the part of many, particularly younger, West Germans. One study, for example, in which schoolchildren were asked to write an essay on what they knew about Hitler, revealed the most extraordinary range of confusion and simple lack of factual knowledge. The showing of the rather sentimental and simplistic American film *Holocaust* in Germany aroused passions and debates which illustrated, if nothing else, the previous relatively dormant nature of any engagement with the topic. Similarly, in 1985 the misjudged visit of America's President Reagan to Bitburg Cemetery with its SS graves – at the last minute counterbalanced by a hastily arranged visit to Belsen concentration camp – further provoked much heated debate on issues which had lain somewhat suppressed in earlier years. The later 1970s and 1980s were characterized by vigorous public interest in German history, as evidenced in the enormous number and range of historical exhibitions that were mounted in West Germany. These included not only the major representations of German history in the Reichstag building in West Berlin, the massive Prussia exhibition, and the diverse exhibitions forming part of Berlin's 750th anniversary celebrations, but also a host of regional and local exhibitions and new museums reflecting a widespread intense popular interest in reinterpreting often forgotten aspects of the German past and representing them in new ways.

However, it can be argued for West Germany as for the East that perceptions of the past, and official views on national identity, were not the key factors affecting the transformation of political culture; to some extent, indeed, they rather reflected changes originating elsewhere. As far as national identity goes, the simple passage of time made the Federal Republic look more and more like the 'natural' political entity to young West Germans, who for the most part had barely a passing interest in the relatively unknown and easily ignored country on the other side of the Iron Curtain dividing the familiar homeland from the drab and easily dismissed GDR. Personal links with the GDR – memories and nostalgia for lost eastern territories – were inevitably dying out. Even in the 1950s, when Adenauer firmly set his face towards the West, material concerns in the age of the economic miracle were more important to many Germans than any prospect of reunification. This was quite evidently the case in the period of *Ostpolitik*, when in the 1972 election – which largely revolved on the issue of support for Brandt's policies effectively conceding the likely permanence of division – there was an extremely high turnout with the SPD for the first time winning more votes than the CDU/CSU. By the later 1980s, few would have questioned the territorial boundaries or fundamental legitimacy of the West German state. In this aspect, there was a key asymmetry between West and East German views of their part of a divided nation: it was relatively easy for westerners to ignore the East (which hardly constituted a tempting tourist destination), in contrast to the great desire to travel to (and experience the consumer delights of) the West felt by many East Germans.

Finally, we may ask the question why both Germanies were developing fundamentally new relationships with their past in the 1970s and 1980s. The answer must of course in part have to do with the consequences of *Ostpolitik* and mutual recognition: despite West Germany's formally continuing commitment to eventual reunification (enshrined in the Basic Law, West Germany's 'temporary' constitution of 1949), both states now appeared to be permanent and would continue to diverge for the foreseeable future. But the answer, perhaps more importantly, has to do with the changed internal characters of the regimes – and of the two societies – which, having passed through a highly painful transitional stage, had become to a considerable degree established. Rather than representing a *precondition* for the development of domestic stability, the new explorations of national identity were rather *predicated on* the prior transformation and stabilization of the two Germanies, which could now afford, from a distance, to reflect more freely on their past.

Changing patterns of political culture

What then of changing political cultures in the two Germanies? Attempts to define and characterize 'political culture' are highly problematic; so problematic that one commentator has likened the task to attempting to nail a milk pudding to the wall. Questions arise concerning what is meant by the concept, in terms of values, attitudes, behaviour; what levels it can be related to ('whole society', region, class or social group); how far it can be used as an explanatory, independent variable, or how far it is the result of other factors, and if so, which. Such debates cannot be entered into in detail here, but a few general points may be made. Of course there are certain inherited patterns of political values, attitudes, and modes of behaviour, which are passed on through socialization and change only slowly over time (although expressions of opinion over specific issues may change very rapidly). But it can be argued that certain sorts of political organization, and certain features of state – society relationships, tend to produce distinctive profiles of political orientation among the populace.[14]

It was suggested, above, that the interventionist nature of the Nazi state, in which 'total' claims were made on the lives of citizens, tended to produce a widespread 'inner emigration', as people learned to lead a double life, conforming in public and reserving their authentic feelings for private spaces and private lives. This phenomenon, frequently termed a *Nischengesellschaft* (niche society), has been widely observed in a number of East

European societies which – in different ways – also tended to make total claims on their citizens. For the GDR the 'niche society' was well described by Günter Gaus, West Germany's former representative in the GDR, in his book *Wo Deutschland liegt.*[15] In Communist East Germany, people participated in their work brigades, their local branches of the SED and FDGB, they belonged to the appropriate youth, sporting, or cultural associations, and the like. They mouthed the appropriate sentiments and slogans at the appropriate times. Yet at weekends they fled to their allotments, with their brightly painted habitable garden sheds (to dignify these with the term 'country cottages' would be an overstatement), where they assiduously cultivated plots blossoming with flowers and fruit. It is true that allotments and gardening have a long tradition in central Europe – and that gardening is a British national pastime, too, under rather different political circumstances – and it is not suggested here that a flight to the land at weekends is of itself something significant and new. What is to be noted, however, is the psychological aspect of the East German pattern: the investment of enthusiasm, the sense of self-expression and free development of individual personality, without the constraints of internal or external censorship. This could of course be found in other private environments – in the family, in church discussion groups, in certain forms of music and literature (which had a heightened political significance) and elsewhere – not only in allotments. The latter was merely a physical symbol of a mode of life: a life characterized by what some East Germans called *Zweigleisigkeit*, living on two tracks, moving between two languages, public conformity and private authenticity. This was not simply an inherited cultural tradition, an aspect of 'traditional' German 'apoliticism'; rather, it was a mode of adapting to life under a particular regime. Nor is it to be equated with a form of 'dissent' or 'opposition'. If anything, it was a safety valve from the point of view of the authorities, and was at times actively encouraged as a stabilizing factor.

The equivalent of this phenomenon in West Germany was simply political passivity. It is quite easy just to ignore politics –

there is no need for active retreat – if the state is not particularly intrusive or demanding on an individual's behaviour. The separation of 'public' and 'private' takes place rather differently. In the occupation period and the 1950s a comparable form of retreatism could be observed in West Germany, partly representing a hangover from the Third Reich, partly arising as a distrustful response to the possibilities of an apparently impermanent political present, in which fear of future reprisals in yet another political climate played some role. Slowly this climate of retreat into the private sphere dissipated, particularly with a process of generational change and the realization that the temporary division of Germany was likely to be long-lasting. After climactic changes in the 1960s, with the development of political activism in some quarters, the 1970s and 1980s saw the possibility for political quiescence and passivity, rather than the retreatism of a double life, on the part of the majority of non-active citizens in the West. From the point of view of the West German political elites, this political passivity was just as contributory to regime stability as would be a more active and explicit assent to official political ideologies – and possibly even more so, since happy but passive citizens make few difficult demands, unlike activists, however supportive the latter may be of the regime's official values. Clearly West German economic performance also played a major role in this set of developments.

Another set of differences has to do with patterns of dissent and opposition in the two Germanies, as related to degrees of toleration and the treatment of dissent in each state. A more tolerant state, in which a wide range of views are permissible, will by definition perceive less 'dissent' from official views than will a state in which orthodoxy is more narrowly defined. Hence in the GDR, anyone not subscribing to Marxism-Leninism as officially defined would inevitably be at least classifiable as a dissenter, a position which was of course rather different to that of the wider spectrum of opinions permissible in West Germany – although even there limits were placed on non-democratic views. However, beyond this rather obvious, even banal, point, there is a more interesting and highly important question to do with the ways in which dissent, however defined, is treated. A curve of sorts may be identified here. If dissent is treated relatively leniently, it may in some ways actually represent a stabilizing factor for the regime, in that discontent which can be expressed can be to some extent defused. If on the other hand it is treated more harshly, it may either be provoked and politicized into active anti-system opposition – which is obviously potentially much more of a problem for regime stability – or it may, if the state is sufficiently draconian, be effectively repressed. There are interesting and subtle dialectics in the oscillations between supportive dissent and destabilizing opposition. The point to be made here is simply this: different state definitions and treatments of dissent, and different political structures, produced notably different patterns of dissent and opposition in the two Germanies, as we have seen in Chapter Ten above. These differences cannot be held to be the result of the inheritance of particular forms of political culture or of different patterns of socialization. The implications of dissent and opposition depend also – crucially – on a wider international context and on the vulnerability of the regime at any particular time, as we shall see in the next chapter.

What about more diffuse modes of orientation towards political activity in general? According to one very widespread and undifferentiated view, 'the Germans' have traditionally been held to have a tendency towards authoritarianism and political conformity: obedience to authority, and lack of civil courage or a sense of democracy. When such a view is predicated on a notion of an enduring 'national character', it is clearly untenable; but some quite sophisticated writers have adopted variants which are initially more appealing. Certain authors perceived a continuity of authoritarian tendencies as a legacy of the Nazi era: Christa Wolf, for instance, suggested that the Nazi heritage for the psyche in East Germany needed to be brought to greater awareness. However, against even the more sensitive of such approaches, it may be argued that tendencies towards conformity were actively fostered by contemporary organizational features of life in the GDR. To take the example of the education system: while the GDR system of 'comprehensive polytechnical education' was structurally far more egalitarian than the predominantly tripartite, hierarchical system in the Federal Republic, with a greater (although by no means complete) equality of opportunity with respect to social background, political conformity was nevertheless as much a prerequisite here for career advancement as was academic proficiency. Moreover, the mode of teaching discouraged independent thought and critical argument, in favour of the exegesis of sacred texts and received viewpoints. Conversely, despite the more hierarchical structure of the West German education system, there was, particularly following the criticisms of the 1960s and the educational reforms of the 1970s, a tendency to attempt to encourage more democratic debate and independent thinking, at least for the privileged minority who were in a position to benefit from it.

Comparable comments could be made about the question of individualism versus collective identities and solidarity. This is a rather complex area, covering a number of fields, but a few remarks may be made about certain avenues worthy of exploration.

It was suggested above that the collective mentalities of the subcultural milieux of Imperial Germany, which continued in changed forms in the Weimar Republic, were to some considerable extent broken down in the Third Reich. In the occupation period, the western occupying powers in particular found it difficult to reintroduce collective notions associated with trade unionism, particularly among younger Germans with no direct experience of independent trade unions. There were similar difficulties for the inculcation of the principle that political parties represent sectional, rather than general, interests, sections which could amicably agree to differ. It is clear that over the decades a new balance of individualism and collectivism, associated with new organizational forms, developed in West Germany. The balance developed rather differently in the East. Most of an East German's working life and organized leisure time fostered a sense of being part of a collective: the work brigades, the work branch of the SED or FDGB, the women's organization, or youth or sporting organization. There is also some evidence that even conscious party attempts to introduce a form of individualist work ethic in East German enterprises were not entirely successful. Despite the assertion of the GDR specialist P.C. Ludz that a career-oriented achievement society was developing in the 1960s, there is evidence to suggest that one of the problems involved in the introduction of the New Economic System at that time was the failure of profit incentives at the individual level. The evidence of East Germans who came to live in the West corroborates the view that they had difficulties learning to act independently, and had become used to collective forms of organization. Many East Germans also took a more total view of society than did West Germans, seeing more clearly the drawbacks of a market economy in combining unemployment and poverty for some with affluence for others, whereas West Germans took a more individualist view of merit and mobility.

Let us turn finally to some aspects of the changing group bases of political culture. There are many possible relevant aspects, including such topics as the importance of regionalism; here, we shall consider only two: class and religion.

There was a radical divergence in the class structure of the two Germanies in a variety of respects, as we have seen above. In relation to East German political culture, of key importance was the early abolition of the old Prussian Junker class, with the Soviet land reform of 1945, and of capitalist industrialists and financiers. While differences of status and privilege were still noticeable in East Germany – based usually on political criteria – one consequence of a general levelling of class structure was the development of what has been classified as a predominantly petty-bourgeois (*kleinbürgerlich*) class culture. (As Gaus calls it, the 'society of the small man'.) The class structure of West Germany changed in rather different ways. Despite the assertions of some western analysts that West Germany was developing a more classless society than Britain (with accents continuing to reflect region rather than class) great social and class-cultural differences could still be observed in the Federal Republic. These differences frequently overrode generational divisions – and generation has been a very strong factor in the differentiation of German political cultures. Among the young, for example, the under-educated, unskilled, and under-employed disproportionately favoured right-wing extremism, while the better-educated tended to hold left-wing radical political views. West German differences in class culture were complicated further by still important regional differences: for instance, right-wing Catholic rural Bavaria was a very different sort of place from industrial North-Rhine–Westphalia or from liberal Protestant urban Hamburg, for all the much-vaunted homogenization of German society. Regional differentiation in East Germany was less marked, perhaps as a result of its smaller size, previous relative homogeneity (predominantly Protestant, for example), and, most importantly, its more centralized political system.

Certain relevant points about the political culture of East German Protestantism have been made above, in connection with the discussion of dissent. German Lutheranism has frequently been declared a major culprit in preparing the path to Hitler, with fingers pointed at the doctrine of obedience to secular authority. The experience of the churches in the Third Reich, from complicity and compliance to courageous opposition, indicates the greater complexity of Christian responses to politics. The political orientation of churches and congregations diverged quite considerably in the two Germanies, largely as a result of the different political locations of religious institutions in the two states. While in West Germany churches as *organizations* still had considerable influence and important formal roles in decision-making processes, there was a noticeable decline in the salience of religious frameworks for individual political orientations, evidenced for example in the decreasing correlations between religion and party preferences. In East Germany a reverse process took place. With the heightened political importance of at least the Protestant Church as a relatively independent institution and discussion partner with the state, as well as increasing space for open discussion, Christianity achieved a new importance for many members of the population. It provided a location for the development of new political views and modes of behaviour, and a variegated set of dissenting political cultures. This salience derived from the structural position of the church in the East

German political system, and not solely from any intrinsic aspects of Protestantism as a belief system.

German national identities and political cultures: conclusions

The discussion in this chapter has focused less on the consequences of different types of political culture – on which the emphasis in much historical and political science writing is placed – but rather on the structural determinants and bases of political orientation. There is undoubtedly an interplay between different levels, with the state responding to particular pressures as well as shaping popular perceptions and patterns of action. However, certain general arguments can be put forward here in relation to the material presented above.

First, a simple materialist view – as characterized some of the GDR's early policies and aspirations – must be qualified. Altering the ownership of the means of production does not produce a changed class-consciousness automatically. In a sense, Max Weber is vindicated over Karl Marx, in the emphasis he laid on the issue of the bureaucratization and growth of the state in would-be socialist societies. Secondly, however, a simple idealist view – which curiously was also present in Ulbricht's GDR, and which forms part of the ambiguity of political Marxism – must also be discounted. The official story about a society's place in history does not of itself greatly affect people's political orientations. Thirdly, a focus on an inherited 'national character' or – more 'scientifically' – on the presumed existence of a 'national political culture' as an 'independent variable' transmitted across generations by some process of socialization must also be subject to qualification.

Rather, the view may be proposed that political cultures represent modes of adapting to diverse aspects of current experience refracted through perceptions and frameworks which are to some degree inherited. It is not only a question of what sort of work is done, but also of how workers are organized, how they relate to work-processes, to decision-making processes, to managers and employers; it is not only a question of what a particular religious ideology potentially entails, but also of what forms of religious organization are present, and of the structural relationships between the latter and the state; it is not only a question of (debatable) biologically determined differences between the sexes, but also of social policies and environmental circumstances affecting gender roles in different forms of society. This list could be elaborated at length, but perhaps enough has been said to demonstrate that, however similar given patterns of political culture may look to their predecessors, their similarity – and survival – has been to a large extent determined by the existence of certain structural arrangements which foster precisely these patterns and not others. So, for example, what appeared to many observers to be a curiously 'traditional' pattern of political culture in the GDR (retreatism, authoritarianism, a widespread lack of democratic notions) was actually produced or shaped by authoritarian features of the SED regime, rather than simply inherited from a rather differently authoritarian past. It must of course be added that this structural conditioning does not mean that actual political cultures are necessarily those desired by political elites: modes of adaptation may be quite subversive, and, despite certain elite theories of history, elites have by and large proved to be notoriously bad at social engineering.

Can one in fact speak at all of national political cultures? In loose parlance, both scholars and others frequently do – particularly when the concept is used as an independent causal factor. However, I would suggest that the answer must in fact be in the negative: there are too many subcultural variations with different bases. What one can attempt to describe is a rather more complex picture of combinations of salient subgroups and varieties of political orientation which make up a rather more differentiated national profile. These profiles do not exactly redescribe social or political structure, since there are mediations of response and cross-cutting foci of identification. We must finally ask about the relationships between such patterns of political culture and changing conceptions and official promotions of national identity.

It is clear that there are no simple and straightforward relationships between changing official conceptions of national identity and changing patterns of political culture. More importantly, perhaps, the amount of energy devoted by political elites to promoting particular versions of national identity may be partly misplaced. Arguably, individuals respond more to particular pressures and constraints in their daily lives, which produce particular modes of behaviour and political attitude, than they do to more ethereal conceptions concerning their society's place in the long sweep of historical development.

Thus, the quest for national identity, while intrinsically fascinating, may be a search not only for something which is perpetually shifting and never to be identified with finality – artefact as it is of contemporary politics – but also for something which does not, in the end, have the importance ascribed to it in relation to national political cultures. The two simply do not neatly correspond.

In any event, the degree to which the two Germanies had diverged became, in the autumn of 1989, what is conventionally known as an 'academic question'. For within a few months, a revolutionary process erupted and snowballed, such that by the beginning of 1990 the division of Germany – and the very existence of *two* Germanies – was for the first time in four decades seriously under question. To many observers, as the revolutions broke out across Eastern Europe, and the Iron Curtain was pulled down, the post-war era appeared to be coming to an end. It is to this radical transformation that we now turn.

THIRTEEN

The East German Revolution and the End of the Post-war Era

In 1989, Eastern Europe was shaken by a series of revolutions, starting in Poland and Hungary, spreading to the GDR and then Czechoslovakia, ultimately even toppling the Romanian communist regime, and heralding the end of the post-war settlement of European and world affairs. Central to the ending of the post-war era were events in Germany. The East German revolution of 1989 inaugurated a process which only a few months earlier would have seemed quite unimaginable: the dismantling of the Iron Curtain between the two Germanies, the destruction of the Berlin Wall, the unification of the two Germanies. How did such dramatic changes come about, and what explains the unique pattern of developments?

To start with, it is worth reconsidering certain features of East Germany's history up until the 1980s. The uprising of 1953 was the only previous moment of serious political unrest in the GDR. It was, as we have seen above, limited in its origins and initial aims – arising out of a protest by workers against a rise in work norms – and only developed into a wider phenomenon, with political demands for the toppling of Ulbricht and reunification with West Germany, as the protests gained momentum. Lacking in leadership, lacking in support from the West, and ultimately repressed by a display of Soviet force, the 1953 uprising was a short-lived phenomenon. From the suppression of the 1953 revolt until the mid-1980s, the GDR was a relatively stable communist state, which gained the reputation of being Moscow's loyal ally, communism effected with Prussian efficiency.

The factors explaining the relative stability of the GDR over thirty-five years or so have been discussed in more detail in preceding chapters. These factors, in new ways, turn out to be important in examining what changed in the mid to later 1980s, and in explaining the background to and nature of the more successful revolutionary upheavals of the autumn of 1989. Three main aspects are of importance.

In the first place, the GDR – unlike its close neighbours, Poland and Czechoslovakia – possessed relatively cohesive elites. On the one hand, the SED, from the purges of the 1950s (1953–4, 1956, 1958) until the generational and other changes of the later 1980s, was a monolithic, well-disciplined party. It did not, to the outside world at least, provide evidence of splits within its midst. This stands in some contrast to the existence of a reform communist wing under the leadership of Alexander Dubček in Czechoslovakia in 1968, giving rise to the Prague Spring – and its repression by Soviet and Warsaw Pact tanks. It also stands in some contrast to the disarray evident within Polish Communism in the late 1970s and early 1980s, which resulted in an ineffectual response to the challenge of the Solidarity movement in 1980–1 and the introduction of military rule under General Jaruzelski (domestic military power, in this case, taking the place of the threat or actuality of Soviet invasion). On the other hand, the SED was in addition not challenged by any serious alliance of potential 'counter-elites'. There was no split with or within the army; nor did the East German technical and cultural intelligentsias even begin to form a potential serious opposition, in the ways that at times they appeared to do in Czechoslovakia. Co-opted, subordinated, politically fragmented, easily exiled or allowed to leave for West Germany – an identical language community, with automatic rights of citizenship – potential counter-elites never developed a serious political momentum in East Germany which could have placed the power and legitimacy of the ruling communist party in question.

This is related to the second factor of importance: the incorporation or isolation and defusing of dissent, over a relatively long period of time. During the 1960s and 1970s, intellectual dissenters remained relatively isolated figures, unable to command a mass following in the GDR. Whether isolated by house arrest – as with Havemann – or by involuntary or voluntary exile to West Germany – Biermann, Bahro – such dissidents failed to gain wide followings in their own country. Many prominent semi-critical writers chose to publish in West Germany, and often – particularly in the later 1970s and early 1980s – actually to leave for West Germany. The ease of publication in, and even emigration to, the west, took away some of the impetus for the development of a kind of samizdat network of underground publication and oppositional organization evident in, for example, Czechoslovakia.

Thirdly, such intellectual dissent as there was – and it should not be underplayed simply because of the distinctive features described above – in part failed to gain a mass following because of the relative lack of serious material discontent in East Germany for much of its history. After the lesson of 1953, the regime made good use of the tactic of consumer concessions to buy off the possibility of mass political unrest. Under Honecker in particular, serious efforts were put into improvements in housing, social policy, the standard of living, the availability of consumer goods, while at the same time there were cultural clamp-downs and reversals of early promises of intellectual liberalization. It should not be suggested that such policies were of a purely cynical, 'bread and circuses' nature: there were very real and genuine attempts to improve the conditions of life of East German citizens, reinforcing the obvious political considerations. What is at issue here, however, is not so much the motives behind such policies, or the causes of the relative (in East European terms) success of the East German economy, as the consequences of East German economic performance. While East Germans of course did not enjoy the standard of living of West Germans, there was nevertheless none of the deprivation which caused food riots in neighbouring Poland. East Germans could disdain the inefficiency of the Poles (thus building on a long established tradition of disdain for their eastern neighbours), and take a modest pride in the way their own economy at least functioned without undue disruption, whatever their grumbles about its shortcomings. In Poland, part of the power of the Solidarity movement of 1980–1 derived from the coalescence of intellectual and material discontents – which had previously erupted separately in post-war Polish history. In East Germany, the two sides failed to come together – until that fragile moment of revolutionary unity in September and October of 1989.

What changed in the 1980s, to alter this picture of stable reproduction of the East German regime? Two separate, but eventually interrelating factors are important in explaining the more immediate background to the revolution of 1989. First, the role of the church since 1978 is important. The – unequal – partnership between church and state represented an inherently unstable and dynamic compromise, with potential benefits for both sides, but also potential risks. For perhaps five or six years – until around 1984 – the experiment appeared to work, from the point of view of the state. Within the officially sanctioned autonomous space of the church, dissenting views could be voiced; but dissenting actions would also be contained, within acceptable bounds, by church leaders who did not want to jeopardize their position *vis-à-vis* the state (as, for example, in the calling off of the 'Swords-into-ploughshares' campaigns of the unofficial peace initiative). But the fostering of a muted dissent under the wing of the church spread beyond the bounds which the church could control. More specialized groups developed, focusing on issues pertaining to human rights and the environment, in addition to peace initiatives, which could no longer so easily be contained by the church.

This proliferation of dissent coincided with, and was to a degree fuelled by, a quite separate factor of major, indeed decisive, importance. In March 1985, Mikhail Gorbachev became leader of the Soviet Union. Inheriting an ailing economy burdened by high defence spending, a world role it could no longer sustain, and political troubles at home, Gorbachev embarked on a radically new course in the Soviet Union, characterized by his slogans of *perestroika* and *glasnost*. Not only did he introduce measures for economic restructuring and increased political openness at home; Gorbachev's reforms, crucially, fostered expectation of change among other eastern European states in addition. This had particular implications in the GDR. Honecker and the top leadership of the SED were by the later 1980s elderly men, and a succession question was in any event in the air. Given the resistance of the East German old guard to Gorbachev's reforms – dismissed as the equivalent of putting up new wallpaper, a simple matter of redecoration which was unnecessary in the GDR – the leadership question inevitably began to entail discussion of whether an East German Gorbachev might be waiting in the wings. The recognized crown prince – insofar as there was one – was a known hardliner, Egon Krenz; but *aficionados* started to mention the name of the relatively unknown moderate, the Dresden party chief Hans Modrow, who was not even a member of the Politburo. Such discussions about a potential alternative future aided a process of what might be called political variegation in the SED. Differences began to emerge more clearly, between regional and local leaderships on the one hand, and the hardline central leadership on the other, and between hardline functionaries and reform-minded pro-Gorbachev communists. This change in the SED revealed a wider range of political principles, aims and strategies than had been seen since the late 1950s, and was to play an important role in the development of events in the autumn of 1989.[1]

What triggered the actual revolution itself? The answer has to do, not so much with dissent or destabilization inside the GDR, as with radical transformations in the external context. These external changes were sufficiently momentous to generate a crisis of authority within the GDR, which could then in turn be exploited by internal dissenters.

Gorbachev's reforms in the Soviet Union were viewed with interest in other communist states. Not only was a climate of reform fostered in other countries; there was also a further, and crucial, element in the new Soviet approach. This was the renunciation of the so-called Brezhnev Doctrine of legitimate interference in the affairs of other states – which had facilitated the military suppression of the Prague Spring in 1968 – and its replacement by what Soviet spokesman Gennady Gerasimov so disarmingly called, in a press conference in the autumn of 1989, the 'Sinatra Doctrine' of 'letting them do it their way'. In this context, in the spring and summer of 1989 the communist regimes in Poland and Hungary underwent radical transformation, inaugurating the whole process of revolutionary change in eastern Europe.

After a decade of dealing with economic difficulty and political unrest, the Polish government collapsed, and on 16 August 1989 was replaced by a Solidarity-led coalition. In Hungary, processes of self-transformation were initiated by the Communist party, and preparations made for a transition to a multi-party democracy in a state which had in any case long experimented with elements of a market economy and a more open approach to the West. It was the changes in Hungary which were to prove the proximate cause of the East German revolution. From May 1989, Hungary began to dismantle the fortified border with Austria which constituted its part of the Iron Curtain. In the summer of 1989, it became increasingly easy to cross from East to West, over the Austro-Hungarian border.

In August 1989, around 220,000 East German holiday-makers were spending their summer holidays in Hungary, which was a popular tourist destination among the rather restricted choices available to GDR citizens. For some, the easing of border restrictions proved an irresistible attraction. As some were successful in their dash to liberty, others decided to follow. Soon camps filled up close to the border, as people congregated in the hope and expectation of seizing the opportunity to flee. At first it remained a risky business, but as more and more were able to pass – despite their East German passports having no valid visa for travel to the west – more and more began to attempt the exodus. Abandoning homes and possessions, jobs, relatives and friends, East Germans fled in increasing numbers across the ever more permeable border to Austria, taking only what possessions they could carry. On 10 September, the Hungarian foreign minister made a decision in principle, with fundamental implications in practice: Hungary's western border would be opened, East Germans would be free to pass as they pleased, and Hungary would no longer officially recognize or sustain the travel restrictions imposed by its fellow communist state, the German Democratic Republic.

The stream of emigrants had been turning into something of

a flood. With aid from the Red Cross, reception camps in the west were set up to give shelter and food to the swelling numbers of refugees. At first, the West German reception was ecstatic. Crowds welcomed the East German arrivals, with balloons and placards and an excited party atmosphere. Even in the cramped and less than comfortable conditions of the refugee camps, East Germans were overwhelmed with gifts of clothes and toys for the children, and offers of employment from predatory West German employers. At the same time, other East Germans – watching such scenes nightly on the West German news programmes on their televisions, at home in East Germany – took the decision to attempt an escape to the West also, while the going appeared to be good. Alternative routes were tried: many flung themselves into the West German embassies in Prague and Warsaw. As these became full to overflowing, with makeshift tent cities sprouting in the elegant grounds of the embassy buildings, negotiations between the affected governments failed to find a means to deal with the escalating crisis. For East Germans at home, added to the scenes of East Germans driving over the Austro-Hungarian border were new scenes of train-loads of East Germans being escorted from the embassies and embarking on a different route to freedom in the West.

The East German leadership proved singularly ineffective in dealing with the refugee crisis, which gave the lie to its claims to legitimacy and challenged the very existence of the regime. (The joke was current in the summer of 1989 that the reunification of the Germans was taking place, but on West German soil.) Erich Honecker, now aged seventy-seven and in poor health, was absent from the political stage for much of the summer following a gall-bladder operation. Others failed to take decisive action in his place. In such a situation of crisis, the way was opened for a challenge from within.

The 'gentle revolution', 26 August–9 November 1989

The period from late August until the opening of the Berlin Wall on 9 November 1989 constituted a distinctive phase in the East German revolution. While its closing date – 9 November – very clearly forms a turning point in German history, the choice of starting date is slightly more arbitrary. Opposition had been building up, with further demonstrations on the Luxemburg–Liebknecht anniversary on 15 January 1989, demanding freedom of expression and organization, and freedom of the press, and resulting in around eighty arrests; there had also been protests against alleged falsification of the results of local elections in May. But the period from late August was distinctively, qualitatively and quantitatively, different. There were three partially overlapping aspects and phases within this period of 'gentle revolution' (taken from the German phrase *sanfte Revolution*). First there was the rise of organized opposition groups, with features marking them as having taken a step beyond earlier forces of opposition, and with increasing support among the population. Secondly, there was the development of new regime policies and tactics, eventuating in the renunciation of the use of force in order to repress the revolution, and the adoption instead of a strategy of attempted 'reform from above'. Thirdly, and following from this, there were the changes in leadership, and the series of dramatic developments which culminated in the breaching of the Berlin Wall on the night of 9 November. This amounted to an opening of the floodgates; and what followed – after the initial euphoria of the long weekend from 10–12 November – amounted to a marked deflection from this early phase of revolution.

At a human rights seminar on 25–6 August, a small group of participants decided, in the words of Ibrahim Böhme, that the situation was so serious ('im Moment das Haus in einer solchen Art und Weise brennt') that it was necessary to rise above general complaints and to attempt instead to organize to change the situation, 'without unnecessary and irresponsible confrontation'.[2] As a result, the Initiative for a Social-Democratic Organization was born, which was later to turn into the official founding (on the significant date of 7 October, the GDR's fortieth anniversary) of an East German SPD. Another important early organization, which was to play a major role in the early phase of revolution, was the New Forum. This was founded on 11 September, after a meeting in the house of Havemann's widow, by a group of people including Bärbel Bohley and Jens Reich. New Forum was intended to represent, not a party with a specific programme or platform for reform, but rather a forum for open and free discussion. It was called *New* Forum to indicate that it was intended to supplement the only existing autonomous forum for discussion, the Church, and was to provide a space for debate for non-Christians outside the Church. On 19 September it requested legalization; this was refused on 21 September; the founders then initiated a major campaign for mass pressure for legalization. While New Forum was the most important initiative for democratization, a number of other groups were also founded at this time: these included the List 2 of environmentalists, Democratic Awakening, Democracy Now, and the Left Platform.

The establishment of these groups marked a new departure in the history of East German dissent. They were no longer content with informal networks of organization under the broad shelter of the Church; rather, they now sought to develop their own nationwide organization. Moreover, they also sought recognition as legally accepted autonomous institutions, in the same way as the Church had been recognized since 1978. At the same time, their defined aims and sphere of interest widened. No longer were they solely concerned specifically with peace, human rights and environmentalism; they now sought also to consider the whole range of policies and problems associated with taking over and dramatically reforming – and then running – a state. Issues considered now included problems of economic policy and reform, and the means of introducing the rule of law in a *Rechtsstaat.* For the first time, dissenting groups conceived the possibility of constituting part of a potential alternative government, which would have to deal with the nitty-gritty of running the country, challenging the previously essentially unquestioned power and future of the ruling SED.[3]

The Churches too came out with demands for reform. From a number of quarters, voices were raised demanding that the regime examine the reasons *why* so many people were trying to flee the GDR, and suggesting that if the regime were to introduce reforms, perhaps East German citizens might be more willing to stay at home, rather than abandoning home and possessions for an uncertain future in the West. Increasing pressure was exerted on the regime to enter into dialogue, to deal with the real issues and bases of unrest, and to introduce some degree of democratization and liberalization, so that people would feel it was worthwhile to stay and work for change from within the GDR. A major centre of this activity was Leipzig. Following a regular Monday evening service in the Nikolaikirche, people would gather to form a procession, marching peacefully around Leipzig's Ringstrasse, demonstrating in favour of democratization. Home-made banners proclaimed such slogans as 'Reisfreiheit statt Massenflucht' ('freedom to travel instead of mass flight'). Consisting at first of a few thousand courageous individuals, demonstrations began to grow in size as people felt growing strength and solidarity – expressed in the simple slogan, 'Wir sind das Volk' ('We are the people'). In East Berlin, the Gethsemane Church became a centre for protest, with sermons on such apparently innocuous texts as Jesus' treatment of the Pharisees gaining intense current political significance, and with peaceful, candlelit vigils for reform. Some demonstrators embarked on fasts, remaining in the church for days without food; others came for short periods of time to discuss and show solidarity. In Halle, Plauen, Dresden and elsewhere, similar demonstrations for peaceful reform began to be organized.

Initially, it was uncertain how the authorities would respond. There were early signs of splits in the ruling bloc, with the LDPD newspaper *Der Morgen* printing speeches by the Liberals' leader Manfred Gerlach in favour of discussions about reform. While some local SED functionaries clearly wanted to adopt a more conciliatory tone, the official responses at first were repressive. Despite the non-violence of demonstrators, there were numerous arrests, and instances of police brutality. Would-be emigrants were dealt with very severely when trains carrying refugees from the Warsaw and Prague embassies passed through East Germany, and there was even the death of a man who lay on the railway tracks in an attempt to halt a trainload of refugees near Dresden to allow others to board. On 3 October the entire population of the GDR was put under virtual house arrest when visa-free travel to Czechoslovakia was banned. Honecker insisted on proceeding with the fortieth anniversary celebrations of the GDR on 7 October, more or less as planned – with the slight qualification that the East German people refused to participate in the self-congratulatory birthday party. Mass demonstrations were met with brutality and numerous arrests. Despite such repression, demonstrators maintained their non-violent stance: young women at the Gethsemane Church, for example, approached members of the militia with flowers, and invited policemen to change out of their uniforms and join them in demanding democratization. Children guarded the candles which were kept alive, symbolically, with the flames of hope for a peaceful revolution. Yet many who joined the protests were deeply afraid, and not without reason. Earlier in the year, the East German regime had officially congratulated the Chinese leadership on the brutal massacre of pro-democracy demonstrators in Peking's Tiananmen Square.

Mikhail Gorbachev came to the GDR, to stand by Honecker's side for the anniversary parades. But he took the opportunity to advise the East German leadership that some willingness to reform was in order – and that it might be time for Honecker, given his age and ill-health, to make way for a more effective leader given the current crisis. These hints were to have dramatic consequences in the next ten days.

An important turning-point in regime responses to the growing crisis came on 9 October. The usual Monday night service in Leipzig's Nikolaikirche and the subsequent demonstration were planned amid growing rumours that there would be a terrible crack-down and brutal suppression along the lines of the Tiananmen Square massacre. A huge, visible presence of police, militia, *Stasi* and works-combat troops gave considerable weight to these rumours. The procession nevertheless set off as planned, leaving the church as usual at about 6 p.m.

Somewhere between 7 and 8 p.m., a curious event – or rather non-event – happened. The *Stasi*, police and armed forces simply melted away. The traffic police aided the procession by halting the traffic to allow it to pass safely. The demonstration was able to conclude peacefully. The authorities appeared to have condoned the protest and refrained from the use of repression as a strategy for dealing with the rising tide of revolution.

But which authorities? What determined this turning-point, this apparent recognition of the legitimacy of protest, this acquiescence in the right to demonstrate? Later, Honecker's short-lived successor, Egon Krenz, was to claim some recognition for his own role on this occasion. But it appears that the initiative for dialogue rather than force came from three local SED functionaries in association with the conductor of the Leipzig Gewandhaus Orchestra, Kurt Masur. In the afternoon they issued a statement in favour of discussion and dialogue about the need for reforms; lacking in authority to call off the troops and police presence themselves, their approach was finally confirmed and given official backing by a telephone call from Krenz, then in charge of security affairs at the national level, at around 7.30 p.m.

This pattern began to be repeated elsewhere: some SED local leaders were, to use the German expression, more *Reformfreudig* ('enthusiastic about reforms') than others. The peaceful outcome of the 9 October demonstration gave courage to more and more people. Numbers demonstrating doubled and doubled again: in Leipzig, from a few thousands in September, to over 100,000 on 16 October, and more than a quarter of a million the following week; and increasing numbers taking to the streets in a peaceful fashion in other towns across the GDR. Support for New Forum also grew, with around twenty-six thousand signatories of the New Forum founding petition acquired by mid-October.

This turning-point inaugurated the third stage in the first, gentle, phase of the East German revolution. The official response was to institute limited reforms from above. On 18 October, at a Politburo meeting where he failed to defend his handling of the crisis, Erich Honecker resigned and was replaced by Krenz, who lost little time in attempting to establish a new reputation as a reformer. Official discussions took place, first with church leaders (planned already by Honecker), and then on 26 October between leaders of the SED and the New Forum. By this time, New Forum had collected more than

100,000 signatures, and clearly constituted a significant force in the land. The meeting resulted in the first authorization in advance of a mass demonstration, to take place in East Berlin on 4 November. There were also local meetings between party officials and reformers in different towns, including Rostock and Dresden. The SED, formerly so uniform and disciplined in its policies, began to respond in diverse ways in different areas, with some local leaders more inclined to enter into dialogue than others. There were increasingly explicit debates about the sort of line the party should take. Splits became more evident at the national level too: fifty-two members of the *Volkskammer* refused to vote for Krenz as head of state, with members of the LDPD prominent among those abstaining or voting against.

The media began to report more accurately what was occurring, and GDR citizens began to read their own newspapers and watch their own television channels with a new interest and even amazement. On 27 October, it was announced that the ban on visa-free travel to Czechoslovakia, imposed on 3 October, would be lifted, and that there would be an amnesty for all those who had been convicted of trying to escape to the West, or who had succeeded in leaving. The line changed from 'weeping no tears' for those who had left to welcoming them back if they wanted to return. But demonstrators did not relax their pressure for further concessions: on Monday 30 October, around half a million people took to the streets in Leipzig, and there were mass demonstrations elsewhere, including, for example, around eighty thousand people on the streets of the moderately small Mecklenburg town of Schwerin. The priorities of the demonstrators began to switch, from the demand for freedom to travel to the demand for free elections, legalization of New Forum, and the disbanding of the *Stasi*.

Krenz made a trip to Moscow at the beginning of November, and returned, after a sort of Road to Damascus, via discussions with Solidarity leaders in Poland, as a supposedly convinced reformer. The first nine days of November saw the culmination of the early phase of revolution. A breathtaking set of reforms were announced, including: the right to travel in the West – although only for a maximum of thirty days in a year, with no guarantee of either a visa or sufficient foreign currency; the establishment of a constitutional court; and the prospect of democratic elections – but no renunciation of the leading role of the SED. Heads began to roll at the top: prominent figures to resign or be sacked included Margot Honecker, Minister of Education and estranged wife of Erich Honecker; Harry Tisch, leader of the FDGB; the leaders of the CDU and NDPD; and certain district SED and trade-union leaders. These were followed by more sweeping purges of the Politburo, removing key members of Honecker's old guard, including Erich Mielke, at eighty-one still in charge of the state security police, and Kurt Hager, at seventy-seven in charge of ideology. Finally, on 7 November the entire East German government resigned, and on 8 November the Politburo – which had been pruned of five more of its members the previous day – resigned *en bloc*. The new, smaller, Politburo was roughly split between hardliners and moderate reformers. The relatively liberal Hans Modrow, party chief in Dresden, who was to play a leading role in the next phase as the country's new Prime Minister, entered the Politburo for the first time. It was announced that there would be a new electoral law, allowing all political forces to compete – and it was acknowledged that this might entail a loss of power for the SED. New Forum was legalized. Meanwhile, the constitutional and legal committee of the *Volkskammer* had refused to ratify the proposed new travel laws, and it had been announced that the refugees in the Prague embassy were free to leave.

The pressure of mass demonstrations was maintained. On 4 November, between half a million and one million people came out onto the streets of Berlin, and gathered to hear speeches made by prominent intellectuals including such figures as Christa Wolf. In Leipzig, on Monday 6 November, around half a million people took to the streets. In the mean time, the mass exodus from the GDR continued unabated; the flood even increased. In particular, East Germans, who now no longer needed a visa to travel to Czechoslovakia, also no longer needed a certificate renouncing GDR citizenship to travel to West Germany over the Czech border; so they could, in effect, simply circumvent the Berlin Wall by making a short detour via Czechoslovakia. East

Germans started pouring out by this route at a rate of about 9000 a day, an average of 375 an hour. It was clear that the Berlin Wall was effectively redundant.

On 9 November 1989 – seventy-one years to the day since the collapse of Imperial Germany – an event of momentous significance occurred, signalling in effect the collapse of the East German communist regime. Towards the end of a late-afternoon press conference, Politburo member and government spokesman Günter Schabowski was asked what the implications of the new freedom to travel were for the status of the Berlin Wall. He responded, wearily, that the Wall would continue to have some sort of function, but of course not the same as before. The effects of this laconic response were electric. Journalists buzzed, rumours flew, huge crowds rapidly massed – on both sides of the Wall; and, on the night of 9–10 November, Berlin celebrated a huge, euphoric party of reunification, with people jumping up onto the Wall, opening bottles of champagne, dancing in the streets, embracing each other, and East German border guards – actually looking human – ceased even attempting any control of visas or stamping of travel documents as people thronged from East to West, West to East, and back again, in their thousands. The following weekend was one of continued euphoria, as millions of East Germans took the opportunity to cross the now permeable borders to the previously forbidden land of plenty, the West, to satisfy their curiosity – and return home again. Roads were clogged, traffic jams built up for miles, as choking and spluttering Wartburgs and Trabants made the journey of a lifetime. The experiment of tearing down the Iron Curtain, in the hope that people would go, look, and return to their home in the GDR, had begun. But the consequences of this dramatic development were ultimately to deflect the whole course of the East German revolution.

The opening of the floodgates and the deflected revolution

At first, the desire, pent-up for decades, to experience at first hand the glittering materialism of western consumer society was given expression. The visual contrast between the East Germans – in their ubiquitous jeans, black leather or denim jackets and third-rate cars – and their affluent West German relatives was marked. After the initial euphoria, West Germans, and particularly West Berliners, began to resent the crowds, the queues for public transport, the traffic jams in border areas, the overcrowding of shops with people who had come largely only to look, with no more western currency than the West German official 'welcome money' of 100 DM, sufficient to buy little more than a bag of oranges and some small treats for the children. More ominously, the opening of the Wall had destabilizing effects for both the West and East German regimes. Far from the calculated gamble coming off – with freedom to travel ensuring the survival of a separate, distinctive democratic socialist GDR – the opening of the floodgates served to subvert and deflect the ideas and aims of both regime supporters and the intellectual opposition in the GDR. The result was a stampede westwards to which there could be only one solution: unification.

It was true that the vast majority of East Germans who rushed to satisfy their curiosity about the West did return, in their spluttering Wartburgs and Trabants, in their hundreds and thousands. But through December, January and February the stream of those seeking permanent residence in the West continued at a rate averaging over two thousand a day, amounting to an estimated total of little under one million people a year seeking to resettle in West Germany. This not only rendered East Germany's already fragile economy increasingly prone to collapse; it also put intolerable strains on West Germany's housing resources and social welfare system, as well as adding heavily to an already worrying unemployment rate. Apart from the obvious social problems entailed in having to house large numbers of people very rapidly, and the longer-term strains that increased demands on welfare benefit payments would put on the taxation system, there were serious immediate political implications in West Germany.

Already in 1989 the right-wing Republican Party had been gaining political ground and exploiting resentment against immigrant populations (mainly *Gastarbeiter*), with considerable success in Berlin, Frankfurt, and parts of Bavaria. Now it was feared that right-wing extremist forces would reap a rich harvest from the social resentments incurred by the influx of East Germans. Attitudes began to change, from the ecstatic reception accorded the East German refugees in the summer of 1989 to a distinctly more reserved response to those East Germans – no longer strictly speaking 'refugees' – seeking to resettle in the West during the winter of 1989–90.

In East Germany, too, there was a change in political mood after the opening of the borders. The fragile sense of a distinctive East German national identity, symbolized in the slogan 'Wir sind das Volk', united in opposition to the communist regime, now proved to have been merely a fleeting phenomenon of the days of 'gentle revolution'. In late November and December 1989, new notes of discord were struck, and new perceptions were gained both of their own and the other Germany. Some East Germans, who had previously remained silent and were absent when demonstrating was still fraught with dangers, now began to speak out. Others simply changed their views, partly as a result of experiencing at first hand what western 'decadent' consumerism was really like, partly as a result of mounting disillusionment with the poverty and pollution of their own country, and of shock as scandals about luxury and corruption in high places broke out. Banners proclaiming 'Wir sind das Volk' were dramatically altered in meaning with the simple substitution of one word: 'Wir sind *ein* Volk'. Calls for democratization now gave way to calls for all-German unity.

In December 1989 and January 1990, the GDR began to crumble. The Communist Party gave up its claim to a monopoly on power at the beginning of December; Krenz was stripped of his offices as party leader and head of state. Although Gregor Gysi replaced Krenz as the leader of the SED, the balance of power now effectively shifted – for the first time in the GDR's history – to the government, led by Prime Minister Hans Modrow. Round-table talks began with leaders of the main opposition groups, the churches, and the increasingly independent coalition parties present. A number of former SED leaders (including Erich Honecker) and other prominent individuals were to undergo investigation and possible criminal proceedings for corruption. A breakdown in law and order threatened, with a rise in apparent neo-Nazi activity; much use was made of this by the government in an attempt to stall the disbanding of the *Stasi*. Revelations continued to appear, not only about the extent of corruption in high places, but also about the true state of the country's economy and environment. In January 1990 it was revealed that the GDR had huge foreign debts, of around £12.9 billion (a greater per capita indebtedness than that of Poland); and that at least £72 billion would be needed simply to clean up East Germany's energy and heat production. Better water and sewerage systems were also essential. Meanwhile, the continued exodus of East Germans was rapidly exacerbating the situation. Those workers who stayed attempted to exploit the labour shortage and capitulation of the authorities with demands for wage and benefit increases worth around £15 billion. The FDGB had long lost authority and new independent unions were being established. Strikes made labour productivity even lower, while a rapidly expanding black market (particularly in Berlin) further dislocated the East German economy. Local government began to disintegrate: many regional and town councils simply dissolved themselves, giving up the attempt to maintain a semblance of administrative efficiency. Many prominent individuals deeply compromised by their activities during Communist rule committed suicide; others succumbed to depression. The domestic mood was characterized by uncertainty and increasing fear for the future.

In such a context, the elections – first planned for 6 May, a date which opposition groups in the autumn had felt might even be too early for their fledgeling organizations – were brought forward to 18 March. When, on 28 November 1989 Chancellor Kohl of West Germany had announced his 'ten-point plan' for a new German confederation, to be achieved through a number of stages lasting several years, he had been denounced as being too hasty. The Soviet Union and the East German Prime Minister Hans Modrow at that time announced that 'reunification was not on the political agenda' (as did Britain's Mrs Thatcher); and East German opposition groups insisted that what they were seeking was not take-over by West German capitalism, but rather a new 'Third Way' of democratic socialism in a continuing GDR. By early February, however, the mood had changed dramatically. In the context of a disintegrating GDR, and a West Germany threatened and burdened by the strains of the opening of the Wall, there was clearly no alternative to an equalization of living conditions and an integration of the economies of the two Germanies – and this inevitably implied political unification. Both Gorbachev and Modrow came to accept German unification as necessary, as did all the major East German opposition groups. When on 6 February, Kohl proposed a monetary union as soon as possible after the March elections, the only dissenting voice was that of the cautious Karl-Otto Pöhl, head of West Germany's Bundesbank – who was soon brought into line, despite that institution's supposed constitutional independence. The question of the unification of the two Germanies increasingly narrowed from 'whether' to 'when and how'.

By early March 1990, the parameters of the question at least had been clarified. Unification of the two Germanies had major international implications, and was not purely a matter of domestic integration of two quite different economies and societies. As far as the major powers of the Second World War were concerned, the formula of 'Two plus Four' was agreed at a meeting of NATO and Warsaw Pact foreign ministers in Ottawa on 13 February 1990. After the East German elections, the (freely elected) governments of the two Germanies would meet to formulate their plans. There would then be a wider conference of the four former wartime Allies – USSR, USA, Britain and France – to approve these plans (and to relinquish their remaining rights in Berlin), plans which would finally be confirmed by a broader group of the nations involved in the Conference on Security and Co-operation in Europe (CSCE) later in the year. A major problem at the international level related to the issue of future security arrangements. While the western powers were intent on a united Germany remaining in NATO, with the possible concession that no NATO troops should be stationed on what was formerly East German soil, the Soviet position was that a united Germany should be neutral. The Warsaw Pact was in any case changing in nature (with the increasing independence of post-revolutionary Poland, Hungary and Czechoslovakia, and the withdrawal of Soviet troops from their territories), and it was clear that in a fundamentally changed world system there would need to be fundamental rethinking of European security arrangements. There were also more easily resolvable questions concerning the membership of what was East Germany, as part of a united Germany, in an enlarged European Community. In addition, for a while the unwillingness of Chancellor Kohl to confirm the inviolability of Poland's western border with Germany – which Kohl legalistically insisted on reserving as a matter for a future all-German government to determine – threatened to add historically resonant frictions and fears of territorial revisionism to the discussions of German unification.

At the domestic level, too, there were a number of serious questions about the manner and outcome of unification. These played a major role in the East German election campaign. By mid-February 1990, the number of 'parties' in the GDR had reached perhaps 160, although 'only' 24 were eventually to contend the elections. However, given the lack of experience and resources – down to the level of typewriters and functioning telephones – for most East German parties, the real issue became that of which East German political forces would gain the support of the major West German parties. In the event, the forces which had spearheaded the autumn revolution – in particular New Forum – were swamped and consigned to political oblivion by the entrance of the West German juggernauts. Kohl's CDU finally threw its not inconsiderable weight behind the centre-right 'Alliance for Germany'. This was made up of the Democratic Awakening (DA), the German Social Union (DSU), which had been founded as a sister party to the Bavarian CSU, and the old East German CDU, now supposedly free of any taint of its forty-year compromise with the Communist regime. The West German SPD supported the East German SPD, which was founded the previous autumn, and which had attempted to resist being infiltrated or flooded by former SED members. The SED itself had now adopted a new image, after two name changes, as the Party of Democratic Socialism (PDS). It received no western support. The West German Greens supported the East German Greens, who were in electoral alliance with a women's party. In addition, there were a number of small parties with no western support. The West German Republicans were very evident in the course of the election campaign, but a Republican party was forbidden to stand in the East German elections.

At first, opinion polls suggested a highly probable victory for the SPD. Fearing for its own future in a united Germany in which the SPD might have an in-built majority, the West German CDU began an energetic campaign to vilify the SPD as a communist party in disguise – conveniently overlooking the complicity of its own partner, the East German CDU, in the Communist regime. Savage CDU attacks on the SPD were somewhat overshadowed by a last-minute scandal, in which the leader of Democratic Awakening was revealed to have worked for the *Stasi* and had to resign and be replaced within a few days of the poll. In the event, however, the East German voters – faced, with the exception of the elderly, with their very first experience of genuinely free elections – voted less for parties as such than on the issue of the manner and speed of unification. Kohl, as Chancellor of West Germany, was clearly in a position to determine the amount of money East Germany would receive – which he had refused to give prior to free elections. He also supported the route of most rapid unification – or effective take-over by West Germany – under Article 23 of the West German Basic Law. This would allow reconstituted *Länder* in East Germany to apply to become part of an expanded West German federal state, with the West German constitution and laws continuing to apply. The SPD, on the other hand, preferred the potentially slower route implied by Article 146 of the Basic Law. This would mean the coming together of the two German governments to devise a new constitution for a new united Germany – in effect, there would be a genuine merger, with the possibility of safeguarding certain rights to social benefits enshrined in East German law. As the prospect of unification became ever more immediate, with West German entrepreneurs exploring the possibilities of acquiring East German enterprises, and West Germans with legal claims to expropriated properties in the East beginning to institute legal proceedings, many East Germans began to be more concerned about safeguarding certain fundamental elements of their existence, particularly in connection with low rents, guaranteed employment, and extensive provisions for child care.

In the event, the vote of 18 March 1990 was a decisive one in favour of rapid unification and the introduction of the West German Deutschmark under conservative auspices. The scale of the centre-right victory, with over forty-eight per cent of the vote, was decisive, even though a coalition would be required for putting through key constitutional changes. The masses, who for decades had suffered in passivity or retreated into their private niches of 'grumbling and making do', finally had their hour; and once again, the dissident intellectuals found themselves isolated. From the point of view of those who had led the peaceful revolution in the autumn, this was a deflection indeed from the vision of democratic socialism which had given them the courage, in the early days, to risk their lives on the streets. The 'Third Way', once again in German history, appeared in this moment of historical transformation to represent, not so much a 'missed opportunity' as an unattainable mirage. The logic of the capitalist economy – in an ironic vindication of the materialistic determination of history – appeared to be having the last word.

The end of a divided nation?

The months following the East German elections saw the detailed discussion of practical aspects of unification of the two Germanies, and the inauguration of radical processes of transformation in a number of areas.

Given continuing economic problems, an equalization of socio-economic conditions across East and West Germany was clearly essential. Currency union was effected on 1 July 1990, with the West German Deutschmark replacing the East German currency at the favourable exchange rate of one to one as far as wages and pensions were concerned (and variable rates for different levels of savings and different age-groups). Overnight, East German shops were stocked with a wide range of West German goods – but at West German prices, with subsidies removed from basic foodstuffs. Fearful of potential rising unemployment, a predictable consequence of the privatization of the economy, most East Germans at first seemed content to remain prudent, stare, and save their new hard currency reserves. Workers in some industries staged strikes in favour of West German wage levels to contend with West German prices. Those less well placed to negotiate, such as pensioners, expressed fears about their ability to pay hugely increased housing costs. There were even fears about whether some people would be entitled to stay in their homes at all, as former owners came from West Germany to stake a claim to property which had been confiscated or abandoned in an earlier period. Agreements were reached in principle over certain issues: the legal claims to ownership of West Germans whose property had been taken by the East German state after 1949 were to be recognized, but not those whose property had been expropriated by the Soviet military government in the period 1945–9. But clearly many individual cases would still be disputed in practice, with difficulties for all concerned. In any event the housing market was likely to change dramatically, as affluent West Germans would pour in to snap up cheap bargains which they had the wherewithal to renovate.

As far as the economy was concerned, a considerable period of dislocation and difficulty was likely to ensue, although the officially expressed hope was that the introduction of market forces into East Germany would eventually render a united Germany as affluent and productive as West Germany had been – and that the West German economy was in any event buoyant enough to carry and buffer the shocks of the transitional period, while its democracy was strong enough to withstand any social and political fall-out. EC partners were assured that the economic giant a united Germany would become eventually could only strengthen, not threaten, the economic well-being of other members of the European Community.

It seemed for some time that most difficulties would be experienced at the international level, over the issue of security arrangements. Faced with increasing political problems at home, Gorbachev's line on a united Germany's membership of NATO wavered between ambiguous and recalcitrant. Yet it was clear that the Warsaw Pact was no longer a cohesive body posing a serious military threat; and by 6 July 1990, a two-day NATO summit was able to issue the 'London Declaration' announcing a radical reconceptualization of its role and effectively declaring peace, as one newspaper headline put it, on the Warsaw Pact. Little over a week later, on 16 July after discussions in Moscow and the Caucasus between Chancellor Kohl and Mikhail Gorbachev, the latter was able to announce that he no longer objected to membership of a united Germany in NATO. Warsaw Pact troops would be withdrawn from the territory of East Germany in phases over a four-year period, and the new, post-unification domestic military force of a united Germany would be reduced from the number produced simply by combining existing East and West German troops. The way finally seemed open for the 'Two-plus-Four' process to work out the remaining problems concerning the external aspects of the unification of two Germanies, catching up with the rapid momentum on the domestic front and paving the way for final political unification. Although precise details of the reorganization of European affairs at the international level had yet to be worked out, with negotiated NATO troop reductions and an enhanced role for the Conference on Security and Co-operation in Europe (CSCE), it was clear that the Cold War had been officially pronounced to be over.

On the national political front, consensus began to be reached among most West and East German political parties that, given the effective economic union, a common political administration was desirable sooner rather than later. Plans were formulated for the official reconstitution of the former East German *Länder* in the autumn of 1990, allowing an orderly application for accession to the Federal Republic under Article 23 of the Basic Law. Yet in the course of the summer of 1990, as the details of the unification treaty were being hammered out between officials in Bonn and East Berlin, conditions in the GDR continued to deteriorate. Far from alleviating the economic problems, currency union seemed merely to have exacerbated East Germany's difficulties.

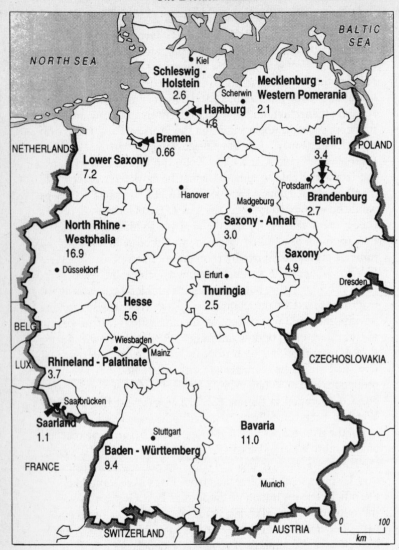

United Germany, 1990

Länder population figures in millions

West German investment failed to materialize on any significant scale; plans for massive privatization of state-owned companies had to be shelved; bankruptcies loomed, and many East Germans found themselves retaining their jobs only on conditions of 'nil hours short-time working'. Women who had relied on state child care facilities were forced to make new decisions about whether they would be able to continue going out to work. Many men and women had no choice at all: they were simply made redundant. Even the East German tourist trade collapsed, despite the West Germans' new-found interest in exploring a long-ignored part of their 'homeland'. After a brief foray, most found it preferable to make day trips from the comfort of West German tourist facilities close to the now-open border, while, with the change to western hard currency, the former flocks of Hungarian and Czechoslovakian visitors could no longer afford their customary fortnight on the Baltic coast.

In such circumstances, the negotiations over the terms of unification were conducted with all the initiative on the West German side. It was exceedingly difficult for East Germans to bargain over the retention of certain social rights when only rapid unification might avert total disaster. Certain issues – particularly the question of the right to abortion on demand in the first twelve weeks of pregnancy, available only to East German women – proved so contentious that they had to be shelved for ultimate resolution by a post-unification all-German parliament. In the East German parliament, tempers frayed, the coalition fell apart, and criticisms mounted of Prime Minister Lothar de Maizière's apparent role as Helmut Kohl's puppet. Finally, at the end of August, the vote was taken: unification was to take place on 3 October 1990, as soon as possible after the CSCE had formally given its approval, and even before the *Länder* elections scheduled for 14 October.

On 3 October 1990 the two Germanies 'celebrated' their unification. Solemn and sombre speeches were made by the key politicians and the President, as Germans entered a new stage of their history with full awareness both of the legacies of the past and the difficulties of the future. While the official ceremonies took place in the centre of Berlin, at the Brandenburg Gate and the Reichstag, demonstrations elsewhere were firmly dealt with by armed police. Less than a year after the fortieth anniversary celebrations of the GDR, the GDR was no more; but the formal unification of the two Germanies was effected in distinctly less euphoric mood than that accompanying the fall of the Berlin Wall only eleven months earlier.

Distinctions between '*Wessis*' (westerners) and '*Ossis*' (from the former GDR) became more vitriolic, as the latter felt they had been downgraded to second-class citizens. Social tensions contributed to a rise in racial tensions. Many Germans felt distinctly uneasy about the new nationalism, the rise in xenophobia and anti-'foreigner' sentiments (thus designated, even when the victims of racial hostility were German citizens). Many, too, felt uneasy about the new problems of 'overcoming the past' with respect, no longer to Nazism but to the GDR. On the one hand, there were serious problems connected with 'de-Stasification'. What roles had now prominent individuals perhaps played in the past? Who had been a *Stasi* collaborator? Which of one's friends could one no longer trust; who might have acted as an informer? What was held on file about oneself, whether true or untrue, and what implications might such information have for the future? What in any event would happen with the *Stasi* archives? On the other hand, there were fears of a witch-hunt including the ousting and professional destruction of the most harmless fellow-travellers of the GDR regime – a regime, it should be noted, which had far more humanitarian and egalitarian goals than its Nazi predecessor, whatever the distortions and repressions in practice. How was the education system to be transformed, and what was to be done in the sphere of the media? Along with the huge material costs of reconstructing the economy of the GDR, there were clearly going to be immense personal and human costs. For the time being, Chancellor Kohl sought to downplay potential problems and suppress anxieties; but the realities – and not only in tax bills and interest rates – would soon have to be faced.

Nevertheless, in the general election of December 1990 – the first all-German free elections since November 1932 – Helmut Kohl and the CDU received a resounding victory, a reward for seizing the initiative and powering the unification process subsequent to the collapse of the GDR. As the crisis in the Gulf, provoked by Iraq's invasion of Kuwait, began to divert attention away from the German and European stage, it rapidly become clear that the new, united, sovereign Germany would have to face up to many hard questions about its future role in a rapidly changing world.

Thus by the end of 1990, the 'post-war period' – the division of Europe, and the world, between the superpowers, which had been inaugurated by a Second World War launched from German soil – had finally come to an end. While the post-unification future in this moment of historical transformation remained open, the immediate past had very clearly been consigned to history. Let us turn, finally, to some wider reflections on the long sweep of German history from 1918 to 1990.

PART THREE

THE DIVIDED CENTURY

FOURTEEN

Tension and Transformation
in Twentieth-century Germany

Germany in the first half of the twentieth century was a country riven with crises: to avert civil war, it entered into world war; defeated in 1918, it was plunged into revolution and counter-revolution. The Weimar Republic was a period of barricades, street-fighting, and political violence, of instability and unresolved tensions. The crises of the late Weimar Republic were 'resolved' in the facade of the 'national community' of the Third Reich only insofar as the state, by appropriating to itself such a high degree of violence, could suppress its enemies at home and pursue foreign policies which were to culminate in a second World War and genocide. The period from the Second World War to 1990 was also not without its violence and its crises: pictures of the East German Uprising of June 1953, or the erection of the Berlin Wall in 1961, are remarkably reminiscent of pictures from earlier decades of Berlin streets filled with demonstrators, police and military vehicles, or of the throwing up of concrete walls and tangles of barbed wire, as in the sudden creation of the ghettos of Łódź and Warsaw in 1940. The techniques and aims of violence of course changed: the sophisticated apparatus of minefields and an electronically policed no man's land which formed the boundary of the German Democratic Republic, and the riot gear and battle-shields deployed by West German police wading into demonstrators at nuclear power plants in the 1970s and 1980s, bore little resemblance to earlier shows of force.

Yet whatever points may be made about continuity and change in manifestations of force, violence and coercion in twentieth-century Germany, something fundamental appeared to have changed. In the physical division of Germany into two states, the domestic tensions and political instability which had beset Germany since the early twentieth century appeared to have been resolved. The two Germanies founded in 1949 survived longer than the preceding political forms, the Weimar Republic and the Third Reich, put together; and they achieved a remarkable stability, considering the arguably more difficult circumstances of their birth. Created as they were as impermanent entities, carved out of a defeated, occupied, and dismembered nation, it was truly extraordinary that the two Germanies should have become such apparently permanent elements of the later twentieth-century world. Moreover, despite the lack of widespread popular support for a relatively drab and repressed existence under the East German regime, the German Democratic Republic had a political system which was capable of reproducing itself: unlike the Third Reich, it was not inherently chaotic, dependent on the non-routinized charisma of one man, or expansionist and ultimately self-destructive. The concept of 'totalitarian', when intended to cover both the Third Reich and the German Democratic Republic, is intrinsically misleading and obscures a multitude of important differences. Yet in 1990, the apparently stable post-war settlement of the German question, and the European – and world – balance of power, was once again shaken open. With a new reshaping of the boundaries of Germany and its place in Europe, another major historical watershed was being passed. It is time, in this concluding chapter, to bring together some elements of the preceding analysis and propose a broader interpretation of the course of twentieth-century German history.

The role of the Third Reich

The Third Reich obviously played a pivotal role in the course of twentieth-century history. Its implications for the reshaping of European and world politics scarcely need elaborating: without Hitler's war, the nature of later twentieth-century Europe, and the involvement and roles of the superpowers, would have been very different – if there had been any such alignment at all. More difficult to determine are the implications of the Third Reich for domestic developments in German politics, economy and society. Did the Nazis' rise to power inaugurate, as many have claimed, a 'national revolution', a 'national awakening', a 'social revolution' producing a *Volksgemeinschaft* in which all was made anew? Did it play a key role, as commentators such as Ralf Dahrendorf would have us believe, in removing 'obstacles to modernization' in German society? Or was it rather – as Nazi ideology also gave grounds for believing – a 'conservative' revolution, against a variety of aspects of 'modernity'? The curious mixture of the use of modern means, modern technology, modern mass mobilization, in pursuit of avowedly anti-modern ends – the unattainable idyll mythicized and idealized in the romantic, agrarian, blood-and-soil ideology – has puzzled many analysts. A still more contentious issue has been the attempt to 'normalize' the history of the Third Reich, and to place the Holocaust in a wider historical context. Let us consider first the question of the degree to which the Nazi era represents a period of social revolution.

In different ways, scholars such as Ralf Dahrendorf and David Schoenbaum argued that, far from being a reactionary, anti-modern movement, Nazism actually played a key role in 'modernization' processes in twentieth-century Germany. Dahrendorf suggested that the Nazi development of the role of 'national comrade' (*Volksgenosse*) helped to break down the earlier 'pillarization' of society: the division into rigid status hierarchies and separate social milieux so characteristic of Imperial and Weimar Germany. This breaking down of old rigidities, according to Dahrendorf, subsequently made possible a more individualistic, mobile society in which the role of 'citizen' was rendered possible (although Dahrendorf, writing in the 1960s, was less than sanguine about the then degree of democratization of West Germans). Schoenbaum's less wide-ranging study, focusing on the years from 1933 to 1939, suggested that while the Nazis failed to effect a social revolution in reality – previous tendencies towards urbanization, concentration of capital and industrialization continuing unabated –

there was nevertheless an important revolution in the field of 'interpreted social reality'. As we have seen in more detail above, these views must be subjected to a range of qualifications. Research sparked off by the debates of the 1960s revealed a far more complex situation, leading to the conclusion, as summarized by Ian Kershaw, that while the Nazis failed to effect a revolution in social reality, their penetration of popular political consciousness was not as deep or as consistent as previously supposed either. Recent research has begun to reveal the variegation of popular opinion among different groups, at different times, under the influence of different factors. Yet it is still not clear where this leaves the role of the Third Reich in long-term processes of change in twentieth-century Germany.

Part of the problem lies in the essentially dated notion of 'modernization', which had considerable appeal in the 1960s, but which has subsequently been the focus of well-founded criticism. It clearly wraps together a number of separate processes – urbanization, industrialization, technological advance, 'secularization' and the like – adding a few dashes of evolutionary optimism, teleology and ethnocentricity to the cocktail, to produce a standard against which very different histories can be measured. Much the simplest way of cutting through the debates is to reject the general intellectual framework of 'modernization', and rather to try to ascertain as accurately as possible what changed, why it changed, how far Nazi policies were preconditions for subsequent developments and how far they were irrelevant to subsequent processes of change in a variety of spheres. Further, to attempt any sort of adequate answer to such questions, the focus must clearly straddle the supposed historical divide of 1945. Hence, a discussion of such issues – however brief and preliminary – can only come at the end of a broad historical survey such as has been undertaken here.

If one pauses to reflect on the processes described in preceding chapters, it becomes apparent that, while Nazi policies (particularly in relation to foreign policy aims and the associated rearmament) had an important immediate impact on the nature of economic recovery and socioeconomic development in the 1930s, more fundamental were the consequences of war and defeat. In the period after 1945, far-reaching changes were effected in the Soviet and western zones of occupation which had a profound impact on the development of the two Germanies over the next four decades. The Marshall Plan and the reorientation of West German industry from the late 1940s to the 1960s effected greater changes in economic structure – and the political orientations of business elites – than had any measures taken by the Nazis. Similarly, East Germany experienced what amounted to a *real* social revolution, under Soviet auspices, on a scale incomparable to any immediate effects of Nazi rule, and as a direct result of the military defeat of the Nazi regime. What the Nazis 'achieved' was less any sort of revolution than self-destruction – and, along with the destruction of an inherently unstable regime, the destruction of the credibility (and even the very existence) of certain old elites. The two German armies of the period after 1955 were very different animals from the army of Weimar and Nazi Germany; the Prussian Junkers found the material basis of their very existence swept away from under them with East German land reform; there was something of a sea-change, with shifting and variegated currents, in the fields of educational, cultural and moral elites in different ways in the two Germanies. But the construction of the new systems in the post-war period was contingent, not only on the effects of military defeat, but also on wider international developments, and in particular the Cold War, which had consequences only tangentially related to processes set in motion by the Nazis. To make great claims for the role of the Third Reich in 'modernization' processes in twentieth-century Germany seems, from this wider perspective, to be somewhat out of focus.

Let us turn then to the question of 'interpreted social reality' and the impact of Nazi ideology. The propaganda campaigns waged by Goebbels have frequently been termed the 'war that Hitler won'. The co-ordinated press, radio, newsreels, the staged mass rallies and parades, the rewritten school textbooks and revised curricula, battered home a consistent message to the German people, whose access to different views was severely restricted. Undoubtedly some of the propaganda – particularly

353

in the peacetime years – must have hit home, or at least struck a chord with pre-existing prejudices. But there is also considerable evidence to suggest a widespread cynicism and scepticism about much Nazi propaganda, particularly in the war-weary years after the invasion of Russia. Moreover, it must not be forgotten that certain elements which are taken to be aspects of 'Nazi ideology' were in fact common, widespread views shared by people other than committed Nazis. (This is true not only of such obvious attitudes as dislike, and desire for revision, of the Versailles Treaty, but also of, for example, eugenic theories, which had a respectable scientific standing.) To disentangle the specifically Nazi from more broadly held presuppositions is a complex task; part of Nazi success in gaining support on certain issues lay in picking up on pre-existing attitudes and placing them in a wider framework of interpretation. But whatever the complexities – which would bear much closer analysis than can be attempted here – it is clear that the Nazis did not succeed in simply 'brainwashing' an entire generation.

More important, arguably, were the ways in which Nazi policies changed the structures of social experience, with important implications for people's perceptions and attitudes. Experiences in everyday life might be more formative of patterns of political orientation than obviously propagandistic messages. (The same can be said in principle – with different substantive contents – of East German attempts at cultivating a 'socialist personality'.) In these areas, the range of effects was wide, and not always in directions intended by the Nazis. What is clear is that the main impact of Nazi reorganization of social life and community structures was negative: while helping to break down previous modes of organization and associated attitudes, the Nazis failed in the more positive (from their point of view) task of attempting to construct a genuine new 'folk community'. Thus, for example, the co-ordination of the range of pre-Nazi youth groups into the Nazi youth organizations did contribute to some partial (though ultimately incomplete) destruction of the 'pillarization' of pre-Nazi society. But the continuity and development of alternative, potentially subversive youth subcultures indicated the failure to achieve a uniform impact on youth in all social positions in Nazi Germany. Similarly, the destruction of trade unions and the co-ordination of workers under the DAF did prevent a whole generation of young workers from gaining experience of trade unionism. The loss of collective bargaining and the introduction of individual pay negotiations and rewards for merit and achievement also induced a greater degree of individualism among some German workers, whittling away at previous notions of collectivism and sentiments of solidarity. But, as in the area of youth organizations, these effects were not universal: many workers quite cynically took advantage of essentially paternalistic schemes, such as the holidays and outings offered by the KDF, without swallowing much of the ideological baggage that went along with such policies.

What the Nazis in the end 'achieved' was essentially negative: a destruction of previous forms of communal organization; a withdrawal of certain forms of experience from a new generation; but an associated failure to put viable new forms in the place of the old. The pressures to conform, to become 'folk comrades' in the new national community, instead led to a very widespread phenomenon: that of leading a dual life, separating public conformity from private authenticity. This duality is encapsulated in numerous jokes of the period, illustrating the ways in which people attempted to retain shreds of honesty and self-respect while simultaneously appearing to conform. One example of such behaviour is the resort to muttering the phrase 'The snow lay this high' ('So hoch lag der Schnee') rather than 'Heil Hitler', when raising the arm in the Hitler-salute. Symbolic forms of 'inner emigration' were not restricted to a minority intellectual elite in Nazi Germany.

What changed in these respects after 1945? Obviously the official ideologies of the two post-war Germanies – liberal democracy and Marxism-Leninism – were very different from the peculiar amalgam of beliefs, prejudices and aims which together made up Nazi ideology. Whatever the failures of Nazis to put across their ideas as a totality, explicit attempts by the occupying powers in the immediate post-war period were also less than entirely successful. Certain pre-existing views – such as a widely prevalent anti-communism – proved useful as transitional ideologies in the West in the 1950s, helping to anchor the new democracy, while other continuing prejudices (such as racialism) were less acceptable. A residual authoritarianism and belief in the virtues of political obedience may have helped in the early years of East Germany's existence, as well as a sense or hope that the division was impermanent and would not last long. More important than explicit instruction in the new political ideologies may have been the changing structures of social and political experience in the two Germanies. A 'pillarization' of German society could not return, in part due to the actions of the occupation powers, and this not only in the East. In the West, too, new patterns of organization were fostered and crystallized, and the resurrection of certain old patterns (such as the SPD's penumbra of social activities and groups) were discouraged. Some orientations which appear to represent continuities may in fact simply be similar forms of behaviour appearing and reappearing under new circumstances. The widespread political apathy of the later 1940s and 1950s, evident in both East and West, and frequently held to be a residual legacy of the Nazi period (or even an eternal, enduring characteristic of the 'apolitical German' since Luther or Kant), might in fact have represented a rational means of responding to new political regimes in which there was a justifiable fear of the possible consequences of 'sticking one's neck out', 'getting one's fingers burnt', by a too-hasty political commitment in circumstances which might again prove to be temporary. Similarly, the later retreatism evident in East German society might largely have been an adaptation to the pressures of an authoritarian political regime. Such questions obviously require further, more detailed exploration.

If one wishes to draw conclusions about the legacies of the Third Reich for the course of twentieth-century German history, there seem to be two main points of importance. These relate to the two areas of very specifically Nazi policy, namely foreign policy and racial policy.

First, the essential legacy of the Third Reich consisted of a negative, indeed suicidal, rather than revolutionary set of processes. It was not so much what the Nazis did to the

German economy and society, as the fact that Hitler unleashed a war which led to total defeat, occupation and division, that had radical consequences for social and economic restructuring in the post-war period. In this sense 1945 did represent a sort of 'zero hour'; obviously not all things could be made anew, but the destructive cycle of the previous seventy-five years of German history had been broken.

Secondly, the racial policies of the Nazis culminated in a genocide which had a profound impact on both the Germanies founded on the ruins of the Third Reich. Both Germanies, in different ways, had to grapple with the problem of 'coming to terms with the past' – whether through distortions and oversimplifications of historical reality, or selective amnesia, or repeated attempts to explain (if not explain away) the ultimately inexplicable. This essentially indigestible moment of Germany's past proved, beyond any other, that all causal accounts in history are also moral indictments, apportioning responsibility and blame. Whether the issue of explaining the Holocaust has been, or ever can be, satisfactorily resolved is another matter. Certainly, with the sheer passage of time, the burden of guilt is one which ever fewer Germans feel it is their part to bear.

In view of the essentially negative 'contributions' of the Nazi regime to twentieth-century German history, perhaps it is time, finally, to jettison some of the arguments about its role in putative processes of 'modernization'. The factors which explain the different patterns of development of the two post-war Germanies were dependent, not so much on processes set in train by the Nazis, as on the consequences of their defeat. Let us turn, finally, to the dynamics of development of the two Germanies from 1945 to 1990.

The double transformation: the two Germanies 1945–89

1945 was not exactly a *Stunde Null*, a zero hour, when Germany became a blank sheet on which to make a completely fresh beginning, as certain post-war apologetics attempted to proclaim.

Yet in many fundamental ways 1945 did constitute a radical break in German history – certainly more fundamental than the break between *Kaiserreich* and democracy in 1918. Continuities there certainly were across this break, in structure, personnel, and political culture – in different ways in *both* Germanies. Yet there were certain radical changes which arguably constituted the key factors helping to explain the relative stability and longevity of the two post-war Germanies in the period before 1989. Four aspects may be singled out as relevant here: first, the structure and interrelations of elites in each state; secondly, the nature and timing of material success in the two Germanies; thirdly, the character and implications of dissent; and finally – and, classically, last but not least! – the changed international system.

It was notable that in the Weimar Republic certain elites acted in ways that undermined the viability of Weimar democracy: opinion formers and moral and cultural leaders – teachers, university professors, priests and pastors, writers and artists, left-wingers and right-wingers – articulated either anti-Republican or anti-capitalist sentiments and denigrated the 'party squabbling' of democratic politics; certain army leaders, notably Schleicher, did their best to undermine democracy and replace it with some form of authoritarian state; certain sectors of industry opposed a system which they perceived as detrimental to their economic interests; debt-ridden landowners of large estates sought desperately for a government which would be particularly friendly to their interests. In the Third Reich, these elites by and large compromised with or condoned – even by silence, inner or real emigration – a system which should have provoked opposition; such resistance as did emanate from elite quarters – uniquely placed to offer effective opposition – was partial, isolated, and belated, certainly never sufficient to overthrow Hitler from within. The track record of German elites before 1945 was at best an ambiguous one. From the foundation of the two Germanies in 1949 to the collapse of the East German regime in 1989, however, the orientations of different elite groups to their respective political systems, and to each other, had rather different implications. This may be illustrated by considering political, military, economic, cultural, moral and educational elites in turn.

There was obviously a radical transfer of power in both Germanies, following the dismantling of the Nazi regime. In the East, the Communists were determined to gain power for themselves, as a new political elite. In the West, it was more a case of the restoration of former politicians who had been excluded or taken an acceptable backstage role in the Third Reich (typified by the re-emergence from semi-retirement of the ex-Mayor of Cologne, Konrad Adenauer, who had spent much of the Nazi period quietly cultivating his roses). However, beyond this rather obvious point, there are some rather more interesting features concerning the development of post-war political elites. After the various purges in the 1950s, Ulbricht effectively led a relatively united party; this was also true of the SED under Honecker until perhaps the mid-1980s, when the challenge of Gorbachev and the succession question fostered greater internal discussion. The relative unity and lack of factionalism in the quarter century or so from the early 1960s to the mid-1980s, in marked contrast to the situation in both the Polish and Czech communist parties, was undoubtedly a major factor in the ability of the SED to sustain its hold on the East German state and society during this period. In West Germany there was of course a plurality of political elites; the notable feature was the willingness on the part of most – whatever their orientations in the Third Reich – to commit themselves to the democratic system. Initially, the constraints imposed by the Allies had much to do with this; so also did Adenauer's policy of incorporating former Nazis into the new Germany.

Military elites played an insidious role in the downfall of the Weimar Republic, and had at best a flawed and ambiguous reputation in the Third Reich. Yet in neither of the post-war Germanies did the refounded armies play a role tending to undermine or destabilize the political system. The West German army, subjected to a range of parliamentary controls and reconstituted as a rather different entity, was constrained to recognize by the 1970s at the latest that it could no longer aspire to any sort of independent political role. The East German army showed no evident distance from the East German communist party; nor was there any perceived need for military, rather than civilian rule, as in Poland when faced with the Solidarity crises of 1980–1. Party and army seemed wholly of one purpose – and determinedly efficient in pursuit of their goals – in the GDR.

Economic elites, both agrarian and industrial, were effectively abolished in East Germany, starting with the land reform and nationalization measures of 1945–6. Yet in a different sense, a potential new economic 'counter-elite', the technical intelligentsia, appeared to be developing as a possible rival for power alongside the SED in the 1960s. Particularly under the New Economic System, it might have proved possible for managers and qualified technical specialists to appropriate more power in important decision-making processes. Yet Ulbricht took care to ensure that decentralization of the economy was not accompanied by political decentralization. Contrary to the claim made by P. C. Ludz, no 'institutionalized counter-elite' developed in the GDR, challenging the party's claim to leadership or seriously influencing important decisions. A high degree of education and specialist qualifications became increasingly important characteristics of the party elite in East Germany under Honecker; but party commitment took precedence over technical expertise, and the latter was definitely placed at the service of the former. In West Germany the situation was different, but the effect – a stabilization of the political system – was comparable. Economic elites were able to salvage their interests across the historical watershed of 1945; their organizations were rapidly resurrected and adapted to the changed conditions of the occupation period; and in the decades following the foundation of the Federal Republic they were able to promote their interests and influence policy formation through a range of pressure groups and organizations. They found that the particular form of corporatism that developed in the Federal Republic was one which they could use to their advantage. Undoubtedly also the early economic successes of the Federal Republic, as well as a changing climate of entrepreneurial opinion, helped to ensure that West German economic elites came to accept parliamentary democracy as a viable political form in which to realize their interests. This stood in marked contrast to the situation in the Weimar Republic.

Turning to the cultural and moral intelligentsias and the leaders of opinion formation in each state, the profiles were again very different but, in different ways, a certain *modus vivendi* appeared to have been achieved by the 1980s. For all the censure made by prominent West German intellectuals of the 'repressive' West German state, or of its failure to confront the past, criticisms were generally directed not *against* democracy but rather against perceived gaps between ideal and reality, and in favour of the extension and fuller realization of democracy. The position of the East German cultural intelligentsia was unique among East European states in that they had another identical language community in which they could publish works censored in their own state and to which they could, if need be, emigrate and yet continue to earn a livelihood by writing in their native tongue. This latter fact had benefits from the point of view of the state, too: disagreeable dissenting voices could be involuntarily exiled, to become thorns in the flesh of West German bourgeois society instead of East German authoritarian bureaucracy. In the event, for the most part of the GDR's history, the cultural intelligentsia – insofar as individuals were not entirely regime hacks knocking out required tracts – maintained a partially supportive critical stance, and exercised a degree of self-imposed censorship. It did not in any case seek to establish itself as a 'counter-elite'.

Church leaders and opinion formers such as the vast majority of school and university teachers in the Federal Republic tended to act positively to sustain democracy. Although widening gulfs developed between church leadership and laity on certain issues (particularly, among Catholics, on matters such as abortion and birth control, also family morality more widely), disputes did not have to do with the political system as such, in contrast to the Weimar situation. In East Germany, the situation with respect particularly to the Protestant churches was more complex and difficult to evaluate. From being, in the 1950s, a persecuted group, East German Christians adapted to changed circumstances and by the 1970s had won from the regime a limited willingness to accept their existence and respect their contribution to GDR society in certain supportive activities. It can be suggested that in the period from the late 1970s to the mid 1980s the asymmetrical partnership between church and state actually helped in curious ways to stabilize the regime by simultaneously providing an outlet for dissent while containing it within certain limits. However, this process itself led to the proliferation of dissenting voices, and ultimately set in motion forces providing a less easily containable challenge to the party's authority. Once changed external circumstances provoked a regime crisis, internal voices for reform were able to inaugurate the popular revolution which ultimately heralded the collapse of the GDR. If one turns from the 'moral' elite to the educational elite in the GDR, the situation appears much simpler: by and large the education system was one serving the interests of the party, and, despite certain recognized difficulties, fulfilling the functions required of it. The main problem from the point of view of goals such as the development of socialist personalities, was that the East German education system tended to breed a certain authoritarian outward conformity rather than an inner commitment to party ideology.

In very different ways, the configurations and orientations of elite groups in the two Germanies up to 1989 tended either to sustain the respective political systems or at the least not to pose serious threats to their stability. What of the masses, the vast majority of the people, in the two Germanies? Much is frequently made of the material privations suffered by people in eastern European countries, with their inefficient, centrally planned economies. Together with restrictions on personal liberties, inability to travel freely, to emigrate, to express their true opinions, to read, discuss, and form autonomous organizations, people in eastern Europe were frequently considered by westerners to be in such a position of subjugation that they could be held back from revolution only by the threat or reality of naked force. How relevant is such a picture in interpreting pre-1989 East Germany, whatever its validity or otherwise in respect of other communist countries? Similarly, much is often made of the commitment of westerners to democratic values, and participation in their political systems. How important were such factors in post-war West German history? However different these questions appear to be, ironically part of the answer in relation to both Germanies seems to be the same: relative material success played a major role in the political trajectories of the two Germanies from the late 1940s to the 1980s. This occurred in different ways, and at different levels in each state; but it provided a crucial margin – however small at times, particularly in East Germany – allowing the new states the space for consolidation and stabilization without the real commitment of a majority of citizens.

Undoubtedly a large number of East Germans did complain about material shortages and personal restrictions. We shall consider the implications of the latter in a moment, in connection with the question of dissent. But in relation to the material shortcomings of life in the GDR, two points must be made. First, whatever their criticisms and grumblings, East Germans did take a certain pride in the performance of their economy, particularly as contrasted with what they considered to be the incompetence of the neighbouring Poles. Secondly, whatever the invidious nature of comparisons with West Germany, for considerable periods one could say that 'es liess sich leben' in East Germany: it was possible to live a relatively comfortable life. The importance of consumer satisfaction was not lost on the regime's leaders: starting with Ulbricht's measures in the wake of the 1953 June Uprising, concessions to consumers periodically and repeatedly were used as a tool of regime stabilization. Certainly under Honecker the material satisfaction of the population was a constant concern; and the rapid expansion of car ownership in the 1980s, as well as the increased availability of formerly scarce luxuries such as real coffee, testified to an improved standard of living for many East Germans. Despite Western criticism of material failings in East Germany, and despite East German discontent about lack of choice or quality, there were not the kinds of economic dislocation and acute shortages or phenomenal price rises which prompted food riots in Poland at various times. In essence, there was not cause enough for mass discontent on a scale which would have persuaded East Germans that it was worth jeopardizing the entire functioning of the economy. This fact tended to isolate and minimize the impact of intellectual dissent for a long period of East Germany's history.

The importance of material success in post-war West German political life can hardly be overstated. Less than five years after its foundation, the Weimar Republic was in serious economic difficulties, with the great inflation of 1923 adding to the more general difficulties and dislocations of the years after the end of the First World War. In contrast, West Germany in the late 1940s and early 1950s, saw the beginnings of a remarkable economic recovery; so rapid and remarkable, indeed, that it soon became widely known as the 'economic miracle'. Sheer pragmatism and concern for personal survival and material well-being brought many West Germans to support the political system which appeared to have initiated, facilitated and sustained this recovery. It was not a principled commitment to democracy as such; but the economic take-off of the 1950s bought valuable time in which the political system could be stabilized, and in which Adenauer could successfully pursue his strategy of western integration. Willingness to jettison East Germany to the Soviets might have been far less, and commitment to an impermanent, severed limb, a partial entity rather than a united nation state, might have been far more difficult, had it not been for this phenomenal economic success. With the passage of time, shifts in factors influencing opinion as well as the passage of generations could effect more fundamental changes in political attitudes. Thus early economic success was crucial in a 'fair weather democracy'; later, economic storms could more easily be weathered and bracketed off from critiques of the political system as a whole. The question became one of which party was held to be the best manager of the economy, rather than one of which political system as a whole would be preferable to the present one, as in the Weimar Republic.

What of the implications of principled dissent and opposition in the two Germanies? In both Germanies, former Nazis were by and large absorbed, in different ways, into the new societies and polities of the 1950s, insofar as they had not been major war criminals (and unfortunately sometimes even when they had been). In both Germanies, new forms of dissent proved more problematic than any serious revisionism. In West Germany, the anti-system opposition of a few extremists, of both left and right, failed to gain any widespread support and generally provoked public hostility and opprobrium. This was in marked contrast to the public reception of anti-system opposition in the Weimar Republic. Articulate intellectual dissent in West Germany tended, while being critical of the regime, to sustain its fundamental values and principles. In East Germany, early purges of dissenting factions in the SED helped Ulbricht consolidate his power. Subsequent dissenting Marxist intellectuals such as Havemann and Bahro remained relatively isolated, without mass followings. The proliferation of wider grass-roots dissent in the 1980s, focusing on issues such as peace, human rights, and the environment, proved ultimately to have more impact on the regime. But for the past, one can say that in the forty years of their divided existence, prior to the international changes providing the revolutionary preconditions in 1989, both Germanies were able to contain dissent in ways not possible in the Weimar Republic.

Finally, there is the question of a changed international situation and its implications for German politics. The war that Germany unleashed in 1939 ultimately radically transformed the nature of the world system. No longer was there a Europe of strong states, jostling for power, influence, and colonies; instead, there was a larger world, divided into spheres of influence between the new superpowers, the USA and USSR, and in its midst a much weakened, dependent, war-ravaged and divided Europe. What developed in the period after the Second World War was a world system very different from that of the first half of the twentieth century. And this changed international system had considerable impact on subsequent German history.

There was of course the obvious set of implications: the division of Germany, the reshaping of the political, economic and social systems of the two new states, the less visible but no less important reshaping of attitudes, values, modes of orientation and expression. There were also the quite obvious constraints imposed by the Allies setting limits on what it was possible for the Germanies to become. In these ways, Allied conquest and occupation of Germany broke the previous spiral of crisis. 1945 did in this sense mark a fundamental break in German history, whatever continuities might be discerned across that divide. In wider ways, changes in the world as a whole meant changes for Germany. In an age of potential nuclear catastrophe, issues of peace and security within a changed framework of international military alliances rendered the 'German question' a very different one from its nineteenth- and early twentieth-century predecessors. As Edwina Moreton put it, the 'German question' of the late twentieth century was no longer one of how Germany affected European security, but rather of how European security affected Germany.[1] This is in itself a measure of the gulf separating Germany in the 1980s from Germany in the 1920s and 1930s.

These factors – the commitment of elites, the relative material success, the containment of dissent, and the changed international system with Germany's changed and divided place in it – together help to explain the longevity of the two German states which succeeded the ill-fated Weimar Republic and Third Reich. Each of these factors itself requires further exploration and more detailed analysis than has been possible in a brief survey such as this; but it may be suggested that they at least provide fruitful clues to the problems of trying to interpret the relative domestic stability of the two Germanies over four decades. Yet nothing in history is unchanging; history is a perpetual process of dynamic development, in which, at certain times, a combination of elements produces a moment of major transformation. Such a watershed was reached at the end of the 1980s.

The international situation had become a very different one from that of the late 1940s. No longer was Europe weak, war-torn, ravaged; rather, western European states were relatively prosperous entities moving towards closer economic, and even political, co-operation and integration, in the framework of a supranational European Community. By contrast, one of the two superpowers, the Soviet Union, was by now a weakened empire beset by domestic problems, and relinquishing its former claims to dominion over Eastern European affairs. Having set in motion processes of increased political openness and economic restructuring at home, with implications for reform movements in its former satellite states, Gorbachev's USSR was content to observe at a distance the playing out of the consequences elsewhere in Eastern Europe. With this *de facto* Soviet withdrawal and condoning, even encouraging, of change, the major precondition for the whole post-war settlement of divided Germany was removed.

The dismantling of the Iron Curtain, predicated on these developments and inaugurated by the reformist Hungarian regime, precipitated – in the form of a flood of refugees – the regime crisis in the GDR. The domestic situation had altered in important respects too: the SED was more differentiated, with many members more willing to contemplate reforms and dialogue; and dissenting voices had proliferated, and developed new strategies of non-violent protest and assertion in pursuit of the aim of democratization by peaceful means. These factors shaped the unique pattern of the gentle revolution of autumn 1989. With its protective shell cracked from without, the East German communist regime capitulated rapidly to mounting pressures from within. But even as dissenting voices pressurized for the development of a democratic socialist GDR, so at the same time the salient focus for material comparison became the now readily attainable consumer paradise of the Federal Republic. In the months following the opening of the borders, it became increasingly clear that an independent East Germany could not hope to survive as a viable economic entity. At the same time, the strains placed on the West German economy and welfare state by the continuing avalanche of immigrants posed serious problems, attacking the very heart of West German material prosperity – which constituted almost the very essence of any real West German identity. It became clear that a resolution of the problems posed for both Germanies by the coming down of the border could only be through a common economy, and common political organization. The division of Germany had effectively collapsed; the problem became that of managing the transition, of designing institutions and allegiances that would provide a secure structure for the future of a united Germany in a changing international system.

It was a long road that Germany travelled in the over seventy years from 1918 to 1990. It may have been a 'twisted road to Auschwitz', but it also must not be forgotten that many more twists and turns have taken place since the collapse of the brutal system that spawned Auschwitz. Is it possible, then, as some Germans are demanding, to 'normalize' the place of the Third Reich in Germany's longer-term historical past?

The answer to this question depends, of course, to some extent on what is meant by 'normalization'. Attempts to diminish the sense of guilt and responsibility for the Holocaust by equating it with, or excusing it with reference to, other atrocities elsewhere must be dismissed as misplaced. On the other hand to wrench the Holocaust out of 'history' and place it on an isolated plane of unique reprehensibility is equally misplaced: this too abstracts evil from its everyday context and represents not only an abdication of the historian's task of attempting to explain, but also evades the moral questions of guilt and responsibility. The Holocaust must be firmly located, and examined, like every other historical phenomenon of note, in its time and place, in its ordinariness and human manner of execution. To this extent, it can be maintained that the Holocaust must be 'normalized' and placed in the long-term patterns and paths of German history.

How should a book on Germany in the twentieth century conclude? With an emphasis on success, or failure; stability, or instability; violence and coercion, or new modes of support and hope? Twentieth-century Germany has witnessed a spectrum of experiences provoking all manner of emotions among those involved and those observing; it is not for the academic analyst to pronounce final judgement. The last words must be ones of caution: it is ultimately impossible either to evoke the totality of the past or to produce a definitive interpretation of its course; all analyses must remain partial and tentative. But an attempt can be made to suggest modes of approach and points for discussion. It is hoped that the present work has gone some small way to putting the worst aspects of the German past in their wider place, and has shifted the emphasis forwards to new problematics: the transformations of the present, which provide the starting-place for human actions in the future.

REFERENCE NOTES

CHAPTER TWO

1. Cf. Dick Geary, 'Working-class Culture in Imperial Germany' in R. Fletcher (ed.), *Bernstein to Brandt* (London: Edward Arnold, 1987).
2. *See* particularly Wolfgang Mommsen, 'The German Revolution 1918–1920: Political Revolution and Social Protest Movement', in Richard Bessel and E. J. Feuchtwanger (eds.), *Social Change and Political Development in Weimar Germany* (London: Croom Helm, 1981).
3. Figures taken from W. Michalka and G. Niedhart (eds.), *Die ungeliebte Republik* (Munich: dtv, 1980), p. 118.
4. E. Kolb, *Die Weimarer Republik* (Munich: Oldenbourg, 1988), pp. 91–106.
5. R. Bessel, 'Why did the Weimar Republic Collapse?' in Ian Kershaw (ed.), *Weimar: Why Did German Democracy Fail?* (London: Weidenfeld and Nicolson, 1990), p. 147.
6. *See* Helen Boak, 'Women in Weimar Germany: The *"Frauenfrage"* and the Female Vote', in Bessel and Feuchtwanger (eds.), op. cit.

CHAPTER THREE

1. Cf. F. L. Carsten, *The Reichswehr and Politics* (Oxford: Clarendon Press, 1966), pp. 397–405; Eberhard Kolb, *Die Weimarer Republik* (Munich: Oldenbourg, 1988), pp. 171–3.
2. *See* particularly Ian Kershaw, *The 'Hitler Myth'* (Oxford: Oxford University Press, 1987), ch. 1.
3. It is important to distinguish between Nazi use of rhetoric and propaganda – as adapted for different audiences – and any putative 'programme'. Hitler's own rabid anti-Semitism was played down in his public speeches after 1923, in favour of an anti-Marxism which would have a wider resonance. See Kershaw, op. cit., ch. 9. *See* also J. P. Stern, *Hitler: The Führer and the People* (London: Fontana Press, 3rd edn, 1990).
4. Harold James, 'Economic reasons for the collapse of the Weimar Republic' in Ian Kershaw (ed.), *Weimar: Why did German democracy fail?* (London: Weidenfeld and Nicolson, 1990), p. 32.

370

5. *See* particularly, Harold James, *The German Slump* (Oxford: Clarendon Press, 1986).
6. *See* Kershaw (ed.), *Weimar*, for an airing of this debate in English.
7. Figures taken from M. Broszat, *Hitler and the Collapse of Weimar Germany* (Leamington Spa: Berg, 1987), pp. 82–3.
8. On the controversial topic of the relations between big business and the Nazis, *see* particularly H. A. Turner, *German Big Business and the Rise of Hitler* (Oxford: Oxford University Press, 1985).
9. *See* particularly Tom Childers, *The Nazi Voter* (Chapel Hill: University of North Carolina Press, 1983), on which this paragraph is largely based.
10. Ibid., pp. 264–5.

CHAPTER FOUR

1. Quoted in J. Noakes and G. Pridham, *Nazism: A Documentary Reader* (Exeter: University of Exeter, revised edn, 1983), vol. 1, p. 160.
2. Quoted in K. D. Bracher, *The German Dictatorship* (Harmondsworth: Penguin, 1980), p. 302.
3. On these debates, *see*, for example: E. N. Peterson, *The Limits of Hitler's Power* (Princeton: Princeton University Press, 1969); M. Broszat, *The Hitler State* (London: Longman, 1981; orig. 1969); Hans Mommsen, 'Hitler's Stellung im national-sozialistischen Herrschaftsystem' and Klaus Hildebrand, 'Monokratie oder Polykratie? Hitlers Herrschaft und das Dritte Reich', both in G. Hirschfeld and L. Kettenacker (eds.), *Der 'Führerstaat': Mythos und Realität* (Stuttgart: Klett-Cotta, 1981); and a seminal discussion in Ian Kershaw, *The Nazi Dictatorship* (London: Edward Arnold, 1985), ch. 4.
4. *Der Volksbrockhaus* (Leipzig: 8th edn, 1939), p. 35.
5. *See* for some examples of such exercises, G. Platner (ed.), *Schule im Dritten Reich* (Munich: dtv, 1983), documents, pp. 195–265.
6. *See* particularly D. Peukert, *Inside Nazi Germany* (London: Batsford, 1987); H. Böll, *Was soll aus dem Jungen bloss werden?* (Bornheim: Lamuv Verlag, 1981).
7. P. Hiron, *Knaur's Gesundheitslexikon: Ein Führer für alle durch das Gesamtgebiet der modernen Medizin* (Berlin: 1940), for example the entries under '*Erbgesundheit*' and '*Eheberatung*'. The former contains – amidst purple passages about the child starting out on life like the traveller setting out on a journey – some chilling euphemisms concerning the way the 'responsible' Nazi state has, for the first time in history, taken practical measures to 'hinder' hereditarily diseased progeny.

8. *See* particularly Jill Stephenson, *The Nazi Organization of Women* (London: Croom Helm, 1981).

9. *See* particularly Ian Kershaw, *Popular Opinion and Political Dissent in the Third Reich* (Oxford: Clarendon Press, 1983).

10. Cf. Heinz Boberach (ed.), *Berichte des SD und der Gestapo über Kirchen und Kirchenvolk in Deutschland, 1933–1944* (Mainz: Matthias-Grünewald Verlag, 1971).

11. *See* ibid., p. 70, on the singing of hymns such as 'aus tiefer Not schrei' ich zu Dir', 'Versage nicht, Du Häuflein klein', 'Und wenn die Welt voll Teufel wär'. *See* also M. Balfour, *Withstanding Hitler* (London: Routledge, 1988), pp. 37–45, for an overview of the role of the churches.

12. Noakes and Pridham, op. cit., vol. II, pp. 262–3.

13. Cf. the entry under 'Reichs-Autobahnen' in the *Volksbrockhaus*, p. 563: 'die nationale Bedeutung der Reichsautobahnen liegt darin, dass sie weite Landesteile dem Verkehr erschliessen und das ineinanderwachsen der deutschen Stämme fördern.'

14. *See* R. J. Overy, *The Nazi Economic Recovery 1932–38* (London: Macmillan, 1982); V. Berghahn, *Modern Germany* (Cambridge: Cambridge University Press, 1982), pp. 148–9.

15. *See* Kershaw, *Nazi Dictatorship*, op. cit., ch. 7; the classic study is David Schoenbaum, *Hitler's Social Revolution* (London: Weidenfeld and Nicolson, 1969; orig. 1966).

16. Quoted in Helmut Krausnick, 'Judenverfolgung' in Hans Buchheim et al., *Anatomie des SS-Staates* (Munich: dtv, 1967), vol. II, p. 279.

17. Cf. David Astor, 'Adam von Trott: A Personal View' in Hedley Bull (ed.), *The Challenge of the Third Reich* (Oxford: Clarendon Press, 1986), pp. 27–32; see also Michael Balfour's discussion of Trott in *Withstanding Hitler*, pp. 179–87.

CHAPTER FIVE

1. On Georg Elser, *see* J. P. Stern, *Hitler: The Führer and the People* (London: Fontana Press, 3rd edn 1990), pp. 123–36.

2. On the transition from a European to a world war, and the connection of the European conflicts with the separate conflicts in the Pacific, *see* W. Carr, *From Poland to Pearl Harbor* (London: Edward Arnold, 1985).

3. The diatribes in Hitler's *Mein Kampf* should have left little doubt as to his real views. For the public downplaying of anti-Semitism, see I. Kershaw, *The 'Hitler Myth'* (Oxford: Oxford University Press, 1987), ch. 9.

4. *See* for example H. Diwald, *Geschichte der Deutschen* (Frankfurt:

Propyläen, 1978), pp. 163–5; M. Stürmer, 'Das industrielle Deutschland' in H. Boockmann et al., *Mitten in Europa: Deutsche Geschichte* (Berlin: Siedler, 1984), pp. 358–9; G. Schulz, *Deutschland seit dem Ersten Weltkrieg, 1918–1945* (Göttingen: Vandenhoek and Ruprecht, 1976), pp. 217–8. The last of these succeeds in dealing with the Holocaust within precisely three sentences, worth discussing in some detail as indicative of a particular approach. The first and longest sentence first places genocide in the context of anti-communism and the fight against 'barbaric Asiatic methods of struggle'; the whole process of mass extermination is then rapidly summarized in half a sentence, which suggests that most extermination camps were within the General Government (no mention of the location of Auschwitz) where killing (no numbers) took place under 'conditions of the strictest secrecy'. The second sentence tells us that the operation was carried out by the SS under the direction of Himmler, SD-chief Heydrich and ultimately Hitler, and that the full extent could not be discovered until the final phase and really only after the war. The third sentence states that this explains the extermination of the majority of European Jewry and casts the greatest shadow over recent German history. The first two sentences are essentially inaccurate in their implications; the third adds nothing. However often words like 'brutality', 'terror' and so on are used in describing the Nazi regime, this sort of slanted brevity on the Holocaust is seriously misleading. On the debate over West German historians' treatment of the Holocaust *see* Chapter Twelve, below.

5. Gerald Fleming, *Hitler and the Final Solution* (London: Hamish Hamilton, 1985), p. 24.

6. *See* Hoess' post-war statement, reprinted in J. Noakes and G. Pridham, *Nazism* (Exeter: University of Exeter, vol. III, 1988), p. 1181.

7. Cf. ibid., p. 1208; for rather different figures, see L. Dawidowicz, *The War against the Jews* (Harmondsworth: Penguin, 1979), p. 480.

8. Fleming, op. cit., p. 2; p. 13.

9. Dawidowicz, op. cit., p. 27.

10. H. Mommsen, 'Anti-Jewish Politics and the Implementation of the Holocaust' in Hedley Bull (ed.), *The Challenge of the Third Reich* (Oxford: Clarendon Press, 1986), p. 131.

11. Ibid., p. 128.

12. *See* M. Broszat, 'Hitler und die Genesis der "Endlösung". Aus Anlass der Thesen von David Irving', *Vierteljahrshefte für Zeitgeschichte*, vol. 25, no. 4 (Oct. 1977): 739–75, p. 746.

13. Cf. Christopher Browning, 'Zur Genesis der "Endlösung": Eine

Antwort an Martin Broszat', *VfZ* vol. 29, no. 1 (1981): 97–109, for
an account differing from Broszat's.

14. Walter Laqueur, *The Terrible Secret* (Harmondsworth: Penguin,
    1980), pp. 31–2.
15. Ibid., p. 92.
16. Ibid., p. 208.
17. *See* for example the extracts reprinted in H. Graml,
    Reichskristallnacht (Munich: dtv, 1988), pp. 262–7.
18. Cf. Hans Buchheim, 'Befehl und Gehorsam' in H. Buchheim et
    al., *Anatomie des SS-Staates*, vol. 1 (Munich: dtv, 1967).
19. Figures taken from M. Broszat, 'The Third Reich and the
    German People', in Hedley Bull (ed.), op. cit., p. 93.
20. On the range of responses to the regime, and means of
    conceptualizing these responses, see Ian Kershaw, ' "Widerstand
    ohne Volk?" Dissens und Widerstand im Dritten Reich' in Jürgen
    Schmädeke and Peter Steinbach (eds.), *Der Widerstand gegen den
    Nationalsozialismus* (Munich: Piper, 1985). *See* also M. Balfour,
    Withstanding Hitler (London: Routledge, 1988).
21. H. Mommsen, 'Social Views and Constitutional Plans of the
    Resistance' in H. Graml et al., *The German Resistance to Hitler*
    (London: Batsford, 1970), p. 62.
22. *See* for example the summer 1944 draft of a 'Regierungserklärung'
    by Ludwig Beck and Carl Goerdeler, reproduced by the Berlin
    Gedenkstätte Widerstand.

CHAPTER SIX

1. Quoted in Rolf Steininger, *Deutsche Geschichte 1945–1961:
   Darstellung und Dokumente* (Frankfurt: Fischer, 1964), vol. I, p. 64.
2. *See* for example: Barbara Marshall, *The Origins of Post-War
   German Politics* (London: Croom Helm, 1988); E. N. Peterson, *The
   American Occupation of Germany* (Detroit: Wayne State University
   Press, 1978); John Gimbel, *The American Occupation of Germany:
   Politics and the Military, 1945–1949* (Stanford: Stanford University
   Press, 1968).
3. L. Niethammer, *Entnazifizierung in Bayern* (Frankfurt: Fischer,
   1972), pp. 126–31; *Süddeutsche Zeitung*, 18 December 1945 and 26
   April 1946, honouring the uprising.
4. Steininger, op. cit., pp. 101–2.
5. Cf. Hermann Weber, 'Geschichte der SED' in Ilse Spittmann
   (ed.), *Die SED in Geschichte und Gegenwart* (Köln: Verlag
   Wissenschaft und Politik, 1987), particularly pp. 10–13. On the
   Soviet zone generally, *see* for example: Gregory Sandford, *From*

Hitler to Ulbricht (Princeton: Princeton University Press, 1983);
J. P. Nettl, *The Eastern Zone and Soviet Policy in Germany 1945–50*
(London: Oxford University Press, 1951).

6. *See* Marshall, op. cit.

7. Rainer Schulze, 'Representation of Interests and Recruitment of
Elites', *German History*, vol. 7, no. 1 (1989): 71–91.

8. Figures from Wolfgang Meinicke, 'Die Entnazifizierung in
der Sowjetischen Besatzungszone 1945 bis 1948', *Zeitschrift für
Geschichtswissenschaft*, vol. 32 (1984) Heft II: 968–979, p. 974.

9. Office of the US High Commissioner for Germany, *Sovietization
of the Public School System in East Germany*, HICOG 5, 1 February
1951, p. 9.

10. *See* for example D. Staritz, *Geschichte der DDR 1949–1985*
(Frankfurt: Suhrkamp, 1985), ch. 1, section I; Christoph
Klessmann, *Die doppelte Staatsgründung* (Göttingen: Vandenhoek
and Ruprecht, 1982), ch. 3, sections 2 and 3.

11. Meinicke, op. cit.

12. Peterson, op. cit., p. 142; see also Niethammer, op. cit., pp. 150–6.

13. *See* the table in Volker Dotterweich, 'Die "Entnazifizierung" ' in
J. Becker, T. Stammen and P. Waldmann (eds.), *Vorgeschichte der
Bundesrepublik Deutschland* (Munich: Wilhelm Frick Verlag, 1979),
p. 147, taken from J. Fürstenau, *Entnazifizierung* (Neuwied and
Berlin: Luchterhand, 1969), pp. 22 ff.

14. *See* the report, *Functional History of Military Government, Bremen
Enclave* 27 April–30 June 1946, Part One, p. 37. (Copy in Institut
für Zeitgeschichte (IfZ), Munich: Fg23.) Other reactions can be
found in the OMGUS opinion surveys (copies also in the IfZ), in
the licensed press of the time, and in a variety of contemporary
reports and pamphlets, such as: W. Lutz, 'Stimmungsbericht aus
Stuttgart', 30 June 1945 (unpublished ms: IfZ: Zs 3067); and Otto
Gritschneder, *Sackgasse Säuberung* (privately produced ms., Passau
1948; copy in the Staatsbibliothek Munich).

15. Cf. James Tent, *Mission on the Rhine* (Chicago: University of
Chicago Press, 1982); on re-education, N. Pronay and K. Wilson
(eds.), *The Political Re-education of Germany and her Allies after
World War Two* (London: Croom Helm, 1985); A. Hearndon (ed.),
The British in Germany (London: Hamish Hamilton, 1978).

16. Evidence of the impact of *Todesmühlen* can be found in a (not
very systematic!) survey reported in the *Süddeutsche Zeitung* of 5
February 1946. Asked why they had not gone to the cinema when
this film was on, people gave answers ranging from 'I see enough
misery around me daily', 'I didn't have anything to do with such
things', 'I was afraid I would not be able to sleep. My nerves can't
take such things', 'I was ashamed to see again what had been done
to tar our name' to 'I only go to the cinema to relax and forget my

worries'. The *Süddeutsche Zeitung* is itself evidence of the beneficial influence of the licensed press on constructing new attitudes and identity among and by the Germans. For the Soviet zone, *see* for example the highly revealing unpublished correspondence between Max Berger and Arnold Plöhn (IfZ: ED10), which provides a range of intriguing insights into social and political conditions and attitudes in one area of the zone.

17. On refugees, *see* for example R. Schulze, 'Growing Discontent: Relations between the Native and Refugee Populations in a Rural District in Western Germany after the Second World War', *German History*, vol. 7, no. 3 (1989): 332–349.

18. Cf. C. von Krockow, *Die Stunde der Frauen* (Stuttgart: Deutsche Verlags-Anstalt, 1988); Annette Kuhn, 'Power and Powerlessness: Women after 1945', *German History*, vol. 7, no. 1, (1989): 35–46.

19. The figures in this and the following paragraph are taken from K. Hardach, *The Political Economy of Germany in the Twentieth Century* (Berkeley: University of California Press, 1980).

20. *See* particularly the shrewd observations of Max Berger in his letter to Arnold Plöhn of 15 January 1946 (IfZ: ED170). Berger comments on the way in which the KPD initially gained considerable popularity from the land reform – until peasants discovered they could do little without cattle or seedcorn. Then they realized how little power even the KPD had with the Russians; and that, given their own lack of materials or money, they would have to go begging to the Russians for collectivization of agriculture. The Russians would then be able to speak of the 'free will of the people'.

21. Quoted in Hardach, op. cit., p. 94. On the Marshall Plan more generally, *see*: Michael Hogan, *The Marshall Plan* (Cambridge: Cambridge University Press, 1987).

22. A. Grosser, *Germany in Our Time* (London: Pall Mall Press, 1971), p. 71.

23. *See* particularly Anthony Carew, *Labour under the Marshall Plan* (Manchester: Manchester University Press, 1987).

24. Steininger, op. cit., p. 174.

CHAPTER SEVEN

1. Quoted in D. P. Conradt, *The German Polity* (London: Longman, 1982), pp. 86–7.

2. On failed attempts at reunification, *see* for example Rolf Steininger, '1952: Eine Chance zur Wiedervereinigung!', *Deutsche Geschichte 1945–1961* (Frankfurt: Fischer, 1985), vol. 2, ch. 16.

3. *See* A. Carew, *Labour under the Marshall Plan* (Manchester:

Manchester University Press, 1987), for an exploration of these aspects of its effects.

4. On socio-economic development, *see* particularly K. Hardach, *The Political Economy of Germany in the Twentieth Century* (Berkeley: University of California Press, 1980). On the development of public opinion, *see* the fascinating surveys undertaken by Elisabeth Noelle and Erich Peter Neumann, in the *Jahrbuch der Öffentlichen Meinung* (Allensbach: Verlag für Demoskopie).

5. On the development of the SPD, *see* for example S. Miller and H. Potthoff, *A History of German Social Democracy* (Leamington Spa: Berg, 1986).

6. Figures taken from Conradt, op. cit., p. 181.

7. *See* for example the attempt at defence of Globke in D. Bark and D. Gress, *A History of West Germany* (Oxford: Basil Blackwell, 1989), vol. 1, pp. 247–8.

8. Chillingly documented in the 'factional' novel by Bernt Engelmann, *Grosses Bundesverdienstkreuz mit Stern* (Göttingen: Steidl Verlag, 1987).

9. *See* for example the increasingly bitter comments of a former member of an anti-Nazi resistance group who subsequently was hounded out of East Germany, only to find no place in the West Germany of the 1950s, Dr Karl Schultes. He comments, for example, in a letter of 16 September 1955, that he feels very unjustly handled in comparison with the 'NSDAP-people' who served Hitler loyally, and now are able to resume their activities in the administration and even be promoted, while he is excluded from any employment. (Unpublished papers in the Munich Institut für Zeitgeschichte: ED 188/2).

10. On this period, *see* the classic insider's view by Wolfgang Leonhard, *Die Revolution entlässt ihre Kinder* (Köln: Verlag Kiepenhauer and Witsch, 1955).

11. On church–state relations, see particularly H. Dähn, *Konfrontation oder Kooperation? Das Verhältnis von Staat und Kirche in der SBZ/DDR 1945–1980* (Opladen: Westdeutscher Verlag, 1982).

12. On the uprising, *see* particularly A. Baring, *Der 17. Juni 1953* (Stuttgart: Deutsche Verlags-Anstalt, 1983).

13. On the 'Third Way', *see* for example Hermann Weber, 'The Third Way', in U. Wolter (ed.), *Rudolf Bahro: Critical Responses* (New York: M. E. Sharpe, 1980).

CHAPTER EIGHT

1. *See* particularly V. Berghahn, *The Americanization of West German Industry* (Leamington Spa: Berg, 1986).

2. Quoted in G. Leptin and M. Melzer, *Economic Reform in East German Industry* (London: Oxford University Press, 1978), p. 10.

3. P. C. Ludz, *The German Democratic Republic from the Sixties to the Seventies* (Harvard Center for International Affairs: Occasional Papers in International Affairs, no. 26, November 1970).

4. *See* the suggestive discussion by Lutz Niethammer, based on his oral history project started well before the 1989 revolution: L. Niethammer, 'Das Volk der DDR und die Revolution', in C. Schüddekopf (ed.), *'Wir sind das Volk!'* (Hamburg: Rowohlt, 1990).

5. *See* Hermann Weber, 'Geschichte der SED' in I. Spittmann (ed.), *Die SED in Geschichte und Gegenwart* (Köln: Verlag Wissenschaft und Politik, 1987), p. 28, p. 31.

6. *See* H. Dähn, *Konfrontation oder Kooperation? Das Verhältnis von Staat und Kirche in der SBZ/DDR 1945–1980* (Opladen: Westdeutscher Verlag, 1982), ch. 3.

7. Figure given by G. Wettig, 'Relations between the two German states', in K. von Beyme and H. Zimmermann (eds.), *Policymaking in the German Democratic Republic* (Aldershot: Gower, 1984), p. 288.

8. Ibid., p. 286. I was somewhat surprised when, on a visit to an old friend in West Berlin in the summer of 1987, I found a mutual East German friend in her flat. A resident of Potsdam, he had not been able to visit West Berlin since the erection of the Wall in 1961; but in 1987 our West Berlin friend had been able to adopt him as her 'step-nephew' and he attended her seventy-first birthday under the heading of 'urgent family business'. Hardly what would have been classified as either 'urgent' or 'family' before then!

CHAPTER NINE

1. *Statistisches Jahrbuch der DDR* (Berlin, East: Staatsverlag der Deutschen Demokratischen Republik, 1984), p. 111.

2. *Zahlenspiegel*, p. 37.

3. Cf. J. Krejci, *Social Structure in Divided Germany* (London: Croom Helm, 1976), p. 119.

4. Figures in this and the following paragraph are taken from the West German official publication *Zahlenspiegel* and the East German official publication *Statistisches Jahrbuch der DDR*.

5. *See Zahlenspiegel*, pp. 6–7.

6. H. Weiler and J. Flasbarth (eds.), *Wirtschaftspartner DDR* (Bonn: Economica Verlag, 1990), p. 18.

7. On comparative living standards, *see* Deutsches Institut für Wirtschaftsforschung Berlin (ed.), *Handbuch DDR-Wirtschaft* (Hamburg: Rowohlt, 4th edn, 1984), ch. 5, section 3.

8. *See* Arthur Hearndon, *Education in the Two Germanies* (Oxford: Basil Blackwell, 1974), ch. 3.

9. *See* for example Hildegard Hamm-Brücher, 'Versäumte Reformen' in K. D. Bracher (ed.), *Nach 25 Jahren: Eine Deutschland-Bilanz* (Munich: Kindler-Verlag, 1970).

10. Cf. H. Weber (ed.), *DDR: Dokumente zur Geschichte der Deutschen Demokratischen Republik* (Munich: dtv, 1986), pp. 71–3.

11. Hearndon, op. cit., pp. 111–23; John Page, 'Education under the Honeckers' in D. Childs (ed.), *Honecker's Germany* (London: Allen and Unwin, 1985).

12. Hearndon, op. cit., p. 86.

13. Ibid., p. 241; D. Childs, *East Germany* (London: Ernest Benn, 1969), pp. 185–6.

14. G.-J. Glaessner, 'Universitäten und Hochschulen' in *DDR-Handbuch* (2nd edn, 1979): 1100–7, p. 1103.

15. Hearndon, op. cit., p. 157, p. 166.

16. Helmut Becker, 'Bildungspolitik' in W. Benz (ed.), *Die Bundesrepublik Deutschland* (Frankfurt: Fischer Taschenbuch Verlag, 1983), vol. II, p. 336.

17. Glaessner, loc. cit., p. 1103; and Glaessner, 'The Education System and Society' in K. von Beyme and H. Zimmermann (eds.), *Policymaking in the GDR* (Aldershot: Gower, 1984), pp. 201–2.

18. Gisela Helwig, *Frau und Familie, Bundesrepublik Deutschland-DDR* (Köln: Verlag Wissenschaft und Politik, 2nd edn, 1987), p. 22.

19. Personal communication in discussion with an East German doctor.

20. Helwig, op. cit., p. 41 and p. 40.

21. Ibid., p. 88, p. 46, p. 49.

22. Ibid., p. 23, p. 33, p. 22, p. 34.

23. Cf. G. E. Edwards, *GDR Society and Social Institutions* (London: Macmillan, 1985).

24. Helwig, op. cit., p. 96.

25. *See* for example the development of Christa Wolf's feminism, as documented in the collection of her speeches and essays, *Die Dimension des Autors* (Darmstadt and Neuwied: Luchterhand, 1987).

26. Cf. for example Christel Lane, 'Women in Socialist Society, with particular reference to the GDR', *Sociology*, vol XVII, no. 4 (November 1983): 489–505.

27. Helwig, op. cit., p. 70.

CHAPTER TEN

1. Figures from Hartmut Zimmermann, 'Power Distribution and Opportunities for Participation: Aspects of the Sociopolitical

System of the GDR', in K. von Beyme and H. Zimmermann (eds.), *Policymaking in the German Democratic Republic* (Aldershot: Gower, 1984), p. 29.

2. *See* for example Franz Loeser, *Die unglaubwürdige Gesellschaft* (Köln: Bund-Verlag, 1984). This sort of insider view is confirmed by conversations I have had with other East Germans on visits prior to the 1989 revolution.

3. The DBD had 95,000 members in 1977; the LDPD had 75,000; the NDPD had 84,000 while the largest of the small parties was the CDU with 115,000 members. In 1987 the figures were 115,000 for the DBD, 104,000 for the LDPD, and 110,000 for the NDPD. Figures taken from Zimmermann, loc. cit., p. 64, and Mike Dennis, *German Democratic Republic* (London: Pinter, 1988), p. 90.

4. Zimmermann, loc. cit., p. 29.

5. Ibid., p. 64.

6. *See* particularly Gero Neugebauer, *Partei und Staatsapparat in der DDR* (Opladen: Westdeutscher Verlag, 1978), ch. 3: 'Instrumentalisierung des Staatsapparats oder Verstaatlichung der Partei?'.

7. *DDR Handbuch*, 3rd edn, 1985, vol. II, pp. 1006–9.

8. P. C. Ludz, *The German Democratic Republic from the Sixties to the Seventies* (Harvard Center for International Affairs: Occasional Papers in International Affairs, no. 26, November 1970); P. C. Ludz, *The Changing Party Elite in East Germany* (Cambridge, Mass.: MIT Press, 1972).

9. T. Baylis, *The Technical Intelligentsia and the East German Elite* (Berkeley: University of California Press, 1974); *see* also M. Sodaru, 'Limits to Dissent in the GDR: Fragmentation, Cooptation and Repression' in Jane Leftwich Curry (ed.), *Dissent in Eastern Europe* (New York: Praeger, 1983), particularly p. 89, where the argument is made that Ulbricht's 'almost obsequious cultivation of the technical elite' actually gave members of the technical intelligentsia such a stake in the existing system that they were unwilling to risk jeopardizing their position; and M. Fulbrook, 'Elites and Politics in the GDR' in J. Trumpbour (ed.), *The Dividing Rhine* (Oxford: Berg, 1989).

10. R. Dahrendorf, *Society and Democracy in Germany* (London: Weidenfeld and Nicolson, 1968), chs. 17, 26, 27; J. Krejci, *Social Structure in Divided Germany* (London: Croom Helm, 1976), ch. 4; S. Thielbeer, 'Ist die DDR ein totalitärer Staat?' in E. Jesse (ed.), *Bundesrepublik Deutschland und Deutsche Demokratische Republik: Die beiden deutschen Staaten im Vergleich* (Berlin: Colloquium Verlag, 3rd edn, 1982).

11. *See* for example Jürgen Seifert, 'Die Verfassung' in Wolfgang Benz (ed.), *Die Bundesrepublik Deutschland* (Frankfurt:

Fischer Taschenbuch Verlag, 3 vols., 1983), vol. I, particularly
p. 53.

12. Lewis Edinger, *West German Politics* (New York: Columbia
University Press, 1986 edn), p. 199.

13. Ibid., p. 200.

14. Gordon Smith, 'Does West Germany have an "Efficient Secret"?'
in W. Paterson and G. Smith (eds.), *The West German Model:
Perspectives on a Stable State* (London: Frank Cass, 1981); *see*
also G. Smith, *Democracy in West Germany* (London: Heinemann,
1979); for a contrasting evaluation, *see* for example J. Hirsch,
'Developments in the Political System of West Germany since
1945' in R. Scase (ed.), *The State in Western Europe* (London:
Croom Helm, 1980).

15. C. Offe and V. Ronge, 'Theses on the Theory of the State',
reprinted in A. Giddens and D. Held (eds.), *Classes, Power and
Conflict* (London: Macmillan, 1982); *see* generally also R. Miliband,
The State in Capitalist Society (London: Weidenfeld and Nicolson,
1969).

16. There are numerous West German books attempting comparison
of systems which have confronted the problem of the two
Germanies' different self-understandings and legitimizations. See
for example Wolfgang Behr, *Bundesrepublik Deutschland–Deutsche
Demokratische Republik. Systemvergleich* (Stuttgart: Kohlhammer,
1979); and E. Jesse (ed.), op. cit.

17. Figures from H. Krisch, *The German Democratic Republic* (Boulder:
Westview Press, 1985), p. 43; p. 45.

18. *See* for example G. Neugebauer, 'Military Policy in the GDR' in
von Beyme and Zimmermann, op. cit.; article on 'Militarisierung'
in *DDR Handbuch*, 3rd edn, op. cit., vol II, p. 892.

19. See Klaus von Schubert, 'Sicherheitspolitik und Bundeswehr', in
Benz (ed.), op. cit., pp. 321–3.

20. Ibid., pp. 320–1.

21. *DDR Handbuch*, op. cit; *see* also 'Der lange Arm der Stasi', *Der
Spiegel*, vol. XLIV, no. 13, March 1990.

22. *Spiegel*, vol. XLII, no. 5, 1988, pp. 18–27.

CHAPTER ELEVEN

1. K. Reyman, 'Preface' to section on East Germany in F. Silnitsky
(ed.), *Communism and Eastern Europe* (Brighton: Harvester Press,
1979), p. 167.

2. *See* D. Staritz, *Geschichte der DDR, 1949–1985* (Frankfurt:
Suhrkamp, 1985), pp. 113–5; and H. Weber, 'The Third Way' in

Uwe Wolter (ed.), *Rudolf Bahro: Critical Responses* (New York: M. E. Sharpe, 1980).

3. *See* for example R. Havemann, *An Alienated Man* (London: Davis Poynter, 1973), the translation of his *Fragen Antworten Fragen*; and Havemann, 'The Socialism of Tomorrow' in Silnitsky (ed.), op. cit.

4. R. Bahro, *The Alternative in Eastern Europe* (London: New Left Books, 1978); *see* also Wolter (ed.), op. cit.

5. A fuller discussion and references on the development of church–state relations can be found in my article, 'Co-option and Commitment: Aspects of Relations between Church and State in the GDR', *Social History*, vol. XII, no. 1, (January 1987), pp. 73–91.

6. On the peace initiatives, *see* for example J. Sandford, *The Sword and the Ploughshare* (London: Merlin Press, 1983); K. Ehring and M. Dallwitz, *Schwerter zu Pflugscharen* (Hamburg: Rowohlt, 1982).

7. On Jews in East Germany, *see* Robin Ostow, *Jews in Contemporary East Germany* (London: Macmillan, 1989).

CHAPTER TWELVE

1. Cf. H. James, *A German Identity, 1700–1990* (London: Weidenfeld and Nicolson, revised edn, 1990); for my own view of the long and problematic sweep of German history in changing political forms and geographical boundaries, *see* M. Fulbrook, *A Concise History of Germany* (Cambridge: Cambridge University Press, 1990).

2. *See* for example, for an autobiographical account of difficulties in gaining access to Brecht by a student of the 1950s, B. Klump, *Das rote Kloster* (Hamburg: Hoffmann and Campe, 1978).

3. *Neues Deutschland*, 18 December 1971.

4. Irma Hanke, 'Continuity and Change: Cultural Policy in the German Democratic Republic since the VIIIth Party Congress in 1971' in K. von Beyme and H. Zimmermann (eds.), *Policymaking in the German Democratic Republic* (Aldershot: Gower, 1984). *See* for a compelling imaginative view by a novelist who fled to West Germany, Monika Maron, *Flugasche*.

5. G. Eckart, *So sehe ick die Sache* (Köln: Kiepenhauer and Witsch, 1985).

6. Cf. the lecture on 'Glasnost and Culture in the GDR' delivered by Klaus Höpke, Deputy Minister of Culture, at London University's School of Slavonic and East European Studies, 31 March 1988.

7. For an overview, *see* for example C. Burdick et al., *Contemporary Germany: Politics and Culture* (Boulder: Westview Press, 1984), Part Two.

8. *See* for example 'Friedrich: ein Denkmal kehrt zurück', *Der Spiegel* 1986, no. 32; Erich Honecker, 'Unsere Zeit verlangt Parteinahme für Fortschritt, Vernunft und Menschlichkeit' in *Martin Luther und unsere Zeit. Konstituierung des Martin-Luther-Komitees der DDR* (Berlin 1980); G. Giles, 'Berlin's 750th anniversary exhibitions', *German History*, vol. VI (1988), pp. 164–70.

9. Cf. J. Kuppe, 'Das Geschichtsbewusstsein in der DDR' in W. Weidenfeld (ed.), *Geschichtsbewusstsein der Deutschen: Materialen zur Spurensuche einer Nation* (Köln: Verlag Wissenschaft und Politik, 1987), pp. 175–7.

10. *See*: *Topographie des Terrors* (Berlin: Verlag Willmuth Arenhövel, 1987).

11. Cf. for example M. Hughes, *Nationalism and Society* (London: Edward Arnold, 1988), ch. 11.

12. Cf. G. Herdegen, 'Einstellungen der Deutschen (Ost) zur nationalen Identität' in D. Berg-Schlosser and J. Schissler (ed.), *Politische Kultur in Deutschland: Bilanz und Perspektiven der Forschung* (Opladen: West-deutscher Verlag, 1987), pp. 216–7.

13. On the *Historikerstreit*, see for the major contributions the Piper collection, *Historikerstreit* (Munich: Piper, 1987); for examples of very different commentaries, Richard J. Evans, *In Hitler's Shadow* (London: I. B. Tauris, 1989), and the quite extraordinary diatribe in D. Bark and D. Gress, *A History of West Germany* (Oxford: Basil Blackwell, 1989), vol. II, Part Ten, ch. 5.

14. I have developed these ideas in my article on 'The State and the Transformation of Political Legitimacy in East and West Germany since 1945', *Comparative Studies in Society and History*, vol. XXIX, no. 2, April 1987, pp. 211–44.

15. G. Gaus, *Wo Deutschland liegt* (München: Deutscher Taschenbuch Verlag, 1986).

CHAPTER THIRTEEN

1. The rest of this chapter is based primarily on contemporary press reports, on television and radio broadcasts, and on discussions with and letters from acquaintances in both Germanies.

2. Radio interview of 13 September 1989, reprinted in *Deutschland Archiv*, vol. XXII, no. 10, October 1989, p. 1180.

3. Cf. ibid., discussion.

CHAPTER FOURTEEN

1. Edwina Moreton, *Germany Between East and West* (Cambridge: Cambridge University Press, 1987).

SELECT BIBLIOGRAPHY OF ENGLISH-LANGUAGE WORKS

Twentieth-century German history is a highly contentious field, with innumerable books on Hitler and the Third Reich alone. It would be impracticable to provide any sort of comprehensive list. This short bibliography includes only selected English-language contributions, which will in turn guide the interested reader to further references. Those works considered to be particularly useful as initial reading, or for teaching purposes, have been marked with an asterisk.

General interpretations and works covering more than one period

*V. Berghahn, *Modern Germany* (Cambridge: Cambridge University Press, 2nd edn, 1987)

D. Calleo, *The German Problem Reconsidered* (Cambridge: Cambridge University Press, 1978)

*W. Carr, *A History of Germany, 1815–1985* (London: Edward Arnold, 3rd edn, 1987)

G. Craig, *The Germans* (Harmondsworth: Penguin, 1978)

*G. Craig, *Germany 1866–1945* (Oxford: Oxford University Press, 1981)

R. Dahrendorf, *Society and Democracy in Germany* (London: Weidenfeld and Nicolson, 1968)

*K. Hardach, *The Political Economy of Germany in the Twentieth Century* (Berkeley: University of California Press, 1980)

S. Miller and H. Potthoff, *A History of German Social Democracy* (Leamington Spa: Berg, 1986)

*D. Orlow, *A History of Modern Germany* (Englewood Cliffs, N.J.: Prentice-Hall, 1987)

The Weimar Republic and the rise of the Nazis

R. Fletcher (ed.), *Bernstein to Brandt: A Short History of German Social Democracy* (London: Edward Arnold, 1987)

*R. Bessel and E. Feuchtwanger (eds.), *Social Change and Political Development in the Weimar Republic* (London: Croom Helm, 1981)

*M. Broszat, *Hitler and the Collapse of Weimar Germany* (Leamington Spa: Berg, 1987)

C. B. Burdick and R. H. Lutz (eds.), *The Political Institutions of the German Revolution, 1918–19* (New York: Praeger, 1966)

F. L. Carsten, *The Reichswehr and Politics* (Oxford: Clarendon Press, 1966)

F. L. Carsten, *The Rise of Fascism* (London: Batsford, 1967)

T. Childers (ed.), *The Formation of the Nazi Constituency* (London: Croom Helm, 1986)

T. Childers, *The Nazi Voter* (Chapel Hill: University of North Carolina Press, 1983)

G. Eley, *From Unification to Nazism* (London: Allen and Unwin, 1986)

E. Eyck, *A History of the Weimar Republic* (Cambridge, Mass.: Harvard University Press, 2nd edn, 1967)

*P. Gay, *Weimar Culture* (New York: Harper and Row, 1968)

J. Hiden, *The Weimar Republic* (Harlow: Longman, 1974)

H. James, *The German Slump* (Oxford: Clarendon Press, 1986)

*I. Kershaw (ed.), *Weimar: Why did German Democracy Fail?* (London: Weidenfeld and Nicolson, 1990)

J. Kocka, *Facing Total War: German Society 1914–1918* (Leamington Spa: Berg, 1984)

*E. Kolb, *The Weimar Republic* (London: Unwin Hyman, 1988)

M. Lee and W. Michalka, *German Foreign Policy 1917–1933: Continuity or Break?* (Leamington Spa: Berg, 1987)

B. Moore, *Injustice,* (London: Macmillan, 1978), chs. 8–11

A. Nicholls, *Weimar and the Rise of Hitler* (London: Macmillan, 2nd edn, 1979)

*J. Noakes and G. Pridham (eds.), *Nazism*, vol. I, 'Hitler's Rise to Power' (Exeter: Exeter Studies in History, 1983)

A. J. Ryder, *The German Revolution of 1918* (Cambridge: Cambridge University Press, 1967)

P. Stachura (ed.), *The Nazi Machtergreifung* (London: Allen and Unwin, 1983)

H. A. Turner, *German Big Business and the Rise of Hitler* (Oxford: Oxford University Press, 1985)

J. Willett, *The New Sobriety: Art and Society in the Weimar Republic* (London: Thames and Hudson, 1978)

The Third Reich

P. Aycoberry, *The Nazi Question* (London: Routledge and Kegan Paul, 1981)

M. Balfour, *Withstanding Hitler* (London: Routledge, 1988)

P. M. Bell, *The Origins of the Second World War in Europe* (London: Longman, 1986)

R. Bessel (ed.), *Life in the Third Reich* (Oxford: Oxford University Press, 1987)

*K. D. Bracher, *The German Dictatorship* (Harmondsworth: Penguin, 1975)

*M. Broszat, *The Hitler State* (London: Longman, 1981)

H. Bull (ed.), *The Challenge of the Third Reich* (Oxford: Clarendon Press, 1986)

W. Carr, *Arms, Autarky and Aggression* (London: Edward Arnold, 1972)

W. Carr, *From Poland to Pearl Harbor* (London: Edward Arnold, 1985)

W. Carr, *Hitler: A Study in Personality and Politics* (London: Edward Arnold, 1978)

L. Dawidowicz, *The War against the Jews* (Harmondsworth: Penguin, 1975)

G. Fleming, *Hitler and the Final Solution* (London: Hamish Hamilton, 1985)

M. Freeman, *Atlas of Nazi Germany* (London: Croom Helm, 1987)

M. Gilbert, *The Holocaust* (London: Collins, 1986)

H. Graml et al., *The German Opposition to Hitler* (London: Batsford, 1970)

R. Grunberger, *A Social History of the Third Reich* (Harmondsworth: Penguin, 1974)

J. Hiden and J. Farquharson, *Explaining Hitler's Germany* (London: Batsford, 1983)

A. Hillgruber, *Germany and the Two World Wars* (Cambridge, Mass.: Harvard University Press, 1981)

G. Hirschfeld and L. Kettenacker (eds.), *Der Führerstaat: Mythos und Realität / The Führer State: Myth and Reality* (in English and German, with important English-language contributions) (Stuttgart: Klett-Cotta, 1981)

P. Hoffman, *German Resistance to Hitler* (Cambridge, Mass.: Harvard University Press, 1988)

M. Kater, *The Nazi Party* (Oxford: Basil Blackwell, 1983)

I. Kershaw, *The Hitler Myth* (Oxford: Oxford University Press, 1987)

*I. Kershaw, *The Nazi Dictatorship* (London: Edward Arnold, 1985)

I. Kershaw, *Popular Opinion and Political Dissent in the Third Reich* (Oxford: Clarendon Press, 1983)

H. W. Koch (ed.), *Aspects of the Third Reich* (London: Macmillan, 1985)

W. Laqueur (ed.), *Fascism: A Reader's Guide* (Harmondsworth: Penguin, 1976)

W. Laqueur, *The Terrible Secret* (Harmondsworth: Penguin, 1980)

G. Martell (ed.), *The Origins of the Second World War Reconsidered: The A. J. P. Taylor Debate after 25 Years* (London: Allen and Unwin, 1986)

J. Noakes and G. Pridham (eds.), *Nazism*, vol. II, 'State, Economy and Society, 1933–1939' (Exeter: Exeter Studies in History, 1984)

J. Noakes and G. Pridham (eds.), *Nazism*, vol. III, 'Foreign Policy, War and Racial Extermination' (Exeter: Exeter Studies in History, 1988)

R. Overy, *The Nazi Economic Recovery, 1932–38* (London: Macmillan, 1982)

R. Overy, *The Origins of the Second World War* (London: Longman, 1987)

E. N. Peterson, *The Limits of Hitler's Power* (Princeton: Princeton University Press, 1969)

D. Peukert, *Inside Nazi Germany* (London: Batsford, 1987)

E. M. Robertson (ed.), *The Origins of the Second World War* (London: Macmillan, 1971)

H. Rothfels, *The German Opposition to Hitler* (London: Oswald Wolff, 1970)

D. Schoenbaum, *Hitler's Social Revolution* (London: Weidenfeld and Nicolson, 1967)

P. Stachura (ed.), *The Shaping of the Nazi State* (London: Croom Helm, 1978)

J. Stephenson, *The Nazi Organization of Women* (London: Croom Helm, 1981)

J. Stephenson, *Women in Nazi Society* (London: Croom Helm, 1975)

J. P. Stern, *Hitler: The Führer and the People* (London: Fontana Press, 3rd edn, 1990)

A. J. P. Taylor, *The Origins of the Second World War* (London: Hamish Hamilton, 1961)

S. J. Woolf (ed.), *European Fascism* (London: Weidenfeld and Nicolson, 1968)

S. J. Woolf (ed.), *The Nature of Fascism* (London: Weidenfeld and Nicolson, 1968)

Germany divided, 1945–1990

J. Backer, *The Decision to Divide Germany* (Durham, N.C.: Duke University Press, 1978)

R. Bahro, *The Alternative in Eastern Europe* (London: New Left Books, 1978)

*M. Balfour, *West Germany: A Contemporary History* (London: Croom Helm, 1982).

A. Baring, *Uprising in East Germany* (New York: Cornell University Press, 1972).

D. Bark and D. Gress, *A History of West Germany*, 2 vols. (Oxford: Basil Blackwell, 1989).

T. Baylis, *The Technical Intelligentsia and the East German Elite* (Berkeley: University of California Press, 1974).

J. Becker, *Hitler's Children* (London: Panther, 1977).

V. Berghahn, *The Americanization of West German Industry, 1945–73* (Leamington Spa: Berg, 1986).

V. Berghahn and D. Karsten, *Industrial Relations in West Germany* (Oxford: Berg, 1987).

*K. von Beyme and H. Zimmermann (eds.), *Policymaking in the German Democratic Republic* (Aldershot: Gower, 1984).

K. von Beyme, *The Political System of the Federal Republic of Germany* (Aldershot: Gower, 1984).

T. Bower, *Blind Eye to Murder* (London: Granada, 1983).

S. Bulmer and W. Paterson, *The Federal Republic of Germany and the European Community* (London: Allen and Unwin, 1987).

C. Burdick et al (eds.), *Contemporary Germany: Politics and Culture* (Boulder, Colorado: Westview Press, 1984).

R. Burns and W. van der Will, *Protest and Democracy in West Germany: Extra-Parliamentary Opposition and the Democratic Agenda* (London: Macmillan, 1988).

A. Carew, *Labour under the Marshall Plan* (Manchester: Manchester University Press, 1987).

*D. Childs, *The GDR: Moscow's German Ally* (London: George Allen and Unwin, 1983).

*D. Childs, (ed.), *Honecker's Germany* (London: Allen and Unwin, 1985).

D. Childs, T. Baylis and M. Rueschemeyer (eds.), *East Germany in Comparative Perspective* (London: Routledge, 1989).

*D. Childs and J. Johnson, *West Germany: Politics and Society* (London: Croom Helm, 1981).

S. Cobler, *Law, Order and Politics in West Germany* (Harmondsworth: Penguin, 1978).

*D. P. Conradt, *The German Polity* (London: Longman, 3rd edn, 1986).

*M. Dennis, *German Democratic Republic* (London: Pinter, 1988).

H. Döring and G. Smith (eds.), *Party Government and Political*

Culture in Western Germany (New York: St. Martin's Press, 1982).

A. Dorpalen, *German History in Marxist Perspective: The East German Approach* (London: I. B. Taurus, 1985).

R. Ebsworth, *Restoring Democracy in Germany* (London: Stevens and Sons Ltd., 1960).

*L. Edinger, *West German Politics* (New York: Columbia University Press, 1986).

*G. E. Edwards, *GDR Society and Social Institutions* (London: Macmillan, 1985).

Richard J. Evans, *In Hitler's Shadow* (London: I. B. Taurus, 1989).

C. Fitzgibbon, *Denazification* (London: Michael Joseph, 1969).

T. Forster, *The East German Army* (London: George Allen and Unwin, 5th edn, 1980).

M. Freund, *From Cold War to Ostpolitik* (London: Oswald Wolff, 1972).

*R. Fritsch-Bournazel, *Confronting the German Question* (Oxford: Berg, 1988).

J. Gimbel, *The American Occupation of Germany: Politics and the Military, 1945–49* (Stanford: Stanford University Press, 1968).

J. Gimbel, *A German Community under American Occupation: Marburg, 1945–52* (Stanford: Stanford University Press, 1961).

*A. Grosser, *Germany In Our Time* (London: Pall Mall Press, 1971).

H. Haftendorn, *Security and Detente: Conflicting Priorities in German Foreign Policy* (New York: Praeger, 1985).

R. Havemann, *An Alienated Man* (London: Davis-Poynter, 1973).

A. Hearndon (ed.), *The British in Germany: Educational Reconstruction after 1945* (London: Hamish Hamilton, 1978).

A. Hearndon, *Education in the Two Germanies* (Oxford: Basil Blackwell, 1974).

A. Heidenheimer, *Adenauer and the CDU* (The Hague, 1960).

H. Heitzer, *GDR: An Historical Outline* (Dresden: Verlag Zeit im Bild, 1981). (Official East German history of GDR in English.)

D. R. Herspring, *East German Civil-military Relations: the Impact of Technology, 1949–72* (New York: Praeger, 1973).

M. Hogan, *The Marshall Plan* (Cambridge: Cambridge University Press.)

W. Hülsberg, *The German Greens: A Social and Political Profile* (London: Verso, 1988).

I. Jeffries and M. Melzer, *The East German Economy* (London: Croom Helm, 1987).

P. Katzenstein, *Policy and Politics in West Germany: The Growth of a Semi-sovereign State* (Philadelphia: Temple University Press, 1987).

P. Katzenstein (ed.), *Industry and Politics in West Germany* (Ithaca: Cornell University Press, 1989).

O. Kirchheimer, 'Germany: The Vanishing Opposition' in R. A. Dahl (ed.), *Political Oppositions in Western Democracies* (New Haven: Yale University Press, 1966).

*E. Kolinsky, *Parties, Opposition and Society in West Germany* (London: Croom Helm, 1984).

E. Kolinsky, *Women in West Germany* (Oxford: Berg, 1989).

J. Krejci, *Social Structure in Divided Germany* (London: Croom Helm, 1976).

*H. Krisch, *The German Democratic Republic* (Boulder, Colorado: Westview Press, 1985).

H. Krisch, *German Politics under Soviet Occupation* (New York: University of Columbia Press, 1984).

*W. Laqueur, *Germany Today: A Personal Report* (London: Weidenfeld and Nicolson, 1985).

J. Leaman, *The Political Economy of West Germany, 1945–85* (London: Macmillan, 1988).

W. Leonard, *Child of the Revolution* (London: Collins, 1957).

G. Lepton and M. Melzer, *Economic Reform in East German Industry* (London: Oxford University Press, 1978).

H. Lippmann, *Honecker and the New Politics of Europe* (New York: Macmillan, 1972).

P. C. Ludz, *The Changing Party Elite in East Germany* (Cambridge, Mass.: MIT Press, 1972).

P. C. Ludz, *The GDR from the Sixties to the Seventies* (Harvard Center for International Affairs: Occasional Papers in International Affairs, no. 26, November 1970).

C. Maier (ed.), *The Origins of the Cold War and Contemporary Europe* (New York: New Viewpoints, 1978).

C. Maier, *The Unmasterable Past: History, Holocaust, and German National Identity* (Cambridge, Mass.: Harvard University Press, 1988).

A. Markovits, *The Politics of West German Trade Unions: Strategies of Class and Interest Representation in Growth and Crisis* (Cambridge: Cambridge University Press, 1986).

B. Marshall, *The Origins of Post-war German Politics* (London: Croom Helm, 1988).

A. J. McAdams, *East Germany and Detente: Building Authority after the Wall* (Cambridge: Cambridge University Press, 1985).

*M. McCauley, *The GDR since 1945* (London: Macmillan, 1983).

M. McCauley, *Marxism-Leninism in the GDR* (London: Macmillan, 1979).

M. McCauley, *The Origins of the Cold War* (London: Longman, 1983).

R. Mellor, *The Two Germanies: A Modern Geography* (London: Harper and Row, 1978).

P. H. Merkl (ed.), *The Federal Republic at Forty* (Cambridge: Cambridge University Press, 1989).

P. H. Merkl, *The Origin of the West German Republic* (New York: Oxford University Press, 1963).

A. J. Merritt and R. L. Merritt (eds.), *Public Opinion in Occupied Germany: The OMGUS Surveys, 1945–49* (Urbana: University of Illinois Press, 1970).

J. Moore-Rinvolucri, *Education in East Germany* (Newton Abbot: David and Charles, 1973).

N. Edwina Moreton (ed.), *Germany between East and West* (Cambridge: Cambridge University Press, 1987).

J. P. Nettl, *The Eastern Zone and Soviet Policy in Germany, 1945–50* (London: Oxford University Press, 1951).

B. Ruhm von Oppen (ed.), *Documents on Germany under Occupation, 1945–55* (London: Oxford University Press, 1955).

Robin Ostow, *Jews in Contemporary East Germany* (London: Macmillan, 1989).

*W. Paterson and G. Smith (eds.), *The West German Model: Perspectives on a Stable State* (London: Frank Cass, 1981).

E. Peterson, *The American Occupation of Germany* (Detroit: Wayne State University Press, 1978).

N. Pronay and K. Wilson (eds.), *The Political Re-education of Germany and her Allies after World War II* (London: Croom Helm, 1985).

J. Reich, 'Reflections on Becoming an East German Dissident, on Losing the Wall and a Country', in G. Prins (eds.), *Spring in Winter: The 1989 Revolutions* (Manchester: Manchester University Press, 1990).

R. Rist, *Guestworkers in Germany: The Prospects for Pluralism* (New York: Praeger, 1978).

M. Rueschemeyer, *Professional Work and Marriage: an East–West Comparison* (London: Macmillan, 1981).

G. Sandford, *From Hitler to Ulbricht: The Communist Reconstruction of East Germany, 1945–6* (Princeton: Princeton University Press, 1983).

J. Sandford, *The Sword and the Ploughshare: Autonomous Peace Initiatives in East Germany* (London: Merlin Press/END, 1983).

C. Bradley Scharf, *Politics and Change in East Germany* (Boulder, Colorado: Westview Press, 1984).

G. Schweigler, *National Consciousness in Divided Germany* (London: Sage, 1975).

*C. C. Schweitzer et al. (eds.), *Politics and Government in the Federal Republic of Germany: Basic Documents* (Leamington Spa: Berg, 1984).

Harry Shaffer, *Women in the Two Germanies* (New York: Pergamon, 1981).

F. Silnitsky (ed.), *Communism in Eastern Europe*, (Brighton: Harvester Press, 1979), section on GDR.

H. Simonian, *The Privileged Partnership: Franco-German Relations in the European Community, 1969–84* (Oxford: Clarendon Press, 1985).

E. Owen Smith, *The West German Economy* (Beckenham: Croom Helm, 1983).

*G. Smith, *Democracy in Western Germany* (Aldershot: Gower, 3rd edn, 1986).

*G. Smith, W. Paterson and Peter H. Merkl (eds.), *Developments in West German Politics* (London: Macmillan, 1989).

*K. Sontheimer and W. Bleek, *The Government and Politics of East Germany* (London: Hutchinson, 1975).

F. Spotts, *The Churches and Politics in Germany* (Middletown, Conn.: Wesleyan University Press, 1973).

J. Steele, *Socialism with a German Face* (London: Jonathan Cape, 1977).

C. Stern, *Ulbricht* (London: Pall Mall Press, 1965).

James F. Tent, *Mission on the Rhine: Re-education and Denazification in American-occupied Germany* (Chicago: University of Chicago Press, 1982).

*J. K. A. Thomanek and J. Mellis (eds.), *Politics, Society and Government in the German Democratic Republic: Basic Documents* (Oxford: Berg, 1988).

R. Tökés (ed.), *Opposition in Eastern Europe* (London: Macmillan, 1979), section on the GDR.

*H. A. Turner, *The Two Germanies since 1945* (New Haven: Yale University Press, 1987).

A. and J. Tusa, *The Nuremberg Trial* (London: Macmillan, 1983).

I. Wallace (ed.), *East Germany*, World Bibliographical Series vol. LXXVII (Oxford: Clio Press, 1987).

I. Wallace (ed.), *The GDR under Honecker, 1971–81* (GDR Monitor Special Series, no. 1, Dundee, 1981).

W. Wessels and E. Regelsberger, *The Federal Republic and the European Community: The Presidency and Beyond* (Bonn: Europa Union Verlag, 1988).

F. Willis, *The French in Germany* (Stanford: Stanford University Press, 1962).

U. Wolters (ed.), *Rudolf Bahro: Critical Responses* (New York: M. E. Sharpe, 1980).

*R. Woods, *Opposition in the GDR under Honecker, 1971–85* (London: Macmillan, 1986).

A. de Zayas, *Nemesis at Potsdam* (London: Routledge and Kegan Paul, 2nd edn, 1979).

Index

397